Elizabeth City County Virginia

Deeds, Wills, Court Orders, Etc.

1715–1721

Compiled by
Rosemary Corley Neal

HERITAGE BOOKS
2015

HERITAGE BOOKS
AN IMPRINT OF HERITAGE BOOKS, INC.

Books, CDs, and more—Worldwide

For our listing of thousands of titles see our website at
www.HeritageBooks.com

Published 2015 by
HERITAGE BOOKS, INC.
Publishing Division
5810 Ruatan Street
Berwyn Heights, Md. 20740

Copyright © 1988 Rosemary Corley Neal

Heritage Books by the author:

*Elizabeth City County, Virginia, (now the City of Hampton):
Deeds, Wills, Court Orders, Etc. 1634, 1659, 1688–1702*

*Elizabeth City County, Virginia:
Deeds, Wills, Court Orders, Etc., 1715–1721*

All rights reserved. No part of this book may be reproduced or transmitted in any form or by any means, electronic or mechanical, including photocopying, recording or by any information storage and retrieval system without written permission from the author, except for the inclusion of brief quotations in a review.

International Standard Book Numbers
Paperbound: 978-1-55613-157-8
Clothbound: 978-0-7884-6263-4

TO

JOHN FREDERICK DORMAN

TABLE OF CONTENTS

INTRODUCTION vii

THE RECORD BOOK 1715 - 1721 xv

DEEDS, WILLS, INVENTORIES 1715 - 1721................... 1

COURT ORDER BOOK 1715 - 1721........................... 75

INDEX..289

INTRODUCTION

Elizabeth City County, Virginia, first settled by Englishmen in 1610, marked its most prosperous days of the Colonial period during the first part of the 18th Century.[1] The town of Hampton was laid off in 1680, lots were sold, and the town began to develop into a bustling port, one of the Council's very few successes in its efforts to establish "Ports ... for the lading and unlading of ships" and for centers of manufacture.[2] The County Court records abstracted herein are all that remain for this period.

The town of Hampton is situated a short distance up Southampton River from its opening into the estuary at the southern end of Chesapeake Bay, the great harbor now called Hampton Roads. The entrance to the Roads, protected by a sand bar and narrow channel, was easily defended and Fort George was erected at Old Point Comfort in 1728.[3] Only small ships and sloops could dock at Hampton, but men-of-war could stand off the shore ready to engage enemy vessels, privateers, or pirates which roamed the coastal waters during England's many wars of that period. Hampton developed quickly as a source of supplies for the fleet and advantageous site for factors to receive European goods and ship out tobacco and other products of the area.

As the port grew, more facilities became necessary. A new Courthouse was constructed in 1716 on land sold by

---

[1] The jurisdiction began life as the Plantation or Burrough of Kecoughtan about 1610, changed its name to Elizabeth City in 1620, and survived until 1952 when it was consolidated into the Independent City of Hampton. See: Rosemary Corley Neal. *Elizabeth City Co., Va. Deeds etc. 1634 ... 1702.* Heritage Books, Inc, 1986

[2] See example: Wm. P. Palmer, ed. *Calendar of Va. State Papers etc.* Richmond, 1875. Vol 1:137, 138. Repeal of Acts ... relating to Ports & Towns dated 1709.

[3] James T. Stensvaag, General Editor. *Hampton From the Sea to the Stars 1610-1685,* Norfolk, 1985, p 22. Ft. George was destroyed by a hurricane in 1749.

William Boswell, in 1719 William Dandridge petitioned to build "a House and Wharf for Conveniency of Storidge and Landing"[4] and in 1721 the inhabitants of the town prayed a patent to build a wharf and key 120 feet long and 18 feet wide of the ground lying within the high water mark, presumably at the foot of King Street.[5] A number of ordinaries were licensed to entertain rowdy sailors, local clientele, and planters who came from outlying areas to deal with the numerous merchants. Hampton was still quite primitive in 1730 and the House of Burgesses found it necessary to pass an Act to prevent swine from running at large within the limits of the town.[6]

Hampton was undoubtedly full of "drifters" of various sorts, as is any port. In 1709 Capt. Geo. Goram of her Majestie's Ship "Maidstone," informed the Council of the desertion of a number of his crew there and offered a reward for their apprehension.[7] In 1720 when seeking seamen to man "His Maty's Ship the Rye ... in case any pirate or privateer should infest this Coast," the Justices of Elizabeth City County were "Impowered and Required to Issue their Warrants for Impressing such Stragling Sailors and other persons not having any visible Imploymt or settled Residence ..."[8] As late as 1736, a petition of sundry inhabitants of Hampton read: "that great numbers of idle and vagrant People come to said Town and others reside therein who are suspected to subsist chiefly by dealing with Servants and Slaves and Praying a Law be made to empower the Justices of the Peace to erect a Work-house for the Reception and Emploiment of such Persons."[9]

From about 1698 until the Revolution, Hampton was headquarters for one of the six Naval Districts in Virginia. First called the Naval District of the Lower James, it became Hampton District after 1736. Naval Officers in charge were: Peter Heyman 1698/1699; William Wilson 1699/1710; Nicholas Curle 1710/1714; John Holloway

---

[4] *Cal Va St Papers.* Vol I:190.

[5] H. R. McIlwaine, ed. *Executive Journals of the Council etc.* Richmond, 1925. Vol II:546

[6] H. R. McIlwaine, ed. *Journals of the House of Burgesses.* Vol 1727-1740:65, 66, 68, 76, 110.

[7] *Cal Va St Papers.* I:128.

[8] H. R. McIlwaine, ed. *Executive Journals of the Council etc.* III:531.

[9] *JHB.* Vol 1727-1740:269.

1714/1716; Henry Irwin 1716/1726; Wilson Cary 1726/1761; Wilson Miles Cary 1761/1775. Each ship entering the waters of the harbor was required to register with the Naval Officer, have cargoes inspected, and pay duties to the Collector of Customs for the Crown. Here, too, pilots licensed by the Council boarded each vessel to navigate the adjacent waters.[10]

There was active shipment of negroes into the District for many years. Large slave ships direct from Africa or England arrived as well as smaller vessels from the West Indies carrying only a few slaves. Among the latter, many of the ships were "plantation built" and had local owners engaged in coastal trade. Between 1710-1718, 743 negroes were brought in on 64 ships. On these same ships came 3 Indian slaves captured in the Carolinas between 1711-1718. 231 slaves had died on the crossings and 103 were "drawn back" as re-exported or died within a certain time after they were purchased. On 10 July 1700 the Pink "St. Johns," a French prize with Master John Atkinson and 160 men aboard, arrived from Barbadoes with a cargo of negroes and on 18 July 1701 the Brigantine "Jane and Margaret" arrived from London. Owned by William Wilson, Roger Jones, Peter Guillam and John Hanson, it brought negroes from Barbadoes. The Pink "Batchellour" departed London 28 Oct 1701 and arrived in the Lower James on 17 Apr 1702 with a cargo of negroes from Barbadoes. Its owners were William Byrd, Willis Wilson and Thomas Ward.

Between 23 Nov and 14 Dec 1713, 13 sloops, including 6 Virginia ships, brought 75 negroes in small lots and 12 more vessels arrived between 1713 and 1716. Of the 37 ships known to have arrived between 29 Apr 1717 and Nov 1718, the largest was the "Nightingale" which brought 157 negroes from Bermuda. Slave trade continued thereafter primarily with small lots.[11]

Obviously negroes were not the only cargo entering Hampton. Mentioned as typical in June of 1745 are two

---

[10] Walter Minchinton, Celia King, & Peter Waite, eds. *Virginia Slave-Trade Statistics, 1698-1775.* (Richmond 1984) Data taken from shipping lists compiled by Naval offices in British colonies in North America & deposited in Public Records Office, London. pp ix, 198. Information below on individual ships taken from various pp in the same source. See pp xiii-xvi, 4-9, 14, 15, 21-35, 47, 54-55, 89, 151, 158-159, 187, 196 et al.

[11] Ibid. See charts throughout book.

ships entered from Glasgow with European goods and several other coastal traders bringing in salt, flour, corn, bread, sugar, ginger and rum and taking out exports of pork, beef, tallow, shingles, and staves, as well as tobacco.

The County also suffered from internal disputes during this period of her history. The precise cause of these troubles is unclear, but may have been part of the larger differences relating to the Reverend Mr. Blair, Commissary of Virginia, and his proclivity for placing his fellow Scotsmen in preferred positions. As early as 1694 there was a serious quarrel among factions of both the Elizabeth City Parish Vestry and the Justices of Peace. The Council received at that time "The complaint of Mr. William Wilson, Mr. Will. Lowrey, Mr. Edmd. Sweeney, Mr. Augustine More, Mr. Coleman Brough, Justices of Elizabeth City County against Capt. Anthony Armistead, Mr. Bertram Servant, Edwd. Mihill, and George Walker, who by petition at Court held 19 February last, accusing Justices of Illegality and Injustice in assessing County and Parish Levys and at the Court appearing with a great number of people, subscribers to the petition, at which time Armistead did assault Mr. James Wallace, Minister, which quarrel and disturbance occasioned the Court's adjournment, all of which proceedings they conceive to be riotous and contrary to law. Referred to the Attorney Genll. to prosecute."[12]

On 24 Apr 1695 a Committee of the House of Burgesses discussed the proposition that Elizabeth City have liberty to elect a new Vestry, but determined that this was not within the jurisdiction of the House. This committee also received a grievance from citizens of the County "touching unwarrantable taxes by Vestries and Court and on 1 Oct 1698 and also resolved that the "Return [that] the Sheriff of Elizabeth City County hath made upon Election of Burgesses is insufficient" and that Mr. Augustin Moor, Sheriff, "be sent for in Custody of the Messenger of the House to amend his return." On 5 Oct 1698, Moor was called into the House and amended his return "by rasing out the words of the Old Returne and entering a new full and sufficient return." Willis Wilson and Anthony Armistead were duly elected Burgesses, but the difficulties persisted. On 3 May 1699, Henry Royall and several other

---

[12] *Executive Journals.* Vol I:309. See also: *Papers Relating to the History of the Church in Virginia,* William Stevens Perry, ed. 1870:34, 35.

freeholders complained against the Sheriff for undue election and return of Anthony Armistead. Others prayed a law to prevent discontinuance of process and Courts by the "not coming of the Justices" to Courts as also by their refusal to sit.[13]

Six years later, on 23 Jan 1705/6, the Council ordered a new Commission of Peace for the County, that Mr. Bertram Servant be put in the place he held in the former Commission and that Capt. Wm. Boswell and Mr. John Bailey be added. The County Levy was not yet laid "to the great prejudice of the County creditors."[14]

In 1710 there was another argument. Mr. Francis Ballard complained of the undue election of William Armistead and the House resolved "That the Sheriff ... hath falsely returned Mr. William Armistead as Burgess ... and that Mr. Francis Ballard is duly elected a Burgess." Armistead complained that Ballard "did make feasts and treats at his house to procure his being Elected a Burgess." The Committee resolved that Armistead's petition was "false and Scandalous the same not being proved."[15]

The Justices again neglected to lay the Levy and the members were summoned to attend a board in 1717[16]. Another petition by Mr. Joshua Curl against an undue election of Anthony Armistead as Burgess caused the House once more to find that a member of the Armistead family had not been duly elected.[17]

The extant County Court records provide us with a letter dated 7 January 1720 from Governor Spotswood to the Justices relating to a dispute between Major Henry Irwin and Mr. Charles Jenings, County Clerk. The Governor replaced Jenings with Irwin, allowing a pension for Jenings. Three of the Justices, James Servant, John Lowry and James Wallace, voted against Irwin's appointment. Irwin tells us when the Justices later repaired to the Court house to vote "in their Passage thither they met with Mr. John Lowry & asked him if he would join with them ... but he rudely answered no ..."[18]

---

[13] *JHB.* Vol 1695-1702:10, 12, 139.
[14] *Executive Journals.* Vol III:70.
[15] *JHB.* Vol 1702-1712:246, 247, 248.
[16] *Executive Journals.* Vol III:464.
[17] *JHB.* Vol 1712-1726:254, 261, 270.
[18] Infra. pp 264, 265.

Finally a new Commission of the Peace was sworn in May, 1721 consisting of Anthony Armistead, Joshua Curle, Robert Armistead, Saml. Sweny, John King, James Ricketts, John Lowry, James Wallace, Joseph Selden and John Selden. This group were presented by the Grand Jury of the General Court for not keeping roads passable in the County and quickly moved to "speedy measures" by hiring labourers to do the necessary work.[19]

On 22 Apr 1726, Anthony Armistead and Simon Hollier petitioned "in behalf of themselves, and the greater number of the Freeholders and Inhabitants of the parish of Elizabeth City, complaining of the great hardships & inconveniences under which the Inhabitants of the said parish have long time laboured by means of the scituation of their parish Church, and other proceedings of a pretended Vestry are still endeavouring to increase the grievances of the people by building a new Church at a place yet more inconvenient than the former, and praying that they may be heard before this Board to shew cause why the said pretended Vestry ought to be dissolved ..." This was followed by a 1727 petition from sundry Inhabitants and the majority of the Vestry "that the Church ... is so ruinous that it is dangerous for them to repair thither for the performing Divine service: and that great differences have arisen ... concerning the place where a new Church should be built."[20] At this point, the Governor heard the petition and the Board gave its opinion that the new Church ought to be built in the Town of Hampton. On 27 March 1728, the House considered "a Bill For Dissolving the Present Vestry ... and for appointing a New Election of Vestry-men ..." and the Act for dissolving the Vestry was passed.[21]

An earlier parish problem occurred in 1704/1705. The Vestry made a supplication to Francis Nicholson, "her Matys Lieu^t and Governor Gen^{ll} of Virginia," to allow Mr. James Wallace, the former minister, to replace Mr. Isaac Grace who had left the Parish. Nicholson replied that Mr. Wallace lacked proper credentials, Mr. Wallace said that he had presented them eleven years earlier when he became

---

[19] Infra. pp 271, 285.

[20] *Executive Journals.* Vol IV:94, 97.

[21] *JHB.* Vol 1727-1740, p 47. St. John's Church, built at this time, is still in use. Also, Waverly K. Winfree. *The Laws of Virginia 1700-1750* (Richmond 1971), pp 322, 323.

Minister of the Parish, and the following letter sent by Wil Robertson as commanded by the Governor ensued. A meeting of the Clergy was called and Wallace was to come if he pleased, "but you being Chaplain to her Matys Ship Strombulo ... intending to sail up the Bay ... your Presence may be necessary on board, and hoped you will have more conscience now than to take her Matys Pay as Chaplain to this Ship and not do your duty as you did when you went Chaplain to her Matys Ship Southampton, but your behaviour since you came into Virginia hath been so very strange that he can expect little good from you in any kind, and he gives you notice that he intends to complain of you ..." Other harsh criticisms follow.[22] Mr. Wallace must have eventually returned to the pulpit in Elizabeth City Parish, since the scanty records of the church indicate that he served until 1712.[23]

By 1735 business at Hampton was declining severely. As the population moved up the rivers and inland, ports were needed closer to the tobacco growing uplands. The sand bar and narrow channel which had protected Hampton in 1700 now proved a detriment and ships preferred to call where navigation was easier. On 2 April 1735 the merchants and owners of vessels of Norfolk, and the Counties of Princess Anne and Nansemond begged relief from the necessity of reporting to the Lower District at the Port of Hampton. The eighteen miles by water from Norfolk Town to Hampton and the twenty-five or thirty miles from Nansemond was "a Difficult and Troublesom Navigation Cross the mouth of James River, and usually requires two Days time and Expence of boat & men ..." The petitioners state that there were no more than three sloops or vessels belonging to Virginia owners and no British ships for many years past that had loaded tobacco on the Hampton side of the James River. All of the major shipping was said to be at Norfolk.[24]

---

[22] *Executive Journals.* Vol II, pp 439-433. Vestrymen who signed were: Collo. Wm. Wilson, Mr. Pasco Curle, Mr. WM. Lowry, Major Wm. Armistead, Mr. Nicho. Curle, Capt Geo. Wauff, Capt Augn Moore, Mr. Robt. Taylor, Mr. Symon Hollier and Lt Collo Antho. Armistead and Capt Henry Royal, Churchwardens.

[23] The Rev. Francis W. Hayes, Jr. Former Rector of St. John's Church. Corrected list of Ministers of Elizabeth City Parish.

[24] *Cal Va St Papers.* I: 221, 222.

As the excitement of constant international contacts waned, Elizabeth City County and Hampton Town settled into a peaceful and productive community of planters, watermen, and merchants and remained thus until modern times.

THE RECORD BOOK 1715 – 1721

The following abstracts were taken from a photostatic copy which was compared with the original volume labeled 1715-1721 on the spine. Both books are housed in the office of the Circuit Clerk of the City of Hampton, Virginia. The original volume was restored in 1937 and is again badly in need of additional work. The flyleaf bears the signature of James Wallace and is dated 4th June 1759. There is no index to the book.

It is possible that there may have initially been two volumes, bound together when restored. The first portion consists primarily of wills, deeds and miscellaneous entries, recorded between 10 July 1715 and 19 July 1721. Pagination seems to be original in this section. The photostat is intact, but pages 9 and 10 of the original have been removed by some vandal.

The second part of the record book contains Court Orders beginning in July 1715 and running through June 1719. Pagination may have been added at restoration and the last page is badly damaged.

Charles Jennings served as County Clerk during most of this period, being superceded by Henry Irwin in 1720/1721. From various entries it can be determined that the practice had been for Mr. Jennings to take the records to his home and that the new Clerk had difficulties in obtaining them. At the Court of 31 January 1720/1721 it was noted that Charles Jenings' son brought some of the "Dockets & Laws" to Irwin, but no entry survives to tell us if all records were eventually returned to the Courthouse.[25]

In preparing the abstracts, all names have been copied exactly as given in the records. Many abbreviations are those used by the Clerks and others are such as are normally employed in works of this type.

Covenants usual and customary to all deeds have been omitted and all land descriptions are given in full.

---

[25]infra. pp 266, 267. The author is greatly indebted to Mr. Donald B. Gibson, who took office as Clerk of the City of Hampton in 1988, for making these records available.

Prefaces of wills expressing religious sentiments, burial arrangements, etc. have been omitted. See the preface of the will of Edwd. Penny, pages 4 and 5 infra, given in full as a typical example of the usual wording.

Some spelling has been modernized, superscripts have been lowered, and occasional punctuation added for clarity.

Since misreadings and other errors may have occurred, readers are advised to examine the original records to be completely sure of the content.

DEEDS, WILLS, INVENTORIES

1715 - 1721

[p 1, damaged] Jos. Curle's deed for town land.--Lowery, Francis Ballard and William Bosell, Gent, Foeffees appt by the Ct of Elizabeth City Co. for the sale of Town Land in pursuance to an Act of Assembly made at James City 16 Apr 1691 and an Act made 2 Mar 1692/3 suspending the Act for Ports made --- 27th 1702 enabling Feoffees to sell the half ac lots for 26- lbs tobo confirmed to Mr. Joshua Curle one lot and a half or 3/4 ac in Hampton Town beg at a hole in the ground on Wine St. and running N ten ---the town ditch S 42 degrees, W six chains 65/100 to --- hole thence S ten degrees, E four chains --- N 81 degrees --- 5 chains 20/100 to the beginning, two poles bounded on the N with the town, on the E with Wine St., on the S with Richd. Kerkin, on the W with Mr. Henry Jenkins. Dated 20 July 1715. Signed: Willm. Lowrey, F. Ballard, William Bosell. Wit: Chas. Jenings CClk. Ack & rec 20 July 1715.

[p 2, damaged] 15 Sept 1713. "I received the letters and bills ... you sent by Capt. Turner and I have protested Murrin's bills. I am very sorry to hear my houses are empty ... You advise me to put them up for sale." The writer continues by stating he would prefer the houses be rented so that he would have "something coming in" and leaves it to the recipient's discretion. "If Mrs. Atkins is in Hampton she may live in one rent free ... Mr. Selden has proved very unkind to me. It had been well for me is I had never met him." The writer is very sorry that the business has been so much trouble. "Capt. Bosell I am sorry I should trouble you ... about the note ... Banister had ... he never paid me [except] £20 paid ... in the office and consigned to Mr. Perry ... As for the salt in William Allen's hand ... I desire you to call him to account ... Perhaps he may say that his negr he had of me died, but I can't help that for I have lost a great many ... Tell Molly Allen that her mother gives her blessing [and says she is very poor] and if she could send her a little something it would be very acceptable. My respects to yourself and wife and family ... hoping I shall have a full [answer by] Capt. M--rin for I hear he is designed [for] England ..."

[pp 3 & 4 are missing.]

[p 5, damaged] and the reversion and remainder sold unto Willm. --- for the term of one whole year, paying rent of one ear of Indian corn at the feast of St. Michaell the Arch[angel] only if demanded. Signed: Tho. Howard, Eliza. (X) Howard. Wit: Emanl. Alkin, ---Mallory, --arles Avera. Ack 17 Aug 1715 by Thomas Howard and Eliza. his wife. Release follows. Thomas Howard and Elizabeth his wife confirm to Wm. Allen a parcel of land lying on the N side of Back R. in Eliz. City Co. containing 50 ac, the same mentioned in a patent granted William Morgan als Brooks dated 22 May 1627, being the land where Thomas Williams and Rebeca his wife lately lived. Signed: Tho. Howard, Eliza. (X) Howard. Ack 18 Aug 1715 by Tho. Howard and Eliza. wife to Tho. Howard [she] being privately examined.

[pp 9, 10 taken from photostatic copy, since these pages have been cut from the original record book.

Probates and Administrations (vizt.)

10 July 1715 - Probate granted to Thomas Howard of Joane Scullie's will.

16 June 1715 - Probate granted to James Servant and Henry Turner of Tho. Westwood's will.

18 May 1715 -Probate granted to Wm. Copland and Eliza. his wife of David Jones nuncupative will.

15 June 1715 -Adm of estate of Peter Proby granted to Bartrand Proby his brother.

Returned to Octobr Genll. Court 1715

-- Janry 1715 - Probate granted Reba. Armistead, Antho., Wm., and John Armistead Execs of Majr. William Armistead's will.

18 Janry 1715 - Probate granted to Eliza. Goodwyne and Wm. More of John More's will.

15 Feb 1715 - Probate granted to Henry Jenkins and Jno. Curle Execs of Nicho. Curle's will.

21 March 1715 –Probate granted to James Ricketts & Jane his wife, late Jane Curle, of Nicho. Curle's will.
Returned to April Genll. Court 1716

16 May 1716 – Adm of Eliza. James, dec'd granted Tho. Wilcox greatest creditor.
15 Aug 1716 – Probate granted to Hannah Watts als Armistead of Mathw. Watts will.
15 Aug 1716 – Probate granted to Saml. Daniel of Ann Daniel's will.
Returned October Genll. Court 1716

-- --- 1716 – Adm of Tho. Proby's estate granted to Barto. Proby his brother.
19 Dec 1716 – Adm with the will annexed granted to Jno. Burtell of James Burtell's estate.
Returned April Genll. Court 1717

15 May 1717 – Probate of the will of Tho. Naylor is granted to Eliza. his wife.
17 Do 1717 –Probate of the will of Wm. Bowtel granted to Eliza. his wife, Exectrx.
17 July 1717 – Probate of the will of Humphry Balis granted to Jane his ...
17 July 1717 – Probate of the will of Tho. Tabb granted to Edwd. Tabb his -----.
Do –Probate of the will of Robt. Bright granted to..
-- March 1717 – Probate of the will of Mrk. Parish granted to Abra. Parish.
Do – Probate of Stephen Lillis' will granted to Kort Norden Exec.
-- 18 1718 – Probate of Tho. Merry's will granted to Wm. Tucker Exec.
--May 1718 – Probate of Robt. Johnson's will granted to John Bordland Exec.
Do – Probate of Jno. Stringer's will granted to Wm. Allen Exec.
Do – Probate of Henry Batts' will granted to Jno. and Thomas Batts Execs.
Do – Adm Of Alexandr. Carver's estate granted to Ann his relict.
-- July 1718 – Probate of Richard Crusell's estate granted to Mary his wife Exectrx.

-- Aug 1718 - Adm of James Gilbert's estate to Mary his relict.

--July 1718 - Adm of Jno. Pett's estate granted to Wm. Smelt.

--July 1718 - Adm of Richd. Hopkins will granted to Joyce his relict.

--July 1718 - Probate of Wm. Hopkins will granted to Mary Bridge, Exctrx.

--Aug 1718 - Adm of T-- Treadway's estate granted to Jno. Bordland

-- ----1718 - Adm of Benja. Smith's estate granted to Susanah Smith his wi---.

[undated] - Adm of Jno. Curles's estate granted to Henry Jenkins.

Returned to Octbr Genll. Court 1718

[p 10. Marginal note: recorded the 22nd Novbr 1715]

[p 10] Ind dated 20th Sept 1715 between Thomas Wood and Ann, his wife, of the Town of Hampton in the Co. of Eliz. City, and Edward Ballard of the same. Thomas Wood and Ann his wife sell for £26 of current silver money of Va. a tract of land sold and ack by Charles Cooper & Barbry, his wife, to the sd Thomas Wood by deed dated 18 Aug 1713. 1/2 ac with houses etc. Signed: Thomas Wood, Anne (X) Wood. Wit: James Servant, --- Wragg, -homas Walker. Thomas Wood ack 16 Nov 1715 and Ann, wife to Thomas Wood, relinquishes dower the same day.

[p 11, damaged] -- Aug 1715. Bond of William More and John More gent both of Eliz. City Co. for £200 lawful money of England. The condition of the obligation is that William More, Adm of Ann More dec'd, make an inventory of the goods, chattels and credits of the estate as required, provided that if a last will was made and Execs named and the Ct approves, this bond to be void. Signed: William More, John More. Wit: Cha. Jenings. Ack 17 Aug 1715.

[p 12] Inv of estate of Thomas Westwood dec'd. Stock, household items. Total value £57:17:0. Signed: --lliam Smelt, ---- Merideth, Tho. Howard.

[pp 12, 13] Last will and testament of Edwd. Penny of Eliz. City Co. "I, Edwd. Penny ... being sick and weak of body but of perfect mind and memory Thanks be to Almighty God do make and appoint this to be my last will and testament in manner and form following revoking and disannulling all wills and testaments by me heretofore made. First I give & bequeath my soul to God that gave it and my [body] to the Earth to be buried after the Christian manner in sure and certain ----through the meritorious sufferings of my Blessed Saviour Jesus Christ to receive a joyfull resurrection at the last day and after my funeral debts together with all other my lawful debts be paid I dispose of what other Estate it hath pleased God to bless me with as follows: "To daughter Hanah Penne my house and lot in the town of Hampton. To wife Elizabeth Penny other lot in Hampton. If the child wife now goes with live, the whole personal estate to be equally divided among wife and children, but if it die, the personal estate to be divided between wife and surviving child to be paid at age of 21 or day of marriage. If both die, all to wife Elizabeth Penne. To Mary Husk as much stuff as will make her a gown and petticoat. Wife Elizabeth Penny to be Exectrx. Dated 31 Mar 1714. Signed: Edwd. Penny. Test: Robt. Armistead, Tho. Read, Wm. Williams. Pro by Tho. Read and William Williams on 15 Sept 1714 and probate granted Exectrx, she giving bond. Signed: Wm. Armistead, Henry Jenkins.

[p 13, 14] Last will and testament of Sarah Curle, sick and weak. To daughter Mary Jenkins, negro Will, provided that son-in-law Capt. Henry Jenkins pay daughter Sarah Curle, wife of Joshua Curle, £10 current money to buy her a negro child. To daughter Judith Bayley, negro child called Judy. To son Joshua Curle, negro Charles. To son John Curle, negro woman called Jone. To son Josa. Curle, working oxen and all the rest of estate as cattle, hogs, and households to be equally divided by son Mr. Nicholas Curle between sons Joshua and John Curle." Son Nicholas is to settle any disputes and any child not agreeing is to forfeit his share. Dated 19 March 1713. Signed: Sarah Curle. Wit: Elizabeth Jenings, Mary Ballard, Euphan Roscow. Pro by oath of Mary Ballard and Eliza. Jenings. No probate date recorded.

[p 14] 16 Nov 1715. Elizabeth Howard, wife of Tho. Howard came into Ct and relinquished her right of dower in houses and lots formerly John Lowery's in Hampton conveyed to William Bossell gent. Signed: Eliza. (X) Howard. Ordered to be recorded.

[p 15] Ind dated 10 Nov 1715. Sam----Selden of Eliz. City Parish and Co. Gent & Rebekah his wife for natural love and affection give to their son Bartholomew Selden, a tract commonly called Downs Field or Strawberry Banks. The land "now being in actual possession by virtue of a sale [lease] thereof made by Samll. Selden Junr dated 11 May 1715 and [release] dated 12 May 1715." If Bartholomew die before age 21 and leaves no lawful issue, the land is to return to S---- and Rebeckah Selden. Signed: Samuell Selden, Rebekah Selden. Wit: George Yeo Junr. Ack 16 Nov 1715 by Saml. Selden. Rebekah relinquishes dower and ack on same day. Recorded 19 Dec 1715.

[p 16] Last will and testament of Katherine Forgison of Elizabeth City, sick and weak. Dated 24 Jan 1713. To grandaughter Elizabeth Dun, one cow & calf and household items to be delivered to her at age 17 or day of marriage. To daughter Ann Dun the wife of Wm. Dunn, all the rest of estate. Son-in-law Wm. Dunn to be Exec. Signed: Katherine (X) Forgison. Wit: Thomas Needham and Charles Avera. No probate date given.

[p 16] 27 Sept 1715. To the Constable of Hampton or his Deputy. Execute and make Return. Complaint is made by William Smelt agst Richard Street "that he did beat and abuse, and mortally wound one Enjon Woman Slave" on Smelt's land. "It is despairing of her life." Therefore "... you are commanded to bring him before me or some other Justice for this County to answer the complaint ..." Signed: William Bossell.

[p 17] Richd. Street was this day brought ... ... More ...Ordered recorded 16 Nov 1715.

[pp 17, 18, 19] Last will and testament of John More of Eliz. City Co. sick and weak. To nephew John More, that "neck of land whereon I now live with the housing thereon and then to have as much on the north side of the branch that makes this neck as will make up one half of my divident and that to be next to Thomas Je-----." To nephew Edward More, the other half of the divident lying next to William Creek. If either die, land reverts to the survivor. To nephew Meritt More, the plantation where John Meritt lives with reversion to Daniell Mo--, nephew. John

Meritt may continue to live on the plantation paying the same rent as he does now. To niece Martha More, negro boy Jack. To niece Ann More, negro girl -udey. To niece Rachell "wife & widdo," negro boy Hump. To niece Susanah Goodwyn, negro child Harry. To sister Elizabeth, three negroes Tobe, York and Sara. To nephew John More, all stock on plantation provided he will be accountable to his brother Meritt More to deliver to him when he comes of age six cows and a bull. To afsd sister Elizabeth Goodwyn, one dozen chairs and all silver plate. Rest of household goods to be divided between sister and nephew John More. To nephew William More, woolen apparel and his choice of one young horse. To Uncle Willm. Lowry and "Ant" Rachell Lowry, each £5 to buy them mourning. Riding horse to "Ant" Lowry. To sister Eliza. Goodwyn, all stock of horses and mares not given above. Silver hilted sword and belt to loving Cozn John Lowry. After debts and funeral expenses are paid, rest of personal estate to sister Eliz. Goodwyn and nephew Willm. More to be equally divided and they to be Execs. Dated 11 Dec 1715. Signed: John More. Wit: Thomas Kirby, Cha. Rowins, Willm. Lowry. Pro 18 Jan 1715 by Tho. Kirby and Cha. Rowin. Recorded 4 Feb 1715/16.

[p 19-21] Last will and testament of William Armistead Senr of Co. of Eliz. City, sick and weak. To loving wife Reba. Armistead for life "all my plantation and tract that I now live on after my mother's decease and after her death to be divided between my two loving sons Anthony Armistead and William Armistead." The dividing line to run from a small cove to a branch between the point of marsh and the landing and from thence to run westward through the --- to the extent of the line. Son William to have that part where dwelling house stands with one half of the orchard. The other half to son Antho. If either son die, his part to fall to next heir at law. To son John Armistead, 350 acs lying on Harrises Cr. with reversion to next surviving male heir. To son Hind Armistead, 160 acs purchased of Tho. Cary and his wife. To son Robert Armistead, 450 acs known as Tony's Quarter. To son Moss Armistead, 100 acs lying near Point Comfort Cr. formerly gr by patent to one John Ingram. To son Edwd. Armistead, 150 acs in Co. of York, formerly leased to Benjamin Cleften? Senr. To two sons Anthony and William, 125 acs on Gullett Run known by the name of the Black Ground to be equally divided. To the infant "my loving wife now bears whether male or female"

132 acs of land called Burton's Quarter with reversion to Hind Armistead. To mother Hanah Armistead, 4 cows, ten sheep and 10 hogs, 5 breeding cows & 5 barrows. Sloop "the Ann and Hanah" to be sold for money or bills of exchange to discharge debts. To sons Anthony and John, "my mill between them." Son Wm. is to have no part of personal estate or negroes & they to be divided between wife and other children in equal shares. Negroes falling to wife to be equally divided after her decease among "my children born of her body." Wife Rebecca and sons Anthony, William and John to be Execs. Dated 5 Jan 1714. Signed: Willm. Armistead. Wit: Anthony Armistead, Robt. Armistead, Thomas Charles, George Cooper. Codicil: Estate to be divided by Antho. Armistead and Robert Armistead and son William Armistead. Dated 5 Jan. Same witnesses and signature. Pro 18 Jan 1715 by Robert Armistead and Anthony Armistead & certificate gr for probate to the Execs [they] giving bond. Rec 17 Feb 1715. Bond of Reba. Armistead, Antho. Armistead, William Armistead, John Armistead, and Robert Armistead for £2000 to Justices William Lowery, Francis Ballard, Thomas Tabb and Wm. Boswell dated 18 Jan 1715. The conditon of bond is to make inventory and give accounts and deliver all legacies. Signed: Rebeccah (X) Armistead, Antho. Armistead, Wm. Armistead, Robt. Armistead. Wit: Samuel Selden Junr, Emanll. Alkin. Ack 18 Jan 1715.

[p 22] 15 Feb 1715. Bond of Henry Jenkins, John Curle, Anthony Armistead Senr, John King, Thomas Wythe, and John Bayley, Execs of will of Nicholas Curle Gent, to William Lowry, Francis Ballard, Thomas Tabb, William Boswell etc Justices of Co. of Eliz. City, for £2000 lawful money of England. Ack 15 Feb 1715.

[p 22-24] Ind dated 13 Mar 1715 between John Butler and William Dandridge, both of Eliz. City Co. John Butler sells for 5 sh current money four lots lying in one square together in Hampton Town, butting on the north side on Mr. James Wallace's lot and from thence extends southward on King St. and makes a corner from which the line lying part on Queene St. side ---land makes a corner and from [damaged] extends northerly on Wine St. butting Mar-Johnson ... signed: John Butler. Wit: Edmd. Kearny, Thomas Wythe, Ja. Wallace. Ack 21 Mar 1715. Release dated 14 Mar 1715 for £200 current money of Va. Ack 21 Mar 1715.

Elizabeth Butler, wife to John Butler, releases her right of dower. Dated 21 Mar 1715. Signed: Elizabeth Butler.

[p 25] Deed of gift. 21 Mar 1715/16. "I, William Winterton of the Town of Hampton, for the tender love and respect I bear unto my Godson George Wauff, the son of George Wauff Junr --- 20 & 5 foot square of land out of my lot of town land joining Widdow Bayley and George W---- and ---- Walker." Signed: William Winterton. Wit: Nathaniel Parker, John (X) Roe, Jo. Wragge. Ack 21 Mar 1715/16.

[pp 25, 26] Ind dated 19 Dec 1715 between William Boswell Gent and Thomas Howard, cordwndr, of Eliz. City Co. for 5 sh grant to his Majts Justices of the Co. of Eliz. City a parcel in Hampton Towne. 42 sq poles for the building of a Courthouse, a prison and other conveniences. Viz: beg upon the town ditch at a hole in the ground. From thence S 5 deg E two chains to another hole in the ground. Thence N 75 deg E 3 chains to another hole in the ground by the ditch side, thence along the ditch to the beg, each chain containing 2 poles. Bounded upon N by town ditch, on W upon Thomas Faulkner's lot, on S by Thomas Howard and on E by Capt. William Boswell's lot and also a passage of 16 foot wide on the E side of this plot of ground through the middle of Capt. Boswell's lot to King St. Signed: William Boswell, Thoms. Howard. Wit: Cha. Jenings. Ack by Howard 18 Jan 1715 and by Boswell 21 Mar 1715.

[p 27, 28] 21 Mar 1715/16. Bond of James Ricketts, Miles Cary of Warwick Co., John Armistead, Anthony Armistead, Robert Armistead, and Hind Armistead, all of Eliz. City Co., for £2000 lawful money of Va. Jane Ricketts, late Jane Curle, Exectrx of will of Nicholas Curle gent dec'd is to make inv of all goods of sd dec'd, etc. Signed: James Ricketts, Miles Cary, Robt. Armistead, Antho. Armistead, John Armistead, Hind Armistead. Wit: Cha. Jenings, William Bossell. Ack 21 Mar 1715.

[p 28] 20 July 1715. Foeffees of Eliz. City Co. grant to Mr. Henry Jenkins one half-acre lot in Hampton Town beg at a hole in the ground on King St. running along the town ditch, thence N 10 --- W 1 chain 60/100 to ---ditch to another hole on Joshua Curle's lot --- Richard Kirkins lot and on 4th side with Mr. James Wallace dec'd, and W with King St. The above granted to Mr. Ja. Wallace dec'd by

deed 28 June 1706 and having relapsed his time in not complying with the law is now granted to Jenkins. Signed: Willm. Lowry, Wm. Bosell. Wit: Robt. Minson, George Wauffe. Ack 16 May 1716 by Foeffees. Rec 18 June 1716.

[pp 29, 30 badly damaged] ---Henry Jenkins for 5 sh unto Peter Baker [the lot described above]. Signed: Henry Je---- -, Mary Jen----. Wit: Cha. Jenings . Ack 16 May 1716 by Henry Jenkins and Mary his w---. Release dated 16 Mar 1716. Ack by Henry Jenkins and Mary his wife.

[p 30-32] Ind dated 14 Feb 1715. William Coopland of Parish and Co. of Eliz. City [and] ------eth his wife of the one part and John Jones of the same. William Coopland and Elizabeth his wife for 10 sh current money [sell] all that plantation or tract late in possession of David Jones lying in Eliz. City Co. at the head of a Creek that parts it from Fort Field on the South and joining ----on N & E. Signed: William Coopland, Eliza. Coopland. Wit: James Servant, James Gilbert. Ack 16 May 1716. Release dated 18 June 1716 for £7:10 dated 18 June 1716. Ack 16 May 1716.

[pp 32, 33] Marginal note: Ricketts & ---- bond per Wilson Curle's estate. James Ricketts and William Bosell, Wm. Smelt, Robert Taylor and Charles Jenings of Eliz. City Co. are bound for £2000 money of England. Condition is that whereas the wife of sd James Ricketts as guardian to her son Wilson Curle, orphan, has taken him into care and management, sd James Ricketts and Jane Ricketts are to yield up [Wilson's share] of estate at full age or marriage and also to educate and bring him up. Signed: James Ricketts, Wm. Bosell, Wm. Smelt, Robt. Taylor, Cha. Jenings. Wit: Thos. Wythe, Cha. Jenings. Ack 20 June 1716. Recorded 25 June 1716.

[pp 33, 34] Appraisal of estate of Elizabeth James taken 8 June 1716. Long and interesting list of household items; one negro woman called Sarah valued at £27:10:0; jewelry, including two gold rings, one gold locket and a necklace of silver "beeds." Total value £80:13:10 1/4. Taken according to Ct Order 16 May 1716 being first sworn by Mr. John King, at the house of Elizabeth James, dec'd. Signed: Thos. Faulkner, John Bordland, Joseph Banister.

[p 34] Appraisal of estate of Johana Smith. "Joan Backhouse her part:" household items. Total £12:18:1. "Elizabeth Backhouse her part:" household items and "one old cow appraised Dec 27th at Thomas Backhouse plantation." Total £1:9:0. "Praised June 19th one young cow and calf." £1:10:0. "To" old bedsteads: 0:6:0 = Total £1:16:0. Appraisal signed by William Smelt, William Loyall.

[pp 35, 36] In obedience to Ct Order 15 --- 1715. Appraisal of estate of Nicholas Curle dec'd that appeared or was shown to us by the Exectrx. Negro men: Jack and Will at £30 per head; Shoreham and Mingo at £25 per head. Total £110:00:00. Dogo? at £20 and Japher? at £23. Total £43:00:00. Male children: Mingo at £10; Will at £6; Strumbelo at £8, Stepney at £6. Total £30:00:00. Negro women: Bess at £18, Jenny at £18, Deberah at £30, Kate at £15. Total £81:00:00. Hannah at £25, Tena at £7:20, Judith at £15, Moll at £15, Beak at £25, Nanny at £25. Total £112:10:00. Female children: Sue at £15, Hannah at £7:10, Abigail at £6, Rachell at £3, Phillis at £5, Frank at £3, Pheby at £7:10. Total £47:00:00. Three negroes given to Mrs. Curle -£123:10:00. By Mr. Curle's will - viz: Martha at £25, Sarah at £30, Moll at £25. Total £80:00:00. Born since Mr. Curle's death of one of the negroes given by Mr. Curle to his wife named Ned. £2:00:00. Total £82:00:00. Long list of livestock, furniture, linens - Total this page £168. Brought over - £591:16:00. More household items including "barrls of port at Barbadoes not valued." Total valuation £674:17:11. Signed: William Bosell, Edmd. Kearny, Tho. Tucker.

[pp 36, 37] Foeffees confirm for 178 lbs tobacco one lot or 1/2 ac in Town of Hampton to William Allen, beg at a hole in the ground on Mr. Anthony Armistead running along Wine St. N 10 d.w., 2 chains 25/100 to another hole in the ground, S 84 deg and 10 chains down to the cove at another hole on sd Armistead's land. The above lot was gr to Abraham Norden by deed dated 19 Sept 1706 and he not complying with the law, it is therefore granted to Wm. Allen. Ack 16 July 1716 by -m. Lowry and Fra. Ballard.

[pp 37-39] Ind dated 6 July 1716 between Charles Jenings and Elizabeth his wife of Co. of Eliz. City and William Westwood of same. Whereas William Naylor, late of Eliz. City Co. dec'd, did by his last will bequeath to Elizabeth his daughter, now wife of sd Charles Jenings, land containing by estimation 50 acs lying in the Co. for 5 sh [convey] the tract wheron Ralph Sidwell late of this Co. dec'd did formerly live and bounded on the N with Mr. Samuell Daniell, on the E by Thomas Naylor's and on the S and W with the land late belonging to Col. William Wilson dec'd etc. Signed: Cha. Jenings, Elizabeth Jenings. Wit: John Armistead, Matt. Ballard. Ack 18 July 1716 by Cha. Jenings & Elizabeth his wife. Release dated 7 July 1716 for 20 sh sterling. Elizabeth wife to sd Charles ack right of dower without compulsion and being privately examined.

[pp 39, 40] Last will and testament of Christopher Coopland, sick and weak. To eldest daughter Ann Poole, the plantation she now lives on according to the deed of gift. To youngest son Falni Coopland, land beg at a marked ash running Sly to the head of the line with reversion to son Elyas Coopland and further reversion to son William Coopland. To eldest son Elyas Coopland, the plantation "I now live on" and all the land binding on William Phrairs' line and upon son Wm. Coopland's line with reversion to son William. To son William Copland that piece of land that William Phrasy is going to seat , that is after the decease of Wm. Phrasy and his wife Mary, the daughter of Christopher Coopland. To son Elyas, the bed "whereon he lyes." To son Falvi Coopland, one cow, one yearling and one mare but daughter Hannah shall have the first foal. To daughter Hannah Coopland, one bed and one heifer yearling. To son William Coopland, household items after the decease of his mother. To son William Coopland and "my fond daughters," Mary Phrasey , Hursley Averitt, Elizabeth Firmer?, Jean Peirce, half a crown apiece. Loving wife to be sole Exectrx. [not named]. Dated 12 Jan 1710/11. Signed: Christopher Coopland. Wit: Thomas Baylis, Moses Davis, William Dunn, Mycall Peirce. Pro 21 March 1715 by Thomas Baylis, William Dunn and Mycall Peirce.

[p 41] Last will and testament of Mathew Watts of Eliz. City Co., sick & weak. Undated. To son Saml. Watts, "my dwelling plantation where I now live, to enjoy at age 21," with reversion to daughter Anne Watts. To daughter Ann Watts, 50 acs lying on the north side of Back River at age 16 with reversion to son Saml. If both die, sd land of 50 acs to brother Samuell Watts. To son Samuel, one negro

woman named Hanah and one boy named Jeffery and one child named Guy. To daughter Anne negro men named Colb and Will. "As for what money is due in England I leave it to my wife and children to be sent for in goods at her discretion." To son and daughter Saml. and Ann, £30 due by brother Samuel Watts to be divided between them when of age. Household goods and stock to be divided betwixt wife and children. Wife and Charles Tucker to be Execs. Signed: Matthew Watts. Wit: Tho. Jones, Wm. Crooke, Cassander Spicer. Pro 15 Aug 1716 by Tho. Jones and Wm. Crooke. Granted for probate to Hanah Armistead, Exectrx thereof. Rec 30 Aug 1716.

[p 42] Last will and testament of Ann Daniell of Eliz. City Co., very sick and weak. Dated 3 Oct 1715. To son Saml. Daniell, one negro boy called Jamey now in his possession, oxen, feather bed and furniture. All cattle that now run at Thomas Skinner's plantation to be equally divided between Ann Skinner, Jonathana Martha Mary and Darby Skinner [sic] To Samll. Skinner, a negro child Indey [or Judey] about 7 mo old and it to be with his mother Eliza. Skinner until he is 18 years old and two cows and calves, two ewes and lambs and one feather bed and what furniture goes with it. To Martha Pett, one heifer. To Sarah Pett, one yearling heifer. To Ann Mitchel, 20 sh current money. To daughter Catherine Pett, two ewes and lambs. To Elizabeth Riddlehurst, one cow. After debts are satisfied all stock, moveables within doors and without, and all the crop of corn and tobacco to son Samuel Daniel and he to serve as Exec. Signed: Ann (X) Daniell. Wit: John King, Edward Richards, Joseph (X) Skinner. Pro 15 Aug 1716 by Jno. King Gent and Joseph Skinner & probate granted to Exec. Rec 30 Aug 1716.

[p 43] Bond of Hinde Armistead and Hanah his wife; Antho. Armistead Senr; and Robert Armistead for £500 money of England dated 16 Aug 1716. Hanah Armistead, wife of Hinde Armistead and Exectrx of Mathew Watts dec'd, is to properly perform as Exectrx. Signed: Hinde Armistead, Hanah (X) Armistead, Antho. Armistead, Robt. Armistead, Antho. Armistead Junr. Wit: Cha. Jenings, Wm. Westwood. Ack 16 Aug. 1716.

[pp 44, 45] Ind dated 10 Sept. 1716. Foeffees [convey] for 5 sh current money of England to Antho. Armistead one lot or 1/2 acre lying in the town of Southampton on Southampton River beg at a stake in a cove running along W 6 chains up to Wine St., thence N 10 degrees W three chains 52/100, thence S 84 degrees E 7 chains down to the cove. Bounded on the N with the lots of the heirs of Col. Wilson dec'd, on the E with the cove, on the S with Capt. Wm. Boswell's lot, and on the W with Wine St. Signed: Willm. Lowery, Wm. Bosell. Ack 19 Sept 1716. Rec 26 Sept 1716. Release of above 11 Sept 1716 for 178 lbs good tobacco.

[p 45] Ind dated 13 Sept 1716. Foeffees [convey] for £5 lawful money of England to William Allen of Eliz. City Co., carpenter, one lot or 1/2 ac in the Town of Southampton on Southampton R. beg at a hole in the ground on Mr. Antho. Armistead running to Wine St. N 10 deg W 2 chains 25/100 to another hole in the ground S 84 deg E 10 chains down to the cove at another hole in the ground, thence along the cove to another hole on the sd Armistead's lot, so along his line N 84 deg W 7 chains to the beg. Signed: Willm. Lowery, Wm. Bosell. Ack 19 Sept 1716. Rec 27 Sept 1716. Release 14 Sept 1716 for 178 lbs good tobacco.

[p 48] "In obedience to a Ct Order dated -- August 1716, [we] have appraised the estate of Dunne Armistead as it was showed us." Signed: Ban. Smith, Francis S. Rogers [does not indicate his mark], Tho. Read. Inv includes household items, stock, "one buckanere Gun," one negro man, one negro man 60 years of age [neither named]. Total value £71:00:00. Rec 19 Sept 1716.

[pp 49, 50] Last will and testament of James Burtell of Eliz. City Co., sick and weak. To Childermus, third son of Madm. Katherine Croft, the house and half "my lott that I now live in" and all the out houses on the sd half lot joining Mr. Robert Taylor's in Hampton, with reversion to Childermus' brother Abraham. If both die, reversion to "my two brothers Edward and John Burtell." To Abraham, Madm. Croft's youngest son, "the other half of my lot and the house in which Mr. Wallace now lives in Hampton," with reversion to Childermus and then to brothers Edward and John Burtell. To Mrs. Marthay Taylor thirty-five pounds "if Please God my goods comes well in it being for her own use the goods I mean is from Mr. Wm. Wilson. Also to Mrs. Marthay Taylor my chariott horses and harness and the sd Mrs. Taylor is to enjoy the sd chariott and to do with it what she pleases Mr. Taylor having nothing to say which is my desire. If anybody will give £75 current money of Va. for my negro woman Kate and her child it is good. If not she and child may be sold by outcry and also my Negro Coffee and Injon Jack. To Abraham, youngest son of Madm. Croft my warfe [wharf] and land belonging to it" with reversion to his brother Childermus and then to brother Edward Burtell, "but in the mean time if anyone will build a house there and pay my Exec £5 a year [he] shall enjoy it until the heir is of age." After debts are paid, remaining goods to be sold and divided between "the two lads afsd." To brother John Burtell, all wearing apparel and it to be sent to him as soon as possible. Friend Mr. Cole Diggs to be Exec. If he refuse, friend Mr. Thomas Nelson of York Town to serve as Exec. Dated 10 Sept 1716. Signed: James Burtell. Wit: George Waffe, Joseph Banister, John Smith. Pro by Joseph Banister 19 Sept 1716 & by George Wauffe and Jno. Smith 20 Sept 1716. Ord rec.

[pp 50, 51] Bond. Tho. Wilcox and Henry Jenkins Gent are bound to Justices for £160 lawful money of England. Tho. Wilcox is Adm of estate of Elizabeth James, dec'd. Signed: Thomas Wilcox. Wit: John Bayley, Cha. Jenkins. Rec 2 Nov. 1716.

[p 51] Henry Jenkins shows the will of Mr. James Burtell and states he is desirous of building a house on the wharf at £5 per year and will comply with the conditions of the will. Signed: Henry Jenkins. Rec -- Sept 1716.

[p 51] "Williamsburgh July the 1st 1715. Mr. John Holloway having this day applyed to me in Behalfe of the Justices of Elizabeth Citty County for leave to Build Their New Court House at Hampton, I doe approve of the Removall and Shall accordingly Order the Sheriff to attend the Court there so soon as the House shall be fit for the Reception of the Justices." A. Spotswood.

[pp 52, 53 damaged] Ind dated 13 Nov. 1716. Foeffees [convey] to Thomas Wythe 25 poles of land in the town of Southampton on Southampton River, beg at a hole in the ground and running along King St. N 10 degrees W 1 chain 22/100 to another hole in the ground on Mr. Henry Jenkins lot, N 81 degrees E 5 chains 20/100 to Richard Kirken's lot and on the S by Mr. James Wallace, dec'd, and on the W by

King St. [formerly gr] to Wallace on 18 June 1706 and he having relapsed his time, it is now sold to Tho. Wythe. Signed: Wm. Lowery and Wm. Bosell. Wit: Cha. Jenings, Henry Jenkins, Saml. Selden, Edmd. Hollier. Ack 21 Nov. 1716. Release dated 14 Nov 1716 for 60 lbs good toba.

[p 54, damaged] "In obedience to the orders of the Genll. and Co. Courts made for a division of the negroes and personal estate of Nicho. Curle, decd. Inventory made 14 Dec 1716 at the House of Mr. James Ricketts in Hampton Town." Signed: Henry Irwin, George Walker. Genll. Ct held at the Capitol at WmBurgh 30 Oct 1716. "Met [on 14 Dec 1716] at Rickett's and the estate was not produced, Rickett's alleging that the Great Part of the Estate was in the hands of Mr. Henry Jenkins and John Curle." Signed: Henry Irwin, George Walker, Wm. Smelt.

[p 55] Inv of Eliza. Andrews estate taken 19 Nov 17--. Household items and stock. No value given. Signed: Richd. Nusum.

[p 55] In obedience to Ct Order of 21 Nov 1716 the estate of Eliza. Andrews is sold. Names mentioned in accts of sale: Richard Nusum, Mr. John Bayley, Francis Rogers, Edmd. Hollier, Geo. Waffe Junr, Mr. Cha. Jenings, Edwd. Andrews. Signed: Simon Hollier, Sheriff. Rec 8 Jan. 1716.

[p 55] 21 Nov 1716. William Coopland and Elizabeth Coopland of Eliz. City Co., for love and respect, deed to brother and sister William Frasey and Mary his wife, both of Co. afsd, a parcel of 16 acs at the head of Harris Cr. Deed is for life, or the longest liver of them. Land adjoins Christopher Coopland, late dec'd. William and Mary Frasey within two years are to plant out 300 Grigson apple trees and must keep the property in good repair. At their deaths the tract reverts to sd William and Elizabeth Coopland or their estate. Signed: Wm. Coopland, Eliza. Coopland. Wit: Cha. Jenings. Ack 19 Dec 1716 by Wm. Coopland and Elizabeth his wife, who also relinquishes dower rights.

[pp 57, 58] 19 Dec 1716. Bond of John Birtell, John King & Robt. Taylor, all of Eliz. City Co., for John Birtell's performance as Adm with will annexed of estate of James Birtell dec'd. Inv ord. Signed: John Burtell, John King,

Robt. Taylor. Wit: Simeon Hollier, Cha. Jenings. Pro 3 July 1716. Ack 19 Dec 1716.

[pp 58-60] Ind dated 6 Dec 1716 between Richard Hopkins of Hampton in Eliz. City Co., carpenter, and Emannuell Alkin of same, chirurgeon. Richard Hopkins [conveys] to Alkin for 5 sh part of the lot where he now lives situate in Wine St. beg on S side of Peter Burten's lot on front of Wine St., then to extend 35 foot in breadth on the sd front to southward and so to continue the breadth of 35 foot the full length and bounds of Hopkin's lot. Wit: Robert Mew , John (X) Roe. Ack 19 Dec 1716 by Richd. Hopkins. Rec 22 Jan 1716. Release 7 Dec 1716 for £15 current money of Va. Same signatures & wit. Ack 9 Dec 1716 by Richd. Hopkins and Joyce his wife.

[p 60] 15 Sept 1714. Bond of Ann Williams, Benjm. Smith & Robt. Armistead, all of Eliz. City Co. Ann Williams, Exectrx of will of William Williams dec'd., is to make inv etc. Signed: Ann (X) Williams, Benjamin Smith. Wit: Cha. Jenings, John Armistead. Marginal note: Ack 15 Sept 1714.

[p 61] 15 Sept 1714. Bond of Margt. Priest and Saml. Snignell, both of Eliz. City Co. Margt. Priest, Exectrx of will of James Priest dec'd, to perform all duties etc. Signed: Margt. (X) Priest, Samll. Snignell.

[pp 62, 63] 21 Jan 1716. John Burtell of the Island of Barmoodas, Adm of estate of his late brother James Burtell, gives power of attorney to friends John King and Robert Taylor of Eliz. City Co. to act for him in any est matters. Signed: John Burtell. Wit: Wm. Bosell, Wm. Smelt, John Mitchal. Pro 28 Feb 1716 by Wm. Bosell and Wm. Smelt. Rec 19 Mar 1716.

[pp 62-64] Ind dated 18 Feb. 1716 between Henery Turner and Sidwell his wife of Co. of Eliz. City and William Westwood of same. Turner conveys land whereon Worlich Westwood, late of this Co. dec'd lived beg at the cleared ground eastward on a spring belonging to the plantation, running westward & southward to Gray's Swamp. Signed: Henery (X) Turner, Sidwell Turner. Wit: Hen. Jenkins, Antho. Armistead Junr, Cha. Jenings. Ack 21 Feb 1716 by Henery Turner & Sidwell his wife. Rec 19 Mar 1716. Release 19 Feb 1716 for £40 current silver money of Va. Same signatures &

wit. Ack 21 Feb 1716 by Henery Turner & Sidwell, wife to Turner.

[p 64] Affadavit of Thomas Francis, witness in the suit by ejectment now depending between Robt. Westlake, plt and Pasco Curle, by James Ricketts and Jane his wife, his guardians, deft. Thomas Francis makes oath that "I very well knew Jane Pool, late of this Co., and also Thomas Pool, the lessor of the plt, is their oldest son and that the same Jane afterwards married one Averit and that I well knew the land claimed by the sd Westlake on demise of Thomas Poole was in the possession of the same Jane at the time of her death and have heard she was an Alien and that after her decease it was found to escheat." Signed: Thomas (X) Francis. "Taken before me in the presence of James Ricketts."11 Oct. 1716. Signed: Willm. Lowry.

[p 65] 3 Nov 1716. "Alexander Spotswood, his Majt. Lieut. Governor and Commander in Cheife of This Dominion" grants adm of Elizabeth James' estate to Thomas Wilcox, Creditor. Signed: A. Spotswood.

[p 66] At Kirkwall 14 Nov 1716. Agreement betwixt Mr. James Liddell, merchant in Leith & supercargo on board the Ship "the Friendship" of Leith, Capt. Walter Keth, Commander, presently in Carston Road in Orkney bound for the West Indies, and Thomas Tomson, cordine., in Kirkwall. Tomson binds himself as servant to Liddell and his assigns in Va. or "Marry land" in America for the accustomed years after his arrival there. Liddell is to furnish Toms<u>one</u> a suit of clothes and other necessaries and to pay his "fraught" and maintain him sufficiently on the voyage. Tomsone cannot write, so the public notary is writing this before Robert Marsone, merchant in Kirkwall, and Hugh Gyer, both of whom sign as witnesses. Rec 10 May 1717.

[pp 66-69] Ind dated 18 March 1717 between Thomas Needham and Margtt. his wife of Co. of Eliz. City and William Dandridge Gent, of afsd Co. Land conveyed is one-half acre lot in Towne of Hampton on South Hampton R. in Co. of Eliz. City, beg at a stake on Joseph Wragg's lot & running along 5 chains to a stake, thence E along a lane 5 1/2 chains to another stake, S on another lane 3 1/2 chains, to another stake, along Joseph Harris 4 1/2 chains to beg, each chain containing two poles. Signed: Thomas Needham, Margt.

Needham. Wit: Edmd. Kearny, Michl. Kearney, Thomas Howard. Ack 16 May 1717 by Tho. Needham & Margtt. his wife. Rec 15 June 1717. Release 19 Mar 1717 for £16 current silver money of Va. Same signatures & witnesses. Ack 16 May 1717.

[pp 69-71] Ind dated 14 Dec 1716. Foefees [convey] to John Roe of Town of Hampton, carpenter, 35 1/2 poles of land & marsh in Hampton Towne, beg at a hole in the ground on the head of a cove and running along Wm. Bayley's lot N 88 deg E 8 poles to another hole on North St, thence along the same 20 deg W four poles to the Cove. Same course continued to 9 poles at a stake in the marsh and from thence 36 deg west 11 poles to beg. Signed: William Lowery, Francis Ballard, William Boswell, Foefees. Wit: Robert Minson. Ack 21 Feb 1716. Rec 5 July 1717. Release 15 Dec 1716 for 80 lbs tobacco. Same signatures and witness. Ack 21 Feb 1716. Rec 5 July 1717.

[p 72] Last will and testament of William Bowtell, sick and weak. The plantation "whereon I live" is to be divided equally between "my two sons William and Adam, my wife to have her third part during life." To son John, land at Fox Hill and wife her third part for life. To daughter Sarah, two young cows and their increase to be delivered to her at age 16. Sons to receive bequests at age 20. All the rest of estate to be used for the bringing up of the children. Dated 11 May 1714. Signed: William Bowtell. Wit: Tho. Naylor, Ann Roe, John (X) Skinner. Pro 16 May 1717 by Jno. Skinner and James Naylor who also proved his brother Thomas Naylor's handwriting. Certificate granted to Eliza. Bowtell, wido [she] giving bond. Rec 11 July 1717.

[pp 72, 73] Last will and testament of Thomas Naylor of Eliz. City Co., sick and weak. To son William Naylor, the plantation where "I now live" and to his heirs with reversion to daughter Mary Naylor and further reversion to wife Elizabeth Naylor. To wife, negro man Harry during her life and afterward to son William Naylor. To daughter Mary Naylor, negro woman called Belle and her child Peter and her increase. To son William, £15 in money at sixteen penny weight for every five shillings and the same to daughter Mary. To wife Elizabeth, the cot she lies on and all furniture belonging to it and horse and colt, two oxen, cart four wheels. To son Wm., household items and stock when he is 16. To daughter Mary, household items when 16. All personal estate to wife Eliza. and she to be sole Exectrx. Dated 30 March 1717. Signed: Thomas Naylor. Wit: Cha. Jenings, William Westwood, Eliza. Jenings. Pro 15 May 1717 by Cha. Jenings and Wm. Westwood. Probate granted to Exectrx, she giving bond. Inv ord. Rec 12 July 1717.

[p 74] Bond of Henry Jenkins and John King to pay rent according to the will of John Burtell dated --June 1717. Jenkins has built a house on the wharf. Signed: Henry Jenkins, John King. Wit: Cha. Jenings, Tho. Wythe. Rec 13 July 1717.

[pp 74, 75] Ind dated 18 Dec. 1716 between the Justices of Eliz. City Co. and William Bosell. The Justices confirm to Bosell for 5 sh all that seller underneath the Court House of the Co. of Eliz. City in the Towne of Hampton on South Hampton R., which sd piece of town land the sd Wm. Boswell sold to the Justices for the building of a Court House. "the sd Celler and premises with appurtenances unto William Bosell." Signed: John Holloway, William Lowry, Francis Ballard, Simeon Hollier, Antho. Armistead, Tho. Wythe, John Bayley, John King, Marke Johnson. Ack 18 July 1717. Release, also for 5 sh, dated 17 Dec 1717. Rec 25 July 1717.

[pp 77-79] Ind dated 9 Jan 1716 between Margaret Bayley, widdow, of Parish and Co. of Eliz. City and Henry Irwin, Gent of Towne of Hampton for 5 sh. Margaret Bayley [conveys] a lot in Hampton bounded as follows: beg at a hole in the ground by a cedar bush on the bank of the river and so along Ann Averson's lot 10 chains to a hole in the ground. Thence along a lane or street 2 chains to a hole in the ground, thence along George Minson's lot 10 chains down to the river... Land was formerly granted to Mr. Walter Bayley dec'd by deed of 18 Oct 1702 and deserted. Then it was surveyed 25 March 1712 by Mr. Wm. Lowery, Surveyor of Eliz. City Co., for Mr. Bayley, son to sd Walter Bayley, and by John Bayley and Judith his wife sold to sd Margt. Bayley. Signed: Margret Bayley. Wit: John Fitzgerald, John Finlason, Henry Wood. Ack & rec -- July 1717. Release 10 July 1716 for £150 current silver money of Va. Ack 17 July 1717. Rec 29 July 1717.

[pp 79-81] Ind dated 7 July 1717 between Antho. Armistead Gent Senr and Ann his wife of Co. of Eliz. City and Robt. Minson of Towne of Hampton. [Armistead conveys] to Minson for 5 sh a lot in Hampton, beg at a stake in a cove running along an old ditch W 6 chains up to Wine St., N 10 deg W 3 52/100 chains thence S 84 deg E 7 chains down to the cove to beg. Bounded by lots of the heirs of Col. Wilson dec'd, on the E with the cove, on the S with Capt. Wm. Bosell and on the W with Wine St. Sold to Antho. Armistead by Foeffees 10 & 11 Sept 1716. Signed: Antho. Armistead, Ann Armistead. Wit: James Servant, Emanl. Alkin. Release 8 July 1717 for £16 current silver money of Virga. Ack 17 July 1717. Rec 29 July 1717.

[pp 82, 83] Ind dated 17 June 1717 between William Allen, carpenter, and Erwin his wife and John Robinson, carpenter, for 5 sh one half of lot [conveyed] in Hampton Towne lying northwardly next to the town ditch taking the half breadth of the whole lot upon the st, running eastward – 1/4 acre. Signed: William Allen, Erwin (X) Allen. Wit: Joseph Wragg, Edmd. Hollier. Ack 17 July 1717. Rec 30 July 1717. Release 18 June 1717 for 40 sh current silver money of Va.

[p 84] Last will and testament of Humphrey Baylis, "being sicke and weake and like to die." To son Jno. Baylis, the upper end of land adj Wm. Baylis. To son Thomas Baylis, the land "I now live on" and to be divided by two men as they see fit so that each son get plantable land. Wife and two sons to be Execs. [Wife not named] Dated 8 Sept 1716. Signed: Humphrey (X) Baylis. Wit: Thomas Baylis, Jno. Whitfield, Tho. (X) Poole. Pro by same witnesses 17 July 1717.

[p 84] 15 Apr 1717. Power of Atty from Rich. Lewis to friend Robert -------- to represent him in the action brought by Mr. Edmd. Kearny. Wit: H. Irwin. Pro by Henry Irwin gent. Rec 19 June 1717.

[p 85] Appraisal made acc to Ct Order of 10 May 17-7. Estate of Mr. Matthew Watts dec'd by Hind Armistead & [blank]. List includes household items and stock values at £45:18:3. Sworn before Fra. Ballard 14 June 1717. Signed: Cha. Jenings, Jno. Howard, Robert (X) Johnson on 15 June 1717.

[p 86] Inv of Wm. Boutwill dec'd taken by Ct Order of 26 May 1717. Stock and household items. Value £20:5:3. Signed: Tho. Tucker, Robt. Bright, Charles Cooper on 17 June 1717. Rec 30 Aug 1717. [Inv includes "one old Indian Slave lame and blind" not named.]

[pp 86-89] Appraisal of Mr. James Burtell taken 24 Dec 1716 as produced by Simon Hollier, Sheriff, and Joseph Banister. Four pages of various household items, fabrics and findings, parts for ships, arms etc. Total £68:10:9. Signed: F. Ballard, Thos. Howard, Wm. Bosell.

[pp 89, 90] Last will and testament of Robert Bright of Eliz. City Co., sick and weak. To son Robt. Bright Junr of Virginia "all my lands, tenements, houses, orchards, cattle, debts, dues or demands, moveables and unmoveable, all rights and titles that ever did lawfully belong to me from the beginning of the World to this Present Day, Negroes also. And that sd Robert Bright Junr shall be Intaile for his lawful heirs." Son to be Exec. Dated 21 Oct. 1717. Signed: Robert (X) Bright. Wit: Thomas Naylor, Charles Cooper, Stephen Lillis. Pro 18 Oct 1717 by Stephen Lillis who also made oath that he saw Tho. Naylor dec'd, one of wit, sign. Pro by Cha. Cooper -- Feb 1717.

[pp 90-92] Last will and testament of Thomas Tabb of Eliz. City Co. Gent, sick and weak. To son John Tabb, part of land beg...by the Marsh running S as far as the parcel reaches, being the plantation "I now dwell on" with reversion to son Henry Tabb. To son Thomas Tabb, all beginning part of the plantation with reversion to son Edward Tabb. To wife, one negro woman named Moll formerly given her by her father Moss, together with five negroes more named Jack, Peter, Tom, Black Betty and Nanny, the last five mentioned given her by her former husband. To wife, "my horse Prince and a new side-saddle together with one bed she had from her father Moss with furniture as valuable as them belonging to the bed." To wife, all the plate left her by her Father and former husband. To son John Tabb, one negro man named Will and a negro woman Fillis and her future increase. To son Thomas Tabb, one negro woman named Moll and her future increase and one negro boy Robin. To son Henry Tabb, one negro woman named Mundingo Sarah and one negro boy Jack. To son Edward Tabb, two negro boys Paul and Will, one negro girl Jenny and her increase. To daughter Diannah Tabb, one negro woman named Frank with her increase and negro boy named Homady. To daughter Mary, one negro boy named Kane & negro girl named Sue and her increase. To daughter Rachel, negro boy Jeffery and girl Breck. To daughter Martha, three negro girls Phillis, Hannah and Judey. Three negroes Watt, Tony and Sarah to be appr and the value thereof together with what plate and cash "I have at present" to be equally divided amongst children. To son John, a young horse of his own choice. To son-in-law Francis Haywerd, one young horse with T+T a blaze in his forehead and one white foot. To daughter-in-law Elisabeth, one young horse, a light roan. To son Thomas Tabb, one seal ring stampt with TT. To daughters Mary and Rachil, each two rings. All remaining estate, to wit, stock, household goods and money in England etc to be sold and, after debts are paid, the value to be equally divided amongst wife and children. Sons are to receive their estates at age 21 and not before, and daughter at age 16 or marriage. Dated 20 Sept 1717. Signed: Thomas Tabb. Wit: ----Hayward, Wm. Tabb, Richard Slater. Pro by Henry Haward, Tabb and Slater 16 Oct 1717. Rec 4 ---1717.

[pp 92, 93] Deed. Elisabeth Tabb, widdow and relict of Thomas Tabb, dec'd, "for natural affection I bear unto my brother-in-law Edwd. Tabb of Charles Parish in the Co. of York and for other considerations ... grant unto him all right, title, claim ... to all the lands ... lying in Eliz. City Co. whereof my late husband Thomas Tabb died seized." Dated 16 Oct 1717. Signed: Elizabeth (X) Tabb. Wit: Wm. More, Meritt Sweny. Ack 16 Oct 1717. Rec -- Nov 1717.

[p 93] Bond of Edward Tabb of Charles Parish in Co. of York, Simon Hollier and Samuel Sweny, both of Eliz. City, for £1000 for Edwd. Tabb's performance as Exec of Thomas Tabb's estate. Inv to be made etc. Dated 16 Oct 1717. Signed: Edward Tabb, Simon Hollier, Saml. Sweny. Wit: Charles Jenings, Tho. Wythe. Rec 22 --- 1717.

[p 94] 18 Dec 1717. Bond of William More and Simon Hollier, both of Eliz. City Co., for £100 for William More's performance as gdn of his brother Lazarus More and the est left him by the last will & testament of John More, dec'd.

Signed: William More, Simon Hollier. Wit: Henry Jenkins, Cha. Jenings. Ack 18 Sept 1717. Rec 11 June 1717.

[pp 94, 95] Ind dated 9 Nov 1717 between William Balis of the Parish and Co. of Eliz. City, planter, and James Brown of the same, for 20 sh current money. [Balis conveys] tract or messuage he has in the dividend called the Black Walnut Ridge containing about 20 acs lying between the lands of Thomas Balis and land late in posession of Humphry Balis dec'd. Signed: William Balis. Wit: Saml. Selden. Ack 18 Dec 1717. Release 10 Dec 1717 for £19. Rec 11 Jan 1717.

[p 96] Bond 10 Nov 1717. William Balis of Parish & Co. of Eliz. City bound unto James Brown, cordwindr. for £40. Signed: William Balis. Wit: Saml. Selden. Ack 18 Dec 1717. Rec 12 Jan 1717.

[p 96] 21 Nov 1716. "We, Tho. Wood and Ann Wood of the Co. of Eliz. City...for the kindness and respect we ... beare unto Sarah Hayes and Henry Hayes her son" give 40 foot square of land within their lot in Hampton at the head of the gardens adj Edwd. Lattimore. Sarah is to have the land for life and at her decease Henry may keep it until he marries, but no longer. Sarah and Henry may not let or rent any portion of the land or any houses they may build on the land. Signed: Tho. Wood, Ann (X) Wood. Wit: James Tompson, James Wilson, Jo. Wragg. Ack 21 Nov 1716.

[p 97] Charles Town, South Carolina. 9 Oct 1717. Power of Atty. John Croft of Charles Town in the Province afsd, Gentleman, to wife Katherine Croft to [act as his agent] in all matters in the Colony of Va., particularly in administering on the estate of James Burtell, late of Va. dec'd, for and on behalf " of my two children Childermus and Abraham, her sons." Signed: John Croft. Wit: Grasinham Salter, Tho. Johnson. Pro 18 Dec 1717 by Grisinham Salter.

[p 98] Power of Atty from the following group of "Mariners or Saylors" to Henry Irwin Gent of Hampton, Eliz. City Co. to recover wages not paid by Capt. Wm. Chappel, on a voyage from Liverpoole to Hampton in the Ship "Eleanor" of Liverpoole. Wages due from 6 Jan 1716/17 to 19 Oct 1717 being nine months and thirteen days.

William Merridel £8:18:6 - Signed: Wm. Mirridel
Edwd. Bowdal £7:10:10 - Signed: Edwd. (X) Bowdal
John Basnett £6:18:6 - Signed: John Basnet
George Smallhane £8:13:00 - Signed: Geo. Smallhane
Wm. Roberts £8:13:11 - Signed: Wm. Roberts
Wit: John Wallace, Tho. Lattimer, Joseph Wragg. Pro 18 Dec 1717 by the oath of Jno. Wallace and affirmation of Jos. Wragg.

Note: Pagination in the photocopy of the original becomes confused, possibly because of a clerical error. The next original page number is "90" with a modern "a" appended. The following badly damaged page is marked "93a" and its reverse "94a. Next comes "95" in original pagination with "a" added through p. 99a.

[pp 99, 90a, 93] the latter two badly damaged] Ind dated 16 Dec 1717 between Robert Minson of Town of Hampton and Tho. Wright of same for 5 sh [Minson conveys] 20 foot of ground on Wine St. next to the lot of William Allen running easterly and 50 foot from sd St. running southerly 20 foot keeping the 20 foot breadth to the end of the sd 50 foot which piece of land together with a greater quantity Robt. Minson bought of Antho. Armistead gent Senr. Signed: Robert Minson. Wit: Cha. Jenings, Eliza. (X) Ballard. Ack 18 Dec 1717. Rec 14 ---1717. Release 17 Dec 1717 for £10 current Spanish money of Virga.

[pp 93a,94a] [Note; Appears to be a deed from Robert Minson to John Middleton. Page is so damaged that a precise land description cannot be given].. six foot ... where he lives ... for a passage into the street and nine foot ... bounds of Anthony Armistead Senr. Date and signature missing. Wit: Cha. Jenings, Eliza. Ballard. Release says 30 foot square.

[pp 95a, 96a] Ind dated 15 Mar 1716 between Elizabeth Selden of Parish and Co. of Eliz. City, spinster, and Samuel Selden of same for £5 current money. Elizabeth Selden "setts over" unto Samuel Selden her father all plantations, messuages and tracts in the Parish and Co. of Eliz. City commonly called by the name of Buckroe, scituate at the head of Mill Cr. and late in the tenure of one Charles Morryson; one other called Old Fields, scituate on or near the head of Hampton R. and late in possession of one Thomas Batt; and one other called Back River Plantation, late the possession of one Henry Robinson lying on the Back R. between the land of George Cooper and the land gr to one Needham. All these plantations were lately sold and transferred by the sd Samuel Selden and Rebeckah his wife to the sd Elizabeth by deed of lease and release. Signed: Elizabeth Selden. Wit: George Yeo, Benjamin Ralph, Samll. White. Ack 15 May 1717. Release 16 March 1716 for £500.

[pp 97a, 98a] Ind dated 18 March 1717 between Thomas Cornelius of Hampton Towne in Eliz. City Co. and Richard Hopkins of same, for 5 sh. [Conveys] a piece of a lot gr to Cornelius by deed under hand of Wm. Lowery and Nicholas Curle, gent Foeffees, dated 18 July 1717. Lot bounded on sd Richard Hopkins northward and running upon Wine St. 30 & 5 foot in breadth and bounding on sd Cornelius and Abraham Mitchell. Signed: Thomas Cornelius. Wit: Bartrand Proby, Richard Nusum, Joseph Wragg. Ack 19 March 1717. Release 19 March for £11 current money of Va.

[p 99a] 18 Mar 1717. Power of Atty to Mr. Henry Jenkins to ack certain deeds for land made to Thomas Jones. Signed: William (X) Hatchell, Ann (X) Hatchell.
Ind dated 18 Mar 1717. William Hatchell and Ann his wife for £6 current money of Va. sell to Tho. Jones, Cordwindr., and Phillis his wife 10 acs in Eliz. City Co., being part of a dividend where sd Wm. Hatchell now dwells lying northeast from his dwelling house [which was] formerly Mr. Pasco Dunn's. Confirmed to Thomas and Phillis Jones during their natural lives. Signed: William (X) Hatchell, Ann (X) Hatchell. Wit: Wm. (X) Hatchell Junr, Mary (X) Hatchell. Ack by Henry Jenkins by power of atty 19 March 1717. Rec 19 June 1718.

[pp 99a-101] Ind dated 17 March 1718. Foefees to John Cooke, carpenter for 5 sh, 12 poles on land in Hampton, beg at a stake running across end of Joseph Wragg's lot N 10 1/2 deg, W 1 & 82/100 chains to another stake S 76 deg 1 & 44/100 chains to beg, each chain 2 poles. Bounded on S with Tho. Needham, on E with ----, N with Cook's own, on W with Joseph Wragg. Signed: Willm. Lowry, Francis Ballard. Ack 19 Mar 1717. Release for 30 lbs tobacco 18 Mar 1718. Rec 13 June 1718.

[pp 102, 103] 20 May 1718. [deed of gift] Ann Parsons, wido and relict of John Parsons late of Charles Parish in the Co. of York, dec'd. For the natural love and affection Ann has for her son William Parsons of Parish and Co. afsd, and in fulfilling the will and desire of her deceased husband, grants to her son a tract in Eliz. City Co. whereon Joseph Hull formerly lived and where Danl. ---- s lated lived, lying on Back R., and bounded on N by Geo. Rogers, by patent 335 acs. Signed: Ann (X) Parsons. Wit: Cha. Jenings. Ack 21 May 1718. Rec 13 June 1718.

[p 103] 20 May 1718. [Deed of gift] Ann Parsons, wido and relict of John Parsons late of Charles Parish in the Co. of York, dec'd. For the natural love and affection Ann has for her son James Parsons. Land on Back R. whereon William Wilson now lives and bounded southerly on a small branch that divides this land and the land belonging to Mark Johnson Gent, and westward on land of Jno. More Gent, dec'd, containing by patent 82 acs. Signed: Ann (X) Parsons. Wit: Cha. Jenings. Ack 21 May 1718. Rec 13 June 1718.

[pp 104-106] Indenture dated 19 May 1718 between Abraham Mitchell and John Henry Rumbagh, both of Hampton in Co. of Eliz. City. [Conveyed] for 5 sh land lying in Hampton beg on North St. on the N side of William Loyall running 5 chains to the head of Thomas Cornelius Wstly 40 foot Nly to sd Mitchall Ely 5 chains along North St. and 45 foot Sly. Signed: Abraham Mitchell. Wit: Cha. Jenings, Robert Minson. Ack 21 May 1718. Release 20 May 1718 for £20 current Spanish money of Va. from Abraham Mitchell and Ann his wife. Signed: Abraham Mitchell and Ann (X) Mitchell. Ack 21 May 1718. Rec 4 June 1718.

[p 106] Bond of William Dandridge, John Holloway Gent, Edmond Kearny & Wm. Smelt, all of Eliz. City Co. 19 Sept 1717. Whereas Col. William Wilson died possessed of a considerable estate , and Wilson Rascow, late of sd Co. [undecipherable] of his Executorship and did possess himself of the greatest part of that est and died also. Euphan, widdow of Wilson Rascow, was Executrx and did possess herself of the estate. Euphan has intermarried with above Wm. Dandridge who is now bound to pay all just debts of both estates and to distribute all bequests.

Signed: William Dandridge, Jno. Holloway, Edmd. Kearny. Rec 19 Sept 1717.

[pp 107, 108] Last will and testament of Mark Parish of Eliz. City Co., sick and weak. To wife Temperance Parish, manor plantation where son Abraham Parish now lives, 50 acs, for life or until marriage; 1/3 part of earnings of mill clear of all charges; long list of household furnishings and stock; and negr. girl Judith. After wife's marriage or decease, all returns to sd Abraham Parish. To grandson Mark Parish, 50 acs beg on E side of Little Mill Dam, Nly into the woods but not running to the Swd, with reversion to his next eldest brother [not named]. To grandson Edwd. Parish, 100 acs. To son Abraham Parish, manor plantation at death or marriage of wife. To grandson Mark Parish, items. To grandson Edwd. Parish, items. All the rest of estate to son Abrm. Parish and he to be Exec. Dated 9 June 1717. Signed: Mrk. Parish. Wit: Henry Jenkins, Jno. Bayley, Jno. Curle. Pro 19 Mar 1717 by Henry Jenkins and Jno. Bayley.

[pp 108, 109] Last will and testament of Stephen Layless, sick and weak. Legacy of £10 left to decedant by his son John and now in the hands of Catherine Norden to be divided equally between wife [unnamed], son Thomas, and daughter [unnamed]. To Mary Henderson, 1/2 of all personal estate and to Catherine Norden, the remaining 1/2. Catherine Norden and John Bordland to be Execs. Dated 17 Dec 1717. Signed: Stephen (X) Layless. Wit: Nathanl. Parker, Jno. Henry Rombogh, Joseph Wragg. Pro 8 Mar 1717 by oath of Rombogh and affirmation of Jos. Wragg.

[pp 109, 110] Ind dated 13 Nov 1717 between Wm. Jones, shipwright, of the Kingdom of Great **Brittan** and James Gilbert of Eliz. City Co., planter, for 20 sh. [Conveyed] tract in Eliz. City Co. lately in possession of William Winter, bounded with a Cr. that divides it from land called Fortfield, and on W by land of Barto. Proby, on N with the Glebe, on E with land of John Jones. Signed: Wm. (X) Jones. Wit: Jno. Selden, George Yeo, Saml. White. Pro by same three wit on 19 Feb 1717. Release 14 Nov 1717 for £74 sterling. Pro 19 Feb 1717. Rec 9 July 1718.

[pp 111, 112] Last will and testament of Thomas Merry of Eliz. City Co., sick and weak. To son Prettyman Merry, negro boy Will. To son Thomas Merry, negro girl Sarah. To son John Merry, negro girl Hanner. To daughter Elizabeth Merry, negro girl Bess. To daughter Mary Merry, negro girl Fillis and £5 current money. To cousin Wm. Brasey, stock. To cousin Mary Brasey, stock. Unto "ten of the poor" of Eliz. City Co., "ten barells of Indian corn and 100 ells of brown oxenbriggs" to be at the disposing of Exec and friend Mr. Wm. Lowery to give to whom they think most in want. If any of the children die before coming of age, [his] negro to be divided between the others. If one of the negroes die, payment of £25 to his owner to be made from estate. All the rest of estate to be divided equally among children. Sons to receive estate at age 18 and daughter at 16 years or marriage. Friend and kinsman William Tucker to be Exec. If he dies, then friend Saml. Roberts to serve. Dated 12 May 1718. Signed: Thomas Merry. Wit: Simon Hollier, Hans Ward, Jno. (X) Wilson. Pro 18 June 1718 by all three witnesses.

[pp 112, 113] Last will and testament of Robert Johnson of Eliz. City Co., sick and weak. To Charles Cely, stock. To Wm. Cely, items. All the rest of estate to son Thos. Johnson with reversion to John Bordland of Hpt. Towne. To Jno. Floyd of Warrick Co., one sh. Mr. James Ricketts and Jno. Bordland to be Execs and John Bordland to bring up son until he comes of age. Dated 27 Mar 1718. Signed: Robert (X) Johnson. Wit: Jo. Wragg, Catherine (X) Whitticar, William (X) Spicer. Pro 22 May 1718 by oaths of William Spicer and Kert. Whittaker and affirmation of Joseph (blank). Rec 11 July 1718.

[pp 113-119] Note: Six pp. relating to the appr of est of Majr. William Armistead dec'd. Dated 16 May 1718. First appears a list of slaves:

```
                                                    £  sh  d
Lucy a girl 26: Mingo a Man 28; Towrey a Man 30-  84:0:0
Mallachi a man 32: Geysa old man 15: Juday,woman  77:0:0
Betty old woman 20: Catty a girl 25: Sary, woman  70:0:0
Frank a girl 13: Nanney a woman distempered 15    28:0:0
Bess a girl 22: Barbery a woman 28                50:0:0
Lemmon? a old sick man 10                         10:0:0
```
Next part headed "In the Porch Chamber"
one and 1/2 pp household items, including beds and bedstead, fabrics, 22 diaper napkins, linens, 2 1/2 doz

silver "brest" buttons, new and old leather chairs both high and low.

Next part is headed "Chamber" and lists feather beds & furnishings, small table and eathern mug etc.

Next part headed "In the Kitchen" and is an inventory of hundreds of items including 48 1/2 of silver plate.[sic] Next part is an inventory of stock.

This portion was made by order of Ct of 9 Mar 1717/18. Signed: 17 May 1718 by Fra. Ballard, John King, Joseph Banister.

Here follow 2 1/4 more pp with no headings. Various household items, tools, farm and carpenter tools, stock etc. "Sume Totall £708:16:16 3/4"

Last: "The following negroes given by will (to wit) Will, Phillis, Moll, Robbin, Mundingo: Sarah, Jack, Paul, Will dec'd since, Jenny, Frank, Hammady, Cain, Sue, Jessy, Beck, Phillis, Hanah, Judy, one Seal Ring and four hoop Rings." Signed: William Lowery, Simon Hollier, Tho. Wythe, Tho. Merry "being first sworn by Mr. Mark Johnson." No date for latter portions of inv.

[pp 119, 120] Inv & appr of est of Thomas Merry, dec'd. 10 June 1718 by Simon Hollier, John King, Edwd. Tabb, Edmond Hollier. Stock, household items, etc. and the following negroes: £ sh d
Man Tom – 40; Woman Pegg – 30   70:0:0
Woman Judy – 25: Man Toney – 25   50:0:0
Woman Nanny   33:0:0
                    Total   289:15:4
Negroes given by will and not appr Vizt: Bess, Wilabey, Sarah, Phillis, Hanah and two cows and calves per Wm. Tucker.

[pp 120, 121] Last will and testament of John Stringer of Co. of Eliz. City, sick and weak. To son John Stringer, stock, bed & furniture & all pewter except 2 dishes and 4 plates given to son Daniel. To sister Elizabeth Wethersby, corn, wheat & hoggs for the use of my son John who is to remain with sister Wethersby until he is 16 "and his estate." To friend Micheal Draper, loom and weaving gear. To son Daniell Stringer, all the rest of estate. Friend William Allen to be Exec. Dated 12 Apr 1718. Signed: John (X) Stringer. Wit: Fra. (X) Rogers, John (X) Crook, John Curle. Pro 21 May 1718 by Rogers and Crook. Inv follows and consists of small list of tools, stock and household items.

[pp 121, 122] Last will and testament of Henry Batts of Eliz. City Co., very sick and weak. To brother John Batts, one-half of lot in Hampton with the house thereon. To brother Tho. Batts, the other half of the lot. To brother John Batts, negroes Peter, Jenny and Frank. To brother Tho. Batts, negroes Will, Judy, Tom. To Godson William Wood, negro girl Miriam with reversion to Tho. Batts. To brother John, items. Negro woman Jenny is now with child. If delivered safely and brother John shall think fit to keep the sd child, he is to pay £10 silver money of Va. to sister Elizabeth Wade and, if not, to deliver the child to sister Elizabeth as a bequest. To brother Thos., stock and plantation during the term of the lease. To "each of my sisters," a ring of 15 sh. All the rest of est to brothers John and Thomas Batts and they to be Execs. Dated 30 Dec 1717. Signed: Henry Batt. Wit: Cha. Jenings, William Westwood, Briget Oharren. Pro 21 May 1718 by Jenings and Bridget Oharen.

[pp 122, 123] Last will and testament of Tho. Casy, sick and weak. To son John Casy, plantation "I now live on" when he comes to age of 21, with reversion to the next brother Tho. Casy and then to his two sisters. Moveable est to be appr and sold and equally divided between "three youngest children [not named]. Exec [not named] is to give children schooling, paid from est. Dated 12 Feb 1718. Signed: Thomas (X) Casy. Wit: Richd. Hawkins, Thomas (X) Powell, John Howard. Pro 21 Mar 1718 by Hawkins and Howard. Appr of Thomas Casey dec'd by order of Ct 21 May 1718. Signed: Hind Armistead, John (X) Skinner, John Howard on 30 May 1718. Stock and household items. Value £19:19:0.

pp 123, 124] Bond of William Allen, Francis Rogers and Phillip Williams, all of Eliz. City Co., for £50 sterling. Dated 16 July 1718. Wm. Allen is to perform duties of Exec of the last will of John Stringer. Wit: Fra. Ballard, Cha. Jenings. Signed: William (X) Allen, Francis (X) Rogers and Phillip (X) Williams. Ack 16 July 1718.

[pp 125, 126] Bond of Joyce Hopkins, James Ricketts, and Jno. Roe, all of Eliz. City Co., for £200. Dated 16 July 1718. Joyce Hopkins is to properly administer the est of

Richd. Hopkins dec'd. Wit: Cha. Jenings. Signed: Joyce (X) Hopkins, James Roberts, John (X) Roe. Ack 16 July.

1718. [pp 126, 127] Ind dated 9 July 1718 between Tho. Wright and Robert Minson, both of Town of Hampton. [Conveyed] for 5 sh 20 ft on Wine St. next to the lot of William Allen and 50 ft from the sd st Ely & running along Sly 20 ft. Tho. Wright bought the same land from Robert Minson by deed 16, 17 Dec 1717. Signed: Thomas Wright. Wit: Charles Jenings, John Cook. Release 10 July 1718 for £10 current money of Va. from Thomas Wright and Jane his wife. Signed: Thomas Wright, Jane (X) Wright. Wit: Cha. Jenings, Richd. Nusum, John Cook. Pro 17 July 1718. Rec 4 Aug 1718.

[p 129] Bond of John More, Henry Robinson, and Brian Penny, all of Eliz. City Co. for £200 sterling dated 16 July 1718. John Moore, having married the relict and Exectrx of Tho. Naylor, dec'd, is to make inv and accting and pay all legacies. Signed: John More, Henry (X) Robinson, Brian Penny. Ack 16 July 1718.

[p 130] Bond of Tho. Hawkins and Richard Hawkins, both of Eliz. City Co., for £30 good and lawful money of England dated 21 May 1718. Thomas Hawkins, Exec of Thomas Casey dec'd, is to make inv etc. Signed: Thomas (X) Hawkins, Richd. Hawkins. Wit: Cha. Jenings. Ack 21 May 1718.

[pp 130-132] Bond of Ann Carver, William Spicer, and Brian Penny of Eliz. City Co. for £100 dated 21 May 1718. Ann Carver, Admx of Alexander Carver dec'd, is to make inv etc., provided if any last will was made by deceased, the Exec therein named will have it proved in Ct. Signed: Ann (X) Carver, William (X) Spicer, Brian Penny. Wit: Cha. Jenings. Ack 21 May 1718. Appr of Carver's est follows. Household items and stock. Value £37:10:8. Made by Ct Order of 18 July 1718. Signed: Frasier? (X) Hogins?, Thos. Allen, Charles (X) Tucker.

[pp 132, 133] Inv of James Gilbert dec'd. Signed: Cha. Jenings. Household items, stock including "4 piggs upon the Island whether dead or alive I cannot tell. I left them there." No value given.

[p 133] Bond of Mary Gilbert, Joseph Wragg and Wm. Winterton, all of Eliz. City Co., for £150 sterling dated 20 Aug 1718. Mary Gilbert, Admx of James Gilbert dec'd, is to make inv etc and to exhibit will, if one be found. Signed: Mary (X) Gilbert, Jo. Wragg, Wm. Winterton. Wit: Cha. Jenings. Ack 20 Aug 1718.

[p 133] Nuncupative will of David James. Christopher Davis and his wife Elizabeth [swear] that at a certain time they asked David James if he should die tomorrow whether Wm. Spicer should have whatever he had. The afsd James said "aye" to the above. Dated 16 July 1718. Signed: Christopher Davis, Eliza. Davis. Rec in Ct. [no date given]

[pp 134, 135] Last will and testament of Richard Crusell [Crussell] dated 8 Apr 1718 in the County of Elizabeth City and Charles Parish, Virga., sick and weak. To wife Mary Crusell, who is to be Executrx, negro woman Nanny and household items and stock. To son Richard Crusell, household items and stock. To daughter Elizabeth Crusell, household items and stock. If child wife goes with is a son, 70 acs of land, but if a daughter, this land to daughter Elizabeth. To unborn child, household items and stock. Signed: Richd. Crusell. Wit: Charles Powers, Wm (X) Wood, Thos. (X) Delaweny?. Pro 16 July 1718 by all three wit.

Bond of Mary Crusell, Charles Powers and Edwd. Myhill for £200 sterling dated 20 Aug 1718. Mary Crusell, Exectrx of Richard Crusell dec'd, to make inv etc. Signed Mary (X) Crusell, Charles Powers, Edwd. Myhill. Wit: Cha. Jenings. Ack 20 Aug 1718.

[pp 135, 136] Bond of Henry Jenkins and Jno. Bordland for £400 sterling dated 21 May 1718. Henry Jenkins, Adm of John Curle dec'd, is to inv etc. Signed: Hen. Jenkins, John Bordland. Wit: Charles Jenings, Simon Hollier. Ack 21 May 1718.

[pp 136, 137] By Ct Order of 17 July 1718, est of Jno. Petts dec'd is appr. Dated 25 July ---- being sworn by Capt. Fra. Ballard. Household items and stock. Value £41:18:4. Signed: Robt. Armistead, Tho. Read, Thos. Allin, Fra. (X) Rogers.

[pp 137-139] Ind dated 8 Aug 1718 between Abraham Parish and Ann his wife and Temperance Parish, widow, all of Parish & Co. of Eliz. City and Thomas Morgan, cooper of same. For 10 sh current Spanish money of Va. [Conveyed] tract containing 50 acs in Par. & Co. of Eliz. City lately in the possession of Mark Parish dec'd. Bounded on N side of Back R. adj Wly on Mr. Robt. Armistead, running Nly into the main woods a mile and Ely on land where sd Abra. Parish now lives including the well within the sd land. Land was bequeathed by Mark Parish dec'd to his wife Temperance for life or widowhood and after to the sd Abra. Signed: Abra. (X) Parish, Ann (X) Parish, Temperance (X) Parish. Wit: Charles Jenings, Richd. Nusum. Ack 20 Aug 1718. Release 9 Aug 1718 for £10 current Spanish money of Va. and "soe much toba at markt price as it is sold for at the fall to the summe of twenty-two pounds like money be paid to the sd Abra. Parish and his wife and the summe of ten pounds like money and to build a dwelling house to and for sd Temperance Parish for her right in [this] parcel." Same signatures and witnesses. Ack 20 Aug 1718.

[p 140] In obedience to Ct Order of 17 July 1718, the "Sloope Boat" and all "her apariall" belonging to Jno. King and Jno. Curle, late dec'd, appr. Value £27:17:6 current money of Va. Dated 18 Aug 1718. Signed: Wm. Smelt, Wm. Loyall, Joseph Banister.

[[140] By Ct Order of 16 July, appr of est of Wm. Hopkins, lately dec'd, taken 15 Aug 1718. Household items, stock, apparel etc. Value £16:10:3. Signed: Hind Armistead, Wm. Spicer, Mrk. Powel, Wm. Crook.

[p 141] 8 Oct 1717. Surveyed by direction of a Jury, wherein Wm. Allen was plt and Hanah Armistead deft. "I began at a white oak an old marked tree & run from thence 65 deg E 76 poles to a stake by the side of the Marsh & thence back to the white oak, from thence N 65 deg W 132 poles to the S side of a branch commonly called the Gullet." Signed: Wm. Lowry, Surveyor.

Ct Order of 18 Sept 1717. "We the Jury met on the land in controversy and found the deft a---- for damages 1 sh sterling." Jurors: James Servant, foreman; James Ricketts, James Naylor, Thos. Francis, Henry Turner, Wm. Tucker, Abram. Mitchell, John Roe, John Mitchell, John Cook, Charles (X) Cely.

[p 141] 20 Oct 1717. Wm. Lowry surveys by direction of a Jury wherein Wm. Westwood was plt and James Ricketts deft. Began at white oak, one of the corners of Wm. Smelt's land, standing on S side of --- and running W 234 poles to a blackgum standing in the Western Br. of Gray's Swamp adj upon Eaton's School Land. Rec 6 Sept 1718.

[pp 142, 143] Last will and testament of Joan Smyth of Town of Hampton in Eliz. City Co., widdow, being old, sick and weak. Dated 12 Aug 1714. To granddaughter Jane Bacchus, eldest daughter of Thomas Bacchus, the improved half of the lot "wherein I now live" adj Widow Bayley's lot, " to Jane and her issue female lawfully begotten, the eldest to take entirely before the younger as well as also the issue female of their issue successively and for want of such issue then to the right heirs of the last issue female for ever." Also granddaughter Jane Bacchus, household items including "one new Gilded Bible with a leather case of covering," and stock. To granddaughter Elizabeth Bacchus, household items. To daughter Amy Bacchus, wife of Thomas Bacchus, for life, the other half of the lot. After her death this is to revert to granddaughter Elizabeth with the same entail as above. Heirs are to enjoy half lots severally and separately for and during the full term and time of their several natural lives to prove all doubtful interpretations which may falaciously be put upon any of the afsd words. To daughter Amy Bacchus, all the rest of estate. Friend Thomas Howard, cordwainer of Hampton, to be Exec and he is appt guardian-in-trust for granddaughter Bacchus. Lot is to be divided within six months and personal estate within forty days after my death and funeral." Granddaughters to receive estate at age 16. If Jane die without lawful female heirs, her portion to Elizabeth. Signed: Joan (X) Smyth. Wit: Jo. Wragg, Nathl. Parker, Chr. Phillipson. Pro by oath of Parker and affirmation of Joseph Wragg 20 July 1715.

[p 144] Deed of Gift 19 June 1717. William Loyall of Hampton in Eliz. City Co, "pilate," for love, good will & affection, to brother John Massenburgh, waterman, and his wife during their lives to live on, but not to rent, 1/2 ac where "I now live." 25 ft on North St. towards Abraham Mitchell. Signed: William Loyall, Elizabeth (X) Loyall. Wit: Nathanl. Parker, Abra. Mitchell. Ack 21 Aug 1717.

[p 145] Ind dated 16 Sept 1718. Samuel Ridlehurst of Hampton "hath put himself Apprentice" to Owen [Owin, Owan] Rain, cooper, with him to dwell for five whole years, during which the apprentice will faithfully serve, his secrets keep and all his lawful commands obey which he will gladly do. The long agreement includes "no matrimony contract." He is to learn occupation of a cooper. Rain is to allow wholesome meat, drink, apparel, washing and lodging and supply at the end of the term one whole suit of apparel or £3 silver money of this Colony and one cooper's axe, an adge, one drawing knife and one taper bit etc. Signed: Samuel Ridlehurst. Wit: Cha. Jenings. Rec 20 Oct 1718.

Second ind with the same terms is signed by: Owen Rain. Ack 17 Sept 1718. Rec 20 Oct 1718.

[pp 146-148] Last will and testament of William Bossell of Eliz. City Co., sick and weak. Dated 27 June 1718. To son Wm. Bossell, plantation and all other land lying at the Southern Br. of Eliza. River, together with housing and stock, when he is 16. To daughter Agness Bosell, plantation in Co. of Nansemond. To son Wm., lot of Town land in Norfolk Town, and lot at the head of the Southern Br. of Elizabeth R. near the bridge, three lots in Hampton vizt: lots bought of Mrs. Lowry by Thomas Howard and now in occupation of Henry Morrisett and Owen Raine; half lot in Hampton next to Thomas Howard and on which a house was built and joining on Esqr Luke; £100 sterling; one-half of new Sloop, two houses and one mare, two [on] the Island and the other at Bryan Penny's; negro man Dick; still and worm; and one pair millstones 3 ft 8 inches across, but wife to have use of these during widowhood; 3 gold rings and one double "Double Loone" of value of 4 pistols; marked silver plate and the Great Bible; one pair pistols and houlsters; and a gun. All to be delivered at age 16. Son also to have the water mill, but wife is to have it during widdowhood. To daughter Agness Bossell, a lot at Hampton Towne Gate, £100 sterling and £100 in goods. To daughter Grace Bossell, a lot in Hampton next the River and now in occupation of Henry Cocke and joining on the other lots bought of Thomas Howard; the other 1/2 lot in Hampton joining on Thomas Howard; negro boy Tom and £100 sterling and £100 in goods. To son Wm. and two daughters Agness and Grace, £160 current silver money to be divided at age

16. To daughter Grace, a lot of town land next Peter Burton and negro woman Sarah. To daughter Ann, large looking glass, marked silver plate, gold rings, ear rings, silver buckles and other household items. To daughter Grace, marked plate, 3 gold rings, silver tankard, porringer, spoons. Stock to be divided between children. All the rest of estate to wife <u>Elenor</u> and after children are raised, the remainder to be at her own disposal. Also to wife, negro Samson and woman Pender. Wife <u>Ellinor</u>, Mr. George Walker and son Wm. to be Execs. If Walker refuse, Mr. Samuel Selden to be Exec. Signed: William Bossell. Wit: William Brough, Eliza. (X) Howard, Jo. Wragg. Pro 17 Sept 1718 by oath of Eliza. Howard and affirmation of Jos. Wragg.

[pp149, 150] Appr of est of Richard Hopkins dec'd made 25 Aug 1718. Household items, tools etc., and one negro girl about 12 years of age. [unnamed] Value £76:00:7. Appr by Ct Order of 16 July 1718. Signed: Ricketts (no first name or mark), Tho. Howard, Jo. Banister. Rec 21 Oct 1718.

[p 150] Bond of Bryan Penny, Charles Jenings and Fra. Ballard, all of Eliz. City Co., for £50 sterling. Bryan Penny, as gdn of Elizabeth Penny, orphan of Edwd. Penny, is to deliver her est at age or marriage. Signed: Bryan Penny, Cha. Jenings, Fra. Ballard. Ack 18 Sept 1718. Rec 21 Oct 1718.

[pp 151-153] Ind dated 18 Sept 1718 between Francis Ballard Gent of the Parish and Co. of Eliz. City and Samuel Sweny Gent of Hampton in the Parish and Co. afsd. [Conveyed] for 5 sh sterling 1/2 ac lot in Hampton on Southampton R., E upon King St. 3 chains 82/100 S upon Queen St. 5 chains 24/100 W on Thomas Poole 3 chains 82/100 and N on Lot No 72 5 chains 24/100. Purchased by Ballard of the Foeffees. Signed: Francis Ballard. Wit: Robert Taylor, John King, Rose Hunt. Ack 19 Oct 1718. Rec 21 Oct 1718. Release 19 Sept 1718 for £52 sterling. Same signatures, witnesses. Rec 21 Oct 1718.

[pp 153-155] Ind dated 7 Oct 1718 between Thomas Cornelius, wheelright, and John Henry Rombough, joyner, both of Hampton, Par. & Co. of Eliz. City. [Conveyed] for 5 sh land in Hampton beg on Wine St., running 28 ft till it joins land that Richard Hopkins bought of Cornelius adj

Abraham Mitchell's lot on Wine St.. Cornelius allows Rombough a lane from the head of the sd piece of ground across the head of Cornelius' lot, to be 34 ft long and 4 1/2 ft wide, for a passage for Rombough to have to his own lot bought of Abram. Mit<u>chel</u>. Signed: Thomas Cornelius. Wit: Cha. Jenings, Jno. Waymouth. Ack 15 Oct 1718. Release 8 Oct 1718 for £10 current silver money of Va. Same signatures and witnesses. Ack 15 Oct 1718.

[p 155] Nuncupative will of Michl. Roberts. Michl. Roberts, living in the house of his daughter Mary Bridge, in Eliz. City Co., was taken sick about the 8th of Nov and died 23 Nov 1718. The subscribers assisted Mary in attending her father and heard him say that if he should die, as he thought he should, daughter Mary Bridge should have his negro during her life and then grandson Jno. Roberts should have him. He also desired that his daughter should have the care of his grandson. Dated 26 Nov 1718. Signed: Francis (X) Williams, Elizabeth (X) Hassellgrove. Pro 21 Jan 1718 by Fra. Williams, Eliza. Crook, and Eliza. Hassellgrove. Pro granted to Mary Bridge, she giving bond. Rec 5 Feb 1718.

[p 156] Last will and testament of James Brown dated 15 Mar 1718. To wife Margrett Brown for life, all land purchased of Wm. Bayley. At her death land reverts in order to: son James Brown or his lawful heirs; son William Brown or his lawful heirs; daughter Sophia or her lawful heirs; daughter Euphan or her lawful heirs. If all children die, reversion to brother William. If he die, to James Wallace. To wife for life (unnamed), furniture, chattels, stock and personal estate "for acting the part of a Double Parent." Signed: James (X) Brown. Wit: Wm. Baylis, Hannah (X) Whitfield, James Wallace. Pro 21 Jan 1718 by both wit. Pro granted to Margtt his relict giving bond etc. Ord rec.

[p 157] Last will and testament of Peter Baker, joiner of Eliza. City Co., sick and weak. To wife Jane Baker, house and half lot in Hampton [to all be disposed of as she shall think fit]; negro woman called Grace; all personal estate and she to be Exectrx. Dated 24 Feb 1717/18. Signed: Peter Baker. Wit: John Bayley, Joseph Banister, Susana (X) Banister. Pro 21 Jan. 1718 by all witnesses.

[p 157] Last will and testament of Thomas Powel, sick and weak. Brother Matthew Powel made full and sole Exec of estate until daughter Hanah Powel comes of age or day of marriage, with reversion to brother Matthew. To brother Mark Powel, one barren cow; also one iron spit for his use until daughter is of age or married. If she die, spit to remain his. Not dated. Signed: Thomas (X) Powell. Wit: Jno. Howard, Michl. (X) Roberts, Marke (X) Powel. Pro 22 Jan 1718 by Howard and Mark Powel. Pro granted to Mark Powel, he giving bond etc.

[p 158] Last will and testament of Thomas Batts Senr of Eliz. City Co., being sick and weak. To son Henry Batts, a cow and calf to be in full of "my whole estate." To daus Elizabeth Wade & Martha Wood each a tumbler of 20 sh; To son John Batts, one silver tumbler of 20 sh "in lew of his share of my estate." Son Thomas Batts to be Exec and to him the rest of the estate in what kind or nature soever. Dated 2 Oct 1717. Signed: Tho. Batts. Wit: Cha. Jenings, Eliz. (X) Cole. Pro 22 Jan 1718 by oath of Cha. Jenings, wit, who says he saw Eliz. Cole also wit will.

[p 158] "This is the last wil of George Gigels speak only by word of mouth before these witnesses and Taken in Wrighting at his departure. Item: I give to my cousin Elizabeth Ridge my bed and furniture and one bull yearling and one bull yearling to Mary Ridge. And I give to William Ceely my chest, and all the rest to Robert Johnson. Take all and pay all and bury me Like a Christian." Wit: William (X) Ceely, Charles (X) Ceely. Dated 7 Dec 1718. Pro 22 Jan 1718 by oaths of both wit. Certificate of Adm granted to Jno. Bordland, giving bond.

[p 159] Last will and testament of George Waffe of Eliz. City. Co., gent, sick and weak. To wife Rebecca Waffe, all goods, chattels & which are now in her possession that she possessed as her own proper goods & chattels when "I intermarried with her," in full of all demands or claims from estate. All the rest of estate to son-in-law Wm. Winterton and daughter Jane Winterton, wife of sd William, except for one large Bible in Folio "which I give to my Grandson George Waffe, son of my own son George Waffe." Son-in-law William Winterton and daughter Jane Winterton to be Execs. Dated 19 July 1718. Signed: George Waffe. Wit: Hen. Jenkins, John Mitchell, Bridgett (X) Jenkins. Pro 22

Jan 1718 by John Mitchel who also swears he saw Capt. Henry Jenkins sign. Pro granted Execs, giving bond and security. Rec 7 Feb 1718.

[p 159] "I doe ... certify that according to a Bill of Saile dated with these presents, have assigned this Pattent unto Bartram Servant ..." Dated 1 Mar 1688. Signed: Elizabeth Claiborne "and if Coll. William Claiborne have assigned I doe confirm the same." Signed: William Claiborne. Rec 4 Mar 1718/19.

[p 160] Ind dated 17 Sept 1718 William Mallory of Eliz. City Co. for £45 current money and for love and affection to son Francis Mallory [conveys] plantation bounded by Mr. Wythe, Mr. Anthony Armistead, etc, divided from plantation where John Berry now lives. [metes and bounds] [Entailed for Francis Mallory and his lawful heirs male.] In default of such heirs, to son William Mallory and his lawful heirs male. Signed: Wm. Mallory. Wit: Thomas Wythe, Rt. Armistead, Geoffrey Pole. Ack 21 Jan 1718.

[p 160] Bond of Francis Mallory of Eliz. City Co. to father Wm. Mallory for £500 sterling. Dated 17 Sept 1718. Condition of obligation is such that whereas Wm. Mallory had sold to Francis Mallory the plantation whereon he now dwells, Francis Mallory is to permit at all time his father to peacefully hold the plantation during his life. Signed: Fra. Mallory. Same wit as entry above. Ack 21 Jan 1718/9. Rec -- Mar 1718.

[pp 161. 163] Ind dated 18 Aug 1718 between Richard Street of the Parish and Co. of Eliz. City, planter, and Samuel Sweny of same, mercht. [conveys] for 5 sh current Spanish money of Va a parcel of 35 acs in sd Par and Co. and now in possession of Richard Street and Mr. Wm. Smelt, being of a pat for a greater quantity and bounded as follows: Beg on the Old Ditch between Wm. Smelt's land and sd Street and running Stly to a cr which issues out of Hampton River including his old orchard and the old house which part of sd land is now leased to Wm. Smelt and commonly called Capp's Point which land was given by the last will & testament of "my father Richard Street, dec'd." [Added below covenants] "Excepted halfe an acre of land where the Burying place now is." Signed: Richard Street, Eliza. (X) Street. Wit: Cha. Jenings. Pro 21 Jan 1718 by both

Richard and Eliza. Street. Release dated 19 Aug 1718 for £28 current Spanish money of Va. Ack 21 Jan 1718 by Richard and Eliza. Street, she being privately examined.

[pp 163, 164] Ind dated 25 Oct 1717 between Thomas Wilcox of Hampton Towne, shipwright, and Wm. Smelt of the same for £20 in Spanish money of Va. [leases] a lot in Hampton being the same lot that Wilcox took up 21 July 1714. Lease is for 99 years with payment of one ear of Indian corn per year if demanded. Signed: Thos. Wilcox. Wit: Henry Morisett, Eliza. (X) Clark. Thomas Wilcox ack the within mortgage for town land on 21 Jan 1718. Ord rec.

[pp 164, 165] Last will and testament of Samuel Daniel of Eliz. City Co., in a sick and weakly condition. To nephew Skinner all wearing apparel and a new chest. To wife Jude Daniel, all tobacco belonging to her before marriage, provided she will not make any claim on the estate, real or personal. In case she makes a claim, then the afsd tobo goes to "my sister Hanah Mitchel and her husband." If wife holds and enjoys whatsoever she had before marriage, then plantation in Eliz. City to be equally divided, one half to the child sister Hanah now goes with if male, but for want of a male, then to eldest female. The other half to nephew Samuel Skinner. Negro boy named Jemmy to sister Hanah Mitchel's child she now goes with "withall." Cattle to be divided equally between sister Hanah and nephew Samuel Skinner. To sister Elizabeth Skinner, a riding horse and items. To sister Hanah Mitchel, a riding horse and items. Two-thirds part of sheep to sister Skinner and the other one-third to sister Hanah. To nephews Robert and Martha Taylor [sic], £4 apiece. Brother-in-law John Mitchel to be Exec. Dated 25 March 1718. Signed: Samuel Daniel. Wit: Abra. Mitchell, Nicholas Parker, Jo. Wragg. Pro 19 Feb 1718 by the oath of Nicholas Parker and the affirmation of Jos. Wragg. Pro granted to Jno. Mitchell giving bond. Ord rec.

[pp 165, 166] Last will and testament of Thomas Tucker Senr of Eliz City Co. being very sick and weak. To grand daughter Elizabeth Cooper, the daughter of Charles Cooper, negro girl called Juno which is now in the possession of Charles Cooper, with her increase to sd Elizabeth and the heirs of her body lawfully begotten. Reversion "to the surviving sister." To the sd Elizabeth Cooper, six new pewter dishes, one doz new pewter plates, two new iron potts about three gallons each. To son Thomas Tucker, plantation "whereon I now live" with all appurtenances, only wife to live there for her natural life. To son Thomas six new pewter dishes and 1 doz new "do" plates and pistols and holsters and sword and belt. To wife Elizabeth Tucker, the use of all Negroes during her widowhood and after to son Thomas Tucker and daughter Mary Tucker: three negroes Harry, Hanah, and Mole to Thomas & two called Minor and Sarah to daughter Mary. ; To son Thomas, furniture, stock, £80 silver money when he is 18. To daughter Mary, 6 new pewter dishes, 1 doz new "do" plates and large looking glass, furniture, stock & £40 silver money. To son Thomas all cooper's tools and carpenter tools and cross cut saw when he is 18. Mary is to receive bequests at age 16. To son Thomas, one brass kettle about 15 gallons. To wife Eliza. all the rest of the estate & she to be Exectrx. Dated 17 March 1717/8. [Added below date] To dau Eliza. More and dau Barbery Cooper, one sh each to be in full of all their part, they having received their portions. Signed: Thom. Tucker. Wit: Cha. Jenings, Robt. Bright, Jno. Batts. Pro by Cha. Jenings and Jno. Batts and certificate for Adm with will annexed granted to Cha. Cooper and Jno. Moore, giving [torn] 15 July 1719.

[pp 167, 168] Last will and testament of Mark Johnson of Eliz City Co. gent, being very sick. To wife Eliza. Johnson for life, dwelling house and part of land adjoining it. [Described in metes and bounds, also mentioning the Creek's side, the Quarter door, Jacob Face's house, to the new road.] Reversion of house and this land to daughter Mary Johnson and her heirs lawfully begotten. Also to daughter Mary the rest of the Manor Plantation and where John Wilson now lives and where Charles Peirce now lives with the new plantation in the Woods. Wife is not to be debarred from getting timber of any of the sd lands for her plantation's use. To daughters Jane and Elizabeth Johnson, house and lot of land in Hampton Town to be equally divided between them at age 16 or marriage. To wife Elizabeth Johnson, negro man Jack and negro woman Frank and "my" horse Ball, to be in full of her thirds. To daughter Marrye Johnson, negro man Absalom and negro boy Peter. To daughter Jane Johnson, negro boy Toney and negro girl Judy. To daughter Elizabeth Johnson, negro boy Martin and negro girl Grace. To daughter Mary Johnson, stock, items and "one hogshead of Tobacco No 2 that is now on Board to goe for England and the Exports to be sent for in goods for her use. Daughter Mary is to have the benefit of her negroes' work, my mare filly and a black mare to harrow her corne" and other stock. Daughter Mary's Negro man is to remain upon the plantation and to have a share of the crop for the succeeding year "the said Mary having nothing to say to any part of my sd estate given away to my wife and her two sister." To William Allen, a broadcloth suit of cloathes. To sister Elizabeth Walker, one cow. The rest of estate to be divided between wife and daugters Jane and Elizabeth, and they to receive their portion at age 16 or day of marriage. Wife Elizabeth Johnson to be Exectrx. Brother-in-law William Westwood to oversee the will performed. To wife the "Nussory" [nursery] behind the Quarter to plant out an Orchard. Dated 10 Feb 1717/18. [Added after date] To wife Elizabeth, a third of the Syder that is made until such time as hers shall bear. Signed: Mark Johnson. Wit: Charles Jenings, Jacob (X) Face, Elizabeth Jenings, Wilwestwood [sic]. Pro 18 Feb 1718 by Charles Jenings and Wm. Westwood. Certificate for probate granted the Exectrx giving bond and sec.

[p 168] John Dixon's nuncupative will. John Dixon, mariner, belonging to his Majestie's Ship called "The Pearle," the 22nd day of Nov 1718, being engaged in a battle, We George Guy and James Cosins did hear the sd John Dixon say to Mr. Evander Meckover and took him by the hands, that the longest liver should take all, meaning their estates, to which Mr. Evander Meckover readily agreed to the offer and both John Dixon and Mr. Evander Meckover desired we bear witness to the afsd agreement. Dated 19 Feb 1718. Signed: George Guy, James Cosins. Noncupative will of John Dixon pro by both witnesses. 19 Feb 1718.

[p 169] Bond of Mary Jenkins, Thos. Wythe, Joshua Curle and John Bayley, all of Eliz City Co. For £2000 money of England. Dated 28 Feb 1718. Condition of obligation is that Mary Jenkins, Admtrx of Henry Jenkins, gent dec'd, is to make an inventory and properly perform all the duties of the Administration. If a will is found, Mary Jenkins is to deliver up her Letters of Adm. Signed: Mary Jenkins, Thos. Wythe, Joshua Curle, John Bayley. Ack 18 Feb 1718. Rec 20 Mar 1718/19.

[p 170] Adm bond of Mary Jenkins, Thos. Wythe, Josa. Curle and John Bayley on the est of Henry Jenkins for £250. Note: exactly as above except for amount of bond and that John Bayley does not sign. Ack 19 Feb 1718. Rec 20 Mar 1718/19.

[p 171] Bond of Easter Minson, Joshua Curle and John Bayley, all of Eliz City Co. Dated 18 Feb 1718. Condition of obligation is proper performance of Easter Minson as Exectrx of Wm. Minson, dec'd. She is to make inventory etc. Signed: Easter (X) Minson, Josa. Curle, John Bayley. Ack 18 Feb 1718. Rec 20 Mar 1718/19.

[p 171, 172] Bond of John Mitchell, Wm. Copland, James Naylor and Thomas Jones, all of Eliz City Co for £200 sterling dated 19 Feb 1718. Condition of obligation is that John Mitchel is to properly perform as Exec of Samuel Daniel. He is to make inventory etc. Signed: John Mitchell, Wm. Copland, James Naylor, Thomas Jones. Ack 19 Feb 1718. Rec 20 Mar 1718/19.

[p 172] Inventory of Thomas Power, dec'd. Dated 16 Feb 1718. Household furniture and items including "two old pockett books." Total value - £19:10:10. In obedience to a ct order of 22 Jan 1718. Inv signed by Hind Armistead, Wm. Spicer, Mattw. Small.

[p 173] Last will and testament of William Minson of the Parish and Co. of Eliz City, weak of body etc. To son Thomas Minson, one-half of plantation "I now live on," the whole being 180 acs, to be divided by a line from the middle of the clear ground into the woods to the extreme bounds, so that one-half clear ground and one-half woodland may be in each part, son Thomas to have that part without the houses and orchards. That half of which the houses and orchards is to remain to eldest son and heir. To son Thomas, negro boy James and negroes Moll and Sarah, after the decease of wife Hester. All children that issue from them during wife's life to be divided equally between "my two sons." To son William, negro boy Peter and negro Sam and negro boy Perrin, but not to have Sam until decease of wife. To wife, the labor of Sam, Moll and Sarah for life. The rest of estate to be divided into three parts and wife and two children to have each one-third. Estate is not to be appraised. Wife Hester is to be Exectrx. Dated 12 Dec

44

1717. Signed: William Minson. Wit: Saml. Selden, Jno. Bushell, Thomas Jones. Pro 18 Feb 1718 & ord rec.

[p 174] Matthew Hilliard gives his Power of Atty to friend Richard FitzWilliams of Eliz City Co. to recover all debts due in the Govet. of Virginia. Dated 19 Nov 1718. Signed: Matthew (X) Hilliard. Wit: Mde. Kelly, Andr. Meade. Pro 18 Feb 1718 & ord rec.

[pp 174, 175] Ind dated 13 Mar 1719. Edward Ballard & Elizabeth his wife of the Town of Hampton in Eliz City Co. [lease] for one year [to] Charles Jenings of Eliz City Co. For 5 sh sterling. One-half ac lot in the Town of Hampton on South Hampton R – N on William Roe – 11 ch E on Thomas Tucker's – 1 ch 41 links S on John Cook – 11 ch W on North St. 141 links each ch containing two poles. Land first taken up by Saml. Dines, dec'd, from the Foefees & by his decease became due to Charles Cooper as marrying Barbery, sister & heir-at-law of the sd Dines, & by them conveyed by ind dated 18 Aug 1713 to Thos. Wood & by sd Thos. Wood & Ann his wife conveyed to sd Edwd. Ballard on 20 Sept 1715. No consideration stated. Signed: Edward (X) Ballard, Elizabeth Ballard. Wit: Richd. Nusum, Penuell Crook, Wm. Tucker. Ack 15 Apr 1719, Eliza. being privately examined, on 7 May 1719. Release dated 14 March 1718/19 for £25.

[pp 177, 178] Last will and testament of Robert Minson of the Town of Hampton, very sick and weak etc. To servant John Proby, the son of Bartd. Proby, a lot of Town land together with the dwelling house thereon, with reversion to Mary Proby, daughter to the afsd Bartd. Proby and further reversion to sd Bartd. Proby. Also to John Proby, one-half of personal estate. The other half of personal estate to Mary Proby. Bartrand Proby is named Exec. Dated 5 Feb 1718/19. Signed: Robt. (X) Minson. Wit: Robert Tenneck, Benja. Rolfe, Joseph Wragg. Memoradum added same date: Exec is to give unto Mary Servant and her daughters Lucy, Mary, and Sidwell Servant each one gold ring of the value of ten shills each. Pro 15 Apr 1719 by the oath of Robt. Tennock and the affirmation of Jos. Wragg. Cert of pro given Exec, giving bond etc, to wit Jas. Ricketts and Wm. Coopland. Ord rec. Rec 5 May 1719.

[pp 178 – 180] Ind dated 12 Apr 1719. Lease. Thomas Williams and Reba. his wife of North Carolina and Wm.

Allen, carpenter of Par. & Co. of Eliz City. For 5 shills current Spanish money of Va. [to] William Allen a parcel of land containing fifty acres insd Par. & Co. being part of a patent granted to one Wm. Morgan als Brooks for 100 acs by Sir John Harvey, Kt, then Gov, bearing date 22 May 1637. The other part of the patent is now in possession of the heirs of Daniel Preedy, dec'd, which land became due to "me the sd Reba. as being the only surviving heir of my father William Morgan dec'd." Term of lease, one year for rent of one ear of Indian corn at the Feast of St. Michael the Archangel if demanded. Signed: Tho. (X) Williams, Reba. (X) Williams. Wit: Cha. Jenings CClk. 15 Apr 1719. Reba. Williams by virtue of a power of atty from her husband Tho. Williams came into Ct and ack deed. Rec 6 May 1719. Release dated 13 Apr 1719.

[p 181] Last will and testament of Margtt. Preist of Eliz City Co, sick and weak. To son James Preist, negro girl Hannah with reversion to son Thomas Preist. To son Thomas Preist, negro woman Judah and negro boy Frank with reversion to son James. To daughter Anfilady Preist, negro woman Fillis with reversion to daughter Martha Preist. To daughter Martha Preist, negro girl Bess with reversion to daughter Anfilady Preist. To son Hugh Ross, feather bed & furniture bought from Selea Langman. To son Wm. Ross, best bed & furniture. To granddaughter Ann Ross, one heifer of three years. To son James Preist, a ring of 15 sh price. To son Thomas Preist, a ring of 15 sh price. To daughter Anfilady "one of my wearing rings and one silver bodkin with her name in it." To daughter Martha Preist, "one of my wearing rings and one silver bodkin with her name in it." To daughter Martha Preist, "one of my wearing rings and one silver bodkin with her name in it." Rest of estate is to be equally divided "amongst all my children – Francis Ross, Hugh Ross, Wm. Ross, James Preist, Anfilady Preist, Martha Preist." Son Hugh Ross to be Exec. Dated 19 Mar 1718/19. Signed: Margtt. (X) Preist. Wit: Edmond Hollier, T. Parris, Ann Pucketts. Pro 20 May 1719 by oath of Thomas Parris and Ann Puckett. Certificate granted and ord rec, the Exec giving bond.

[pp 182, 183] Last will and testament of Edmond Hollier, sick and weak. To loving nephew [sic] Mary Stuckey, negro man Leby?, bed & furniture "I lie on," and a 15 sh ring with reversion to her sister Eliza. Stuckey. To nephew

Elizabeth Stuckey, negro girl Tenah and a 15 sh ring with reversion to her sister Mary Stuckey. To nephew Edmond Stuckey, negro girl Judy with reversion to his bro Simon Stuckey. To nephew Simon Stuckey, negro woman Moll and a 15 sh ring with reversion to his bro Edmond Stuckey. To bro Penuel Crooke, a gun and all wearing clothes. To Abraham Pukett, two barrels Indian corn. To John Berry, 15 ells linen. To Wm. Wilson Junr, 9 ells linen. To Wm. Flenn, 9 ells linen and 2 barrels Indian corn. To Florence Dreskell, 1 barrel Indina corn. To George Paine, 1 barrel Indian corn. All the rest of estate whatsoever to be equally divided between nephews Simon Hollier, Simon Stuckey, Edmond Stuckey, Robert Crooke, Penuel Crooke Junr, Debra Crooke, Martha Crooke, Mary Stuckey, and Elizabeth Stuckey. Brothers Simon Hollier and Penuell Crooke to be Execs. Dated 24 Apr 1719. Signed: Edmond Hollier. Wit: Tho. Wythe, Edward Tabb. Pro 20 May 1719. Certificate granted Exec, giving bond etc.

[p 183] " Whereas Francis Parker of the Isle of Wight Co in Va, dec'd, did by his last will & testament bequeath among other things a lot of 1/2 ac lying in the Town of Hampton to be equally divided between his two sons, vizt Nathaniel and Nicholas Parker, and whereas they are very desirous to have their Father's will fulfilled in all its parts as far as can be," they agree that Nicholas shall have the half adj Abraham Mitchel's lot and on North St keeping the same breadth through the lot to the head thereof that it has on North St together with dwelling house now standing included. Nathaniel shall have all that remaining part or moiety joining on Joan Smith's lot near Thomas Ba--ss and on North St. Dated 20 May 1719. Signed: Nathll. Parker, Nicho. Parker. Wit: Cha. Jenings, Tho. Howard. Ack 20 May 1719 by both parties and ord rec. Rec 27 May 1719.

[p 184] Ind dated 2 Dec 1718 between Francis Ballard and Charles Jenings both of Par & Co of Eliz City. For 5 sh silver money of Va. 1/2 ac lot in the Town of Hampton south on Queens St 5 chains, W on Wine St 4 ch, E on Francis Rogers 4 ch and N on Matthew Small 5 ch, each ch conta two poles, which lot was purchased by Ballard from Nicho. Curle gent, foeffee of the Co, by deed dated 18 May 1708. Signed: Fra. Ballard. Wit: John King, Josha. Curle. Ack 21 May 1719. Rec 27 May 1719. Release for £52 current silver money. Ack 21 May 1719. Rec 27 May 1719.

[p 185, 187] Ind dated 30 Apr 1719 between Hind Armistead and Cha--- Tucker, both of Eliz. City Co. For 5 sh. 25 acs wood land ground in Co. of Eliz. City bounded Stly on Hayle's land & Nthy & Esty on William Creek's land. Lease for one year paying one ear of Indian corn at the Feast of St. Michael the Archangel if demanded. Signed Hinde Armistead. Wit: Fra. Ballard & Mattw. (X) Tuell. Ack 21 May 1719 & ord rec.

[p 187 - damaged] Release of lease above. --- Hind Armistead & Hanah my wife of Eliz. City Co. to Charles Tucker ... parcel of wood land ... which land is taken out of John Chandler ... Divident in Co. bounded Sthy by John Haile's divident, Ntly & cutting Estly on Wm. Creek's land. No consideration given. Signed: Hind Armistead, Hanah (X) Armistead. Wit: Fra. Ballard & Mattw. (X) Tuell. Ack by Hind Armistead 21 May 1719. Hanah (X) Armistead reliquishes dower same day. Ord rec.

[p 189] Bond dated 28 May 1719 of Hugh Ross, Francis Ross & Fra. Mallory, all of Eliz. City Co., for £300 lawful money of England. Hugh Ross is Exec of the last will of Margtt. Preist dec'd. He is to make inventory etc. Signed: Hugh Ross, Francis Ross & Fra. Ballard. Wit: Cha. Jenings CClk. Rec 5 June 1719.

[p 190] Power of Atty of Richard Kirkin of Town of Hampton in Co. of Eliz. City to friend Joseph Wragg to convey unto Richard Nusum a dwelling house & land. Signed: Richd. (X) Kirkin. Wit: Nicho. Parker, Wm. Brough, John Robinson [who may have used mark. Unclear] Pro by Parker & Brough 20 May 1719.

[p 190] Bond of Hind Armistead and Hannah his wife for £20 on their bargain and sale to Charles Tucker. 25 acs. Securites F. Ballard & Matthew (X) Tuell. Signed: Hind Armistead. Ack by Hind & ord rec.

[pp 191, 192] North Carolina, 10 Mar 1718/19. "I, Thomas Williams of the Presinke of Pasquotanke of the afsd Colony, planter..." had given Wm. Allin of the Co. of Hampton [sic] living in Little Towne upon the narrows of Back River, a Power of Atty. "Wm. Allin, by colour of the sd authority...behaved himselfe greatly to my disadvantage..." Power of Atty is hereby revoked. Signed: Thomas (X) Williams. Wit: Ro. Watson, James Collings, Chr. Hind Jr. Pro 15 Apr 1719.

10 Mar 1718/19. Thomas Williams gives to his wife Hanah Williams his power of atty in place of the above to Wm. Allin. Signed: Thos. (X) Williams. Same witnesses. Pro 15 Apr 1719 by Christopher Hinds. Ord rec.

[pp 192, 193] Ind dated 13 Mar 1718/19 between Richard Kirkin and Richard Nusum, both of Towne of Hampton in Eliz City Co. For 5 sh [sells] the part of that lot and 1/2 ac lying in Hampton on South Hampton R bounded as follows: one dwelling house & so much land upon the st now in occupation of Richard Kirkin together with so much of Kirkin's lot upon Wine St as shall be within 5 ft joining to his new house vizt: the Brick Gable end of the house & also from Mr. Batt's line so deep as to run down the line 8 ft upon the ground on which a new Clabboard house now stands vizt: joining on Richard Kirkin & so to be measured with a square nthwd & running estwd up along without Kirkin's Brick Chimney 5 ft etc. Signed: Richard (X) Kirkin. Wit: Nicho. Parker, Wm. Brough, Jno. (X) Robinson. Ack 20 May 1719 by Joseph Wragg by virtue of a power of atty. Release dated 14 Mar 1718/9 for £25 current Spanish money of Va.

[pp 194, 195] Last will and testament of Edward Myhill of Parish and Co. of Eliz. City. Dated 23 Oct 1718. For serving well and faithfully for many years past, two negro slaves Nicholas Manuell and Bungey his wife are to be freed immediately. All lands including slaves Hanah Manuell, David Manuell, William Manuell, George Manuell, Nicholas Manuell the younger, and Elizabeth Manuell are devised to dau Elizabeth Myhill for life. After her decease land and slaves to be divided: 1/2 to cosen Edward Myhill son of cosen Lockey Myhill and to his lawful heirs male with reversion to cosen Josuah [sic] Myhill and the other 1/2 to cosen Josuah Myhill and his heirs male with further reversion to heirs female and to cosen Lockey Myhill and his lawful heirs male. All personal estate, stock, household goods etc. to daughter Elizabeth for life and following her decease divided to the sd Josuah & Edward. "And, whereas to my unspeakable grief my wife Anne did elope from me and hath ever since lived in adultery and hath lately bore a child of her body I not haveing had any carnal knowledge of my sd wife for severall years Last past

Therefore I doe not think fitt to...bequeath...any part of my Estate real or Personall to my sd wife or her Child." Cosen Lockey Myhill & Josuah Myhill to be Gdns of dau Elizabeth and also to be Execs. Signed: Edward Myhill. Wit: Edward Ward, Gerard Roberts, Pasco Ward, Edwd (X) Ward Jnr. Pro -- May 1719 by all witnesses but Edward Ward. Cert of probate granted, Execs giving bond.

[p 195] Last will and testament of Francis Rogers of Co. and Parish of Eliz. City, sick and weak... To son Francis Rogers and his heirs male the plantation "I now live on that I purchased of Thos. Read & his wife" with reversion to daughters Ann & Bathia Rogers & their lawful heirs. To wife's daughter Martha £8 in current silver money & two cows when of age or married. Remainder of estate, as Negroes, household goods, stock etc. to be divided equally between wife & three children: Francis, Ann & Bathia Rogers. Negroes which fall to wife should, after her decease, fall equally to surviving children. Wife together with all three children to be Execs. Dated 13 Feb 1717. Signed: Fra. (X) Rogers. Wit: Robt. Armistead, Brien Penne, Henry (X) Cumblin. Pro by Armistead & Penne on 17 May 1719.

[p 196] Inv of est of Samuel Daniel 3 Apr 1718. Here follows a long list of household & farm items, stock etc. "This given in by me Chas. Jenings."

[p 196] Inv of est of Humphrey Baylis, dec'd. Aug 1717. List of household and farm items, stock etc. Signed: Jane (X) Baylis. Rec 2 July 1719.

[p 197] Appr of such part of est of Mr. Samuel Daniels taken 16 Mar 1718/19 as was produced by John Mitchell. Household & farm items, stock. Total value £94:19:7. In obedience to Ct Order of 19 Feb last past, Joseph Banister & Samuel Sweny being first sworn & Joseph Wragg giving his affirmation. Ret dated 9 June 1719. Signed: Saml. Sweny, Joseph Banister, Jo. Wragg. Rec 2 July 1719.

[p 197] 1717 [no mo or day] Inv of Mr. John Rabb dec'd. List of clothing follows. Signed: Henry Moriset. Ret 3 July 1719.

[p 198] Bond of William Barber and Susana his wife and Robert Armistead, all of Eliz. City Co., for £200 sterl. Wm. Barber & Susana are to properly perform duties as Admtrs. of est of Sarah Smith, dec'd. Signed: Wm. Barber, Susa. (X) Barber, Robt. Armistead. Wit: Cha. Jenings. Ack 18 June 1719.

[p 198] Bond of Elizabeth Tabb, Antho. Armistead, Robert Armistead & Merritt Sweny, all of Eliz. City Co., for £700 lawful money of England. Elizabeth Tabb has the gdnship & tuition of her two children, Edward Tabb & Martha Tabb & is to deliver all their est when they shall come to age or day of marriage. Signed: Eliza. Tabb, Antho. Armistead, Robt. Armistead, Merritt Sweny. Wit: F. Hayward, Will Westwood. Rec 13 July ----.

[p 199] 17 June 1719. Bond of Lockey Myhill of York Co., Jos. Myhill, Saml. Sweny & Wm. Marshall, all of Eliz. City Co. for £1000 sterl. Locky & Jos. Myhill are to perform all proper duties as Execs of est of Edward Myhill dec'd. Signed by all parties. Ack 17 June 1719. Rec. 13 July 1719.

[pp 199, 200] 19 May 1719. Bond of Simon Hollier & Edwd. Tabb, both of Eliz. City Co, for £500 sterl. Simon Hollier is to perform all proper duties as Exec of est of Edmond Hollier dec'd. Signed: Simon Hollier, Edward Tabb. Wit: Cha. Jenings. Ack 20 May 1719. Rec 13 July 1719.

[p 200] 20 Apr 1719. Bartrand Proby, James Ricketts, Wm. Coopland & Charles Jenings, all of Eliz. City Co. Bond for £100 sterl. Barto. Proby is to perform all proper duties as Exec of est of Robt. Minson. Signed: Bartrand Proby, Ricketts [sic], Wm. Coopland, Cha. Jenings. Wit: John Smith, Wm. Riddouch. Rec 13 July 1719.

[p 201] 17 June 1719. Bond of Eliza. Rogers, Penuell Crooke, John Cook, all of Eliz. City Co. for £500 sterl. Elizabeth is to perform all duties as Exectrx of est of Francis Rogers. Signed: Eliza. (X) Rogers, Penuell Crooke, John Cook. Wit: Cha. Jenings. Ack 17 June 1719. Rec 13 July 1719.

[pp 201, 202] Bond of Mary Bridge & Thomas Jones, cordwinder, both of Eliz. City Co., for £50 sterl. Mary is to perform all duties as Exectrx of est of Micheal Roberts. Wit: Cha. Jenings. No ack. Rec 13 July 1719.

[p 203] Last will and testament of Eliza. Tucker of Eliz. City Co., very sick & weak etc. Dated 16 Jan 1718. To son Thomas Tucker & daughter Mary Tucker, the sum of twenty-three pounds silver money of sixteen penny weight & over five shillings to be equally divided between them & paid at age of 16 or marriage. If either die survivor gets all. To sd Thomas & Mary, "all my thirds of estate left by will of my dec'd husband Thomas Tucker" to be equally divided. To Jno. More, "the debt That he Oweth me." To Carter Cooper, "the debt That he Oweth me." Jno. More to be Gdn to son Thomas. Charles Cooper to be Gdn to daughter Mary. Brother-in-law Charles Tucker to be Overseer. Signed: Eliza. (X) Tucker. Wit: Cha. Jenings, WILLISWOOD (sic). Pro by Cha. Jenings & Wm. Westwood 15 July 1719. Cert of probate granted Extrx giving bond etc. Rec 15 Aug 1719.

[p 204] 17 June 1719. Appr of Fra. Rogers dec'd. Household items etc. One negro woman called Judy; one negro boy about 7 yrs old; one negro boy about 5 yrs old; one negro girl about 10 yrs old. No total given. Signed: Tho. Read, Cha. Tucker, John Roe. Rec 15 Aug 1719.

[p 205] 6 June 1719. Inv of "my Late Decd Husband Benjm. Smith" Five negroes [unnamed], stock, household items. Signed: Susa. (X) Barber. Rec 15 Aug 1719.

[p 205] 16 July 1719. Power of Atty to Mr. Robt. Armistead. "Pray appear... and suffer Judgments to Pass agt me to Mr. Maximilian Boush & Executors of Capt. Christopher Coe-- dec'd for the Debts due them from my dec'd Husband, Capt. Henry Jenkins..." Signed: Mary Jenkins. Pro 15 July 1719. Rec 15 Aug 1719.

[p 205] 21 May 1719. Bond of Mark Powell, Hind Armistead & Wm. Spicer for £100 lawful money of England. Mark Powell is to perform duties as Exec of estate of Thomas Powell dec'd. Signed: Mark (X) Powell, Hinde (sic) Armistead, Wm. Spicer. Wit: Cha. Jenings. Rec 17 Aug 1719.

[p 205] 9 June 1719. Inv of estate of Henry Noblin, dec'd. Household items, stock etc. Signed: F. Ballard. Rec 17 Aug 1719.

[p 206] 18 June 1719. Bond of Mary Gilbert, Henry Robinson & Wm. Sorrell for £300 lawful money of England. Mary Gilbert is to perform all duties as Admx of estate of James Gilbert dec'd. Signed: Mary Gilbert, Hen. Robinson, Wm. (X) Sorrell. Wit: Cha. Jenings, WMWESTWOOD. Rec 17 Aug 1719.

[p 207] 1 June 1719. Inv & Appr of part of estate of Edmond Hollier, dec'd. Full page of stock, household items etc. Total value £76:2:1 1/2. Not appr: Negroes Sey, Moll, Tenah, Judy and other items. In obedience to Ct Ord dated 21 May 1719, appraisers met 26 June 1719. Signed: Willm. Lowry, Edwd. Tabb, Wm. Tucker. Rec 17 Aug 1719.

[p 208] Inv & Appr of estate of Capt. Henry Jenkins dec'd taken 13 Mar 1718. Jack, negro man about 28 - £26; Frank, negro man about 20 - £26; Moll, negro woman about 30 - £26; Bobb, a young woman about 18 - £26; Sarah, a Melatto girl about --, £20; Venus, a young slave about 9 - £18; Ann about 7 yrs old & Stepney about 5 yrs - £30. Full page of household items, stock etc. Peter, a negro man about 18 - £26; America, a negro man about 19 but somewhat sickly - £28; one negro woman well in years - Marea - £18; one woman very old called Jenny - £14; Dianna about 20 yrs old & a woman child a month old - £30. The half of the Sloop Hampton & her apperell - £16; the 1/2 of half of Sloop Mary - £50; the New Sloop 27 Foot & --- £35. Total value £533:14:7. By Ct Ord dated 18 Feb 1718/19. Ret 17 June 1719 by John King, H. Irwin, Fra. Ballard, Jos. Banister. Rec 17 Aug 1719.

[p 209] Inv & Appr of est of Margt. Preist dec'd taken 8 June 1719. Household items, stock. Total value £44:7:11. Signed: Simon Hollier, Edward Tabb, Antho. Armistead Jnr. [Under signatures are listed] Judah, Fillis, Hanah, Bess, Frank - Negroes, and items not valued. Signed: Hugh Ross. Rec 17 Aug 1719.

[p 210] Inv & Appr of Mr. Mark Johnson dec'd. Full page of household and farm items. No total given. Ct Ord dated 21 May 1719. Appraisers met at house of Antho. Armistead. Ret 13 June 1719. Signed: Tho. Wythe, Edwd. Tabb, Jos. Banister. Rec 22 Aug 1719.

[p 211] Last will and testament of Thomas House of Eliz. City Co., sick & weak etc. To two sons John House and William House, devidend of land "I now live on containing 50 acres more or less" to be equally divided between them and their heirs. After wife's decease "son Jno. to have the first [choice]." To son Thomas, one cow. To daughter Mary Baylis, one cow. To wife Eliza. the rest of personal estate during her natural life and after her decease to be divided between "my children, that is to say, Jno. House, Anthony House, Elizabeth House, Ann House, and Martha House." Wife and son John to be Execs. Dated 7 Nov 1702 [sic]. Signed: Thomas House. Wit: Jno. (X) Bushell, Jno. Bushell Junr., Jno. Dunn. Pro 18 May 1703. [sic] Rec 25 Aug 1719.

[p 211] Inv & Appr dated 15 June 1719. Ct Ord of 26 May 1719. Est of Humphry Baylis dec'd. Stock, household items. Total value £24:11:11. Signed: Edwd. Lattemore, James Naylor, Wm. Coopland.

[p 212] Power of Atty. Thomas Wood to Saml. Selden. Signed: Thomas Wood. Wit: Geo. Yeo, Richard (X) Kirkin. Pro 16 July 1719 by witnesses thereto. Rec 25 Aug 1719.

[p 213] Inv & Appr of est of Eliza. Prescott dec'd taken 16 July 1719. Stock etc. Total value £6:10:0. Ret 16 July 1719. Jas. Ricketts, Joseph Banister.

[p 213] Ind dated 6 July 1719 between Thomas Wood of Eliz. City Co., Mar[iner] & John Pugh of the Co. of Nansemond for £5. Dwelling house upon the north side of his lot in Hampton Towne with the half of his lot adj on Edwd. Lattemore on which the house stands to be divided by a straight line from the St to the East between part of lot now or late in possession of Thos. Wood. By Saml. Selden. Wit: Jo. Wragg, Jos. Selden, Thomas Ramy. Ack 16 July 1719. Rec 28 Aug 1719. Release for £45 dated 10 July 1719.

[pp 214, 215] Inv & Appr of Edwd. Mihill dec'd taken 1 Aug 1719. Entire page of stock, household items etc. Ct Ord dated 15 June ----. Signed: Lockey Myhill, Simon Hollier, Joshua Myhill.

[p 215] Appr of what part of est of Mr. Thos. Fry is in the possession of Mrs. Katherine Croft. Dated 18 Aug 1719.

Personal items and clothing. Total Value £9:27:6. Ct ord of 15 July 1719. Ret by Saml. Selden, Joseph Banister.

[pp 216, 217] Ind dated 6 July 1719. Thomas Wood, Marrinor, [sells to] John Pugh of Co. of Nansend. for £5. Dwelling house situate on north side of his lot in Hampton Towne, west half of lot adj Edward Lattimor on which the house stands to be divided by a straight line from the st to the East Extream part of his lot. By Saml. Selden. Wit: Jos. Wragg, Jos. Selden, Tho. ---- Ack 6 July 1719. Release for £45 dated 10 July 1719. Ack 16 July 1719.

[pp 219-221] Ind dated 17 July 1719 between William Winterton and Henry Irwin Gent both of Hampton in Eliz. City Co. Parcel bounded on the lot now in the tenure of Irwin to the westwd thence to estwd 16 foot in breadth & in length from north to south 80 foot...on the part "whereof a well is now built and houses erected, erecting & building." Signed: William Winterton. Wit: William Brand, Dunn Armistead, Isaac Rambow, Godfrey Pole. Receipt signed: Wm. Winterton. Pro by Wm. Brand & Isaac Rambow on 17 Sept 1719. Winterton gives his bond for £500 sterl.

[pp 221-223] Inv & appr of est of Capt. Wm. Boswell dec'd. One and 1/2 pp of inventory of goods, probably of a general store follow. Next a list of Negroes: Dick @ £35; Sarah @ £35; Tom @ £32:10:00. Next household goods & stock. Total value £599:62:93/4. Ret by Tho. Wythe, Joseph Curle, J. Ricketts on 7 July 1719.

[p 223] 4 May 1714 [sic] Wm. Minson, Henry Dunn, & James Nayler, having been sworn by Mr. John King, appraise two negro boys, they being seized for debt of David Jones dec'd and now in the hands of William Coopland. Jack @ £12 and Peter @ £4.

[p 224] An account of Probates and Administrations etc. Dated 21 July 1718. [Note: marginal note by most entries indicates whether instrument has been recorded. Abbreviation used by Clerk is "recd."]

21 July 1718 - Probate of James Brown to Margt. his wife.
         Recd.
         Nuncupative will of Michael Roberts granted

	to Mary Bridge his daughter. Recd.
	Probate of Peter Baker granted to Jane his relict.
22 do	Geo. Waffe Senr. To Wm. Winterton and Jane his wife, Exectrx named in will. Recd.
	Probate with will annexed to Jno. Boardland of George Jeggells est.
	Adm of Mathew Powell's est to Mrk. Powell his brother.
	Adm with will annexed of Thos. Powell during minority of the heirs granted to Mark Powell his brother.
	Probate of Thos. Batts est granted to Thos. Batts his son. Recd.
	Adm granted to Thos. Batts on est of Eliza. his late wife, daughter of Jno. Sheppard decd.
-- Feb do	Adm granted to Mary Jenkins on Henry Jenkins est. Recd.
	Adm granted to Mary Jenkins on Jno. Curle's est. Recd.
	Probate granted to Easter Minson of Wm. Minson's est. Recd.
	Probate granted to Eliza. Johnson of Mrk. Johnson's will.
	Probate of Saml. Daniel's will granted to Jno. Mitchell. Recd.
15 Apr do	Probate of Robt. Minson's will granted to Bartd. Proby. Recd.
20 May do	Probate of Edwd. Hollier's will granted to Simon Hollier. Recd.
	Margt. Prest's will granted to Fr. Rose her son. Recd.
17 June do	Probate of Edwd. Mihill's will granted to Lockey & Jos. Mihill. Recd.
	Fras. Rogers' will granted to his wife. Recd. [She is not named.]
18 June do	Adm. granted to Wm. Barber & Susa. his wife on Susa. Smith's est their daughter. Recd.
15 July do	Probate of Eliza. Tucker's est granted to Jno. More & Cha. Cooper her Execs. Not recd.
	Adm with will annexed of Tho. Tucker's est granted to Jno. More & Cha. Cooper. Not recd.

16 ---- do	Adm granted to Jno. Bayley on Jno. Davis' est. Recd. Returned to Oct. Genll Ct.
18 Nov 1719	Probate of Capt. Fra. Ballard's will granted to Joshua Curle as his Exec. Not recd. Note: this entry has been struck through in its entirety.
18 Nov 1719	Adm of Andr. Thompson's est granted to Ann Wallace & Thomas Wythe. Recd.
20 Jan do	Probate of Robert Taylor's will granted to Martha Taylor his Exectrx. Recd.
16 Mar 1719	Probate of Capt. Fra. Ballard's will granted to Joshua [sic] his Exec. Not recd.
18 May 1720	Probate of Jno. Bayley's will granted to Judith Bayley his relict & Exectrx.
20 July 1720	Probate of Margt. Bayley's will granted to Margt. Needham her Exectrx.

These returned to Octbr Genll Ct 1720.

[p 224] An Account of Marriage Lysenses
Lenrd. Whiting and Easter Minson
Thomas Wythe and Margt. Walker
Thos. [blotted] Milner and Mary Selden
Wm. Greenwood and Mrs. Harrington
George Yeo and Ellinor Boswell
John King and Reba. Armistead
Robert Greiset? and Elinor Wandless
John Young and Eliza. Ryland
Francis Mallory and Ann Myhill
Marginal note: All Retnd to Genll Ct in 1719 & 20.

[p 225] Appr of James Gilbert decd taken by Fra. Ballard, James Ricketts, Wm. Smelt 1 Sept 1718. Stock and household items. Total value £87:2:1.

[p 226] Ind dated 6 Aug 1719. Thos. Jenings of Eliz. City Co., son and heir of Cha. Jenings late of sd Co. dec'd of the first part and Chas. Jenings son of sd. Chas. Jening of the other part. For natural love and affection and for £30 current money being part of the personal est of Cha. Jenings, Father of the sd. Thos. & Charles, which by law did belong to Chas. Jenings Party to these Presents which he the sd. Thos. Jenings do own & do hereby acquit and discharge Chas. Jenings [for] 154 acs commonly called Leanffeilds situate on the head of Hampton River and lying between the land of Saml. Selden & the land where Richd.

Hursly formerly lived. Signed: Thos. Jenings. Wit. Wilwestwood, James Baker, Henry Cork. Ack 19 Aug 1719. Recd 24 Sept 1719.

[pp 227, 228] Ind dated 26 Aug 1719. Thos. Wilcox and Parrish Shipwright [sic] of the one part and Chas. Jenings of the second part, all of the Co. and Parish of Eliz. City. For 5 shill [sell] 1/2 acre lot in the Town of Hampton on Southampton R beg at a hole in the ground on the river side running thence N 83 deg W 10 chains joining on Mr. Edmd. Kersey's lot to a hole in the ground thence N 7 deg E 2 chains to a hole in the ground thence S 80 deg E 8 chains joining on Edwd. Penny's decd down to the River, each chain two poles as by a deed from the Foeffees made to the sd Thos. Wilcox bearing date 21 July 1714. Signed: Thos. Wilcox. Wit: Jo. Wragg, John Massenburg, Sarah (X) Hayes. Ack 16 Sept 1719. Recd 25 Sept 1719. Release for £40 dated 27 Aug 1719. Signed: Thomas Willcox of the Parish & Co. of Eliz. City and Elizabeth his wife of the Kingdom of England. Ack by Thomas Willcox on 16 Sept 1719 & ord rec.

[pp 229, 230] Ind dated 14 Sept 1719. Anthony Armistead Senr [sells to] Robt. Armistead son of Majr. Wm. Armistead dec'd late of Co. & Parish of Eliz. City for 5 shil 123 acs lying on the Cener Dams in Parish & Co. afsd which was purchased of Wm. Ewings, blacksmith and Eliza. his wife on 31 Mar 1707. Signed: Antho. Armistead. Wit: J. ----. Ack 16 Sept 1719. Relase for £20 current silver money of Va. dated 15 Sept 1719 between Anthony Armistead Senr and Elizabeth his wife, according to the will of the afsd Wm. Armistead dec'd. Signed: Anthony Armistead, Elizabeth Armistead. Ack by both 16 Sept 1719. Ord rec.

[pp 231, 232] Ind dated 18 Oct 1719. Francis Ballard, Henry Irwin & Josa. Curle Gent Foeffees [to] Abra. Mitchell, shipwright for 5 shil. Lot on South Hampton R containing 31 sq poles 575 sq links. Beg at a stake in the ground on the side of a Cove running N 14 deg W [to] the corner of John Mitchell's lot on Queen St to a stake in the ground thence the course of the St N 89 deg E six chains down the river to another stake thence S 38 links to a stake. Bounded on W with John Mitchell's lot, on N with Queen St, on E & S with Hampton River, each chain 2 poles. Surveyed by John Lowery

Surveyor of Co. on 17 Oct 1719. Ack 18 Nov 1719. Release dated 19 Oct 1719. No amount stated.

[p 233] 17 Nov 1719. Appr of residue of est of Mr. John Curle dec'd at the house of Mrs. Mary Jenkins by Ct ord of 8 Sept last. Household goods and cattle. Total value £8:10:00. "In the Sloop Hampton not appraised & seven head of cattle." Signed: Mary Jenkins, Hind Armistead, John Moore, Henry Irwin.

[pp 233, 234] Inv & appr of est of Robt. Minson dec'd taken 6 Oct 1719. Household goods, stock etc. Total value £36:15:04 in obedience to Ct ord of 16 Sept 1719. Signed: Joseph Banister, Samuel Sweny, Thos. Howard.

[pp 234, 235] Last will and testament of Robert Taylor of the Town of Hampton in Co. of Eliz. City. Dated 18 July 1719. To nephew Daniel Taylor, 1 shil sterl money of England. To nephew Cathern Taylor alis Knight, 1 shil sterl money of England. To nephew Sarah Taylor, 1 shil sterl money of England. Above to be in full of any claim agst the estate. To daughter Martha Taylor and her lawful heirs, one dwelling house & lot in Hampton Town and now in occupation of Samuel Sweny, with reversion to son Robt. Taylor and his heirs with further reversion to wife Martha Taylor. To daughter Martha, one negro woman Bess & one silver Can & 6 silver spoons. To son Robt. and his lawful heirs, land and negroes not already given him with reversion to daughter Martha. All the rest of estate is to be divided equally between wife, son & daughter. Wife and son Robt. to be Execs. If wife marries again, son shall have liberty to choose a guardian to demand and receive children's portion. Signed: Robert Taylor. Wit: Josha. Curle, Saml. Sweney, Jo. Wragg. Pro 20 July 1719 by oaths of Curle and Sweney and affirmation of Jo. Wragg. Cert of probate granted Execs giving bond.

[pp 236, 237, 238. Right edge of p torn] Ind dated 5 Dec 1719. Foeffees of Eliz. City Co. sell to George Walker for 70 lbs tobacco a parcel adj two lots formerly granted to Thomas Curle Cordwainer on E side of two lots between them in a Cove that runs up the side of the two lots. Signed: William Lowry, F. Ballard, Josha. Curle. Ack 20 Jan 1719. Release dated 5 Dec 1719 [and additional description given] Beg at S part of Jening's lot running N 81 deg E 86

---- to E side of sd Jenings lot thence S -- 7 deg -- along a long row of Pailes -- now standing N 81 deg E --- to the Head of the Cove -- along low water mark S 7 deg E 4 chains to Boardland's lot -- S 81 deg W -- N 7 deg to beg. Signed and ack by same 20 Jan 1719.

[pp 238, 239] Ind dated 20 Jan 1719. Rebeckah Avera of Co. of Eliz. City widow [to] Joseph Wragg for £3:10 current money of Va. Quit claim for her right of dower. Lot bounded N on Samuel Dynes 11 chains E on Wm. Bowtell's 1 chain 41 links S on Joseph Harris 11 chains & W on North St 1 chain 41 links & all the houses situate thereon which was Thomas Avera's her late husband. Signed: Reba. (X) Avera. Wit: F. Ballard, George Yeo, C. Jenings. Ack 20 Jan 1719.

[pp 239, 240] Ind dated 15 Nov 1714. Antho. Armistead of Co. of Eliz. City [sells] to Emanl. Alkin of same Chirurgeon for 5 sh cur Spanish money. 5 ac, pt of land whereon sd Armistead now lives and lying in the woods at the head thereof. Signed: Antho. Armistead. Wit: Wm. Malory, Matthew Watts. Ack 17 Nov 1714 & ord rec. Release dated 16 Nov 1714 for one thousand lbs of good sweet scented tobo. Same signature, wit, ack, rec.

[pp 241, 242] Ind dated 17 July 1719. Dunn Armistead of Eliz. City Co. [sells] to Antho. Armistead Senr a plantation commonly known as Ridge of Land containing 600 acs and whereon one Pasco Dunn dec'd formerly lived, which land was by the last will of sd Pasco Dunn devised to sd Dunn Armistead and his heirs. Signed: Dunn Armistead. Wit: F. Ballard, Hinde Armistead, John King, W. Westwood. Proved by all four witnesses on -- Jan 1719. Release for £140 current money of Va. dated 18 Jan 1719. Same signature, witnesses. Proved 21 Jan 1719 & ord rec.

[p 243] Ind dated 9 Feb 1719. Thomas Wilcox and Eliza. his wife of Eliz. City Co. [sell] to Isaac Velline of the Co. of Gloster Shipwright for £8 current silver money a low sunken parcel of land containing 214 acs. Bounded on Mark Johnson's land, south 3 deg W 220 poles, 79 deg W, on N by Thos. Robert's, on the E by Mark Johnson's land, on S by Benjamin Smith's land, and on W with land of the heirs of Tho. Curle Merch. dec'd. Gr to Wilcox by patent dated 14 Jan 1719. Signed: Thomas Wilcox. Wit: Thomas Howard, John Smith, Jo. Wragg. Ack 17 Feb 1719 & ord rec.

[pp 244, 245] Last will and testament of Francis Ballard, very sick and weak. To son Servant Ballard one silver tankard, "my silver-hilted sword and my silver watch." To dau Frances Ballard six silver spoons, a cordial silver cup and the ?coyer?, six silver guilt tea spoons and the "choyce" of feather bed, one pr holland sheets, one boulster, two pillows, a Silk Quilt and Callicow Curtains and Vallens. To daughter Mary one silver porringer and one Silver Spoon, one Silver Salver and the Second best feather bed, boulster and two pillows, one pr of Holland Sheets. To daughter Lucey one Silver Porringer and one silver spoon and a Dram Silver Tumbler, one feather bed, one boulster, two pillows, one Rugg, two blanketts, one pr sheets. To daughter Ann one silver porringer and one Silver Spoon and one Small Silver Spoon. To son Francis one Pint Silver Tumbler and a Silver Tobo box and one half-pint Tumbler. Rest of plate to be divided between sons Servant and Francis. To daughter Mary one Rugg and one pr Blanketts, one new black hood. To daughter Ann one feather bed, one boulster, two pillows, one Rugg and one Pr sheets, Two Blanketts. To daughter Frances a Silk Scarfe and the Best black hood. To daughters Mary and Ann a Remnt of Callico to be equally divided and all the Remnt of Stuff to be divided between daughters Lucy and Ann. All the rest of personal estate may be sold at public outcry. To son Servt. Ballard all my land upon James Riverside joining on Mr. Jening's corner, 100 acs to him and the male heirs of his body. To son Frans. Ballard and the male heirs of his body the remainder of land being 84 acs, the remainder of "my pattent." If sons die without male heirs, the land is to be divided between four daughters: Frances, Mary, Lucey, and Ann. £54 to be paid to Mr. Perry out of personal estate. Mr. Josa. Curle Senr, Mr. Alexandr. McKenzie, and son Servant Ballard to be Execs. Dated 10 March 1719. Signed: F. Ballard. Wit: Robt. Armistead, Mary Jenkins, Jo. Wragg. Pro 16 Mar 1719 by oaths of Armistead and Jenkins and the affirmation of Joseph Wragg. Certificate for probate granted Execs. Ord rec.

[p 245] Bond of Joyce Simons and Matthew Small, both of Eliz City Co., for £35 current money. Joyce Simons is appt Gdn to Susa. Peirce, orphan of Edwd. Peirce dec'd. Joyce is to deliver estate to Susa. Peirce when she shall

come of age or be married. Signed: Joyce Simons, Matthew (X) Small. Wit: Cha. Jenings, Geo. (X) Lewis.

[pp 246, 247] Appraismt of est of Mr. Robt. Taylor dec'd as was produced by Mrs. Taylor, Exectrx on 3 Mar 1719. [1 1/2 pp of household and farming items follow, plus the following servants] "one negro man named Tom, one named Adam and do Dempsey all vallued £90:00:00. One old negro woman named Hanah – one do woman named Bess – 55:00:00 – and one white servt woman having three years to serve – 05:00:00." No total valuation of est given.

[pp 247, 248] Ind dated 15 Mar 1720. Edmund Kerney of Co. of Nansemond [leases] to Wm. Lowry of Eliz. City Co. for 5 sh current money of Va. a lot in the Town of Hampton gr to Kerney by Foeffees 21 July 1714. Signed: Edmd. Kerney. Wit: Simon Hollier, Joseph Selden. Ack 6 Mar 1719 & ord rec. No release.

[pp 248, 249] Last will and testament of John Baley of Eliz. City Co., "being in a very sick and weak condition of body." To eldest son Walter Baley all land, being three plantations in Eliz. City Co. excepting wife's third. To wife Judeth Baley four negroes: two negro men called Prince and Tom and two negro women Labella and Abby. The other negroes, Mount & Gomery (sic), Bob, Venus, Nanny & Will, and all personal estate to be equally divided between wife and "all my children and the child sd. wife is now bigg with." Wife Judeth Byley appt sole Exectrx. Dated 25 Mar 1720. Signed: John Bayley. Wit: Jo. Wragg, Josa. Curle, Margaret Needham. Pro 18 May 1720 by Curle and Needham and affirmed by Wragg. Certificate for pro granted & ord rec.

[pp 249, 250] Ind dated 15 Apr 1720. Jonas Tow and Douglas alias Brogal Reed of Province of NC, of the first part, and Thos. Lattimore of Parish and Co. of Eliz. City of the second part. For £3 current money [sell] a tract lying at the mouth of Back R containing by estimation 100 ac lately in the tenure of one Richd. Reed. Bounded Estly by the land of Edwd. Lattimore, Stly on land of Wm. Brown, Wstly on land of Humphrey Balis. Signed: Doglas (X) Brogal Reed, Jonas (X) Tow. Wit: Wm. Roe, Edwd. Lattimore, James (X) Baker. Pro 18 May 1720 by Lattimore & Baker. Ord rec. Release for £32. Same signatures and wit. Pro 18 May 1720. Rec 2 June 1720.

[pp 251, 252] Ind dated 15 May 1720. Foefees Henry Irwin and Joshua Curle, Gent [sell] to Edwd. Lattimore of Eliz. City, planter, for 20 lbs tobo two lots on the head of North St. in Hampton. Bounded on east by sd Edwd. Lattimore, on south with Tho. Woods, running north on the st to a creek called Col. Wilson's Cr. One halfacre formerly gr to Eliza. Penny and since recovered by a judmt of this Ct. Signed: Henry Irwin, Joshua Curle. Ack 18 May 1720 & ord rec. Release for 336 lbs tobo. Signed: H. Irwin, Joshua Curle. Ack 18 May 1720. Ord rec.

[p 253] "I have rec'd of Mr. Thomas Wilcox and Charles Jenings the sum of twenty-two pounds current money being the within morgage money with interest ... and do discharge the within indenture of Morgage 18 May 1720." Signed: William Smelt. Wit: Tho. Wythe, Wm. Westwood, John Bordland. Ack 18 May 1720 & ord rec.

[pp 253, 254, 255] Ind dated 16 Mar 1720 [sic]. Edmd. Kerney of Co. of Nansemond [to] Willm. Lowery of Co. of Eliz. City for £35 sterling. "That lot in Hampton gr unto sd Edmd. Kerney by deed of saile from Foefees on 21 July 1714." Signed: Edmond Kearny [sic]. Wit: Simon Hollier, Joseph Selden. Ack 16 Mar 1719 [sic] & ord rec.

[p 255] Inv of Thos. Tucker's est taken [no date] Includes a short list of household items. Also: "£90:07:00 left by Tho. Tucker in silver money weighed before Jas. Baker & Jno. Cooper; £6:5:0 in gold by weight before Jas. Nayler, James Baker, & Jno. Cooper." Also a total of 192 ells of various types of cloth. No total valuation given. No signature of appraisers given.

[pp 255, 256] In obedience to an Order of Court dated 17 June 1719. Appr & valuation of est of Frans. Rogers dec'd. Household items, stock etc. Total valuation £117:13:4. Signed: Thos. Read, Charles (X) Tucker, John Ro-----. "Look in the original appraismt and their you will find a mistake in the same set down and cast up as I think of £49:15:00."

[pp 256, 257] Ind dated 20 Apr 1720. William Dandridge, late of Hampton in the Co. of Eliz. City but now of King William Co. in the Colony and Domn. of Virga. Gentleman [sells to] Henry Irwin of Hampton for 5 sh a lot in Hampton on South Hampton R and running along Joseph Wragg 5 chains to a stake thence on the South another lane, on East 3 chains and 1/2 to another stake, thence along on Joseph Harris' lot 4 1/2 chains to the beg, each chain containing 2 poles. Signed: William Dandridge. Wit: John Mathers, Peter Thiboult, Godfrey Pole. Ack 19 May 1720 & ord rec. Release dated 21 Apr 1720 for £30 current money of Va. Same signature & wit. Ack & ord rec.

[p 259] Performance bond of William Dandridge for 100 pounds lawful money of Great Britain dated 21 Apr 1720. Signed: Wm. Dandridge. Wit: John Mathers, Peter Thiboult, Godfrey Pole. Ack 19 May 1720 & ord rec.

[pp 259, 260, 261] Ind dated 18 May 1720. Henry Irwin and Joshua Curle Gent, Foefees, [to] James Rascow Esqr. of the Co. of Warrick for 5 sh current money of Va. Two lots in Hampton on South Hampton R upon Kings St and Queen St, adj. Estly lots purchased by James Ricketts of William Dandridge. Signed: Henry Irwin, Joshua Curle. Wit: Cha. Jenings. Ack 19 May 1720 & ord rec. Release dated 19 May 1720 for 356 lbs tobo. Same signatures and wit: Ack 19 May 1720 and ord rec.

[pp 261, 262, 263] Apprismt of est of Capt. Fras. Ballard Gent dec'd "as was produced to us by Joshua Curle Gent 30 Apr 1720." A long list of household items follows including books: <u>Plutarch's Lives</u>, Dictionary, law books etc. Total valuation £118:01:71 1/2. Signed: James Ricketts, Joseph Banister, John Bordland, Joseph Wragg.

[pp 263, 264] Inv & Appr of est of Mr. Andr. Thomson dec'd taken 14 June 1720. Household items, clothing etc., including a parcel of old Hebrew and Greek books, English books and a Bible. Total valuation £50:02:06. "In obedience to an order of Court of 18 May we did meet at the house of Mrs. Ann Wallace and valued what was tendered us." Dated 14 June 1720. Signed: Simon Hollier, John Lowery, Edwd. Lattemore. "Part of estate not appraised viz: a hog, boy called Titus and old watch, a gown and cassock, a piece of Black Silk used for a pall to the Coffin, a Walking Cane, Cash in his Chest 93-4-9. To be ?Levyed? for him 1450 but not all Rec'd. A True Acct of the sd Estate. Error Excepted." Signed: Ann Wallace, Tho. Wythe.

[p 264] Estate of Mr. Andr. Thomson deceased. Dr to funeral and other charges July 1720. To: cash paid Jno. Bordland for Medeara Wine -6-; Brandy spice and 6 yds Silk for the Coffin 7-2-0; St--llone for the Coffin 15/ to a Coffin 1-15-0; Holland Sheet a napkin & hand kerchiefe to burie him in 1-5-0; 35 lb Musquerado Sugr @7 1/2 ... at 1/ used at ffuneral 2-2-4 1/2; a Hhd of Sider at his funeral 1-0-0; Tending on him in his Sickness and other Trouble and Charges about his funeral 3-0-0; 3 lbs Double Refined Sugr at his funeral at 2 - 0-6-0; Doctr. McKenzie for ?Means? and attendce & ps Silk for his Pall & Coffin 3-1-6; pd Jno. Bordland acct for work don him in his lifetime 7-0-1; his own boys board remaining unpaid being about 7 1/2 months 10-0-7 1/2; a Kersey Waskoat & briches for his boy 0-10-4; a pr Shoes and Stockins for do and Shirt and briches 0-10-00; pd Jno. Skinner the balla of theire accotts 0-3-0; Total 37-15-7. Commission on 37-15-7 at 5 pr cent 1-17-9. Total 39-13-4. Signed: Ann Wallace, Thos. Wythe.

[p 265] Inv of est of Wm. Williams dec'd taken by ord of Ct 23 May 1720. List includes household items, tools etc. and the following debts to est: Mary Bridge owes 60 lbs tobo; Ann Allen is indebted ten shills; Sarah Duberry is indebted 27 shills; Cha. Peirce 12 Cheires [chairs]; John Wilson & Wm. Armistead owe 25 d; Joshua Curle Senr owes 20 lbs tobo. Signed: Fras. Malory Subsheriff.

[pp 265, 266] Apprsmt of est of John Bayley Gent dec'd taken 9 June 1720. One and one-half pp of household items, stock etc. Includes the following negroes: 1 young man named Gomery @30:0:0; do Mount @30; do Bobb @27; girl Nanny @ 19; girl Venus @ 19; boy Will @7. Total valuation of est 304:0:0. Signed: Sarah Sweny, Joseph Banister, John Moore.

[p 267] Last will and testament of Margt. Bayley, Wido of Eliz City Co., being weak in body. To granddaughter Margt. Bayley, daughter of son Walter and her lawful heirs, three young negroes now with her sd father named Martin, Nell & Janey with reversion to two granddaughters Mary Bayley & Betty Bayley, daughters of sd son Walter Bayley. To Sarah Bayley, daughter of son Walter, two negrs called Jenny & Sarah with reversion to Mary & Betty. To grandson Christopher Needham, son of Thos. Needham, one negr man called Thos. Oxford [sic]. To dau Margt. Needham two

negro women, Judey & Cuckow. To sons Walter Bayley & Jno. Bayley one shill to each, they being already Preferred. Son Walter & daughter Margt. Needham to be Execs. Dated 8 Dec 1719. Signed: Margaret Bayley. Wit: Saml. Selden, John Selden, Thos. Jones. Pro 20 July 1720 by Jno. Selden & Thos. Jones. Cert for probate granted Margt. Needham, she giving bond, & ord rec.

[pp 268, 269] Last will and testament of Saml. Selden of Par & Co of Eliz City, being weak of body. To wife Reba. Selden, all the plantation "I now live upon called Buckrow" during her life in full recompense of dower & after her decease to remain to "my Right heire at law." To son Joseph, plantation on Potomack Cr & to his heirs forever, if he pay unto his two sisters the sums of money hereafter given two daughters. If he refuse to pay, then the same plantation to son John Selden under the same terms. To son John Selden, two plantations called Back River Plantation, being the tract lately in occupation of Leonard Yeo, and Old Fortes, being the tract on Hampton River late in the tenure of one Thos. Batts. To son Bartholomew, all the tobacco & money "he oweth me and five pounds to put him in a mourning suit and thirty pounds to buy him a Negr in case he gain none of his wife ?Akleys? negroes." To daughter Elizabeth Selden £60 sterling & to daughter Mary Milner £60 sterling, to be paid in two able negrs [to be bought] out of the plantation at Potomack, "that is to say by son Joseph within two years after my decease." If he does not, then to John Selden. If he does not pay, plantation goes to daughters. To wife, Negroes old Jack, Old Bess, and girl Pegg for life with reversion to son Joseph. Also to wife, boy Tom to be given by her to which child she pleases. To daughter Elizabeth £100 current money & two negrs Dick & Jenny, also 10 sheep, 6 cows or heifers of 3 yrs, and 3rd best bed. To daughter Mary Milner, use of the negr now with her, Harry, with reversion to son Joseph if Mary die without lawful heirs of her body. To son Joseph, negro man Tony & boy Will. To son John, negr man Pompi & boy Jack & 4th best bed & items. All the rest of personal estate to wife & son Joseph & they to be Execs. Estate not to be appr. Dated 9 May 1720. Signed: Samuel Selden. Wit: George Yeo, Wm. Brough, Margt. (X) Welch. Pro by all three wit at July Ct 1720. Cert for probate granted & ord rec.

[pp 269, 270] Power of Atty of Richd. Tookerman, late of the Province of South Carolina but now of Colony of Virga. gent. "By virtue of the several powers & authorities unto me given & made by my wife Katherine, formerly Katherine Grant before that Katherine English and theretofore Katherine Harrison, relict & Excutrix of Josias Harrison Merchant of Barbadoes." Henry Irwin of Hampton is appointed to handle any business or legal matter for Tookerman or his wife. Dated 18 June 1720. Signed: Richd. Tookerman. Wit: Emanl. Alkin, Wm. Brand, Fras. Malory, Saml. Sweny. Pro by all wit 23 July 1720 & ord rec.

[pp 270, 271] Ind dated 15 Aug 1720. Deed of gift from Wm. Lowery of Par & Co of Eliz. City to son John Lowery, "now being in actual possession by marreing Frances one of the Daughters and Coe heirs of Thos. Purifie of the Par & Co afsd dec'd and mother to the sd John Lowery," all of the plantation "whereon I now live," beg at a small branch on the W side of Wils Quarter & running from the head of the same Nthly to the uppermost bounds of sd land, adj. Mr. Simon Hollier's land & on E side with land of Mrs. Hannah Booker & upon the S with Back River. 200 acs known as Purifies Old Fields. Signed: William Lowery. Wit: Thos. Kerby, Peter Manson. Ack 17 Aug 1720.

[pp 271, 272] Ind dated 15 Aug 1720. Wm. Lowery Senr's deed of gift to son Wm. Lowery Junr. Lot with houses etc. in Hampton Town bought by Wm. Lowery Senr from Edmd. Kearney 15 Mar 1719. Signed: William Lowery. Wit: Thos. Kerby, Peter Manson. Ack 17 Aug 1720.

[pp 272, 273] Ind dated 16 Aug 1720. William Lowery, Henry Irwin & Joshua Curle, all of Eliz. City Co Gent, Surviving Foefees appt by the Ct of sd Co [to] Joseph Banister Gent for 200 lbs tobo. 36 square poles in Hampton Town, pt being low sunken land, beg at bank of the Watering Cove & running along bank S 62 1/2 deg W 70/100 chain to above Banister's lot, along lot N 42 deg E 7 chains to the backlane, thence to Esqr. Lukes lot S 62 deg E 34/100 chains, thence along Esqr. Lukes lot S 10 1/2 Wstly 3 68/100 to a stake ... Signed: Willm. Lowery, Joshua Curle. Wit: Cha. Jenings CClk. Ack 17 1720 by Willm. Lowery.

[p 273] 21 May 1683 [sic]. Surveyed for John Hayles. [metes and bounds. Following persons and landmarks mentioned.]

Part butting S on mouth of Broad Cr at James River between land of Mr. Augustine More formerly Mr. Sherley's land & land of John Chandler, running from the point to a br of Broad Cr ... Tarpitt Spring & and by agreement of Jno. Chandler & John Hayles crossing Slippery Pine Br. 150 acs first gr as follows: 50 ac to Eliza. Lupo by pat dated 20 Sept 1629 & 100 gr to Wm. Perry by pat dated Janry 1661 & 10 acs overplus. Ord rec on motion of Cha. Jenings 15 June 1720.

[p 274] Power of Atty of Hannah Booker of Abbingdon Par in Co of Glocester to Wm. Lowery Senr of Eliz. City Co. When requested by Thos. Kerby of Charles Par in Co of York, Lowery is to ack lease & release to Kerby. Dated 11 Aug 1720. Signed: Hanh. (X) Booker. Wit: Peter Manson, Wm. Lowery, Edwd. Booker. Pro by Manson & Lowery 17 Aug 1720 & ord rec.

[pp 274 - 277] Ind dated 10 Aug 1720. Hannah Booker of the Co of Gloster [to] Thos. Kerby of Co of York, planter for 5 sh lawful money of Va. Tract in Eliz. City Co. 100 acs [on] line between Wm. Lowery & sd Hannah Booker ... Mr. Simon Hollier's line near head of Price's Cr crossing main br of sd Cr to S side. Signed: Hanh. Booker. Wit: Peter Manson, Wm. Lowery, Edwd. Booker. Ack by Wm. Lowery as Atty on 17 Aug 1720 & ord rec. Release for £100 dated 11 Aug 1720. Same signature, witnesses, acknowledgement etc.

[pp 277 - 280] Ind dated 15 Aug 1720. Wm. Lowery, Henry Irwin, & Joshua Curle, Foefees [to] John Bordland In holder. For 50 lbs tobo. Piece of Wast or lapsed land. 32 sq poles on S side of lot Bordland now lives on ... to George Walker's lot ... down to Cove. Signed: Wm. Lowery, Joshua Curle. Wit: Cha. Jenings CClk. Ack by all 17 Aug 1720 & ord rec. Release dated 16 Aug 1720 for 72 lbs good sweet-scented tobo. Signed: Josha. Curle. Ack & ord rec 17 Aug 1720.

[pp 280-282] Ind dated 3 June 1720. Joshua Curle & Wm. Lowery, Feofees [to] Henry Irwin Gent for 20 lbs tobo. Wast or lapsed land. 39 sq poles beg at head of Will Winterton's across heads of Henry Irwin's & Wilson Curle's lot to Josa. Curle's lot...to stake near head of Cove...to George Wauffe's lot. Signed: Wm. Lowery. Ack 17 Aug 1720 & ord rec. Release dated 4 June 1720 for 79 lbs tobo. Signature, wit, ack same.

[pp 282, 283] In obedience to Ct Ord dated 19 June 1720, the appraismt of est of Wm. Williams dec'd. Household items etc. Total valuation £62:10:7 3/4. Also includes: To debts due estate: Mary Bridge, Josa. Curle Senr, Giles Duberry's est, Mr. Allen's est, Charles Peirce. Signed: Brian Penne, Richd. Nusum, Tho. Batts.

[283, 283] Inv of est of Mr. John Moore dec'd. Seven negroes, unnamed; household items, implements etc; two cows at Richd. Haneys. Signed: Elizabeth Gooding, William Moore. No valuation given.

[p 284] Last will and testament of William Hopkins of Eliz. City Co, sick & weak. To Henry Noblin, clothing. To Edwd. Jones, clothing & items. To Mary Bridge, bed; Bible, Prayer Book & old horse. To nephew Wm. Calicote, heiffer. To James Calicote, heifer. To Mary Bridge items & stock. To Wm. Creek, clothing. To Mark Powell, clothing. To Jno. Meredith, items. To Mary Bridge, more stock & the lease "of this land where I now live." Mary Bridge & Myhill Roberts to be Execs. Dated 20 May 1717. Signed: William Hopkins. Wit: Mark (X) Powell, Wm. Creek, Thos. Jones. Pro in Ct 18 June 1718 (sic) & ord rec.

[p 285] Bond dated 19 July 1720 of Reba. Selden, Joseph Selden, George Yeo and Jno. Selden, all of Eliz. City Co for £2000. Reba. and Joseph Selden are to make an inv and properly perform the duties of Execs of est of Saml. Selden dec'd. Signed: Reba. (X) Selden, Joseph Selden, George Yeo, Jno. Selden. Wit: Cha. Jennings CClk, Fra. Mallory, Godfrey Pole.

[pp 285, 286] Bond of Mary Gilbert, James Ricketts, Bart. Proby, all of Eliz. City Co, for £140. Dated 21 July 1720. Mary Gilbert, Admx of est of James Gilbert dec'd is to make inv and properly perform the duties of Admx. Ack 21 July 1720.

[p 286] Bond of Mary Bridge, Brian Penny & Richd. Nusum for £100 dated 16 June 1720. Mary Bridge is appt Gdn to Ann Williams, orphan of Wm. Williams, taking her into her custody & care together with her est. Mary Bridge is to

pay all of est when Ann comes to age or marries. Signed: Mary (X) Bridge, Brian Penny, Richd. Nusum. Act 16 June 1720.

[p 287] Inv & appr of est of John Dunn taken 9 Nov 1719 in obedience to an ord of Ct 16 Sept 1719. To three bbls of Cyder due from Wm. Dunn. Total value £5:06. The undersigned met at house of John Bayley Gent. Signed: Thomas Batts, Bryan Penny, John (X) Chandler.

[p 287, 288] Last will and testament of William Willson, planter. To son William Willson, 1 shill of silver money of Va. To son John Willson, 1 shill of silver money of Va. To daughter Frances Skinner, 1 shill of silver money of Va. To daughter Martha Willson, items & stock. To daughter Jane Willson, items & stock. To son Edward Willson, rest of whole est, personal & real and he to be Exec. Dated 11 Apr 1720. Signed: William (X) Willson. Wit: Jaccob (X) Face, George (X) Pain, Mary (X) Pain. Pro 17 May 1721 by George Pain and Jacob Face & adm to rec.

[p 289] Last will and testament of Wm. Malory dated 17 Aug 1719. Sick & weak. To son Francis Mallory, the plantation "Whereon I now live" bounded by a line of markt from Mr. Tho. Wythe to Mr. Antho. Armistead. To son Wm. Malory, all residue of lands to enjoy at age 16. Personal est to be equally divided between son William and daughters Mary & Anne, except one copper kettle to son William. To son Francis, negro Will and small brass kettle & "Liberty over my whole land to get timber for his plantation use." Two sons Frances (sic) & William to be joint Execs. Interlined: "& do appt Mr. Thos. Wyth overseer." Signed: Wm. Malory. Wit: Jno. (X) Bean, Ann (X) Bean. Pro 15 Feb 1720 by Jno. Bean & Ann his wife & adm to rec.

[pp 289 - 291] Ind dated 17 Jan 1720. Thomas Curle of Co of Eliz. City, planter [to] Matthew Williams of Par & Co afsd, planter, for 5 sh current money of Va. Parcel of 50 acs, that part of Thos. Curle's Manr Planta which lies next to land given to Ann Curle dec'd, sister to sd Thos. Curle. Signed: Thomas (X) Curle. Wit: Willm. Westwood, Thomas (X) Morgan. Release dated 18 Jan 1720 for £19 current money of Va. Ack 19 May 1721 & adm to rec.

[pp 291-293] Ind dated 20 Sept 1720. Jane Baker of Town of Hampton, Widdow [to] John Wallis Junr for 5 sh silver money of Va. One-half lot gr to late husband Peter Baker by Henry Jenkins Gent dec'd. Bounded N on Henry Jenkins Junr, E on Richard Kirkin, S on Thomas Wyth Gent, and on King St W. Signed: Jane (X) Baker. Wit: Rosana Huntt, Martha Pett, Jo. Wragg. Ack -- May 1721. Release Sept 1720 for £50 current silver money of Va. & adm to rec.

[pp 293-295] Ind dated 15 May 1721. Hind [and Hinde] Armistead & Hanah his wife [to] Joshua Curle Gent for 5 sh. All that tract of hers bounded Wstly on lands late of Collo. Wm. Wilson's dec'd, Sthly on James R, Estly upon a Cr which divides the sd land from land whereon Hinde Armistead now lives, Nthly running up Cr. 40 ac. Signed: Hind Armistead, Hanah (X) Armistead. Wit: Jam. Falconar, Leonard Whiting. Ack 18 May 1721. Release for £40 lawful money of Va. Same signatures, ack etc.

[pp 295, 296] Ind dated 13 Mar 1720/21. Abm. Mitchell of Town of Hampton, Par & Co of Eliz. City, Shipwright [to] Wm. Westwood for 5 sh. Parcel in Town of Hampton on South Hampton R. 31 sq poles, 575 sq links. On side of Cove, E of John Mitchel's lot on Queens St, bounded on W with John Mitchels lot, on N with Queens St, on E & SW with Hampton R. Purchased by Mitchell from Foefees 18, 19 Oct 1719. Signed Abraham Mitchell. Wit: Henry Irwin, Wm. Loyall. Ack 18 May 1721. Release dated 14 May 1721 for £5 current money of Va. from Abram. Mitchel & Ann his wife. Signed: Abram. Mitchel, Ann (X) Mitchel. Wit same. Ack by Abraham and Ann, who relinquishes right of dower 18 May 1721.

[pp 299, 300] Ind dated 19 June 1721. Thos. Curle & Ann his wife, and Judith Preedy, daus of Danl. Preedy dec'd [to] Joseph Otterson, all of Eliz. City Co., for 20 shill current money. Tract of 50 acs joining land of Thos. Williams now Wm. Allens & land late belonging to Thos. Lewis now Samll. Watts & butting E on Back R as by survey from Wm. Lowry Gent Surveyor dated 13 Sept 1714. Sold by Wm. Morgan alis Brooks to Ralph Mourton by deed dated 16 Mar 1639 & by the sd Mourton given to Robt. Preedy & the sd Robt. devised the land by will dated 1 Mar 1667 to his son Danl. Preedy & he to daus Judith & Ann. Signed: Thos. (X) Curle, Ann (X) Curle, Judith (X) Preedy. Wit: Cha. Jenings, Fra. Mallory. Ack 21 June 1721. Marginal note reads: It is to be noted that the burying place upon the said land is excepted. Release dated 20 June 1721 for £42 current money. Adm to rec.

[pp 302, 303] Ind dated 20 June 1721. Joseph Otterson [to] Wm. Allen carpenter for 25 sh current money. 50 acs joining land of Thos. Williams now Wm. Allens & land late belonging to Thos. Lewis now Samll. Watts & butting E on Back R. as by survey from Wm. Lowry Gent Surveyor dated 13 Sept 1714. [Note: see land chain above for this same property] and conveyed to the sd Joseph Otterson. Signed: Joseph Otterson. Wit: John Smith, Fra. Mallory. Ack -- June 1721 & adm to rec. Release from Joseph Otterson and Mary his wife [to] Wm. Allen dated 21 June 1721 for £42 current money. Signed: Joseph Otterson, Mary Otterson. Same wit. Ack 21 June 1721 & adm to rec.

[pp 304, 305] Ind dated 16 May 1721. Richd. Kirkin [Kerkin & Kirken etc] of Town of Hampton & Par & Co of Eliz. City [to] Mary Floyd for 5 sh current money of Va. Part of a lot, 35 foot square within sd Kerkins's lot, bounded on Tho. Wyth Gent W, on Kerkin N & E, & John Batts Sthly, together with an outlet of five foot in breadth into the street by the Brick Gable end of sd Kerkin's dwelling house. Signed: Richd. (X) Kerkin. Wit: Bartrand Proby, Jo. Wragge. Ack 22 June 1721. Release dated 17 May 1721 for £5. Same signatures & ack.

[pp 305, 306] Will of Wm. Cole of Eliz. City Co, weak in body. To Cozen Henry Robinson all land and he appt Exec. Dated 22 Sept 1720. Signed: Willm(X) Cole. Wit: Jenings (sic), Benjamin (X) Ralph, Joseph (X) Milby. Pro 21 June 1721 by Charles Jenings & Benjamin Ralph. Adm to rec.

[p 306] Inv of est of Mr. Samll. Selden dec'd. Short list. Outstanding debts about £400; of Cattle 120 head; of horses 4 head; pigs 20; sheep 74; household items. Signed: Rebekah Selden & Joseph Selden. No date.

[p 306] Inv of certain things Expended for the use of the famaly ... already come to their hand. Household items etc. £38:3:11. In obedience to ord of Ct we met at the house of Mrs. Yeo & appr goods above being the remaining pt of Capt. Boswell's Decd his estate. Dated 22 Sept 1720.

Signed: Tho. Wythe, Joshua Curle, Jas. Ricketts. Ret 22 June 1721 & ord rec.

[p 307] Inv & appr of est of Giles Duberry dec'd taken 20 June 1721. List of household items etc including a Bible. £38:14:3. In obedience to Ct Ord of 18 May. Signed: Wm. Armistead, Thos. Read, John Cook [or Coak]. Ret 22 June 1721 & ord rec.

[p 307] The Ct ord on 18 May 1721 an appr of the remaining pt of John Pett's est. Wm. Smelt informs the Ct that persons formerly appt to appr refused. Ct ord Joseph Wragg, John Smith Senr & John Bordland to appr. Ret 22 June 1721. Two negroes & 14 pounds. Appr dated 20 June 1721.

[p 308] Bond of John King, Robt. Armistead & Henry Irwin for £2000. John King having been appt High Sheriffe of Eliz City Co & sworn 21 June 1721, is to well & truly perform the duties of his office. Signed: John King, Robt. Armistead, H. Irwin. Wit: Jas. Ricketts, Samll. Sweny. Ack 21 June 1721 & ord rec.

[308] Mary Cary made oath that Cary Haslett, Mariner, is indebted to her for £30. She has lost the Bill & Writing Obligatory he wrote in his own proper hand. She swears she has received no part of the debt. Dated 22 June 1721. Signed: Mary Cary. Ord rec.

[pp 308, 309] Ind dated 13 July 1721. Henry Jenkins of Par & Co of Eliz. City, Mariner, [to] Samuel Sweny of Town of Hampton for 5 sh sterl. 1/2 lot in Town of Hampton on South Hampton R. N on land formerly belonging to Collo. Wm. Wilson & now in possession of Mr. James Ricketts, W with Queens St, S with other half lot purchased by Peter Baker of Capt. Henry Jenkins dec'd, & E by Mr. ----. Land assigned to sd Henry Jenkins as heir at law to his late father dec'd. Signed: Henry Jenkins. Wit: Frans. Gugh or Pugh, Miles Cary. Ack 19 July 1721. Release dated 14 July 1721 for £6:10. Same signatures. Ack & adm to rec 19 July 1721.

[311, 312] Ind dated 17 July 1721. Joseph Harris of Par & Co of Eliz. City, planter [to] Wm. Whitfield, Mariner of Town of Hampton for 5 sh. Parcel in Town of Hampton. 4 sq chains & 1/2 taken out of lot of sd Harris, adj. Harris, Josa. Ragg. Signed: Joseph (X) Harris. Wit: Henry Irwin, Wm. Fyfe, Wm. Winterton. Release dated 18 July 1721 for £11:05 current silver money of Va. Same signatures. Ack 3rd Wed in July (18 July 1721) & ord rec.

[pp 313, 314] Ind dated 15 July 1721. William Hachell of Co of Eliz. City [to] Thos. Baker of Worwick [sic] Co for 5 sh lawful money of Va. 74 acs in Eliz. City as by pat bearing date 19 Dec 1711. Signed: William (X) Hachell. Wit: Simon Hollier, John Bordland, Wm. Bordland. Release for £10 lawful money of Va. dated 16 July 1721. Same signatures. Ack 19 July 1721 & ord rec.

COURT ORDER BOOK

1715-1721

At a Court held 3rd Wednesday of July 1715
Present: Mr. Wm. Lowery, Mr. John Bayley, Mr. Tho.
Tabb, Mr. Tho. Wythe, Mr. Antho. Armistead, Mr. John
King, Capt. Wm. Bosell, Mr. Marke Johnson
His Majt.'s Justices.

[p 1] John Sweatman is presented by the Grand Jury for ----coming to Church. Ordered that he be fined and pay fine to Churchwardens.

Dority Floyd, presented for having a bastard child, was not summoned. Ordered she be summoned to answer for her crime.

Suit by Emanl. Alkin agt John Stringer in an action of the case for 50 sh. Attachmt to be executed.

John Bayley, next friend to his son William complains agst Wm. Dandridge and Euphan his wife, Exectrx of Wills. Roscoe dec'd, deft for legacy of £50 left to sd William by Roscoe. Dandridge not appearing, attachment is granted. Return to next Ct for further trial.

In suit of Tho. Walker, pltf, agt B----- Penny, deft in action of trespass, damage twenty --- sterling and pltf's attachmt being returned executed ---

An Wallace, Admx of James Wallace dec'd, agt William Coopland in an action upon the case for 50 sh ended between themselves -- Mr. Selden --

Bill in chancery brought by Tho. Jones agt ---Coopland and Eliza. his wife, Admx of David Jones dec'd.

[p 2] In suit brought by Geo. Luke Esqr agt Jane Curle, Exectrx of Nicho. Curle gent dec'd. Action on the case for £20. Nonsuit granted her & ord paymt to deft.

Capt. William Bosell produced two letters and the sale by outcry of two lots in Hampton Town and also made oath that he rec'd the lots from England from Mrs. Jane Lowery. Ordered recorded.

Last will of Joane Smith dec'd proved by oath of Nathl. Parker & affirmation of Joseph Wragg. Ordered recorded. Probate granted to Execs, having given bond.

Ordered appraisal of estate of Joane Smith dec'd by Mr. Robt. Taylor, Joseph Banister, Mr. Wm. Loyall, & Mr. Wm. Smelt, or any two of them & return to next Ct.

Foeffees ack deed for town land to Joshua Curle. Ordered recorded.

Petition of Henry Bowcock for license to keep Ordinary in town, granted, he giving bond & duty & having pd the Governor.

"The Building of the Court House and Prison being Considered of by the Court and having what Each workman offered to build the Court House and Prison Cheapest, Mr. Simon Hollier has undertaken to build the sd Prison for Thirty Pounds in Money or Tobo at fifteen shills per hundred, according to the Demensions set down in a Former order for building the sd Prison. And Mr. Saml. Sweny undertakes to Build the Court House at the same Demensions as in the former order and to Furnish the Same for one hundred and thirty-seven Pounds Money or Tobo at fifteen shills per hundrd. Each Undertaker obliging themselves to do the said worke workman like giving bond and Security to Performe the Same."

Rachel Provine complains agt Tho. Wilcox and James Talbert for beating sd Provine and four Enids. [Indians?] being sworn by the Ct but the Enids not making anything appear – [balance of entry missing]

Eliza. Harety complains that her master Brian Penny beats and abuses her & gives her no diet sufficient for a white servant. It appears to the Ct that Eliza. is an indented servant to the Revend. Mr. John [Note: this name is very difficult to decipher. It may be Winston or Umston or even Vimston.] of North Carolina. Ordered that the servant be set free from Penny & safely conveyed to her former Master, being delivered from Constable to Constable till she shall [be] out of this Government.

Court adjourns till Tomorrow Ten a Clock. John Holloway [signs]

At a Court held the 3rd Wednesday of Augst being the 17th day 1715

Present – Mr. Thomas Tabb, Capt. Fra. Ballard, Mr. Antho.

Armistead, Mr. John More, Mr. John Bayley, Mr. Tho. Wyth

Upon petition of William Marloe for his estate, ordered that William Wilson be summoned to next Ct to answer.

Suit by Robt. Taylor pltf agt Henry Sandwich deft in an action of debt for £7:7:10 & he not to be found, attchmt granted agt his estate with costs.

Tho. Poole being presented for not coming to Church & he promising to ----- offences, ordered fine be remitted.

Alexdr. Avery presented for not coming to Church & he not excusing himself is to pay fine to Churchwardens for use of sd Parish.

John Whitfield presented for not coming to Church and not excusing himself is ordered to pay fine to Churchwardens for use of sd Parish.

Tho. Taylor presented for not coming to Church & he excusing himself, ordered that fine be remitted.

[p 4] Humphry Baylis presented for not coming to Church and he not excusing himself, ordered to pay fine to Churchwardens.

Tho. Avery presented for not coming to Church and he not excusing himself, ordered he pay fine of 5 sh or 50 lbs tobo.

Wm. Baylis presented for not coming to Church and he not excusing himself, ordered to pay fine of 5 sh or 50 lbs tobo.

Richd. Rowton Junr presented for not coming to Church and not excusing himself, ordered to pay fine of 5 sh or 50 lbs tobo.

Michl. Peirce presented for not coming to Church and he not excusing himself, ordered to pay fine of 5 sh or 50 lbs tobo.

John Wilson presented for not coming to Church and he excusing himself, fine is remitted.

Matthew Watts presented for not coming to Church and he excusing himself, fine is remitted.

Saml. Watts presented for not coming to Church and he excusing himself, fine is remitted.

Abm. Parish presented for not keeping scales and weights in his mill and he excusing himself, fine is remitted.

John Phillips presented for a common swearer and he excusing himself, fine is remitted.

Michl. Roberts presented for a common swearer and he being convicted, ordered fined 5 sh or 50 lbs toba and pay to Churchwardens.

Wm. Wilson presented for not coming to Church and he excusing himself, fine is remitted and he is to pay costs.

James Floyd presented for not coming to Church and he not excusing himself, ordered fined 5 sh or 50 lbs tobo.

[p 5 – damaged. Top entry missing]

Cost granted to Wm. Marshall Junr for taking up a Runaway of John Clarke of Gloster Co. having made oath & never rec'd any satisfaction for the same.

The action brought by Robt. Taylor agt William Roger deft for 20 sterling refd to next Ct.

Suit brought by Tho. Walker agt Edwd. Mihill in an action of the case for £2:17:6 for ... sidesaddle refd to next Ct.

The ejectmt brought by William Symons agt John Tracy on ... Jane Curle ... the last Ct & deft pleading not guilty, refd to next Ct.

Tho. Howard and Eliza. his wife ack [deed] to William Allen.

In the suit brought by Antho. Armistead agt Edwd. Mihill...action of trespass, damage £100 sterling for trespass on pltf's land. It is ordered that the pltf have judgmt on the Verdict and that deft pay damages assessed by the Jury of one shilling & costs.

Wm. Dandridge and Euphan his wife, Exectrx of Wilso. Rascow dec'd agt Rich'd. K--kin and Margt. his wife, action upon the case...£100 sterling refd to next Ct for trial.

Ord that Antho. Armistead pay Fra. Malory for – days attendance for him agt Edwd. Mihill with costs.

John More. Suit agt Tho. Powell deft in action of trespass. Refd to next Ct for trial.

Robt. Taylor. Suit agt Tho. [Balance of entry torn off]

[p 6 – top entry missing]

Edwd. Lattimore agt Phillip Prescott. Action of trespass...£10 sterl...

Judgmt granted by nilil dicet agt Jane Curle Exectrx of Nicho. Curle dec'd to answer suit of Mathw. Small.

Judgmt granted by nihil dicet agt Jos. Curle to answer suit of Matthew Small.

In the suit brought by Eliza. James agt Jno. Sweetman for 45 sh, deft appearing, judgmt is discharged [since] he ack himself [indebted] for £3 with the condition that if he do not acct with plt for goods rec'd of her between this and next Ct before Capt. Wm. Bosell, Mr. Saml. Selden Jr and Mr. Banister or any two of them, the above recognizance to be void. To make report to next Ct.

It is ordered that if Mr. Phillip Prescott do not within two days come to the Clk's office and give security for the estate of Edwd. Penny's orphan, the Sheriff is ordered to take the estate into his possession for the children. Signed: Wm. Lowery.

At a Court held the 3rd Wednesday of Septbr
being the 21st day 1715.
Majr. John Holloway, Mr. Wm. Lowry, Capt. Fra. Ballard,
Mr. John Bayley, Majr. Wm. Armistead, ... More,
Mr. Anthony Armistead, Mr. Thomas Tabb, ... Wythe,
Mr. Mark Johnson – His Majt. Justices.

[torn]... to build a "watter" mill is rejected.
...Thomas Badley is postponed...

[p 7] ...Samuel Selden plt agt...

In the suit brought by John Sweetman agt Wm. ------In an action upon the case for £7:5 and Francis Ballard late Sheriff ... Summoned to give acct of what has become of the attachmt agt deft ... [Ballard] pleading that there was not any estate to be found to serve attachmt upon, whereupon the plt discharged the deft. Attachmt continued.

Judgmt granted by nihil dicet agt Bryan Penny to answer the suit of Thomas Walker in an action of trespass damage £20 sterling.

Upon the motion of Geo. Walker, Edmd. Kearny, John Smith and Josa. Curle, Securities for estate of Nicho. Curle dec'd, ordered that James Ricketts and Jane his wife be summoned to answer and that Jane Curle Exectrx of sd Curle's will be summoned.

Henry Robinson's suit agt Samll. Seldon is refd to next Ct in an action of debt for £100 ...

William Armistead's suit agt Simon Hollier dismissed.

Prince, a negro belonging to Mr. John Bayley, being brought to Ct for stealing a hog from John Pett. Ordered that sd negro receive thirty-nine lashes well laid on his bare back and the master ordered to pay Pet 200 lbs tobo.

William Coopland's suit agt Charles Avery...
[Balance of page missing]

[p 8] Emanuell Alkins suit...
    Daniell Lewis. Suit agt Emanuell Alkin.
    John Curle. Suit agt Elexder. Avery, dismist.
    Judgement confirmed by Bryan Penny for £4:1:6 to William Smelt with costs.
    Jane Curle Exectrx of Nicho. Curle dec'd. Suit agt John Bayley dismist.
    Christopher Phillipson. Suit agt Geo. Luke Esqr dismist.
    Robert Taylor. Suit agt Francis Ballard. Deft appears & prays time to next Ct. Granted.
    Imparlence granted to Wm. Newberry to answer suit of Joseph Wragg, damage £50 sterling in action of trover.
    Imparlence granted to Wm. Coopland to answer suit of Nicholas Phillips.
    Upon petition of Wm. Marloe agt Wm. Wilson for his estate, his atty prays time to next Ct for trial which is granted.
    Robt. Taylor. Suit agt Wm. Rogers refd to next Ct.
    Robt. Wayslock lessee of Thomas Poole agt Jane Curle is dismist because the deft is married.
    John More. Suit agt Tho. Powell for trespass, damage £10. Jury's verdict dated 16 June 1715 being returned, the plt put in reasons in stay of judgmt. The deft prayd time to next Ct to argue the same. Granted.
    --- Faulkner. Suit agt Thomas Roberts --- [missing]

[p 9] Edward Lattemore. Suit agt Phillip Prescott refd to next Ct for trial.
    Matthew Small. Suit agt Josa. Curle in action of debt, deft pleads nihil dicet. Refd to next Ct for further trial.
    Matthew Small. Suit agt Jane Curle Exectrx dismist, she being married.
    Matthew Small. Suit agt Josa. Curle in action of trespass upon the case - £10 sterling. Deft pleads non assumpsit. Refd to next Ct.
    Elizabeth James. Action accts to render agt Jno. Sweetman for 45 sh. Ordered he is to acct before Capt. William Bossell, Jos. Banister and Samll. Selden Junr or any two of them between this and next Ct. [If he does not] to pay £3 sterling to James.

William Dandridge. Suit agt Richd. Kirkin & Margtt. his wife postponed till tomorrow for trial if Mr. Chapple, one of the Evidences, be here. If not to come to trial next Ct.

Robert Taylor. Suit agt Henry Sandwich dismist.

Dority Floyd, being presented by the Grand Jury for having a bastard child and she being married to the father of the sd child, ordered that her fine be remitted only paying costs.

Thomas Roberts obliges himself to pay the fine acc to law for Abigall Bushall for having a bastard child born of her body and to save the Parish harmless from the sd child till she confesses the father, and to pay costs.

Ordered that the Sheriff summon Mary Randy to answer the presentation of the Grand Jury for having a bastard child.

The Proclamation concerning Grievances was published. Ordered to --- special Imparlence granted to Antho. Armistead gent to answer ---

Marke Johnson gent. Action of trespass - damage £10

Imparlence granted to William Malory to answer suit of Francis [Ballard] in action of debt for £4 sterling.

Upon the summons in Chancery brought by Thomas Jones Senr, --- Coopland and Eliza. his wife, Exectrx of David Jones dec'd, the deft putting in his answer ---

[p 10] Suit brought by --- Proby in action of acct rendered for £150 sterling, summons returned executed & deft not appearing, attchmt agt his body granted.

Action of accts for £7:5 brought by Richd. Kirkin agt Richd. Adams Pltf failing to appear, non-suit is granted.

Richd. Kirkin's action agst Jane Curle, wido, Exectrx of Nicho. Curle gent, dismist, she being married.

Order granted agt Sheriff for non-appearance of John Sampson to answer suit of Edward Mihill in an action upon the case for damages, 300 lbs tobo.

Special imparlence granted to John Curle to answer suit of Matthew Small in an action on the case for 35 sh.

Ordered that Edwd. Mihill pay Eliza. Malory for four days attendance as an evidence for him agt his wife with costs.

In an action brought by Brian Penny agt Tho. Walker, deft prays time. Granted.

Edmd. Henry and Joshua Curle. Suit agt Richd. Mosely is dismist. No prosecution.

In the suit brought by Wm. Tracey agt Henry Batts in action of trespass, damages £10 sterl. Writ not being executed but a Copia left at deft's house and he not appearing, attchmt granted for sd sum. Return to next Ct for further trial.

In the suit brought by Henery Cake and Mary his wife agt Francis Ballard in an action upon the case for an assault and battery, damages £100 sterling. Copia of writ being left at deft's house, attchmt granted. Return to next Ct for further trial.

In the suit brought by Jane Curle, Exectrx of Nicho. Curle gent dec'd, agt Joshua Curle, Henry Jenkins and Mary his wife in an action on the case for £53 sterling, dismist, pltf being married.

Emanl. Alkin. Suit agt Wm. Coopland dismist.

Joseph Milbee. Suit agt Wm. Coopland in an action upon the case for 45 sh, deft prayed time. Granted.

Imparlence granted Richd. Kirkin to answer suit of Edward Mihill in an action upon the case, damage £30 current money.

Imparlence granted to John Smith to answer -----

[p 11] William Bosell Gent in an action upon the case agt Rachell Provine. Dismist.

Court adjourned till tomorrow morning Nine O Clock. John Holloway Signed. Test: Cha. Jenings CClk.

At a Court held the 22nd day of Septembr 1715
Majr. John Holloway, Mr. William Lowery, Capt. Francis Ballard, Mr. Marke Johnson – His Majt Justices

Upon motion of Mr. Saml. Selden on behalf of Mr. Wm. Dandridge and Euphan his wife, Execs of Wilson Rascow dec'd, agt Richd. Kirkin and Margt. his wife. Affadavit of John Chapple, a seafaring man, as Evidence in this cause, is to be taken before one of the Justices and defts to have timely notice "of the taken of the same." Affadavit is to be used in case Chapple be not in the Country.

Richd. Kirkin's suit agt Thomas Badely dismist.

In the suit brought by Wm. Dandridge and Euphan his wife, Execs of Wilso. Rascow late dec'd, agt Richd. Kirkin and Margt. his wife in an action upon the case, damages £500 sterling, refd to next Ct for trial for want of a Jury.

Then the Court adjourned Till the Court in Course. John Holloway.

At a Court held 8 Wednesday of Novembr being the 16th day 1715
Majr. John Holloway, Mr. Tho. Tabb, Capt. John More, Majr. Wm. Armistead, Mr. Antho. Armistead, Mr. John Bayley, Mr. Fra. Ballard, Capt. Wm. Bosell, Mr. John King, Mr. Marke Johnson – His Majt. Justices

Upon petition of Thomas Curle for his est in the hands of Benja. Smith, it is ordered that Smith be summoned to answer.

In an ejection brought by Robt. Westlake agt William Symons. On 10 May 171-, one Tho. Roote at the Parish of Eliza. City had demised "and to farm let" to Westlake one dwelling house, one gardian [garden], 60 acs of land, 30 acs of woodland, 30 acs of cleared land in the Parish and Co afsd. On 1 May 1715, Wm. Symons did enter with force of arms and eject him, his term not ended
[p 12] and other Enormities did do to damages of £10 current money. Oath being made by Alexdr. Avery on 16 Nov 1715 he had delivered a Copia of the ejection with endorsement to John Stores and Fracey, tenants in possession of the land in question. Ordered that Jno. Stores and Wm. Fracey appear at next Ct and in this cause plead.

Samuell Selden and Rebeckah his wife ack their deed of gift to Bartholomew Selden.

Upon Capt. William Bosell & Mr. Thomas Howard's proposal to give land in Towne enough to build a Courthouse upon which land they did show to Mr. John Holloway, Mr. William Lowry & Mr. Anthony Armistead, and to give sixteen foot wide for a way to the High Street & to give also five pounds toward the building of the same and the privilege of a house for the workmen whilst building it. It's agreed by the Ct that the same be accordingly built on the sd land, that Mr. Wm. Lowery lay off the land, and that deeds be prepared against next Ct for sd Bosell & Howard to convey to the Justices & their successors for this use.

Upon the motion of Capt. Henry Jenkins that appraisal of Mr. Nicholas Curle be not recorded. Motion granted and time given Jenkins till next Ct.

Mr. George Walker comes into Ct and relinquishes Execship of Mr. Nicho. Curle and desires same be rec. Granted.

Samuell Selden. Suit agt Bryan Penny. Action upon the case for £4 damage. Refd to next Ct.

John Sweetman's attachmt agt Wm. Weston continued for £17:5. Attachmt issued.

Elizabeth Howard, wife to Thomas Howard, came into Ct and ack her right of dower of certain town lots to Capt. Wm. Bossell & ordered recorded.

Tho. Wood [is licensed] to keep an ordinary at his house in Hampton Towne, he giving security acc to law.

[p 13] Eliza. James [is licensed] to keep an ordinary at her house in Hampton Towne, she giving security acc to law.

Tho. Wood and his wife came into Ct and ack their deed to Edward Ballard. Ordered recorded.

Thomas Walker's suit agt Bryan Penny. Plt not appearing, dismist.

Wm. Coopeland's suit agt Charles Avera refd to next Ct.

Thomas Faulkner's suit agt Tho. Roberts refd to next Ct.

Henery Robinson's suit agt Samll. Selden in an action of debt for £100. Deft prayed time. Granted.

John Jones' suit agt Wm. Coopland dismist, the action not being brought right.

Judgmt confessed by Edwd. Myhill for costs and damages he is liable by law to pay Wm. Armistead Junr in an action of debt for £20 sterling -- for John Sampson with costs at execution.

Emanll. Alkin's suit agt Danll. Lewis. Refd to next Ct, his atty not being here.

Joseph Wragg's suit agt Wm. Newbery. Refd to next Ct, his atty not being here.

Nicholas Phillips' suit agt Wm. Coopland dismist, deft agreeing to pay costs.

Upon petition of Wm. Marloe for his estate in the hands of Wm. Wilson. Refd to tomorrow for deft to produce the record.

Robert Taylor's suit agt Wm. Rodgers refd to next Ct for trial.

Robt. Taylor's suit agt Fra. Ballard. Deft pleading he owes nothing, continued to next Ct.

Robt. Taylor's suit agt Tho. Badely dismist.

Suit brought by John More agt Tho. Powell wherein Tho. Jenings is admitted deft in action of trespass, damages £10 sterling. Plt moved for new trial which was opposed by deft and argued. Refd to next Ct to hear Evidences on both sides.

[p 14] Ordered that James Ricketts and Jane his wife attend next Ct to give security for Wilson Curle's est.

Martine Beane's suit agt Joseph Wragg. Dismist.

In the suit brought by Edward Lattemore agt Phillip Prescott, an action of trespass, damages £10 for hindering the Surveyor from surveying and laying out a certain lot in Hampton. Jury being impannelled and sworn, namely Tho. Merry etc. [sic] Pltf not appearing, non suit is granted and plt to pay with costs.

Richard Street being bound over to answer the complaint of Wm. Smelt for beating an Indian woman. [Smelt] failing to prosecute, ordered Street discharged.

Petition of Geo. Walker, Edmund Kearney, Jos. Curle & John Smith, securities of Nicholas Curle's estate, to be released. Ordered that upon James Rickett's giving bond for £4000 sterling, they be discharged. Ct approves of Majr. William Armistead, William Smelt and James Servant [to be] securities for Ricketts.

Judgmt confessed by Cha. Peirce for 115 lbs tobo to Phillip Lightfoot with costs.

Then Court adjourns till twomorrow morning Ten a Clock. John Holladay Signe.

At a Court held the 17th day of November 1716
Present: Majr. John Holloway, Mr. Wm. Armistead, Capt. John More, Mr. Fra. Ballard, Capt. Wm. Bosell, Mr. Antho. Armistead, Mr. Mark Johnson - His Majt's Justices

In the suit of Matthew Small agt Josa. Curle Senr. Action of debt for £13:5 being for rent refd to next Ct.

[p 15] Elizabeth James' acct to render agt John Sweetman continued.

Judgmt granted by nihil dicet agt William Mallory to answer the suit of Francis Ballard in an action of debt for £6:10:0.

Judgmt granted by nihil dicet agt Fra. Mallory to answer the suit of Francis Ballard in an action of debt for £4:4:0.

Judgmt granted by nihil dicet agt Fra. Ballard to answer the suit of Samll. Selden in an action of trespass, damages £10.

Samuell Selden, next friend to Bartholomew Selden, plt. Suit agt John Roe deft. In an action of trespass, damage £10 current money for a trespass committed on plt's land in pulling down his hedge as is set forth in the deed. Deft pleads not guilty. It's ordered that the Sheriff summon an able Jury of the Visonage to meet the surveyor of this Co on the land in controversy and lay out the same on 8 Dec if fair, if not on the first fair day, having regard to all patents and Evidences and that a Justice of the Peace be there. Report to next Court.

Samuel Selden's attchmt agt Tho. Lewis is continued.

Upon the petition of Wm. Marloe for his estate in the hands of Willm. Wilson and arguments being heard on both sides & being considered of by the Ct, ordered that the suit be dismist, plt paying costs.

Marke Johnson's suit agt Anthony Armistead Senr in an action of trespass, damages £10 sterling. Deft pleads not guilty. Refd to next Ct for trial.

Symon Stacey's Scire Facies agt Johnathon Jones. Deft pleads not guilty and prays time to next Ct. Granted.

Bill in Chancery brought by Tho. Jones Senr, complainant agt Willm. Coopland & Eliza. his wife, late Eliza. Jones, wido of David Jones, dec'd for maintenance abroad & arguments being heard on both sides & being considered of by the Ct. It is ord that Coopland pay to Jones towards his maintenance abroad the sum of 20 sh to be paid him either in "corne, porke, wheete, or toba to be yearly at price current, each party paying their costs."

Suit brought by Willm. Dandridge and Euphan his wife, Execs of Wilson Rascoe dec'd, petitioners agst Richd. Kirkin and Margt. his wife in an action upon the case, damage £500 sterling. Plt failing to prosecute, suit is dismist.

Ordered that Mr. Wm. Dandridge pay to Celer [?] Cole for her seven days attendance as Evidence for him agt Richd. Kirkin with costs.

[p 16] In the suit brought by Barto. Proby agt Francis Ballard in an action for accts render for £150 sterling.

Deft not appearing, attchmt ordered agt deft's body. Return to next Ct for further trial.

Ordered that Richd Kirkin pay Kert Jeele for her seven days attendance as Evidence for him agt Wm. Dandridge.

Ordered that Wm. Dandridge pay to Hage Symons for two days attendance agt Richd. Kirkin.

Suit brought by Edward Mihill agt John Sampson. Action upon the case, damage 300 lbs toba. Deft pleads he owes nothing. Refd to next Ct and that he remain in custody.

Matthw. Small in an action upon the case for £2:2:06. The plt's wife being dec'd and he not appearing, refd to next Ct at plt's charge.

Judgmt granted by nihil dicet agt Thos. Walker to answer the suit of Brian Penny. Action upon the case, damages £10 sterling.

Imparlence granted Henry Batts to answer the suit of William Fracey in an action of trespass for £10 sterling.

Action of trespass upon the case for assault and battery, damages of £50 sterling brought by Henry Cocke and Mary his wife agt Francis Ballard gent [who] pleads not guilty. Refd to next Ct for trial.

Joseph Milbee's action upon the case for 40 sh brought agt William Coopland [who] pleads he owes nothing. Refd to next Ct for trial.

Judgmt granted by nihil dicet agt Richd. Kirkin to answer the suit of Edwd. Mihill in an action of trespass upon the case, damages £30 current money.

James Naylor's suit agt William Brown [who] pleads the Genll Issue. Refd to next Ct for trial.

Judgmt granted by nihill dicet agt John Smith to answer the suit of Jacob Leghman in an action upon the case for slander, damages £50 sterling.

Special imparlence granted William Malory to answer the suit of Anthony Armistead Senr in an action upon the case, damages £15 sterling.

Special imparlence granted Francis Malory to answer the suit of Anthony Armistead in an action upon the case.

The action brought by Wm. Starke agt Wm. Coopland for ---[blank] Plt failing to prosecute, upon the motion of the deft non-suit granted him and plt to pay same with costs.

Action upon the case brought by Wm. Marshall Senr agt Wm. Coopland for 40 sh, deft prays time to next Ct. Granted.

Action brought by Mathw. Small agt James Ricketts and Jane his wife Exectrx of Nicho. Curle dec'd in an action upon the case. Plt failing to file his declaration, upon the motion of the deft non-suit granted. Plt to pay the same to deft with costs at exon.

Imparlence granted to Alexandr. Alkins to answer the suit of Joshua Curle in an action upon the case, damages £12 sterling.

Imparlence granted to Peter Baker to answer the suit of Josa. Curle in an action upon the case for breach of covenant, damages £20 sterling.

[p 17] Florence Driscoll's suit agt Richard Ellis dismist, plt not appearing.

Benja. Smith. Suit agt Emanl. Alkin. Parties not appearing, dismist.

Ord granted agt Abr. Mitchel, John Cook, and Sarah Jones, securities for the non-appearance of Saml. Neele and Alexdr. Alkins to answer the suit of Brian Penny. Debt for £3.

Order granted agt Sarah Jones, Security for the non-appearance of Saml. Neele to answer the suit of Cha. Jenings in an action upon the case for 212 lbs tobo.

Order granted agt Tho. Roberts and Richd. Hopkins, security for sd Hopkins non-appearance to answer the suit of Richd. Kirkin in an action upon the case for 44 sh.

Mary Cary, wido. Bill in Chancery agt William Dandridge and Euphan his wife, Exectrx of Wilson Roscoe dec'd. Ordered that a Supa. issue agt defts. Refd to next Ct.

Capt. Henry Jenkins made oath of service of an ejectmt brought by John Thomas agt Richd. Rogers wherein Cha. Jenings is tenant in possession. The sd lessor of plt prays for the Common order. Granted.

Robert Mew came into Ct & made oath that he imported himself into this Colony to dwell in the year 1715. Certificate granted him for taking up 50 acs of land acc to the Charter of King Charles the Second.

Then the Court adjourned till the Court in Course. John Holloway signed.

At a Court held the 3rd Wednesday of Decembr being the 23rd day 1716
Present: Majr. John Holloway, Mr. Wm. Lowery, Mr. Tho.

Tabb, Mr. Antho. Armistead, Mr. John Bayley, Mr. Mark Johnson, Mr. Thomas Wythe – His Majt's Justices

Petition of Thomas Curle for his estate in the hands of Benja. Smith. Ord that Smith deliver all & singular the plt's estate.

Robt. Westlake's ejectmt agt Wm. Symons. Pasco Curle (by James Ricketts and Jane his wife being admitted guardian to the sd Pasco Curle appear) and desires to be admitted deft in sd suit and confesses lease entry & ouster.

[p 18] In the suit brought by Samuell Selden agt Bryan Penny in an action upon the case for 36 shillings. Parties joining in demurrer & arguments being heard, both parties confronting to put the Justice of the Cause upon the Ct for trial, the Ct considering the cause ord that deft pay to the plt 25 shillings with costs.

In the suit brought by John Sweetman agt William Weston for £17:5, attachmt being executed upon Edmd. Kearny, Wm. Dandridge, Henry Jenkins and John Smith. Ordered the several persons mentioned in the return be summoned to the next Ct to give acct of what estate they have in their hands of sd Weston.

John Armistead producing a Commission from the Honble. the Governor Elexander Spotswood to be agent of this County which he has entered into bond with security and is acc sworn.

Thomas Faulkner's action agt Thomas Roberts postponed till tomorrow for plt to reply.

In the suit brought by Emanll. Alkin agt Danll. Lewis in an action upon the case for £2:10, parties agree to put the cause upon the Ct for trial, the plt swearing to his acct, the Ct setting the price of the articles. Judgmt is granted agt the deft for 40 sh to plt with costs at exon.

Joseph Wragg's suit agt William Newberry is by consent of plt refd to next Ct, deft being sick.

The Presentments of the Grand Jury being returned, ordered the several persons presented be summoned to next Ct to answer.

The Ct. agrees that the County Levey be laid on the tenth day of Jan and ordered the Sheriff give notice to the People of the Same.

Mark Johnson's suit agt Anthony Armistead is refd to next Ct.

Justices Sworne - Majr. John Holloway, Mr. William Lowry, Mr. Tho. Tabb, Mr. John Bayley, Mr. Thomas Wyth, Mr. Mark Johnson and Mr. Antho. Armistead has this day taken the oath appt by law and signed the Test and also taken the oath of Justices of the Peace and Chancery acc to the Govns. Commission dated the 8th day of Dec 1715.

[p 19] Order of last Ct for laying out land in Towne to build a Ct house upon not being complied with. It's ordered that Mr. William Lowry lay out the same land acc to the former order and return the plott Time enough against the Ct for the Clerk to prepare deeds.

Then the Court adjourns till tomorrow morning Ten a Clock.
John Holloway

At a Court held 18 Jan 1715
Present: Majr. John Holloway, Mr. William Lowery, Mr. John Bayley, Mr. John King, Mr. Thomas Tabb, Mr. Thomas Wythe, Mr. Marke Johnson - Justices

The last will & testament of John More Gent dec'd proved by oaths of Tho. Kirby and Charles Rowin, wits. Certificate for probate granted the Exectrx & ordered recorded.

Thomas Howard ack his lease & release for town land to build a Court house for the uses within mentioned.

The estate of Mr. Nicho. Curle being offered to Mr. George Walker and John Smith, securities for the estate, and they refusing to take the same, ordered estate remain in possession of James Ricketts and his wife upon the former's security.

The last will & testament of William Armistead gent dec'd is proved by the oath of Robert Armistead, one of the wit. Certificate for probate granted to the Exec, he giving bond & security. Ordered recorded.

Petition of Edward Ballard agt his maidservant Martha Carman for having a bastard child, for one years service for the trouble of his house, she making oath that one John Conley of New York is the father of the child. Her master Edwd. Ballard answers to pay fine of 50 shillings and 500 lbs tobo for her fine to the Churchwardens for the use of the Parish, Martha agreeing to serve one year after her time is expired by indenture.

Upon the petition of Tho., an Indian Man, agt Majr. Wm. Armistead for his freedom. Ordered the Exec of the sd Armistead be summoned to the next Ct to answer.

Then the Court adjourned to the Court in course. John Holloway.

[p 20]
At a Court held 15 Febry 1715
Present: Mr. Wm. Lowery, Capt. Francis Ballard, Mr. Tho. Tabb, Mr. Antho. Armistead, Mr. John Bayley, Mr. Mark Johnson – Justices

Capt. Fra. Ballard and Capt. Wm. Bosell is sworn Justice of the Peace and also [have] taken oath and signed the Test acc to the Govn's Commission.

Whereas it is apparent to the Ct that there was a mistake in laying of the last County Levy in omitting to raise the four pounds of tobo per head for the Govner acc to law and in --- the number of Tithables. Ordered that all mistakes be regulated & amended & that the Sherf. Mr. Simon Hollier collect & receive of every tithable person in this County the just sum of twenty-four pounds of tobo per head & upon non-payers to make distress for the same.

Henry Jenkins and John Curle, two of the Execs of Nicho. Curle's will, having given bond and security, certificate of probate granted.

The last will & testament of Wm. Armistead gent is pro by the oath of Antho. Armistead, one of the wit.

Francis Ballard signed.

At a Court held the 3rd Wednesday of March being the 22nd day 1715/16
Majr. John Holloway, Mr. Wm. Lowery, Capt. Fra. Ballard, Mr. Antho. Armistead, Mr. John Bayley, Capt. Wm. Bosell, Mr. Thomas Wythe, Mr. Marke Johnson – Justices

John Butler ack deed for lots in Hampton Towne to William Dandridge and Elizabeth Butler, wife to John, ack release of her right of dower.

Pluto, a negro boy belonging to George Walker, is adjudged to be ten years old and to pay levy acc to law.

William Winterton ack deed for town land to George Wauffe.

Upon the petition of Robt. Taylor for license to keep an ordinary in Hampton Towne, granted, he giving bond and security to keep good rules etc. having pd the Govrn's dues.

Wm. Smelt's petition for an ordinary License granted.

[p 21] The last will & testament of Chr. Coopland pro by Thomas Balis, Wm. Dunn and Michael Peirce, wit. Probate granted & ordered recorded, Execs to give bond.

The motion of George Walker, Edward Kerny, John Smith, & Joshua Curle that they be discharged from being securities of Nicho. Curle's estate, James Ricketts as marrying Jane Curle Exectrx. So ordered.

Upon petition of John Wallace for license to keep ordinary. Granted, he giving bond & security.

Complaint of Richd. Street agt Phillis & Meriere, Indian servants to Wm. Smelt, & Isa, a negr man belonging to Geo. Luke Esqr for sheep stealing and the slaves being examined & Meriere & Isa confessing, ordered that Merieare receive ten lashes & Isa receive thirty-nine, well laid on.

Petition of William Smelt for license to keep ordinary is granted, he giving bond & security.

Wm. Bosell ack his lease & release for town land to build a Courthouse upon.

Petition of Thomas, an Indian man, suing Execs of Willm. Armistead gent dec'd for his freedom, and the parties agreeing to put the matter upon the Ct for trial, and two Evidences being sworn for the Indian, it appears to the Ct that the Indian was sold "but for thirty-one years" and it also appears that the time is expired. Ordered that the Indian be set free.

Geo. Beckett, servant to Joseph Banister, is adjudged to be thirteen years old and to pay Levy acc to law.
Court adjourns till the Court in Course. John Holloway.

At a Court held the 3rd Wednesday of May being the 16th day 1716
Mr. Wm. Lowrey, Capt. Fra. Ballard, Capt. Wm. Bosell, Mr. John King, Mr. Thomas Tabb, Mr. Tho. Wythe, Mr. Marke Johnson – Justices

James Servant made oath that he never rec'd satisfaction for a Bill of Exchange drawn by Nicho. Phillips upon "Robt wife March --- in London nor noe body for him to his knowledge." It's ordered that certificate be granted him accordingly.

Upon petition of Robert Minson for license to keep an ordinary in Towne. Granted, giving bond & security.

[p 22] It's ordered that Thomas Wilcox be sworn Constable in the Town of Hampton for one year in the room of Jno. Bordland.

Foeffees ack deed for town land to Capt. Henry Jenkins.

Henry Jenkins ack lease & release for land to Peter Baker.

Upon petition of Eliza. Hill for license to keep an ordinary in Hampton, granted, [she] giving security acc to law for the same.

Upon petition of Thomas Wilcox for adm of estate of Eliza. James dec'd, he alleging he is greatest creditor and the children consenting thereto. It's ordered that Adm be granted to him, giving bond & security acc to law.

Ordered that the estate of Eliza. James dec'd be appraised by Jno. Bordland, Joseph Banister, Wm. Lyall & Tho. Faulkner. Report to next Ct.

Mary Jenkins, wife of Henry Jenkins, ack release of right of dower to town land sold to Peter Baker.

Also William Coopland ack lease & release to John Jones. Elizabeth [his] wife ack dower rights being privately examined.

In the suit brought by Wm. Coopland agt Cha. Avery in an action of debt for 1150 lbs tobo being due for rent parties joining issue & coming to trial & arguments bein heard, and the Ct considering are of opinion & order de to pay 1150 lbs of sweet scented tobo with costs at exc Ct.

Robert Taylor's suit agst Wm. Rogers is refd to ne debt

Henry Robinson's suit agt Saml. Selden in an action for £100 sterling. Refd to next Ct.

next Robert Taylor's suit agt Francis Ballard. Refd Ct.

Spi Ordered that Tho. Jenings pay to Jno. Theadom & for cer for their ten days attendance each as an Evid him agt Jno. More with costs at exon.

to Ordered that William Coopland pay to James Gilber law for six days attendance for him agt Cha. Av [p 23] Upon the return of the Grand jury. It's ordered that the several persons presented be summoned to next Ct.

Ordered that William Coopland pay Wm. Fracey for four days attendance as an Evidence for him agt Cha. Avery with costs at exon.

Ordered that Cha. Avery pay Henry Batts for four days attendance as an Evidence for him agt Wm. Coopland.

John More's suit agt Tho. Powell is continued to next Ct to consider what cost the plt ought to pay, he being deceased. [sic]

Upon petition of Richd. Kirkin agt James Ricketts and Jane his wife, Exectrx of Nicho. Curle, dec'd. The petitioner proving his acct, judgmt granted agt Ricketts and wife for £5:14:03 out of deft's estate.

"The Surveyor of the Highways and the Gentlemen appt. to take the list of tithables look for the particulars in the Ruffe order books."

Ordered that the rates of "lyquors" be sold at same price sold last season.

William Lowery signs.

At a Court held the 17th May 1716
Mr. Wm. Lowrey, Mr. Antho. Armistead, Mr. John Bayley, Mr. Marke Johnson – Justices

Eliza. James' suit agt John Sweetman in an action of accts render for 45 sh is ordered dismist, plt being deceased.

Matthew Small's suit agst Joshua Curle in an action of debt for £13:5. Plt not appearing, suit is dismist.

Bartholomew Selden by Saml. Selden, his next friend, brought an action of trespass agt John Roe, damage £10 current money, for pulling down the hedge on plt's land. Deft pleads not guilty, and the last order for survey not being complied with, it is ordered that the Sheriff summon a Jury of the Visonage to meet the surveyor on the land in difference on the third Friday in June if fair, if not on the first fair day, and try the trespass having regard to all patents and evidences and that a Justice of the Peace be there to swear the Jury and Evidence and the Jury is to return Verdict to next Ct.

Saml. Selden's suit agt Thomas Lewis in an action of debt for 20 sh. Deft being gone out of the Country and no estate to be found, ordered dismist on plt's request.

Action by scire facias brought by Simon Staycey agt Johnathon Jones for 700 lbs tobo & 10 shillings in money. Refd to next Ct.

Edward Mihill's action agt John Sampson, damage 3000 lbs tobo, is ended between themselves.

Mathw. Small agst Jno. Curle in an action upon the case for 35 shillings is dismist. Non-appearance of the parties.

[p 24] Action upon the case brought by Brian Penny agt Tho. Walker. Deft pleading time to next Ct. Granted.

Action of trespass, damages £10 sterling, brought by Wm. Frasey agt Henry Batts. Dismist.

Action of trespass upon the case for assault and battery, damages £20 sterling, brought by Henry Cock and Mary his wife agt Francis Ballard. Dismist because of appearance of neither party.

Joseph Milbee's suit agt Wm. Copland is dismist, the decl being found faulty.

Edward Mihill's suit agt Richd. Kirkin in an action of trespass upon the case, damages £30. Deft pleaded not guilty. Plt requests time to next Ct to summon Evidences. Granted.

James Naylor's suit agt Wm. Brown in an action upon the case. Deft prayed time to next Ct to bring in his discount. Granted.

In the suit brought by Jacob Leghman agt John Smith in an action upon the case for slander for damages £50 sterling. Deft pleads not guilty and one Evidence being sworn for the plt. A Jury being impannelled and sworn, namely: Henry Robinson, John Poole, Edwd. Lattemore, Jno. Curle, James Ricketts, Wm. Minson, Wm. Brown, Wm. Allen, Wm. Fracey, Wm. Coopland, James Naylor, and Jos. Banister, and having heard arguments on both sides & rec'd their charge, went in trial and being out some time, returned for verdict these words. We of the Jury find for the plt damage of 5 shillings & costs. Jos. Banister, foreman. On motion of plt, the verdict is recorded, whereupon the deft moves an arrest of judgmt & "saith the words are not actionable," and therefore ordered to be refd to next Ct to be argued.

Action upon the case brought by Antho. Armistead agt William Malory is ended between themselves.

Action brought by Joshua Curle agt Alexandr. Alkins is dismist. No appearance of either party.

Non-suit granted to Peter Baker agt estate of Joshua Curle, the plt's declaration being found faulty. Ordered that he pay the same to Baker with costs at exon.

Action of debt brought by Brian Penny agt Alexdr. Alkins and Saml. Neele. Deft prays oyer of the bill. Granted.

Action of debt for rent brought by Th. Wood agt Robert By--see dismist, the deft being "ded."

Order granted agt Saml. Neele and Sarah Jones security to answer suit of Cha. Jenings in an action upon the case for 320 lbs tobo.

Judgmt confirmed agt Tho. Roberts & Richd. Hopkins, securities, to answer the suit of Richd. Kirkin in an action upon the case for what shall appear due at next Ct. Ordered that a Jury of Inquiry
[p 25] be summoned to next Ct to inquire what damages the plt has sustained by the deft.

The bill in Chancery brought by Mrs. Mary Cary, wido of Miles Cary of Warwick Co., dec'd, complains agt William Dandridge and Euphan his wife, Exectrx of Wilson Roscow dec'd for £500 sterling, and they not appearing in defence, it is ordered that attachmt be granted agt the bodys of the sd Wm. Dandridge and his wife for their appearance at next Ct to answer sd bill.

In the suit brought by Saml. Selden agt Fra. Ballard in an action of trespass, damage £10 sterl for stopping the Surveyor from laying out the --- land as is set forth in the decla, the deft pleads the Genll Issue. The plt moved for trial at barr which the deft approved. It is considered and ordered that the Sheriff summon a Jury to meet the Surveyor upon the land in controversy on 16 June if fair ... and lay out the same having regard to all patents and Evidences and that a Justice of the Peace be there to swear the Jury and Evidences and that the Jury ret the verdict to next Ct.

The Ejectione firmione brought by Robert Westlake agt William Symmons for land and tenements, the Parties joining issue. Refd to next Ct for trial at deft's charge.

Jno. Sweetman's suit agt Wm. Walker in an action upon the case for £17:5. It's ordered that Edwd. Kerny, Wm. Dandridge, and John Smith be summoned to next Ct to give acct if they have any of Walker's estate in their hands.

Suit brought by Tho. Faulkner agt Tho. Roberts in an action of the case, damage £35, and neither appearing, order suit dismist.

It's ordered that the Sheriff summon Mr. Wilcox's maids Hannah Scott and Mary Floyd for their appearance at next Ct to answer the presentment of the Grand Jury for having bastard children born of their bodies.

Mark Johnson brought an action upon the case, damage £5, agt Antho. Armistead. Ordered refd to next Ct for Petitioner to prove his action.

The difference depending between Joseph Wragg, plt and William Newberry, deft is refd to next Ct.

Nath. James being thirteen years old puts himself by the consent of the Ct as apprentice unto Thomas Wilcox until he comes of age, he "larning" the appr the trade of carpenter and to read and "wright" and to find him during his apprenticeship what is necessary for an appr

Mary Frizell's suit agt James Birtell in an action of the case for assault & battery, damage £20 sterling, deft appearing and confessing the fact. Ordered that a Jury of Inquiry be sworn to inquire what damage plt has sustained.

Order granted agt the Security Jno. Sweetman for the non-appearance of Alexdr. Alkins to answer the suit of Stephen Lillis in an action upon the case for 20 sh.

[p 26] Attchmt granted to An Wallace Admx of James Wallace dec'd agt William Minson in an action upon the case for 250 lbs toba. Returnable to next Ct for further trial.

Thomas Howard's suit agt John King in an action upon the case, damage £6. Deft prays special imparlence. Granted.

Attchmt granted to Cha. Jenings agt the estate of Wm. Browne, damage 1000 lbs tobo. Returnable to next Ct for further trial.

William Smelt's suit agt Thomas Wilcox is refd to next Ct upon request of both parties.

Special imparlence granted to Phillip Prescott to answer the suit of Edwd. Lattemore in an action of trespass, damage £10 sterling.

Special imparlence granted Richard Kirkin to answer the suit of Thomas Wood in an action upon the case for £4:4:4.

Elizabeth James' suit agt Thomas Badely. Dismist, plt being dec'd.

Order granted agt John Armistead, Security for the non-appearance of Joseph Wragg to answer the suit of Stephen Lillis.

Fra. Ballard's suit agt William Mallory in an action of debt for £6 is ended.

Fra. Ballard's suit agt Fra. Mallory in an action of debt for £4 is ended.

Ord that Jacob Leghman pay unto James Hide for 4 days attendance as Evidence for him agt John Smith with costs at exon.

Bartrand Proby, Adm of Peter Proby dec'd agt Francis Ballard. Accts to render for £150 sterl. The deft pleading, plt prayed time to next Ct to consider his plea, which is granted.

In the suit brought by Jacob Leghman agt John Smith. Dismist for non-appearance.

In the suit brought by James Servant agt Danll. Lewis. Dismist for non-appearance.

In the suit brought by Augustine Moore agt Florence Dreskill. Dismist for non-appearance.

Special imparlence granted Jacob Leghman to answer the suit of John Smith. Damages £20 sterl.

John Wilson's suit agt William Marloe is dismist for non-appearance.

In the suit brought by Willm. Coopeland agt James Ricketts and Jane his wife, Exectrx of Nicho. Curle dec'd, in an action upon the case. Refd to next Ct for the parties to settle their accts.

In the suit brought by Wm. Coopland & Eliz. his wife, Exectrx of David Jones dec'd, agt James Ricketts and Jane his wife, Exectrx of Nicho. Curle dec'd, in an action upon the case. Refd to next Ct for parties to settle their accts.

[p 27] Edward Myhill's suit agt Richard Kirkin in an action of trespass upon the case, damage £30 sterling, deft pleading not guilty, the plt prayed till next Ct, which is granted. "This order recorded already."

In the suit brought by James Naylor agt William Browne. Deft prayd time to next Ct to bring in his discount. Granted. "This order already recorded."

Order granted agt the ----- Wm. Armistead for the non-appearance of ---- Parish to answer the suit of William Lowry gent.

Non-suit granted to Robert Armistead agt John Sampson, plt not appearing and order plt to pay to deft with costs at exon.

Jacob Leghman's suit agt John Smith scire facias. Deft prays time to next Ct to answer. Granted.

Judgmt granted by nihil dicet agt William Coopland to answer the suit of William Marshall in an action of debt for 40 sh or 400 lbs tobo.

Non-suit granted to Thomas Walker acc to law agt Henry Batts & ordered he pay same to deft with costs at exon.

Attchmt granted agt the estate of Samll. Watts. The suit of Charles Jenings in an action upon the case, damage 600 lbs toba.

Order granted agt Wm. Bossell, Security for the non-appearance of Elexandr. A--- to answer the suit of Thomas Wood.

Capt. Henry Jenkins' motion about the recording of Mr. Nicho. Curles' appraisement is refd to next Ct.

Ordered that James Ricketts & Jane his wife give security for Wilson Curle's estate at next Ct.

Non-suit is granted agt the estate of Bryan Penny to Joshua Curle & ordered he pay 5 shillings with costs at exon.

Order granted agt the Sheriff for the non- appearance of Rashell Provine ---- suit of Mary Frizell's. Assault & battery. Damages £5 sterling.

Imparlence granted to John Kembell at the suit of Emall. Alkin in an action upon the case for 40 shillings.

William Mallory's suit agt Jacob Leghman granted the deft with costs at exon. Issued 25 May 1716.

Imparlence granted John Jones to answer the suit of John Curle. Trespass --- £100 sterling.

John Gibbons' suit agt William Mallory for 500 - --in an action upon the case refd to next Ct.

Stephen Lillis' suit agt John Sweetman. Refd to next Ct [balance of entry torn away]

Thomas Wood's suit agt Thomas -ryer and he not appearing, order granted agt Willm. Smelt, Security.

Special imparlence granted to Danll. Lewis at the suit of Thos. Wood.

Order granted agt the Sheriff for non-appearance of Thomas Wilcox to answer the suit of William Walker in an action upon the case for £7.

Special imparlence granted to John King gent to answer the suit of William Smelt in an action upon the case, damage £40 sterling.

Order granted agt Nathll. Parker, Security, for non-appearance of Joseph Wragg to answer suit of John Cooke.

John Franklin's suit agt Francis Mallory. Special imparlence granted deft.

Special imparlence granted to Darby Dunaway to answer the suit of Pasco Curle by James Ricketts & Jane his wife, his next friends in an action of trespass.

Special imparlence granted to Henry Jenkins to answer the suit of James Ricketts & Jane his wife Exectrx etc. [sic]

Attchmt granted to John Curle agt the estate of James Naylor in an action upon the case for 34 shillings and 7 pence.

Upon petition of Sarah Jones for license to keep an ordinary. Granted, giving bond and security acc to law and paymt be made of the Governor's dues.

Ordered that the Rates of liquor be settled at the rates they were last year.

Court adjourned to the Court in course. Willm. Lowery.

At a Court held the 3rd Wednesday of June being the 20th day 1716
Present: Majr. John Holloway, Mr. William Lowry, Mr. Tho. Tabb, Mr. Jno. King, Capt. Fra. Ballard, Capt. Wm. Bossell, Mr. Mark Johnson, Mr. Anthony Armistead —His Majt's Justices

Upon petition of Mrs. Mary Luke for a license to keep an ordinary at her home in Hampton Towne. Granted, she giving bond and security acc to law.

[C]harles Jenings producing a Commission from Mr. Secretary Cork [?] for to be [torn away] the Ct ordered it read and thereupon put the [ ] among themselves whether they were willing to admit him Clerke, to which [unani]mously agreed and thereupon he was accordly sworn and admitted.

[p 29] Ordered that the appraisement of Elizabeth James be recorded.

Capt. William Bossell petitioned for to have a "seller" under the Courthouse. It's considered by the Ct that the petition be granted, he paying for the building of the same.

Robert Taylor's suit agt William Rodger is continued to next Ct.

Presentment of the Grand Jury agt Anthony Armistead Senr about mending the Mill Dam and they promising to mend the same. Ordered that his fine be remitted paying costs at exon.

Presentment of the Grand Jury agt Mrs. Ann Wallace for felling a tree across the road. It's ordered dismist, it being cognizeable before a Justice of the Peace, paying costs.

Presentment of the Grand Jury agt Michll. Peirse for turning the road, he excusing himself. Ordered dismist, paying costs, he making the road as good as the former.

Presentment of the Grand Jury agt Florence Dreskell for stopping a road and he excusing himself, ordered fine remitted only paying costs.

Presentment of the Grand Jury agt William Walker for stopping a road and he excusing himself, ordered fine remitted only paying costs.

Presentment of the Grand Jury agt William More for stopping a road and he excusing himeself, ordered fine remitted only paying costs.

Thomas Merry being presented by the Grand Jury for stopping a road and he excusing himself, ordered fine be remitted, paying costs at exon, provided he clear the old road.

Allexander Alkins and Jane his wife being presented by the Grand Jury for Swearing and Drinking on the Sabbath Day and they excusing themselves. Ordered fine be remitted only paying costs.

It's ordered that the Sheriff take in custody Mary Peirse till she give bond and security acc to law for her appearance at next Ct to answer the presentment of the Grand Jury for having a bastard child born of her body.

Frances George being presented by the Grand Jury for having a bastard child born of her body. She swearing that Richd. Ellis is the father, ordered that sd George pay her fine which the father assumes. 500 lbs tobo of £50 and he ack himself to be indebted to the King for £40 sterling. Condition is that he will "safe the Parish Harmless from Maintayning the Child and pay Frances George's fine."

Francis Mallory and Ann Myhill being presented by the Grand Jury for living in adultery. It's ordered that indictment be brought agt them to next Ct and that Willm. Allen and Frances Ross be summoned to sd next Ct to Evidence agt the sd persons.

Wm. Hopkins and Mary Bridge being presented by the Grand Jury for living in adultery. It's ordered that indictment be brought agt them to next Ct and that Capt.

Fra. Ballard, Edward Jones, and Wm. Spiser be summoned to next Ct to Evidence agt the sd persons.

Elizabeth Haynes being presented by the Grand Jury for keeping a bawdy house, she excusing herself, ordered fine be remitted only paying costs at exon.

[p 30] Ceely Cole being presented by the Grand Jury for keeping a bawdy house and she not appearing. Ordered the Sheriff to take her into custody till next Ct.

Richard Ellis and Frances George being presented by the Grand Jury for living in fornication and they excusing themselves. Ordered fine remitted paying costs at exon.

Upon the petition of Henry Irwin agt Henry Bowcock for dealing with his servant and receiving money of the sd servant, the plt not having the Law ready, prays time to next Ct to produce sd law. Granted.

Henry Robinson's suit agt Samuell Selden in an action of debt for £100 sterling, the plt putting in a surjoynder. It's refd to next Ct for arguing the issues & demurrer for the trial.

In an action of trespass brought by John More damages £10 agt Thomas Powell wherein Thomas Jenings was admitted deft and a Jury's Verdict being returned in this case and arguments being heard about what costs the plt ought to pay the deft. It's considered of by the Ct and ordered the suit be dismist with costs at exon and that the sd More's Execs pay sd costs unto Jenings.

Bartholomew Selden by Samll. Selden his next friend brought his suit agt John Roe in a trespass, damage £10. [This portion struck over by Clerk and not clear.] Ordered that the Sheriff summon a Jury of Visenage to meet the Surveyor on the land in difference and try the trespass on the 2nd Tuesday in July if fair, if not on the first fair day, having regard for all Pattents and Evidences and that a Justice be there to swear [them] and that Jury return their report to next Ct.

Simon Stasey's suit agt Johnathan Jones is refd to next Ct by consent.

Bryan Penny's suit agt Thomas Walker, plt prayed time to consider the De-----. Granted.

Joseph Wragg's suit agt William Newberry is dismist, it being agreed.

Ord Joseph Wragg pay Thomas Walker for seven days attendance as Evidence for him agt William Newberry with costs at exon.

Ord Joseph Wragg pay Sarah Hayes for five days attendance as Evidence for him agt William Newberry with costs at exon.

Judgmt confirmed by nihil dicet agt Alexder. Alkins & Samll. Neale to answer the suit of Bryan Penny in an action upon the case for £3.

Judgmt granted agt Samuell Neale for paymt of 25 sh unto Charles Jenings with costs at exon.

Richard Kirkin's suit agt Thomas Roberts is ended.

Mark Johnson's suit agt Antho. Armistead is dismist.

Mrs. Mary Cary's bill in Chancery agt William Dandridge and Euphan his wife, Execs of Wilson Roscow dec'd, for £500 sterling. Deft prays time to answer. Granted.

In a suit brought by James Naylor agt William Browne in an action upon the case for £1:15, deft pleads nonassumpsit and the parties referring the cause to the Ct for trial and the Ct having settled the accts on both sides and there appearing due to the plt 9 shillings 9d. Ordered that deft pay same to plt with costs at exon.

Its ordered that the Sheriff or Constable take into custody Hago Symo upon suspicion of felony and commit her to the Gaol of the county till she be thence delivered and that he make search in all suspected places for money or goods and if he find any ---- till the Ct of Oyer & Terminer. "Copia gave Wilcox Const."

Edward Myhill's suit agt Richd. Kirkin refd to next Ct upon deft's charge and it's agreed that the Enid's [Indians?] depositions be taken and allowed as good Evidence in the Cause upon Trial.

Robt. Taylor's suit agt Fra. Ballard in an action of debt, damage £10 sterling, deft prays time to next Ct to answer. Granted.

Suit brought by Jacob Leghman agt John Smith in an action for slander, damage £50 sterling. The last Ct the Jury found for the plt which deft moved in arrest of judgmt and coming to trial and arguments being heard, the Ct are of the opinion and do ord judgmt be arrested.

James Ricketts entered into bond for Wilson Curle's est. Ord rec.

The appraisal of Joane Smith's est being returned, ord rec.

John Sweetman's attchmt agt Willm. Weston for £17:5 continued to next Ct.

Ord that the Sheriff take Hanah Scott & Mary Floyd in custody for their appearance at next Ct to answer the presentment of the Grand Jury for having bastard children.

Ann Wallace, Admx of James Wallace dec'd, suit agt William Minson for 250 lbs toba. Deft making oath that he has paid debt, ord dismist.

Judgmt granted by nihil dicet agt John King to answer the suit of Tho. Howard.

Attachmt is continued to Cha. Jenings agt the est of Willm. Browne with costs for 710 lbs toba.

Mary Frissle's suit agt James Burtell refd to next Ct, deft not being here.

Judgmt confessed by nihil dicet agt Alexndr. Alkins to answer the suit of Stephen Lillis.

William Smelt's suit agt Tho. Wilcox refd by consent to next Ct.

Judgmt confessed by nihil dicet agt Phillip Prescott at the suit of Edwd. Lattemore in an action of trespass, damages £10 sterling.

[p 32] Thomas Wilcox affirms paymt of 500 lbs toba or 50 sh for his maid's fine for having a bastard child and also ack himself indebted to the King and his successors for £40 sterling to save the Parish harmless for maintaining the child and fine to be paid to Churchwardens at the laying of the next levy for the use of the Parish.

Thomas Wood's suit agt Richard Kirkin. Deft prays of the [plavits?]. Granted.

Judgmt confessed by nihil dicet agt Joseph Wragg at the suit of Stephen Lillis.

Samuell Selden's suit agt Francis Ballard in an action of trespass, damage £10 sterling, for stopping the Surveyor as laid down in ... the last order for survey not being complied with. It is ordered that the Sheriff cause an able Jury of good and lawful men of the Visenage to meet on the land in difference with the Surveyor and try the trespass on the second Wednesday of July if fair and if not on the first fair day having regard to all Patents and Evidences and a Justice be there to swear the Jury. Returnable to next Ct.

Bartrand Proby, Adm of Peter Proby dec'd, suit agt Fra. Ballard in an action of accts to render for £150 sterling. Pltf prays time to consider deft's plea. Granted.

John Smith's suit agt Jacob Leghman. Deft pleading be owes nothing, pltf prays time to next Ct to consider. Granted.

[The following entry was made twice by Clerk] William Coopeland's suit agt James Ricketts & Jane his wife, Exectrx. Refd to next Ct by consent of both parties.

William Lowery's suit agt Abraham Parish is refd to next Ct for pltf to make his debt appear.

Judgmt granted by nihil dicet agt John Smith to answer the suit of Jacob Leghman scire facias for 443 lbs tobo and 5 sh in money.

William Marshall's suit agt William Coopland dismist, deft paying costs at exon.

Attchmt continued agt the est of Samuell Watts to answer the suit of Charles Jenings, damage 600 lbs tobo.

Judgmt confessed by nihil dicet agt Alexandr. Alkins at the suit of Thomas Wood.

Capt. Henry Jenkins withdrawing his motion agt the recording of Nicho. Curles' appraisement. Ordered recorded

Judgmt confessed by nihil dicet agt Rashell Provine at the suit of Mary Frizel in an action upon the case for assault and battery.

Danll. Lewis' suit agt Thomas Wood is ended.

[p 33] Judgmt confessed by John Kemball for payment of 140 sh to Emall. Alkin with costs at exon. Only exon to be stayed till two months.

Judgmt confessed by nihil dicet agt John Jones. Suit of John Curle.

John Gibbon's suit agt William Mallory. Refd to next Ct.

Stephen Lillis' suit agt John Sweetman. Deft confessed judgmt for payment of 40 sh to be paid in corn and wheat, the wheat at 3 sh per bushel, the corn at 2 sh per bushel with costs at exon.

Thomas Wood's suit agt Edward Bryer in an action upon the case. The plt putting in his acott. the deft prays oyer of the same. Granted.

Thomas Wood's suit agt Daniell Lewis is dismist, being agreed.

William Walker's suit agt Thomas Wilcox is continued as it was.

Wm. Smelt's suit agt John King in an action upon the case, damaged £40 sterling. Judgmt granted agt King.

Jugdmt granted by nihil dicet agt Joseph Wragg to answer the suit of John Cooke in an action upon the case.

John Franklin's suit agt Francis Malory is dismist, being agreed.

Tho. Wood's suit agt Noah Barefoot in an action upon the case, damage £27 sterling. Deft prays oyer of the pltf accordingly granted.

Judgmt granted by nihil dicet agt Darby Dunaway to answer the suit of James Ricketts & Jane his wife, next friends to Pasco Curle, in an action of trespass, damage £50.

Judgmt granted Henry Jenkins by nihil dicet to answer the suit of Pasco Curle by James Ricketts and Jane his wife, his next friends, in an action of trespass.

In the suit brought by Jno. Curle agt James Naylor in an action of debt for 34 sh and 3 pence. A copia of the writ being left at his house and he not appearing in defense. Upon motion of the plt attchmt is granted agt his est for the sd sum, returnable to next Ct for further trial.

Then the Court adjourned till the Court in course. John Holloway.

[p 34]
The Court held of Oyer & Terminer the 23rd day of June 1716 for Trying of Jack and Cesar Negr and mellato belonging to John Smith and Joa an Indian Man belonging to Mr. Edmond Kearny and Hago Symo belonging to Mr. George Walker. Present Majr. John Holloway, Mr. Fra. Ballard, Mr. Antho. Armistead, Mr. John Bayley, Mr. John King, Mr. Mark Johnson – His Majt's Justices of Oyer & Terminer.

The Commissioners having taken oath appointed by the Dedimus and subscribed the Test & the Commission read etc and there being no Evidence agt Hago Symo, the attorney prepared no indictment agt her. The other prisoners were arraigned for felony and burglary and plead not guilty. Mr. Henry Irwin sworn for the King -- - Giles [damaged] swore - - Jacob - - Mr. Markem Sesman sworn. Thomas Wilcox sworn.- - - agt the prisoners. Whereupon the indictment being read & Evidences being heard and nothing being proved agt Cesar and he is acquitted. Negr Jack is to receive on his bare back thirty-nine lashes and Joa twenty-five well laid on on Munday morning at 10 o'clock and the Sheriff is to return them to their Masters and it appears to the Justices that Giles Tidmarsh [appears guilty also] and ought to be tried for the same at Genll Ct. Remanded to the Co. Gaol. Signed: John Holloway.

At a Court held the 3rd Wednesday of July being the 18th day 1716
Present Mr. Antho. Armistead, Mr. Thomas Wyth, Mr. Jno. King, Capt. Fra. Ballard, Mr. Jno. Bayley, Mr. Mark Johnson – His Majt. Justices

Upon the petition of Mr. George Walker to build a "watter" Mill in this Co on John's Cr having land lying on one side. Ord the petition be refd to next Ct upon the motion of Samuell Selden.

William Mallory complains agt Hugh Ross that he went in danger of his life. No person appearing to prosecute. Dismist.

[p 35] Charles Jenings ack lease & release for land unto William Westwood. Also Elizabeth wife to sd Jenings came into Ct and ack her release of deed, being privately examined. Admitted to record.

Upon complaint of John Addeston Rodgers agt Edward Richardson for breaking open the sd Rodgers' house and two Evidences being found on behalf of complainant. Being considered by the Ct, ordered Richardson to receive ten lashes on his bare back and laid on forthwith.

Upon petition of Thomas Wilcox, Constable, agt Richard Kirkin and Margett his wife about abusing the Ct and himself. Ordered that the Sheriff take Kirkin and wife into Custody till they give bond and security for their good behavior and for their appearance at next Ct.

Upon the petition of Edwd. Ballard for a license to keep an ordinary at his in Hampton Towne. Granted paying Governor's fees etc.

Robert Taylor's suit agt William Rodger continued to next Ct.

Upon the presentment of the Grand Jury agt Mary Peirse for having a bastard child and she confessing the fact. John Lattemore and James Naylor came into Ct and confessed judgmt for paying the fine of 500 lb tobo or 50 sh in money to the Churchwardens for the use of the Parish at the next laying of the Levy.

The Foeffees ack their deed for town land to William Allen. Ordered recorded.

William Hopkins and Mary Bridge, Fra. Mallory and Ann Myhill being presented by the Grand Jury. Refd to next Ct.

Upon the presentment of the Grand Jury agt Mary Floyd for having a bastard child and she confessing and swearing that Richard Barber was the father. Barber is to be summoned to next Ct to give Sec to save the Parish harmless for maintaining sd child and Mary Floyd
[p 36] assumes with Mr. Saml. Selden for to assign over a Judgmt that she has agt William Browne for 500 lbs tobo at next Ct, the Clerk to have the remaining part after Mr. Selden has had 400 out of it.

Upon the petition of Henry Irvine Gent agt Henry Bowcock setting forth that he received some money from his servant and therefore prays that Bowcock be suppressed from keeping an Ordinary. He confessed that his servant spent about 4 sh 6 pence and also had lodged him in his house one whole night. Ordered that Bowcock be fined 10 sh acc to law and pay the same to Irwin with costs.

Upon the petition of Henery Bowcock for a license to keep an Ordinary. Granted, he giving bond and sec and paying fees.

Bartholomew Selden by Saml. Selden his next friend brought an action of trespass, damage £10, agt John Roe for pulling down the hedge of the plt, to which the deft pleads not guilty & the last order for survey not being complied with. It's ordered that the Sheriff summon an able Jury to meet the Surveyor on the land in difference on the 2nd Wednesday in Aug if fair or the next fair day. Report to be returned to next Ct.

Judgmt confessed agt Abraham Parish and Wm. Armistead, Securities, for 500 lbs of tobo to Wm. Lowery being due by Specialty, he having made oath to his debt, with costs at exon.

Mr. Thos. Wyth informing to this Ct that Wm. Smelt swore these oaths. It's ordered that he be fined acc to law which is 15 sh and that he pay Churchwardens for the use of the Parish.

Jane Grimes being bound over on suspicion of stealing money from Mr. Henry Irwin and six Evidences being sworn and nothing being proved. Ord she be from thence discharged, paying costs at exon.

Upon complaint of Mr. Mark Johnson agt Jane Grimes for abusing him, ordered that she receive on her bare back ten lashes well laid on forthwith.

The Ct adjourns till the Ct in course. Willm. Lowery signs.

[p 37]
At a Court held the 3rd Wednesday August 15 1716
Present Majr. John Holloway, Mr. Wm. Lowery, Mr. Antho. Armistead, Mr. Thomas Tabb, Mr. Thomas Wythe, Capt. Fra. Ballard, Mr. John King – His Majt's Justices

Upon petition of George Walker for building a Water Mill on John's Cr, the Ct are of the opinion that the petitioner has not pursued the law. Rejected.

Upon petition of Saml. Selden for the building of a Publick Water Mill on John's Cr. Rejected by reason the sd Selden has not complied with the law.

Upon petition of John Armistead, one of the Execs of Maj. Wm. Armistead dec'd, to appr the est of Dun Armistead. It's ordered that Francis Rogers, Benja. Smith and Tho. Read or any two of them being first sworn do appr the est and return report to next Ct.

Upon petition of Tho. Wilcox, Constable, agt Richd. Kirkin and Margt. his wife about abusing the Governor and Ct. Ordered that Kirkin and Margt. his wife make a personal appearance before the Honble. the Genll Ct on the fourth day to answer.

Bond of Richd. Kirkin and Margreat his wife for £40 sterl to appear on the fourth day of Genll Ct. Wm. Smelt is Security & ack himself to owe £20 sterl for Margrt's appearance. The parties ack same in Open Ct.

Upon petition Richd. Kirkin is granted license to keep an Ordinary, giving bond and security acc to law.

Upon petition of James Ricketts and Jane his wife to be appt gdn to her children and to divide the est betwixt her and her children. On motion of Henry Jenkins and Jno. Curle, Execs of Nicho. Curle's est, prays time to Next Ct to answer the petition.

[p 38] Upon the petition of George Walker to build a Water Mill on John's Cr and two Evidences being sworn for the petitioner concerning giving Saml. Selden a paper wherein

he demanded an acre of land. Mr. Selden being asked whether he would let Mr. Walker have an acre of land who answered that he had no land there, but the Justices agreeing. Mr. Selden consents that Walker have liberty to build the Mill and offers to give Walker sufficient deed "for to joyn" his dam to his land & that he will not molest Walker etc. Mr. Walker is not to waste Selden's land.

Simon Staycey's scire facias agt Johnathen Jones. Refd to next Ct for trial.

Brian Penny's suit agt Tho. Walker is refd to next Ct for trial.

Brian Penny agt Saml. Neele and Alexdr. Alkins. Prayed time to next Ct. Granted.

Mary Cary's bill in Chancery agt Wm. Dandridge and Euphan his wife, Exectrx of Wilson Rascow dec'd. Complainant prays time to next Ct. Granted.

Robert Taylor agt Francis Ballard in an action of debt for £5 and 201 lbs tobo. The Cause lies as it does and deft obliges himself to come to trial next Ct if plt urges for it.

Jno. Sweetman's attachmt agt William Weston for £35 sterl. Attchmt continued.

Judgmt confessed agt John King Gent for paymt of four barrels of pitch to Tho. Howard with costs at exon.

In the suit brought by Mary Frizell agt James Birtell for assault and battery, damage £20. Jury [Edwd Lattemore, Tho. Merry, John Poole, Benja. Smith, Saml. Daniel, Henry Batts, James Ricketts, Wm. Coopland, Wm. Fracey, Barto. Proby, Tho. Howard and Wm. Creeks]. Verdict for the plt, damage £2:06. Tho. Merry, foreman. On the motion of the plt, the verdict is recorded. Refd to next Ct to consider costs to be allowed.

Emaml. Alkin and Mary Luke being summoned to give evidence for Mary Frizell agt James Birtell and they not appearing. Ordered to be fined unless thay appear at next Ct and show Cause.

Judgmt confessed by Alexdr. Alkins for 20 sh unto Stephen Lillis with costs at exon.

[p 39] Suit of Wm. Smelt agt Thomas Wilcox, dismist.

Edwd. Lattemore's suit agt Phillip Prescott on an action of trespass, damages £10 sterl, deft putting in his plea, plt prays time. Granted.

Tho. Wood's suit agt Richd. Kirkin. Deft pleads he owes nothing. Cause continued to next Ct.

Judgmt confessed by Joseph Wragg for payment of £2:12:4 to Stephen Lillis with costs at exon.

The last will & testament of Matthew Watts dec'd proved by Thomas Jones and William Creek wit. Cert of probate granted Hanah Armistead, one of the Execs, who has taken the oath.

Samuel Selden's suit agt Francis Ballard. Ord that the Verdict be opened by the Clark and copias to be given the parties if they require the same. Cause continued to next Ct.

In the suit brought by John Smith agt Jacob Loughman in an action upon the case for £13:8:3 1/2 and one Evidence being sworn for the deft who pleads he owes nothing and producing his Anott which the Ct settling the Anott on both sides. There appears due to plt £1:11. To be paid with costs at exon.

Ordered Jacob Loughman pay James Hyde for 3 days attendance as Evidence for him agt John Smith with costs at exon.

The last will of Ann Daniell proved by John King and Joseph Skiner wit. Probate granted Exec & ordered recorded.

The Court adjourns till Tomorrow Morning Ten a Clock.

At a Court held 16 August 1716
Majr. John Holloway, Mr. Wm. Lowery, Mr. John King,
Mr. John Bayley, Mr. Thomas Tabb, Mr. Thomas Wythe,
Mr. Antho. Armistead – His Majt's Justices

Robt. Westlock, lessee of Thomas Poole. Ejectmt agt Wm. Simons wherein James Ricketts etc is admitted deft. Deft prays time to next Ct to search for his paper evidence. Granted.

Henry Robinson's suit agt Saml. Selden in an action of debt, damages £100 sterl. Refd to next Ct.

Barto. Proby's suit agt Francis Ballard in an acct Render for £150 sterl. Refd to next Ct for plt to find his replyquation.

Chas. Jenings' attachmt agt Saml. Watts for 350 lbs tobo continued.

[p 40] Judgmt confessed agt Alexandr. Alkins for £1:10 to Francis Wood with costs at exon.

Judgmt confessed agt James Ricketts and Jane his wife, Exectrx of Nicho. Curle, for £1:1:3 to William Coopland with costs at exon.

Wm. Coopland and Eliza. his wife, Exectrx of David Jones dec'd, agt James Ricketts and Jane his wife Exectrx of Nicho. Curle dec'd, in an action upon the case. It's ordered that Edwd. Lattemore, Tho. Tucker and Mr. Tho. Wythe or any two of them do meet and determine the accts. Refd to next Ct.

Mary Frizell's suit agt Rachell Provine, damages £5 sterl in a trespass upon the case for assault and battery. Judgmt by nihil dicet confessed and ordered that writ of Judgmt be executed at next Ct.

John Curle's suit agt John Jones in action of trespass, £100 sterl, deft pleading, plt prays time to next Ct. Granted.

Judgmt granted by nihil dicet agt William Malory at the suit of John Gibins of York Co. in an action upon the case, 1000 lbs tobo.

Judgmt granted by nihil dicet agt Edwd. Brier at the suit of Tho. Wood, damages £5.

Suit brought by Jacob Loghman agt John Smith in an action of scire facias for the recovering of a judgmt for 443 lbs tobo and £5 money. Deft demurring but consenting that judgmt be confessed, plt allowing all just discounts.

Wm. Walker's suit agt Tho. Wilcox dismist.

William Smelt's suit agt John King gent, in an action upon the case, damage £40 sterl. Continued to next Ct.

Edward Mihill agt Richd. Kirkin in an action of trespass upon the case for £30, deft prays time which is granted to consider paper evidences & ordered plt put same into the office.

Thomas Roberts agt Joseph ---ylis dismist.

Judgmt by nihil dicet granted agt Noah Barefoot at the suit of Thomas Wood in an action on the case, damage £27 silver money.

Pascow Curle by James Ricketts and Jane his wife next Friends in an action of trespass, damage £50 sterl agt Darby Dunaway is dismist, the deft being "ded."

John Curle's suit agt James Naylor in an action of debt for 34 sh & 6 pence. The attachmt being ret executed. It's ordered that the Sher summon Edwd. Lattemore, James Baker and Tho. Tucker and they or any two of them being first sworn appr what was attached and report to next Ct.

[p 41] John Cooke agt Joseph Wragg in an action upon the case, damage £10 sterl, deft has time till next Ct provided he put in his pleas 6 days before Ct.

James Ricketts agt Henry Jenkins in an action of trespass upon the case, damage £50 sterl. Time given deft to next Ct provided he file his plea 10 days before next Ct or judgmt by nihill dicet will be confessed.

Hanah Scott being presented by the Grand Jury for having a bastard child. Ordered to be taken into Custody for her appearance at next Ct.

The suit brought by Tho. Babb agt Edwd. Cursill. Plt failing to file declr upon motion of the deft, non-suit granted him agt Babb's est and ordered he pay same to deft with costs at exon.

Joseph Milbes's suit agt Wm. Coopland and Eliza. his wife, Exectrx of David Jones dec'd, in an action upon the case for 40 sh, deft pleading he owes nothing and refers cause to Ct for trial and plt likewise. Judgmt confessed agt Coopland and wife for 20 sh being the ball of accotts unto Jos. Milbee with costs at exon.

Imparlence granted to Francis Malory to answer the suit of Mary Wright of Yorke Co in an action of debt.

Special imparlence granted to Saml. Browedge at the suit of Edwd. Pursil in an action upon the case, damage £6.

Wm. Smelt's suit agt Francis Wright. Deft prays oyer of the accott. Granted.

James Ricketts, Henry Jenkins and John Curle, Execs of Nicho. Curle dec'd, agt Mattw. Jones in an action on the case, damage £50 sterl. Deft prays oyer of the accott. Granted.

Brian Penny's suit agt Joshua Curle, damage £6, copia of the writ being left at deft's house and he not appearing. Upon motion of the plt, attachmt granted agt his est returnable to next Ct for further trial.

Special imparlence granted to Saml. Browedge to answer the suit of Robert Wells.

Attachmt granted to William Allen agt the est of Antho. Armistead Junr in an action of trespass, damage £10 sterl.

Attchmt granted to James Servant and Henry Turner, Execs of Tho. Westwood dec'd, agt Richd. Street in an action of the case, damage £4.

Order granted agt Richd. Kirkin Sec, for non-appearance of Tho. Johnson to answer the suit of Susa. Allen. The plt was admitted to swear to her acct.

Henry Jenkins' suit agt Brian Penny is dismist no decltion being filed.

[p 42] Barto. Selden by Saml. Selden his next friend brought an action of trespass, damage £10 current money agt John Roe for pulling down the hedge. Deft pleading not guilty and last order for survey not being complied with. Ord that the Sherf summon a Jury to meet on the land in question on the 2nd Tuesday in Sept if fair, if not, on the first fair day and try the trespass.

James Servant and Henry Turner, Execs of Thomas Westwood dec'd, in an action upon the case agt Abraham Parish. Refd to next Ct.

Order granted agt Joseph Wragg, Security, and Tho. Skinner for his non-appearance to answer the suit of James Servant and Henry Turner, Execs of Tho. Westwood dec'd.

Suit brought by James Servant and Henry Turner, Execs of Tho. Westwood dec'd, agt Wm. Spicer on an action of the case for 1200 pine boards and 2 sh in money. Dismist.

Order granted agt the Sheriff for the non-appearance of Tho. Allen to answer the suit of James Servant and Henry Turner, Execs of Tho. Westwood dec'd.

Order granted agt the Sheriff for the non-appearance of Edmd. Kerney to answer the suit of Antho. Armistead gent in an action upon the case for £24 money.

Order granted agt Robert Mew and Henry Bowcock his Sec for his non-appearance to answer the suit of John Wallace.

Antho. Armistead's suit agt John Merrideth in an action upon the case, deft not appearing. Plt prays time. Refd to next Ct.

Order granted agt Tho. Wilcox and John Faulkner his Sec for his non-appearance to answer the suit of Richard Kirkin.

Imparlence granted to Robert Armistead to answer the suit of John Sampson in an action upon the case for 600 lbs tobo.

Imparlence granted to Katherine Norden at the suit of Geo. Luke and Mary his wife in an action of trespass upon the case and "sclander," damage £50.

Robert Taylor's action upon the case, damage £10 sterl agt Wm. Rogers, is by consent continued to next Ct being upon Arbitration.

Upon the petition of James Ricketts and Jane his wife, Exectrx of Nicho. Curle dec'd, agt John Curle also one of the other sd Execs concerning cattle. The sd Curle appeared and prayed time to next Ct. Granted.

Judgmt confessed by Peter Burton for 50 sh to the Churchwardens of this Parish for the fine of Mary Floyd for having a bastard child born of her body. The same to be paid by Christmas with costs at exon and Saml. Selden discharged from paymt of 500 lbs tobo fine.

[p 43] Wm. Hopkins, Mary Bridge, Francis Malory & Ann Mihill being presented by the Grand Jury for living in adultery. Ord continued to next Ct and sd Persons to appear to answer an Indictment to be exhibited agt them. Note: Marginal note says: "Richd. Barber, Ricketts etc..." James Ricketts and Wm. Coopland ack themselves indebted to the Churchwardens of the Parish for £20 to keep the Parish of Eliz City harmless from maintaining the bastard child that Barber had by Mary Floyd.

Order granted agt Robert Mew and Tho. Wilcox his Sec for his non-appearance to answer the suit of Emall. Alkin in an action of the case for £5.

Order granted agt Tho. Wilcox, Cha. Jenings and Joseph Wragg his Secs for his non-appearance to answer the suit of Emal. Alkin.

Order granted agt Daniel Lewis and John Wallace Sec for his non-appearance to answer the suit of Wm. Smelt in an action upon the case.

Order granted agt Mr. Mark Johnson gent for the non-appearance of Jacob Face to answer the suit of Tho. Buttler of Warwick Co. in an action of debt for 250 lbs tobo.

Upon complaint of Mary Frizell agt Richd. Kirkin and Margt. his wife and she making oath that she went in danger of her life. Ordered that Richd. Kirkin and Margt. his wife for their good behavior towards all His Majt. Liege People and especially toward the complainant for the full term of one whole year and the Sheriff take them into Custody till they give such Security.

Wm. Smelt's suit agt Tho. Baddely. Deft appears in the Custody of the Sheriff and had time granted him to plead at next Ct.

John Holloway signed

At a Court held the 3rd Wednesday of Septembr being the 19th day 1716

Majr. John Holloway, Mr. Wm. Lowry, Mr. Antho. Armistead, Mr. Thomas Wythe, Capt. Wm. Boswell, Mr. John King – Justices

On petition of Tho. Wilcox, Adm of Eliza. James dec'd, and Susa. Bird orphan of the sd James, setting forth for auditor to be appt to audit the accts between them and the est. Ord that Joseph Banister, Wm. Smelt and Henry Turner or any two of them do between this and next Ct audit the accts and report to next Ct.

Edwd. Mihill's petition concerning what cost he ought to pay in the suit between him and Antho. Armistead. Whereupon the Ct appts Mr. Tho. Wythe and Mr. Jno. King to examine the charge and report to next Ct.

Upon Scire Facias brought by Simon Stacey agt Joshua [blotted] for 715 lbs tobo and 10 sh in money and parties joining issue. Ct hearing arguments on both sides are of the opinion that the suit be dismist with costs at exon.

In the suit brought by Brian Penny agt Tho. Walker in an action upon the case, damage £10.
Parties joined in demurrer and coming to trial. Upon argument demurrer is overruled and the issue also joined upon the Country & Evidences sworn for the plt and jury impanneled and sworn, namely: Jno. Armistead, Wm. Spicer, Hind Armistead, Wm. Fracey, Francis Rogers, Tho. Allen, Ja. Naylor, Tho. Howard, Richd. Street, Jno. Roe, Cha. Cooper, and Jno. Poole, foreman. Returned verdict for plt £4:09. Judgmt gr agt deft for paymt with costs at exon.

Upon the petition of James Ricketts and Jane his wife to be admitted gdn to her children and to divide est. At the last Ct Henry Jenkins and Jno. Curle, Execs of Nicho. Curle's will, stated that there is a personal est of considerable value bequeathed in his will dated 12 Aug 1714, that all debts are not yet paid, and that the children have not yet attained the respective ages specified in the will for receiving their bequests. The Ct are of the opinion and do ordered that the sd Jane be appt gdn to her children and that Mr. George Walker, Mr. Joshua Curle, Mr. Wm. Smelt and Mr. Henry Irwin or any three of them[p 45] divide the personal est acc to the will of Nicho. Curle and report to next Ct. Deft appeals to the seventh day of the Honble Genll Ct. Granted giving bond and security.

In an action of debt brought by Brian Penny agt Saml. Noble and Alexr. Alkins for £4:00:06. At the last Ct deft pled, then plt prayed time to answer. Refd to next Ct for trial.

Ordered that Edwd. Mihill pay to Matthew Whitfield acc to law for his one days attendance at Ct and for coming six miles and going six miles and for ferriage 5 sh for coming and 5 sh for ferriage going over James River as an Evidence agt Richd. Kirkin with costs at exon.

Bill in Chancery brought by Mary Cary of Warwick Co. agt Wm. Dandridge and Euphan his wife, Exectrx of Wilson Rascow dec'd, respondents, for £500. Complt filing her replycation, respondents pray time to consider. Granted.

Suit brought by Robt. Taylor agt Fra. Ballard in an action of debt for £5 and 201 lbs of tobo. Deft pleading, plt joins and puts it upon the Ct for trial. Two Evidences being sworn for the plt and two for the deft and arguments heard, Ct ordered suit be dismist with costs.

Ordered that Fra. Ballard pay unto James Servant for his one days attendance as Evidence for him agt Robert Taylor with costs at exon.

Ordered that Fra. Ballard pay to Tho. Baddely for his twelve days attendance as Evidence for him agt Robt. Taylor with costs at exon, one day of which to be allowed in the bill of cost agt Taylor.

John Sweetman's suit agt Wm. Weston for £17:05. Attachmt not being executed, upon the motion of plt is continued.

The suit brought by Mary Frizel agt James Birtell in an action of trespass for assault and battery, damages £20. At last Ct refd to consider what cost ought to be allowed and now being called and heard, Ct confirms the Jury's verdict. Ordered deft pay to plt £2:06 with costs at exon.

The action of trespass, damage £10, brought by Edwd. Lattemore agt Phillip Prescott for stopping the chain of the Surveyor then surveying a certain lot in Hampton. Pltf filing his replycation, deft prays time to consider. Granted.

Tho. Wood's suit agt Richd. Kirkin in an action upon the case for £3:02:04. Deft pleaded he owes nothing and exhibiting his acct. Ordered accts be settled. Joseph Wragg, Jos. Banister and Wm. Smelt or any two of them to examine accts and report to next Ct.

In a suit brought by Saml. Selden agt Fra. Ballard in an action of trespass, damage £10, from hindering the Surveyor from surveying the plt's land, the last order being for the Clk to open the Jury's verdict and report to be given and none being called and arguments heard what each party had to offer the Ct. Ord that the Sherf summon the same Jury, as many as can be had, to meet upon the same land. Refd to next Ct to fix a time for Survey.

[p 46] Robert Westlake, lessee of Tho. Poole, ejectmt agt William Simons wherein James Ricketts and Jane his wife, next friend to Pasco Curle are admitted defts, damage £10. The last ord was for deft to search for their paper Evidences and being called, deft not having paper Evidence, moves for a longer time which is granted. Examination of Richd. Rowton and Thomas Francis Senr is to be taken before a Justice and to be allowed good Evidence upon trial in case they are not alive or not able to come, deft paying Ct's charges.

Wm. Lowry and William Bosell, Foeffees, ack their lease & release for Town Land unto Antho. Armistead gent. Ordered recorded.

Upon the petition of Thomas Howard for a license to keep an ordinary at Town, which is granted, giving bond and security acc to law.

Upon petition of William Morgan for his freedom. Ordered that Mrs. Luke, his mistress, be summoned to next Ct to answer the petitioner.

Upon complaint of Kort. Neele agt Tho. Roberts about beating and abusing of her and taking her oath of the same, the Ct ordered that Roberts be summoned to next Ct to answer and the Sheriff take him into Custody till he give bond and sec for £20 in the meantime for his good behaviour towards all his Majt's Liege People especially toward the complt.

Upon the petition of Cha. Jenings agt John Curle for 234 lbs tobo. Curle appears and consents to refer it to Ct for judgmt. Ordered refd to next Ct for proof.

Ordered that John Allen Jones pay to Wm. Green of Ile White Co for his four days attendance at Ct as Evidence agt Simon Stacey and for coming 20 miles and going 20 miles and 5 sh for passing and 5 sh for repassing for ferriage over James River from Newport News to Pagan Creek with costs at exon.

Feoffees ack their lease & release for Town Land to William Allen. Ordered recorded.

James Rose, servant boy belonging to Saml. Sweny, adjudged to be twelve years old and ordered to serve acc to law.

Jane Borthwick, servant girl to James Ricketts, is adjudged to be thirteen years old and ordered to serve sd Master acc to law.

Jno. Armistead having returned the inv of Dun Armistead's est and he having made oath to the same and orderer recorded, he offers Capt. Jenkins and Mr. James Ricketts Sec for sd est. Ct approves and he is ordered to give bond to the Clk of the Ct.

In the suit brought by Edward Mihill agt Richd. Kirkin in an action of trespass upon the case, damage £30 money setting forth for a Negr woman which the deft took away from the plt. Deft pleading not guilty in manner and form, and three Evidences being sworn for the plt and Jury impannelled and sworn, namely: John Armistead, Hind Armistead, Fra. Rogers, Wm. Spicer, Tho. Howard, John Bordland, Richd. Street, John Roe, Tho. Allen, John Poole, Tho. Wood and Cha. Cooper.

[p 47] "and having heard the Arguments on both sides and received their Charge went in Tryall of the said Suit and being out some Time, Returne for Verdict in These Words Wee of the Jury do find" for the plt damage £10 current money which on motion of the plt ordered recorded and that deft to pay sd sum with costs at exon.

Ordered that Edwd. Mihill pay to James Brown for his five days attendance as an Evidence for him agt Richd. Kirkin with costs at exon.

Ordered that Edwd. Mihill pay to Ann Wood for her five days attendance as an Evidence for him agt Richd. Kirkin with costs at exon.

Ordered that Edwd. Mihill pay to Saml. Brown for one days attendance and for coming 40 miles and going 40 miles and 5 sh for coming and 5 sh for going for ferriage over the James River at Newport News with costs at exon.

Mr. Cole Diggs and Mr. Tho. Nelson came into Ct in order to have James Birtell's will probated but refuse to take the Executorship, they being appt Execs in the will. The Ct therefore appts Mr. Simon Hollier, Sheriff, and Mr. Joseph Banister with the Clk of sd Ct to take an inv. of the est and keep the same in their hands and return to Ct when required except what is perishing to be disposed of.

The last will of James Birtell dec'd is proved by the oath of Joseph Banister, one of the wit, and ord that the granting of a certificate for probate or adm be delayed till the time be expired by law to see if any body will appear to probate the will or admst.

Court adjourns till Tomorrow Ten a Clock.

At a Court held the 20th day of September 1716
Present – Majr. John Holloway, Mr. William Lowery, Mr. Antho. Armistead, Capt. Francis Ballard, Capt. William Boswell, Mr. Mark Johnson.

Upon the petition of Henry Jenkins for to build a house upon a warff on Mr. James Birtell's land in Hampton and to pay the rent expressed in the will of Birtell, ord that petitioner be granted the building of sd house and paying the rent and that he give bond and sec to the Ct for the performance of same. Six months liberty is given to build the house and to pay rent from that time and ordered that the petition be recorded.

Upon the petition of Capt. Wm. Boswell for Adm of James Birtell's est, the Ct having yesterday committed the care of the est to the Sheriff and Jos. Banister. It's ordered petition be refd till they return an acct of est to Ct and then petition be considered.

Henry Robinson's suit agt Saml. Selden in an action of debt for £100, deft prays time to next Ct. Granted.

The last w & t of James Birtell is proved by the oaths of John Smith and George Wauff, wit thereto, the Question being settled with Banister whether the "Razurs" in the will was before it was signed and delivered who declared it was. Ordered recorded.

[p 48] In the suit brought by Wm. Coopland and Eliza. his wife Exectrx of David Jones dec'd, agt James Ricketts and Jane his wife, Henry Jenkins and John Curle Execs of Nicho. Curle gent dec'd in an action upon the case for £5:10. The audit being returned, judgmt granted agt the defts for £4 out of Curle's est with costs at exon, the plt first making oath before a Justice of the Peace that "he never rec'd No Part of Sattisfaction of the Sd accott."

Mary Frizell's suit agt Rachel Provine in an action of assault and battery, damage £50, to be refd to next Ct to execute a Writ of Reply to inquire as to damages.

Action of trespass, damage £100, brought by John Curle agt John Jones. Deft prays time to consider plt's replycation. Granted.

John Gibin's suit agt William Malory is dismist.

Tho. Wood's suit agt Edward Brier in an action upon the case. Deft pleads non-assumpsit. Ordered refd to Tho. Wilcox, Joseph Banister and William Loyall or any two of them to settle accts and report to next Ct.

Wm. Smelt's suit agt John King gent in an action upon the case, damage £40 by consent of both parties. The Cause if refd to Mr. Michel Gerny [?Henry or Kerny?] to arbitrate the accts on both sides & report to next Ct.

Thomas Wood's suit agt Noah Barefoot in an action upon the case, damage £20. Judgmt by nihil dicet confirmed and ordered writ of inquiry to inquire into damages at next Ct.

Judgmt confessed by James Naylor for paymt of 34 sh 7 d to John Curle with costs at exon due by specialty.

John Cook's suit agt Joseph Wragg, damage £10 in an action of trespass upon the case. Deft pleading, the plt joins. Refd to next Ct for trial.

James Ricketts' suit agt Henry Jenkins, deft pleading. Pltf prays time to next Ct to consider plea. Granted.

Ordered that the Sheriff take Hanah Scott into Custody for her appearance at next Ct to answer the presentment of the Grand Jury for Bastardy.

Judgment confessed by Fra. Malory for paymt of 52 sh according to the written agreement unto Mary Wright with costs at exon.

Judgmt gr by nihil dicet agt Saml. Browige at the suit of Edward Pursill.

[p 49] Wm. Smelt agt Francis Wright. Deft prays leave to plead as many pleas as he thinks fit which is granted and according pled which plt joined. Refd to next Ct for trial.

James Ricketts, Henry Jenkins and John Curle, Execs of Nicho. Curle dec'd, brought their action on the case, damage £50, agt Mattw. Jones as marrying the Exectrx of John George dec'd. Deft prays oyer of the acct. Ord suit be refd.

In the suit brought by Brian Penny agt Jno. Curle Junr in an action upon the case for £5:10:06, plt failing to prosecute his suit, non-suit is awarded the deft and plt is to pay 5 sh to deft with costs at exon.

Judgmt granted by nihil dicet agt Saml. Browige at the suit of Robert Wells in an action upon the case.

Wm. Allen's suit agt Antho. Armistead Junr in a trespass, damage £10. Deft appears and prays time to plead. Granted.

James Servant and Henry Turner, Execs of Tho. Westwood dec'd, brought an action upon the case for £3 silver money agt Richd. Street. Judgmt granted agt the deft for 34 sh 3d to be paid in corn at the rate of 10 sh the barrel and 185 foot clapboard being the bal of the acct to the sd Exec with costs at exon.

Susanah Allen's suit agt Tho. Johnson in an action upon the case, damage £28. Richd. Kirkin being his Sec which he now becomes special bail for sd Johnson to pay the condemnation of the Ct or else to surrender the deft up to prison. Judgmt granted agt the deft by nihil dicet at the suit of sd Susa. Allen.

In the suit brought by Antho. Armistead agt Edmd. Kerny in an action upon the case for £24 silver money. The parties consenting to put the Case upon the Ct for trial and plt by oath proving that he delivered the deft 6000 pipe staves at £4 per 1000, plt has judgmt for 24 sh out of which the deft is to be allowed all just discounts that he can make appear.

James Servant and Henry Turner, Execs of Tho. Westwood dec'd, brought their action upon the case agt --- ba. Parish. Pltf prays it be continued. Granted.

James Servant and Henry Turner, Execs of Tho. Westwood dec'd, brought an action upon the case agt Tho. Allen. Pltf prays it be continued. Granted.

James Servant and Henry Turner, Execs of Tho. Westwood dec'd, brought suit agt Tho. Skinner and neither party appearing, ord dismist.

Court adjourns till the Court in Cource. John Holloway.

[p 50]
At a Court held the 3rd Wednesday of November
being the 21st day 1716
Present: Majr. John Holloway, Mr. William Lowery, Capt. Wm. Boswell, Mr. John King, Mr. Thomas Wythe, Mr. Antho. Armistead, Mr. Marke Johnson - His Majt Justices

Petition of Thomas Wilcox, Adm of Elizabeth James dec'd, and Susanna Bird, orphan of sd James to have accounts settled between them. The last order for auditing not being complied with, ord that the former order be performed & report to next Ct.

Petition of James Gilbert for license to keep an ordinary at the Fort at Pt Comfort. Granted, he giving bond & paying Govs. & other fees.

Petition of Martha Taylor for two pieces of stuff which she left in Mr. Ja. Birtell's store. Referred to next Ct.

Petition of Robert Taylor for the " Chariott of Horses" left to his wife by Mr. James Birtell in his last will. Granted. Chariott & horses to be appr & that Mr. Jos. Banister deliver them upon his giving bond & sec to return value thereof to the Adm in case there be not sufficient to pay Birtell's debts without it.

Joseph Banister returns the inv of est of James Birtell. Ord appr by Mr. Wm. Smelt, Mr. Henry Irwin, Mr. Saml. Sweny & Mr. Henry Bowcocke? & return to next Ct.

Thomas Wood ack his deed of gift to Sarah Hayes & her son Henry Hayes. Also Ann, wife to sd Thos. Wood, ack right of dower to sd Sarah Hayes & her son Henry Hayes. Ordered recorded.

Thomas Brittin confesses judgement for 500 lbs tobo or 50 sh in money to the Churchwardens of this Parish for the fine of Hannah Scott for having a bastard child born of her body. Upon non-payment Execution to issue to keep the Parish harmless from the maintaining of the sd child.

[p 51] The Order from Genl Ct agt Margt. Kirkin being read. It appearing to the Ct that she is very sick, the Execution of order is suspended till next Ct.

Richd. Nusome ret the inv of Eliza. Andrew's est. Ord that he take est in his custody and sell the same at an outcry & ret the acct to next Ct.

Mr. Marke Johnson is this day sworn one of his Maj.'s Corronrs for the Co. of Eliz City.

The Grand Jury returns presentment. Ordered that James Naylor be summoned to next Ct to answer.

Wm. Lowery & Wm. Bosell, Foefees, execute lease & release for land to Thomas Wythe, Gent., the same being pro by witnesses subscribed to sd deeds. Ordered recorded.

Court adjourned to the Court in course to be held at Hampton Town in this Court. John Holloway Signed.

At a Court held the 3rd Wednes of Decembr being the 19th day 1716

Present – Majr. John Holloway, Mr. William Lowery, Capt. Wm. Bosell, Capt. Fra. Ballard, Mr. John Bayley, Mr. Tho. Tabb, Mr. Tho. Wythe, Mr. Antho. Armistead, Mr. John King, Mr. Mark Johnson – His Majt. Justices.

James Miller brought before the Ct on suspicion of Felony of breaking open the storehouse of George Walker in Hampton Town and the house of Saml. Sweny & taking away several goods. Several evidences being heard & Ct receiving several matters of fact. Ct is of the opinion that James Miller be taken to the public Gaol in WmBurgh in order to have his trial at Genll Ct.

Kort Norden, Saml. Sweny, George Walker, Wm. Walker, & Tho. Peirce give their bond for £20 that each will appear before the Genll Ct on the 4th day thereof to give evidence agt James Miller, prisoner.

[p 52] Wm. Bayley gives his bond for £40 sterling for good behaviour for twelve months & a day. Saml. Sweny likewise gives his bond for £20 as security. Ordered that the Sheriff take William Bayley into his custody & secure him till he deliver him to the Public Gaol.

Richd. Hopkins ack his deed for town land to Emanl. Alkin. Ordered recorded.

Auditors appt to divide the est of Nicho. Curle report they could not comply with the order of Genll & Co Cts, James Ricketts alleging that parts of the est are in the hands of Henry Jenkins & John Curle. Ct orders that John Curle & James Ricketts produce the Negroes and personal est of sd Nicho. Curle before Mr. Antho. Armistead Senr in the room of George Walker, Mr. Henry Irwin, Mr. Edmond Kerney, and Mr. Josa. Curle or any three of them & they are to report the division to next Ct.

Mary Andrews being twelve years old is bound apprentice unto John Bayley & Judeath his wife until she be eighteen years of age. They are to teach her to spin ---- household work and at expiration "cloathe her decently."

Upon petition of Jno. Birtell for Adm with the will annexed of est of James Birtell, dec'd. Granted, he giving bond & sec. Robert Taylor & John King offer as sec & Ct approves. The Sheriff & Joseph Banister are to deliver the est to Jno. Birtell, retaining sufficient for their trouble & expense. Appr to be made by Mr. Fra. Ballard, Mr. Tho.

Wythe, Mr. Tho. Howard & Mr. Wm. Bosell, or any three of them, & report made to next Ct.

Wm. Coopland and Eliza. his wife ack their deed of gift for land unto Wm. Fracey. Ordered recorded.

[p 53] Joseph Banister has returned his part of the inv of Mr. Birtell's est. Ordered recorded.

The Court adjourns till Tomorrow Ten a Clock. John Holloway signed.

At a Court held the 3rd Wednesday of Janry being 16 day 1716

Present – Majr. John Holloway, Capt. Francis Ballard, Capt. Wm. Bosell, Mr. John King, Mr. Tho. Tabb, Mr. John Bayley, Mr. Mark Johnson

Petition of Thomas Howard for cleaning the Courthouse, Capt. Bosell approving the same. Ordered refd to a fuller Ct.

Petition of Eliza. Dunaway agt John Curle for a share of her husband's crop as being his overseer. Ordered Curle be summoned to next Ct to answer.

Suit brought by Mary Frizell agt Rachel Provine in an action upon the case for assault & battery, damage £5 sterling. Four evidences sworn for the plt. A Jury was impanelled to inquire into damages, namely: Edward Lattamore foreman, John Poole, Richd. Cursell, Tho. Allen, Fra. Rogers, Wm. Coopland, Joseph Haris, Brian Penny, Peter Baker, Edwd. Ballard, Barto. Proby and Henry Robinson. Jury finds for the plt 4d damages. Verdict ordered recorded. Deft to pay 4 d.

Tho. Poole's ejectment agt James Ricketts on behalf of Pasco Curle, infant, refd to next Ct, Ricketts not being at Ct, deft paying this Ct's charge.

Ordered Mary Frizell pay Joseph Wragg for two days attendance as an evidence agt Rachel Provine with costs at execution.

Ordered that Tho. Wilcox accts agt Eliza. James est and Susanah Bird's accts be audited by Capt. Wm. Bosell in the room of Henry Turner, Mr. Wm. Smelt & Mr. Jos. Banister or any two of them & report to next Ct.

[p 54] Action of debt brought by Brian Penny agt Alexander Alkins and Saml. Neele for £4:6. Defts demurring, judgmt

granted agt defts for paymt of sd sum with costs at execution.

Wm. Bayley brought before the Ct on suspicion of Felony of breaking open the storehouse of George Walker in Hampton Town and taking away several goods. Eliza. Lashley & Wm. Walker giving evidence agt Bayley. Ct are of the opinion that Bayley ought to have his trial at the Honble the Genll Ct. Ordered Bayley be remanded to County Gaol.

Florance Driscoll brought before the Ct on suspicion of receiving & concealing stolen goods from Wm. Bayley & James Miller. Ct is of the opinion that he have trial on the 4th day. Whereupon he enters with recognizance in the sum of £20 sterling and Simon Hollier & Edmd. Hollier each of them in the sum of £10 for his appearance at Genll Ct.

Tho. Tucker, Constable, & Eliza. Lashley give an appearance bond for £20 sterling to give evidence at Genll Ct agt Wm. Bayley, James Miller & Florance Driscoll.

Petition of Edwd. Mihill, plt, about what cost ought to be allowed in the suit between him & Antho. Armistead. Ct ordered petition be dismist.

Ordered that Mary Frizell pay Eliza. Walker & Sarah Hayes for two days each attendance agt Rachel Provine with costs at execution.

Court adjourned till Tomorrow Ten a Clock.

At a Court held 17 Janry 1716
Majr. John Holloway, Capt. Fra. Ballard, Capt. Wm. Bosell, Mr. Tho. Wythe, Mr. Tho. Tabb, Mr. John Bayley, Mr. John King, Mr. Mark Johnson.

Petition of Martha Taylor for two pieces of stuff or silk left in the store of James Birtell is rejected.

Petition of Cha. Jenkins for the turning of the road at his plantation at Hampton River. Ordered Mr. John King & Mr. James Ricketts to lay off another convenient road & report to next Ct.

[p 55] Mr. Simon Hollier is appt overseer to make a good road where Mr. Armistead's Mill Dam was & he to [summon] as many persons in the County as he thinks fit to repair the road & that he keep an exact acct of charges & that before any person builds a Mill house they pay such charges the County is at. [sic]

Saml. Sweny brought John Sampson, his servant, for running away & arguments heard. Accts amount to 200 lbs tobo and £1 money, being absent thirty days. Ordered that he serve sd master 60 days for his absence & 6 months for the charges in taking him up and pay costs.

Ordered Saml. Sweny pay John George & James Shells for one days attendance each as evidence agt John Sampson with costs.

Ordered John Sampson pay Edwd. Mihill & Fran. Rose for one days attendance each as evidences agt Saml. Sweny with costs.

Fra. Ballard agt John Sampson for his Levys which is 147 lbs tobo. Mr. Saml. Sweny will pay & John Sampson is to serve him two months for the same after his other time expires.

Ordered that Henry Robinson pay Frances Ballard & Robt. Taylor for their four days attendance each as evidences agt Saml. Selden in the action with ---- -- --
[missing]

[p 56] Suit brought by Henry Robinson agt Saml. Selden in an action of debt for £100 sterling for Breach of Articles. Dismist.

Petition of William Westwood agt the est of Eliza. Andre-- for 400 lbs tobo. Ordered he be pd out of the est with costs, the same being due for the building of a house for sd Andrews.

Ordered that the Levys be laid on Monday next, if fair etc.

Then the Court adjourns till the Court in Course. John Holloway signs.

At a Court held 20th Febr 1716
Majr. John Holloway, Mr. Wm. Lowery, Mr. John Bayley, Capt. Fra. Ballard, Mr. John King, Capt. Wm. Bosell, Mr. Mark Johnson, His Majt's Justices

John Hampton, twelve year old orphan, is by his own consent bound an apprentice to Robt. Taylor or his heirs until he comes of age, he learning the boy to read and write and at end of time to clothe him according to law.

Upon petition of Saml. Sweny for payment for building a Courthouse and Prison. Ordered that when High Sheriff Simon Hollier as appt to lay the levy as soon as he receives enough tobacco is to discharge debt to Sweny first, either in tobo or money at 15 pct.

Petition of Bartd. Proby for adm of his brother Tho. Proby's est. Ordered that cert be granted, he giving bond and security.

Order granted agt Tho. Ryland, Sec for the non-appearance of John Merrideth to answer the suit of Antho. Armistead.

Richd. Nusum makes oath that the est of Eliza. Andrews dec'd is indebted to him for 505 lbs tobo & 23 sh & 10 pence. Ordered that he be paid from est.

Upon the motion of Wm. More, he is appt gdn to his brother Merritt More, giving bond & security.

[p 57] Upon petition of Eliza. Dunaway agt Jno. Curle for a share of her husband's crop, the Petnr being --- Denied.

John Burtell's power of atty to Robt. Taylor and Jno. King pro by the oaths of William Bosell and Wm. Smelt, wit.

In the ejectmt brought by Robert Westlock on the demise of Tho. Poole, plt, agt Pasco Curle, infant. Deft pleads not guilty. Evidences examined on both sides, Jury is impannelled and sworn, namely: Joseph Banister, Tho. Merry, Cha. Tucker, Bartd. Proby, Thomas Howard, Henry Dun, Wm. Allen, Brian Penny, Hind Armistead, Richd. Hopkins, Edwd. Ballard and Jno. Howard. Jury brought in Special Verdict. Refd to next Ct for a Matter of Law to be argued.

Ordered that Pasco Curle pay to Edwd. Lattemore, Henry Robinson and Jos. Harris for their four days attendance as evidences for him agt Tho. Poole with costs at exon.

In the suit brought by Wm. Smelt agt Fra. Wright in an action upon the case for ten barrels of Indian corn and five casks. Ct ordered that the deft give the plt notes for 22 1/2 bushels of Indian corn upon those persons in whose hands the corn lies. Ordered dismst with costs at exon.

Mr. Henry Irwin being bound over to the Ct at the complaint of Edith Smith for beating of her etc. Ordered Irwin be bound for his good behaviour for twelve months and a day from the 20th of Jan last. Irwin gives his bond for £100 sterling to be of good behaviour toward all his Majesty's Liege people and especially towards complainant.

Court adjourns till tomorrow at 10 a clock.

[p 58] At a Court held the 21st day Febr 1716

Majr. John Holloway, Mr. Wm. Sweny, Mr. John King, Mr. John Bayley, Mr. Mark Johnson — His Majesty's Justices

William Neele, Servant to Mr. Fitch Williams, is adjudged to be 16 years old & ordered to serve his master or assigns according to law.

Mr. John King, Undertaker, is to build a "Paire of Stocks, Pillory and Whiping post according to the patten [pattern] of them at Williamsborough, the finding Iron worke and what Else Convenient and to build a Ducking Stoole to Goe upon three wheeles Three foot High to the Liking of the Court for all which he is to have Eight Pounds in Money."

Henry Turner ack his lease & release to William Westwood. Also Sidwell his wife being present and ack her deeds to Wm. Westwood.

William Lowery & Wm. Bosell, foefees, ack their deed for town land unto John Roe.

It is ordered that Tho. Poole Senr pay to Tho. Jones for two days attendance as evidences for him agt Pasco Curle with costs at exon.

Cha. Jenings producing his accts agt the est of Mrs. Mary Jenings dec'd and making oath to same. Ordered accts [be] recorded.

John Holloway, Antho. Armistead, John Bayley, John King, and Marke Johnson gent ack their deeds to William Bosell gent for the celler under the Courthouse. Ordered recorded.

Court adjourns to the Court in course. John Holloway signed.

At a Court held the 2nd Wed of March
being the 20th day 1716.
Mr. Wm. Lowery, Capt. Fra. Ballard, Mr. John Bayley, Mr. Tho. Tabb, Capt. Wm. Bosell, Mr. Antho. Armistead, Mr. John King, Mr. Mark Johnson

Petition of John Bordland for a license to keep an ordinary in the Towne of Hampton. Granted giving bond & security.

Complaint of Geo. Walker agt Richd. Fitch Williams for striking and ill usage. Having heard evidences, the Justices are of the opinion that sd Williams give a bond of £25 that he keep the peace. Mr. Alexdr. Meckenzie and Robt. Armistead are securities for £10 each for Williams.

Motion of Benja. Smith and Tho. Thompson to have an instrument of writing between them recorded. So ordered and also Thompson ack to serve Smith or his assigns five years.

Richd. Kirkin's suit agt Tho. Wilcox, Adm of Eliz. James dec'd in an action upon the case. Deft prays time to next Ct, Capt. Jenkins his Atty not being at Ct. Granted.

[Same entry repeated]

John Sampson's suit agt Robt. Armistead in an action upon the case, damages 1000 lbs tobo. Ordered refd to next Ct.

Robt. Taylor in an action upon the case, damages £40 sterl agt Wm. Rogers. Ordered dismst, parties being agreed.

Bart. Selden by Saml. Selden his next friend, brought action of trespass, damages -- pounds agt John Roe. Refd to next Ct.

Petition of James Ricketts on behalf of Pasco Curle infant agt John Curle for cattle etc. Order is granted agt sd Curle by nihill dicett to answer.

Emanl. Alkin's suit agt Tho. Wilcox, Adm of Eliza. James dec'd in an action upon the case. Deft prays time to next Ct. Granted.

Emanl. Alkin's action agt Robert Mew ordered dismst, neither party appearing.

William Smelt in an action upon the case agt Daniel Lewis is ordered dismst, the defendant being deceased.

Tho. Butler of Warwick Co. Suit agt Jacob Face ord dismst, the plaintiff being deceased.

Action of debt brought by Henry Robinson agt Edward Colwell for £4:10. Deft prays oyer of the bill. Granted.

Wm. Smelt's suit agt Tho. Baddely. Deft prays time to next Ct. Granted.

[p 60] Ct represents to his Honor Alexdr. Spotswood, his Majt's Lt. Gov. and Commander in Chief of the Colony of Va., Capt. Wm. Bosell, Mr. John Bayley and Mr. John King to be fit and proper persons to be High Sheriff of Eliz. City Co. for the preceeding years. William Lowery signed.

At a Court held the 3rd Wednesday of May
being the 15th day 1717
Majr. John Holloway, Mr. Wm. Lowery, Capt. Wm. Bosell, Capt. Fra. Ballard, Mr. Thos. Wythe, Mr. Thos. Tabb, Mr. Mark Johnson - His Majt's Justices

Petition of Joseph Rusell "for to be clear from paying his county Levy" granted.

Petition of Moses Marsh for his freedom from Capt. Ballard. Heard and considered and ordered rejected.

Hind Armistead and Hanah his wife, Execs of Mattw. Watts dec'd agt Saml. Watts in an action upon the case, damages £10 sterl. Upon motion of deft, imparlence is granted.

Suit brought by Saml. Watts agt Hind Armistead, damages £40 in money. Trespass. Upon motion of deft Speciall Imparlence is granted him.

John Wallard [Wallace?] appt Constable for the Towne of Hampton in room of Thos. Wilcox and to be sworn. Wilcox is not to be discharged until the other is sworn.

Upon petition of Margtt. Seton agt ill usuage of her master & mistress Josa. Curle and his wife. Dismissed.

Joshua Curle bringing Margtt. Seton his servant before the Ct to have charge allowed him that he was out in getting Seton when she was runaway. Ordered he be allowed at next Ct for what expense he was at in getting sd servant again and for her time.

[p 61] Ordered est of Matthew Watts dec'd be appr by Charles Jenings, John Howard, Robert Johnson, and Jo. Banister.

Special Imparlence granted to John Byregee? at his suit of Wm. Smelt. £5.

William Smelt's suit agt Thomas Wood is ended.

John Sweetman's attachment agt Wm. West is continued.

In action of Accts Render for £150 brought by Bartrand Proby, Adm of Peter Proby, agt Fra. Ballard, deft. Jury impannelled: Edwd. Lattimore, Wm. Coopland, Hind Armistead, Thomas Merry, Bryan Penny, Jno. Poole, Edwd. Ballard, Thomas Howard, James Gilbert, Phillip Prescott, Thomas Jones and Joseph Banister foreman. Jury finds deft Adm to sd Peter Proby. Verdict rec. It is ord that deft acct before Mr. Thomas Wythe, Mr. Joseph Banister and Mr. George Walker or any two of them at such time and place as auditors shall appt giving Ballard four days notice. Ordered to audit to next Ct.

Edwd. Lattemore agt Phillip Prescott, damages £10 sterl. Deft pleads not guilty. Ordered surveyor with jury meet and lay out land in controversy on 2nd Tuesday in June if fair etc having good regard to all pattens and evidences. To return report to next Ct.

[p 62] Judgment granted by nihill dicett agt Jno. Curle to answer suit of Charles Jenings.

John Curle agt Jno. Jones, damages £100 sterl, trespass. Deft demurring, plt prayed time to next Ct. Granted.

John Cook agt Jos. Wragg in action of trespass, damages £10, is dismist, parties being agreed.

James Ricketts agt Henry Jenkins. Trespass, damages £50, is dismist, parties agreeing.

James Ricketts and Jane his wife, Henry Jenkins and Jno. Curle, Execs of Nicho. Curle dec'd, agt Makhew Jones in an action upon the case, damages £50 sterl. Deft having prayed Oyer of the Accts and pltfs not producing any, ord dismist.

Robert Wells agt Samll. Broomage, damages £10 sterl. Capt. Henry Jenkins enters himself speciall bayle for to pay the condemnation of the Ct for the deft to which he pleads. Plt prays time to next Ct. Granted.

William Allen agt Antho. Armistead Junr. Trespass upon the case, damages £10 sterl. Upon petition of Mrs. Hanah Armistead she is admitted deft in sd cause and ack to pay all costs and damages. Whereupon judgment granted by nihill dicett agt deft to answer suit of Wm. Allen.

Last will & testament of Tho. Nayler pro by Cha. Jenings and Wm. Westwood. Cert for probate granted Exectrx giving bond, she having taken oath and ordered to return inventory to next Ct.

Richard Lukas, orphan being 16 the 25th day of January next is bound apprentice until he be of age unto Wm. Walker, he learning the boy the art of a lawyer and to give him a year and a half of schooling, directly, and at the expiration of his time to give him according to law. [sic]

Judgment confirmed agt Tho. Johnson and Richd. Kirkin his sec for £7:15:09 unto Susa. Allen with costs at exon.

[p 63] Suit brought by James Servant and Henry Turner, Execs of Tho. Westwood dec'd agt Abraham Parish is dismist, being agreed.

Upon the motion of Richd. Kirkin for an attachmt agt est of Tho. Johnson. Granted for £7:15:09 with costs.

Order granted agt Thomas Backas and Richd. Hopkins, Sec for his non-appearance to answer suit of Thomas Howard in an action upon the case for £6.

Alexander Alkins and Jane his wife agt Tho. Wood and Ann his wife in action upon the case for slander, damages £50. No declr being filed, ordered dismist.

Ordered that Alexdr. Alkins pay to Mary Hartwell for her five days attendance as an evidence for him agt Tho. Wood with costs at exon.

Special Imparlence granted to Mary Frizell to answer the suit of William Smelt in an action upon the case for 20 sh.

Order granted agt Thomas Roberts and Tho. Ryland Sec for his non-appearance to answer the suit of Samll. Neele and <u>Kert.</u> his wife, damages £4.

Order granted agt James Marke and John Smith Junr, Sec for non-appearance to answer suit of Robert Armistead.

Order granted agt John ?Vuelage? and William Dandridge Sec for his non-appearance to answer suit of Richard Hopkins in action of trespass upon the case, damages £50 sterl.

Suit brought by Alexdr. Alkins agt Robert Tennoch in an action of trespass upon the case for an assault damage £20 and no declr being filed, ordered dismist.

Ordered Alexdr. Alkins pay to John Wallace and his wife and to each for their four days attendance as evidences for him agt Robt. Tannoch with costs at exon.

In the suit brought by Brian Penny agt Joshua Curle Junr, deft in an action upon the case, damages £5:04 and he pleading a copy of the writt being left at his house and he not appearing to defend. Pltf's motion of attchmt granted agsts est for same with costs. Ret to next Ct for further trial.

Petition of Robert Taylor and Martha his wife agt James Burtell's est for two pieces of stuff. Dismist.

William Smelt agt Henry Irwin for £5 being due by notes accepted by Irwin and the plt loosing [losing] the note, ordered dismist.

Mrs. Margt. Bayley ack deeds for town land to Andrew Laws. Ordered recorded.

Joseph Banister's petition for Adm of James Burtell's est is dismist, his brother having one granted before.

[p 63] James Burtell's appr of est by Joseph Banister ord rec.

Special Imparlence granted to Samll. Sweny to answer the suit of Cha. Chiswell.

Special Imparlence granted to George Luke, Esq, and Mary his wife at the suit of Emanl. Aikin, damages £12.

Attchmt granted Cha. Jenings agt the est of Geo. Luke for £5:02:06 with costs. Returnable to next Ct.

Attchmt granted Cha. Jenings agt the est of Tho. Read and Ann his wife, Execs of William dec'd [sic] for 600 lbs of tobo. Ret to next Ct for further trial.

Order granted agt Benja. Smith and the Sheriff for his non-appearance to answer the suit of Richard Basford, damages £3.

Order granted agt James Ricketts and the Sheriff for non-appearance at the suit of Richd. Basford, damages 400 lbs tobo.

Ordered Sheriff take James Naylor into Custody for his appearance at next Ct to answer the presentment of the Grand Jury for not keeping the Highway clear.

Upon the motion of John Burtell, Adm of James Burtell dec'd, for non-suit to be granted him agt the est of James Ricketts and Jane his wife as guardian to Pasco Curle for bringing an action of debt agt Burtell's est and then failing to prosecute. Granted.

Special Imparlence granted to John Burtell, Adm of James Burtell, to answer the suit of James Ricketts in an action upon the case.

Order granted agt Tho. Wilcox and Tho. Roberts Sec for his non-appearance to answer the suit of Tho. Howard, damages £6.

The suit brought by Edwd. Ballard agt Tho. Wood in an action upon the case, damages [blank] and no declr being filed. Non-suit granted agt Edwd. Ballard's est.

Eliza. Selden ack deed for land to Saml. Selden. Ordered recorded.

Order granted agt Antho. Armistead Senr and the Sheriff for his non-appearance to answer the suit of John Smith Senr, damages £20.

Order granted agt Joseph Wragg and Tho. Roberts Sec for non-appearance to answer the suit of Henry Batts in an action upon the case for £6.

Order granted agt Jos. Wragg and Tho. Roberts Sec for non-appearance to answer the suit of Henry Batts in an action upon the case.

[p 65] Judgment granted agt John Burtell, Adm of James Burtell dec'd, for £26:13:07 1/2 sterl and £18:17:05 to Archibald Blair, the plt having made oath to his acct to be paid from est with costs at exon.

Cha. Jenings suing John Burtell, Adm of James Burtell dec'd, for Clerk's fees. 2092 lbs tobo. Deft prayed oyer of accts. Granted.

Judgment confessed by Tho. Wilcox for 500 lbs tobo to Wm. Lowery gent, with costs at exon.

Wm. Bosell gent brought an action of debt agt Jno. Burtell, Adm. of James Burtell dec'd. Deft payed oyer of the bond. Granted.

Then the Court adjourned "tel Tommorrow Ten a Clock."

At a Court held the 16th day May 1717
Present – Majr. John Holloway, Mr. Wm. Lowry,
Mr. Thomas Wythe, Capt. Fra. Ballard,
Mr. John King – His Majt's Justices

Ordered that Thomas Allen as Surveyor of the Highways from Scones Dam to Holmes Bridge, do, between this and next Ct, meet the Surveyor of the Highways of Warwick Co. of that Parish and make the sd bridge according to law.

Ann Phillips, Exectrx of Nicho. Phillips dec'd, agt Johnathon Rogers. Ordered dismist for non- appearance.

Petition of Robert Taylor for License to keep an ordinary at his house in Hampton. Granted giving bond according to law.

John Poole's suit agt Thomas Jones, damage £50. Dismist for non-appearance.

Order granted agt John Brittain and John House Sec for his non-appearance to answer the suit of John Curle, damage 600 lb tobo.

Fra. Ballard, late High Sheriff, and Antho. Armistead, late Church[warden] of Parish of Eliz. City, pltfs. agt William Walker, deft, in an action upon the case to the Ct for Judgmt and arguments being heard. Ct do order that Walker pay Ballard 213 1/2 lbs tobo being the balance with costs.

[p 66] Wm. Dandridge hath this day taken the oath of allegiance and supremacy to his Majt. King George and signed the test and produced a Cert under the Minister and Churchwardens' hands that he has rec'd the Sacrement.

Suit brt by Fra. Ballard and Antho. Armistead etc. agt Tho. Read in an action upon the case for the sum of [blank] tobo by consent of the Justices dismist, deft. paying costs.

Tho. Dawk brt his action upon the case, damages 40 sh. Deft prays time. Granted.

Suit brt by John Smith and Edith his wife agt Henry Irwin Gent in an action of trespass upon the case, damages £100 sterl for an assault and battery. Deft prays Special Imparlence which is granted without giving speciall bayle by the unanimous judgmt of the Ct.

Action of trespass upon the case for an assault and battry, damages £20 brt by Jno. Smith Senr agt Henry Irwin Gent. Deft prayed time. Granted.

Action of trespass upon the case for an assault and battry, damages £5 brt by Jno. Smith agt Henry Irwin gent. Deft prayed time. Granted.

Fra. Ballard, late High Sheriff of Eliz. City Co. and Anthoy. Armistead, late Churchwarden of sd Parish brt their action upon the case agt Jno. Pett. Deft confesses judgmt for paymt of 538 1/2 lbs tobo with costs at exon.

Judgmt confessed by Francis Rogers for 747 lbs tobo to Fra. Ballard, late High Sheriff and Churchwarden of Eliz. City Parish with costs at exon.

Action upon the case, damages £10 sterl brt by Robt. Taylor and Martha his wife agt Jno. Burtell, Adm of James Burtell dec'd for two pieces of stuffe, petitioners making oath they never rec'd any satisfaction. Judgmt is confirmed agt Burtell for delivery to plt with cost.

Judgmt granted agt Saml. Watts for 550 lbs sweet-scented tobo to Cha. Tucker with costs at exon.

[p 67] John Curle's suit agt Charles ?Cluery? Deft prays time to plead. Granted.

Judgmt confessed by Jno. Merrideth for 28 sh unto Antho. Armistead Senr with costs at exon, the plt having taken his oath to the balance.

In the ejecmt brt by Robert Westlock on the demise of Thomas Poole, plt agt Pasco Curle, infant. Whereon James Ricketts and Jane his wife was admitted defts for lands and tenaments in the --- to wit: One dwelling house, one garden, sixty acs land, 30 acs wood and 30 acs of --- land with appurtenances in the Parish and Co. of Eliz. City, which Thomas Poole to the sd Robert had demnified for a term not yet expired, did enter and force him from his farm afsd and did eject and other Enormities to him did do to the great damage of him the sd Robert and agt the peace of our Lord the King that now is, and whereupon Robert by Samuell Selden his Atty complains that when the afsd Tho. Poole the 10th day of May 1715 at Eliz. City had demnified to the afsd Robert the tenemants to be held and occupied by him the sd Robert and his assigns from the first day of the same May until the end of five years not yet expired. The sd Pasco on the 12th day of May 1715 with force and arms, damages £10 current money to which deft pleads not guilty. Whereupon evidence being heard and Jury impanneled finds for the deft. "We find the last will and testament of John Poole dec'd pro and rec in Eliz. City Co. Ct dated 17 Mar 1667 with an endorsement thereon from John Poole the [p 68] younger to Robt. Beverley dated 10 of 8br 1702 and hereunto annexed. We find that sd John Poole the Elder died seized of fee in the land in question. We find pattent granted to Jane Poole dated 6 Apr 1671 of land in question and annexed. We find a deed ack and rec in Eliz. City Co. Ct from Jane Avery to her three sons, vizt Thos. Poole, John Poole and William Poole dated 5 Jan 1688 with indorsement thereon from John Poole to Robt. Beverly dated 23 8br 1701 both of the land in question and hereto annexed. We find a deed from John Poole to Robert Beverly dated 13 8br 1701 of land in question hereto annexed and ack and rec in the Genll Ct. We find the last will and testament of Nicho. Curle hereunto annexed whereon is devised to his son Pasco Curle the land in question. We find that Jane Poole who had been the wife of Jno. Poole the Elder dec'd mother to Tho. and John Poole now living and Wm. Poole now dec'd by her husband the sd John Poole the Elder after the death of sd Poole was marryed to one Henry Avery of this Co. and he died before Jane and she died afterward when she was Avery's widdow and went by the name of Jane Avery at her death. We find an inquisition dated 26th day Nov 1702 under hand and seal of Jerom Ham, Deputie of John Lightfoot Esq, Escheator of Eliz. City Co. and a Jury sworne before him to Enquire whether 474 acs of land late in the possession of Jane Poole did escheat to her Majt and hereunto annexed. We find the land in question to be the 474 mentioned in the inquisition. We find a pattent from Francis Nicholson Govrnr date 16th day Apr 1704 by which the land in the Declr mentioned is granted to sd Thomas Poole, lessor of the plt. We find that Thomas Poole the lessor of the Pltf is the Eldest Son and heir of sd Jane Poole, afterward Jane Avery, and if upon the whole matter the Law be with Pltf, we find for Pltf one shilling damage. If not, we find for the Deft. Joseph Banister foreman. Which on motion of the Parties was ref'd for the matter of law to be augued. Now being called and argument being heard, the Ct considering the same are of the opinion that the law is for the Pltf." Therefore ord that plt recover the lands and tenaments in the declr mentioned which is granted giving sec according to law.

[p 69] Ordered that Thomas Poole pay to Tho. Avery acc to law for 15 days attendance for him agt Pasco Curle with costs at exon.

Tho. Needham and Margt. his wife ack their deeds to Wm. Dandridge, she being privately examined. Adm to rec.

Order granted agt James Naylor and Tho. Balis Sec for his non-appearance to answer the suit of Emanl. Alkin in an action upon the case, damages £4.

Lewis Delany's suit agt Wm. Smelt. The plt being sick and by consent of deft refd to next Ct.

Order granted agt Richd. Adams and John Dunn Sec for non-appearance to answer the suit of Tho. Wood, action on the case, damages £6.

Special Imparlence granted to John Burtell, Adm. of James Burtell dec'd to answer suit of Bartd. Proby, Adm of ---Proby in an acct render for £130.

Order granted agt Thomas Jenings and Cha. Jenings Sec to answer suit of Fra. Ballard in an action of debt for £20.

Richard Kirkin's suit agt Thomas Wilcox, Adm of Eliza. James dec'd, damages £3. Upon motion of plt refd to next Ct for plt to prove his acct.

Richard Kirkin's suit agt Thomas Wilcox, damages £4 in an action upon the case. Parties by consent refer accts to Capt. Henry Jenkins and Charles Jenings to audit and report to next Ct.

John Sampson's suit agt Robert Armistead <u>action case</u> damages 1000 lbs tobo. Ord Thos. Read and Abra. Parish do view the house plt built for deft and return value thereof to next Ct.

Emanuel Alkin's suit agt Thomas Wilcox is ended they being agreed.

[Exact repeat of above entry]

Judgmt by nihil dicell granted agt Edmd. Colwell at the suit of Henry Robinson for action of debt for £4:10.

Presentments agt Fra. Mallory, Ann Myhill, Wm. Hopkins and Mary Bridge refd to next Ct for defts to plead.

Special Imparlence granted to James Ricketts to answer suit of Wm. Westwood by Cha. Jenings his next friend in an action of trespass, damages £100 sterl.

[p 70] George Allen agt Jno. Adduston Rodgers in an action upon the case, damages £3 refd to next Ct.

Order granted agt Richd. Lewis and Thomas Tucker in an action upon the case, damages £20 sterl to answer suit of Edmond Kearny.

Order granted Johnathan ?Clift? and Richd. Kirkin Senr to answer suit of Thomas Wood in action upon the case, Damages £40.

Thomas Wood's suit agt Jno. Knott in action upon the case for £6:11:3 3/4 refd to next Ct for Mr. Servant to be at Ct to prove some matters and ord that he remain in Sheriff's Custody till he gives bails.

Order granted agt Saml. Daniell and George Wauffe Senr to a suit of Emanl. Alkins. action case, damages £4.

Henry Irwin's suit agt Saml. Bosworth dismst. No declr.

Willm. Smelt petitions for an ordinary licence. Granted, giving bond and sec acc to law.

Samuel Smith's suit agt Jno. Burtell, Adm with will annexed of Ja. Burtell dec'd. Deft prays oyer of the bill. Granted.

Order granted agt Bryan Penny and Hind Armistead Sec to answer suit of Fra. Ross, assignee of Margtt. Preist for 300 lbs tobo.

Order granted agt Robert Bright and the Sheriff Sec to answer suit of Richard Kirkin action case, damages £5:2.

Order granted agt Alexandr. Alkins and Richd. Kirkin Sec to answer suit of Thomas Faulkner in action of the case, damages £4.

Edmond Kearny's suit agt Richard Lewis, damages £28 sterl, action being brt to Apll Ct and no declr filed, dismist.

Saml. Selden's suit agt Jno. Roe refd to next Ct to know which action either agt Roe or Ballard was fixt upon the dockett.

Last will & t of Wm. Boutwil is pro by the oath of John Skinner, one of the wit and James Naylor being sworn to prove his brother Thomas Naylor's hand, one of the wit and also declares he heard Boutwil
[p 71] desire Mr. George Walker to make his will and ord to be rec. Exec being sworn, probate is granted by giving bond etc. Ordered that est be appr by Edward Lattemore, Thomas Tucker, Robert Bright and Cha. Cooper or any three and ret appr to next Ct.

Wilson Curle by James Ricketts etc. Petition agt John Curle etc refd to next Ct.

Simon Hollier and Joseph Banister's acct of James Burtell's est refd to next Ct for acct to be considered.

John Holloway Signed. Test: Cha. Jenings CClk.

At a Court held the 3rd Wed June
being the 19th day 1717
Present - Mr. Wm. Lowery, Capt. Francis Ballard,
Mr. Antho. Armistead, Mr. Thomas Tabb, Mr. Thomas Wythe, Mr. John King, Mr. Mark Johnson
His Majt's Justices

William Boswell gent is sworn High Sheriff of this Co. of Eliz. City acc to the Govrns' Commission and entered into bond to perform his office and ack the same. Jno. Dunn and Robert Brough are sworn his Subsheriffs.

Richard Lewis' p of atty to Mr. Robert Tucker pro by oath of Henery Irwin gent and ordered recorded.

Upon motion of Mr. Robert Tucker, Capt. Henry Jenkins is ordered to be recorded his Atty.

Janny, a negr girl belonging to Richard Hopkins is adjudged to be seven years old and to pay Levy acc to law.

Appr of Matthew Watts est is ret and ordered recorded.

Henry Irwin's suit agt Robert Moss is dismst, no declr being filed.

Henry Irwin's suit agt Robert Mewden is dismst, no declr being filed.

Upon petition of Robert Mew agt Henry Irwin for Lying in Prison at sd Irwin's suit and no declr being filed agt him, ordered that he be set at Lyberty.

Upon petition of Saml. Miles for to be acquitted from paying his Levy for the future. Granted.

[p 72] Petition of Jno. Loyall as marrying Hannah Scott for her est. Ordered that Madam Wallace be summoned to next Ct to answer petition.

In the suit in Chancery brt by Mary Cary complnt agt William Dandridge respondent for £500 sterl. Upon request of Mr. Thos. Wythe suit refd to next Ct because neither the Respnt nor Majr. Holloway who is his Atty is here.

In the suit brt by Thomas Wood agt Noah Barefoot in an action upon the case for £13 and one penny 1/2 penny the Ct settling accts between them ordered deft pay plt £12:12:11, it being balance due with costs at exon.

Upon petition of James Thompson, Mariner, agt est of Jno. Schaverall for £3:4 for funeral charges and he having returned an acct of the sd est, ordered that Mr. Jos. Banister appr est that is shewed him by Thompson and ret appr to next Ct & that Thompson be pd out of the same.

At a Ct held the 3rd Wed of July being the 17th day 1717. The orders of the last Ct was read and then the Ct. proceeded to business. Present – Majr. John Holloway, Mr. William Bayley, Mr. John Bayley, Capt. Fra. Ballard, Mr. Tho. Wythe, Mr. Simon Hollier, Mr. John King, Mr. Antho. Armistead, Mr. Mark Johnson – His Majt's Justices.

Upon motion of John Burtell Adm of James Burtell dec'd agt Joseph Banister and Simon Hollier praying to have Banister and Hollier's accts agt est settled. Ct ord ... due to Banister £24:10 and £6:10. Ordered that Banister and Hollier retain so much in their hands as will satisfy sd sums.

[p 73] Ordered that Banister and Hollier deliver the remainder of est to Adm of James Burtell dec'd.

Judgmt by nihil dicet granted agt Saml. Watts to answer suit of Hind Armistead and Hanah his wife, Exectrx of Matthew Watts dec'd in an action upon the case for £10.

Judgmt by nihil dicel granted agt Hind Armistead to answer the suit of Saml. Watts in an action upon the case for £40.

Judgmt by nihil dicet granted agt John Byresee to answer Wm. Smelt in and action upon the case for £5 sterl.

Francis Ballard, one of the Execs of Bartd. Servant dec'd praying to have accts of est audited, Ct ordered petition be granted and appt Mr. Tho. Wythe and Mr. Jno. King Gent to audit and ret to next Ct.

Upon the motion of Coffee a Negro Man praying to have some relief being in a miserable condition concerning his ulcerated leg. Ct ord Robt. Taylor take care of the Negro Man and endeavor to get his leg cured.

John Sweetman's suit agt Wm. Weston in an action upon the case damages £35 current money dismist, plt not producing his accts.

The action of accts render for £150 brt by Bartd. Proby Adm of Petr. Proby dec'd agt Fra. Ballard. Auditors report in these words that the sd Ballard would not account alleging that he owed Peter nothing. Ct ord that deft do acct upon oath before Mr. Tho. Wythe, Mr. Jos. Banister and Mr. Geo. Walker or any two of them, plt giving deft four days notice. Report to be ret to next Ct.

The last will and testament of Humphrey Balis is hereby pro by oath of --- Balis, John Whitfield and Tho. Poole, wit. Cert for pro gr Exec giving bond etc & ordered will rec & est appr between this and next Ct by Mr. Edwd. Lattemore, James Naylor and Wm. Coopland or any two of the & ret appr to next Ct.

Edwd. Lattemore brt his action of trespass damages £10 agt Phillip Prescott. Deft prays time. Granted.

Thos. Wood brt his action upon the case for £3:2:4 agt Richd. Kirkin. Refd to next Ct.

Judgmt granted agt John Curle for 234 lbs tobo to Cha. Jenings he having made oath that he never had any satisfaction.

[p 74] John Curle brt his action of trespass damage £100 sterl agt Jno. Jones. Plt not appearing, dismist with costs at exon.

Robt. Wells action upon the case agt Saml. Bromage. Pltf prays time to consider deft pleas. Granted.

Suit brt by Saml. Selden agt Fra. Ballard in an action of trespass damages £10 sterl. Several orders for survey not being complied with, ordered Sheriff to summon a Jury to meet the Surveyor on the land in controversy and lay out land on the 2nd Tuesday in Aug if fair etc. having regard to Pattens and evidence and ord if Jury see fit to lay out any other lands relating to the Cause & a Justice is desired to be there. Retnble to next Ct.

Wm. Allen's suit agt Antho. Armistead Junr action trespass damages £10 sterl. Deft pleads not guilty. Refd to next Ct.

Tho. Howard's suit agt Thomas Baccas is ended between themselves.

Judgmt by nihil dicet granted agt Mary Frizel to answer the suit of William Smelt in an action upon the case for £1.

Mrs. Margreat Bayley, wido, ack her lease and release for Town land to Henry Irwin Gent. Ordered recorded.

In the suit brt by Saml. Neele and Kort. his wife agt Thomas Roberts in an action of debt for 40 sh, plts making oath they never received any satisfaction. Judgmt confirmed agt deft and Tho. Ryland Sec with costs at exon.

Robt. Armistead's suit agt James Marke for 40 sh cont to next Ct.

Capt. Henry Jenkins enters himself special bayle for Jno. Vilage to pay condemnation of Ct if lost in the suit brt by Richd. Hopkins. Deft not appearing, judgmt granted by nihil dicet agt Vilage to answer.

Antho. Armistead Senr ack his lease & release for Town land to Robt. Minson. Also Ann his wife came into Ct and relinquished her right of dower. Ordered recorded.

Suit brt by Brian Penny agt Josa. Curle Junr in an action upon the case for £5:10:06 and several orders of attchmt being awarded plt but not executed. Ordered that attchmt be granted him. Ret to next Ct for further proceedings.

[p 75] Charles Chiswell gent agt Saml. Sweny in an action upon the case, damages £20, deft pleads he owes nothing. Refd to next Ct.

Judgmt granted by nihil dicett agt Geo. Luke and Mary his wife to answer the suit of Emanl. Aikin in an action upon the case, damages £12.

Ordered that Saml. Neale pay to Nicho. Benton for his one days attendance as an evidence agt Thomas Roberts with costs at exon, the deft not to pay this charge.

Cha. Jenings' suit agt Thomas Read and Ann his wife action case, damages 600 lbs tobo. Ordered attchmt be confirmed at next Ct.

Richd. Basford's suit agt Benja. Smith in an action upon the case damages £3. Deft pleads he owes nothing. Refd to next Ct for trial.

Richd. Basford's suit agt James Ricketts is dismist, parties being agreed.

Richd. Basford's suit agt Thomas Curle in an action upon the case damages 200 lbs tobo. Parties refer the cause to the Ct for trial. Ct ordered suit be dismist.

William Allen ack his deed for Town land to Jno. Robinson and his heirs. Also Erwin his wife came into Ct & relinquished her right of dower. Ordered recorded.

The presentment of the Grand Jury agt James Naylor is dismst, paying costs at exon.

Upon the motion of William Westwood for turning of the Highway that lies southward of his house at the Church, the same being considered that it was very prejudicial to the Plantation. Ordered that Westwood have liberty to stop the sd road and bridge.

Wm. Westwood is appt Surveyor of the Highway from Broad Creek Bridge to Scowins Dam Bridge.

[p 76] James Ricketts & Extrs & suit agt Jno. Burtell Adm & of James Burtell. Action upon the case damages £60. Ordered plt amend his declr. When done deft pleads nothing is due. Ord accts be auditted by Mr. Saml. Sweney, Jos. Wragg & Mr. Henry Irwin and ret to next Ct.

Upon petition of Edward Andross to chose his gdn and makes choice of Charles Jenings. Granted.

Ordered est of James Burtell dec'd pay Thomas Howard for four days attendance at the appraisal of Burtell's est with costs at exon.

Petition of Elizabeth Hill for a license to keep an Ordinary at her house in Hampton Town. Granted provided she pay all fees and give bond & security.

Then the Court adjourns till to morrow ten a Clock.

At a Court held the 18th July 1717

Majr. Jno. Holloway, Mr. Wm. Lowery, Mr. Jno. Bayley, Capt. Fra. Ballard, Mr. Thos. Wythe, Mr. Antho. Armistead Mr. Mark Johnson, Mr. Simon Hollier — His Majts Justices

Petition of Emanl. Alkin agt est of Ja. Burtell for £5:09 dismist.

Thomas Howard agt Tho. Wilcox action upon the case damages £6. Special bayle demanded. It is thought not reasonable. Judgmt granted by nihil dicet agt deft.

Cha. Jenings attachmt agt Geo. Luke for £5:2:6 continued.

Jno. Smith's suit agt Antho. Armistead Senr. Deft pleads he owes nothing. Ordered refd to next Ct for tryall.

[p 77] Henry Batts agt Joseph Wragg, action upon the case damages £6. Judgmt granted by nihil dicet agt deft.

Judgmt by nihil dicet granted agt Jos. Wragg to answer the suit of Henry Batts for £6.

Judgmt granted by nihil agt Jno. Burtell Adm & to answer suit of Charles Jenings in action of debt for 3000 lb tobo.

Judgmt confessed to Wm. Boswel agt Jno. Burtell Adm etc for £35 current money. To be paid out of assets of Burtell's est with costs at exon.

Judgmt confessed agt Jno. Brittin for 346 lbs tobo to John Curle with costs at exon.

Judgmt granted by nihil dicet agt Thomas Roberts to answer the suit of Thomas Dawk.

Judgmt by nihil dicet granted agt Henry Irwin Gent to answer the suit of John Smith and Edith his wife in action of trespass for assault & battery, damages £100.

Judgmt by nihil dicet granted agt Henry Irwin Gent to answer the suit of John Smith in an action of trespass for assault and battery, damages £5 sterling.

Judgmt by nihil dicet granted agt Henry Irwin Gen to answer suit of John Smith in an action of trespass, damages £10 sterling.

Judgmt granted agt James Naylor in an action upon the case, damages £4. Deft not appearing the plt making oath to his acct. Ordered deft pay £1:07 being the balance with costs.

[p 78] Suit of Lewis Delany agt Wm. Smelt in an action upon the case damages £30 current money. Parties consent to appt Mr. Merritt Sweny and Mr. Peter Parker to view the dwelling house of deft where he lives to see whether the work be finished acc to the agreemt & ordered to report to next Ct.

Barto. Proby Adm of Tho. Proby dec'd agt John Burtel Adm with will annexed of James Burtell dec'd in an action of accts. Render damage £130. Deft consents to answer before audittors. Mr. Tho. Wythe, Mr. Geo. Walker and Mr. Joseph Banister are to audit & report to next Ct.

In a suit brt by Fra. Ballard agt Thomas Jenings in an action of debt for £10 current money. Complaint refd to

Capt. Henry Jenkins to settle accts between them & report to next Ct.

Richd. Kirkin agt Tho. Wilcox. Parties not appearing, dismist.

John Sampson agt Robt. Armistead in action of debt 1000 lb tobo. By consent of parties refd to next Ct.

Henry Robinson agt Edwd. Colwil in an action of debt £4:10. Deft pleading, plt prays time to consider. Granted.

The Presentmt of the Grand Jury agt Fra. Malory and Ann Mihill for living in common adultry, deft pleads not guilty. Refd to next Ct for tryall.

Presentmt of the Grand Jury agt Wm. Hopkins & Mary Bridge for living in common adultry. Defts pleading not guilty, refd to next Ct for tryall.

Wm. Westwood by Cha. Jenings his next friend in action of trespass £100 sterl agt James Ricketts, deft appearing & not pleading. Judgmt granted by nihil dicet agt deft.

[p 79] George Allen agt John Adderston Roger dismist, parties being agreed.

Edward Kerny agt Richd. Lewis in an action upon the case damages £28 sterl. Capt. Henry Jenkins appearing in behalf of deft & Sec & prays that the last Ct order agt deft & Sec may be confessed as it is till next Ct & he undertakes then to plead if the cause is not agreed & consents if he does not then plead that then the judgmt shall be confessed agt deft & Sec.

Judgmt by nihil dicet granted agt Johnathen Clift to answer the suit of Tho. Wood in an action upon the case damage 40 sh.

Tho. Wood agt John Knott in an action upon the case damage £4. Deft pleads he does not owe so much of the acct. Refd to next Ct for tryall.

Judgmt by nihil dicet granted agt John Burtell Adm of James Burtell dec'd to answer suit of Saml. Smith in an action of debt for £35:10.

Judgmt confessed by Brian Penny for 300 lbs tobo acc to specialty to Fra. Rose, assignee of Margt. Prest with costs at exon. Ordered exon be stayed till Novembr next coming.

Judgmt confessed by Alexdr. Alkins for £2:00:07 1/2 penny to Tho. Faulkner with costs at exon. Exon to be stayed two months by consent of plt's atty.

Bartholomew Selden by Saml. Selden his next friend brt an action of trespass damage £10 current money agt John Roe deft for pulling down the hedge of plt as is set forth in the Declr, to which deft pleads not guilty & several orders for survey not being complied with. Ord Sheriff summon Jury to meet the Survey of Co. for land in contention on the 2nd Tuesday in Aug or second Wed if faire if not on next fair day etc.

James Ricketts & His wife as Gdns to Pasco Curle infant. Petition agt John Curle concerning his Detayning (sic) of Pasco's cattle. By consent dismist.

[p 80] Judgmt confessed by Cha. Avery for paymt of £16:01:04 to Cha. Jenings with costs at execution only execution stayed two months.

Judgmt gr agt John King Gent for paymt of £4:18:09 1/2 and 1655 lbs tobo to William Smelt, which Smelt confessed to take 9 bbls tarr & 4 bbls pitch in lieu of tobo.

In the suit brt by James Servant agt Tho. Baddely action upon the case damage £12, the deft appears in discharge of his Security & confessed the acct. Judgmt gr plt & by plt he is suffered to go at large.

In the suit in Chancery brt by Mary Cary agt Wm. Dandridge and Euphan his wife for £500 sterl. Respondents pleading time to join in. Ct gives the Respondents time till next Ct to consider the Demurrer.

Emanl. Alkin's suit agt Mark Parish & Temperance his wife is ord dismst, the male deft being "ded."

Imparlance granted Michael Peirce to answer the suit of Mary Savoy action on the case damage £3.

The Ct having viewed the stops at the Courthouse doors ordered that Saml. Sweny be paid for same £4, which Capt. Bosell is to pay £3 on his own acct & the parish the remainder for the County for which County is to repay him at laying the next Levy in discount, he owing the County £5.

[p 81] **At a Court held the 3rd Wednesday of Augt being the 21st day 1717**
Present: Mr. Wm. Lowery, Capt. Fra. Ballard, Mr. Simon Hollier, Mr. John King, Mr. Mark Johnson – Justices

Upon the petition of Cornelas Dolich & Rachel his wife to keep an ordinary at his town house in Hampton. Granted giving bond & security.

In the suit brt by Fra. Bracey his next friend agt John Burtell, Admr of James Burtell dec'd, in an action upon the case damage £5. Deft failing to appear, attachmt awarded plt with cost. Ret to next Ct for further tryall.

The action upon the case damage £80 brt by Jno. Smith Senr agt John Burtell, Admr of James Burtell dec'd, the deft prays oyer of the acct. Granted.

Robert Taylor's suit agt Richd. Kirkin in an action upon the case damage £50, imparlance granted deft.

John Burtell, Admr of James Burtell dec'd. Petition agt Simon Hollier & Joseph Banister for detaining the est in their hands, Mr. Hollier not having notice. Ordered petition be referd for former order to be complied with.

Joshua Curle Senr bringing his acct of charges agt his servant Margreat Seeton for absenting herself from his services. Acct amounts to 16 shilling & 3 pence & 400 lbs tobo for taking of her up twice & being absent 8 weeks. Ordered that Margt. serve her Master for satisfaction of that time after her time is expired by Indenture.

Henry Robinson's suit agt Saml. Selden in an action of debt damage £100 sterl, deft prays oyer of the writing. Granted.

Joshua Curle Senr enters himself Security or Speciall Bayle to pay the condemnation of the Ct if lost in the suit brt by Brian Penny agt Joshua Curle Junr in an action upon the case for £5:10 and thereupon ord that the Negr. woman that is attached be returned to sd Curle Junr.

Special imparlence gr to Emanl. Alkin to answer the suit of Mary Henderson in an action upon the case for Salt and Battry [sic] damage £10.
[Note: this entry is repeated by the Clerk.]

[p 82] Non-suit granted to John Burtell, Admr of James Burtell dec'd, agt Robt. Tannoch in an action upon the case damage £6 silver money, the plt filing no declaration. Ord Tannoch pay same to Burtell with costs at exec.

Order granted agt John Knot & Thos. Wood his Security for his non-appearance to answer the suit of Thos. Howard in an action upon the case £2.

Emanl. Alkin's suit agt Fra. Ballard gent in an action upon the case damage £50. Deft prays time to next Ct. Granted.

Mark Johnson gent. Suit agt Thos. Wood in an action upon the case damage £10. Deft confessed judgmt for paymt of £4, being the balance with costs at exec, only exec stayed two months.

Upon the petition of John Massenburgh for his wife's est in hands of Matthew Small. Ordered Small be summoned to next Ct to answer the petition.

Non-suit granted to John Standly agt Benj. Hill & Eliza. his wife, the plt failing to file their declaration, with costs at exec.

In a suit brt by Antho. Armistead gent agt Fra. Ballard gent in an action upon the dase damage £500 sterling, deft appears & prays an Imparlence. Granted.

Wm. Malory's suit agt Richd. Kirkin action of debt for £1:3, deft not appearing. Order granted agt deft & Jno. Merrideth Security.

William Smelt's suit agt James Servant & Tho. Wilcox in action of debt damage £12, deft not appearing. Order granted agt deft Robt. Taylor & Thos. Roberts their Security.

Imparlence granted to Antho. Armistead Senr to answer Fra. Ballard in action of debt for 3021 lbs tobo.

Francis Ballard's suit agt Antho. Armistead Senr in action of debt for 546 lbs tobo, deft prays imparlence. Granted.

Imparlence granted to Eliza. Goodwyn & Wm. More, Execs of Jno. More gent dec'd, to answer suit of Fra. Ballard in an action upon the case for 1426 lbs tobo.

Francis Ballard gent brt his action upon the case damage £40 agt John Burtell, Admr of James Burtell dec'd. Deft prays oyer of acct. Granted.

Imparlence granted Emanl. Alkin to answer the suit of Francis Ballard gent in an action upon the case damage £13.

Imparlence granted Emanl. Alkin to answer the suit of Francis Ballard gent in an action upon the case damage 2000 lbs. tobo.

Fra. Ballard's suit agt John Burtell, Admr of James Burtell dec'd, in an action upon the case damage 1400 lbs tobo, deft prays oyer of acct. Granted.

[p 83] Upon the Summons by Scire facias brt by Nicho. Curle gent, late Naval Officer of the Lower District of James River late dec'd, her Maj. Queen Ann and the Governr. of this Dominion agt Francis Ballard & John King Gent, Security for John Vanburgh for £100 sterl, wherin the Pltf

recovered Judgmt agt Vanburgh, defts prays time to next Ct to put in their Plea. Granted.

Wm. Loyall & Eliza. his wife came into Ct & ack their deed of gift for land to John Massenburgh. Ordered recorded.

The inv of Humphrey Balis' est being ret, ordered the est be appr by Edwd. Lattimore, Tho. Tucker & John Parish. Ret to next Ct.

Then the Ct adjourned to the Ct in cource. Wm. Lowery Signed.

At a Court held the 3rd Wednesday of Septembr the 16 day 1717
Present: Majr. John Holloway, Mr. William Lowery, Mr. Simon Hollier, Mr. John Bayley, Mr. Thomas Wythe, Mr. Mark Johnson – Justices

Upon petition of John Wallace to keep an ordinary. Granted giving bond & security.

Upon petition of Sarah Robinson to keep an ordinary. Granted giving bond & security.

In suit brt by Hind Armistead & Hanah his wife, Execs of Mathw. Watts dec'd, pltfs agt Saml. Watts in an action upon the case damage £10 sterl, deft prays time to next Ct. Granted.

Suit brt by Saml. Watts agt Hind Armistead in an action of trespass damage £40, deft pleads not guilty. Ordered refd to next Ct for trial.

Upon petition of Charles Powers to be discharged from being Constable, it's ordered petition be granted & that Fra. Malory be sworn Constable in his room in sd Persinks [sic].

Martin Bean is appt Constable for Back River & to be sworn.

Upon petition of Martha Hill, orphan of Justinian Hill dec'd, for her est in hands of Cha. Powers being spent. It's ordered that Cha. Powers pay & deliver to plt all & singular her est according to Bill & appraismt.

Wm. Smelt brt his action upon the case damage £5 sterl agt John Byreree. Deft pleads not guilty & parties consenting to refer cause to the Ct. Ct ordered suit be dismist with costs at exec.

[p 84] Upon petition of Capt. Fra. Ballard to have his acct agt Mr. Servant's est admitted. It's ordered that former order be continued.

Barto. Proby, Admr of Peter Proby dec'd, brt action agt Fra. Ballard, acct render for £150, which upon return of acct is ordered dismist.

Edward Lattemore agt Phillip Prescott in action of trespass damage £10 sterl, refd to next Ct for tryal.

Saml. Selden agt Fra. Ballard in action of trespass damage £10 sterl. Jury's Verdict being returned, plt moved to have verdict recorded, which was opposed by deft. Ct's opinion is Verdict ought not to be received or recorded, but ord that James Servant & Fra. Ballard attend at next Ct to answer to such exceptions as Henry Jenkins has excepted, the sd Servant with his wife.

The presentment of the Grand Jury agt Wm. Hopkins & Mary Bridge for living in common Adultery to which defts plead not guilty. A Jury being impanneled, namely: John Curle etc [sic] & no evidences being here to prove the fact, the Jury "withdrawed" & return verdict "We of the Jury find deft not guilty." Verdict recorded & presentment dismist.

Ordered that Wm. Spicer & Edwd. Jones be summoned to next Ct to show cause if any why judgmt should not be confessed agt them for their non-appearance to give evidence between our Sov. Lord the King, Wm. Hopkins & Mary Bridge.

Upon petition of Tho. Allen to be discharged from being Surveyor of the High Ways. Ordered he be acquitted & Alexr. Carver be appt Surveyor of sd Persink [sic].

Upon petition of Temperance Parish, wido, to have husband's will probated, ordered that Abr. Parish the deceased's son be ordered to next Ct to have will proved.

Robt. Wells brt his action upon the case damage £10 sterl agt Saml. Bromage. Ordered refd to next Ct for deft to reply.

In the suit brt by Wm. Allen agt Antho. Armistead Junr wherein Hanah Armistead is Admrx, deft in an action of trespass damage £10 sterl, to which deft pleads not guilty. It's ordered that the Sheriff summon a Jury to meet the Surveyor on the land in controversy and lay out the same on the second Tuesday in Oct. etc. Ret to next Ct.

Wm. Smelt's suit agt Mary Frizell in an action upon the case damage 40 shill. Deft pleads she owes nothing. Ordered refd to next Ct for tryal.

[p 85] Richd. Hopkins brt his action of trespass upon the case damage £50 sterl agt John Velage. Deft pleads he owes nothing. Refd to next Ct for tryal.

Brian Penny's suit agt Joshua Curle Junr in an action upon the case for £5:10. Deft prayed Liberty to plead as many mattrs. as he thinks fit. Gr. Plt prays time. Granted.

Cha. Chickwell brt his action agt Saml. Sweny. Refd to next Ct.

The action upon the case brt by Emanl. Alkin agt Geo. Luke Esqr & Mary his wife for £12 silver money refd to next Ct.

Suit brt by James Ricketts & Jane his wife, Execs of Nicho. Curle gent dec'd, agt John Burtell Admr of James Burtell dec'd, in an action upon the case damage £60. Auditors returned their audit. It's refd till tomorrow for Mr. Ricketts to be at Ct.

Judmt by Nihill Dicet is confessed agt Tho. Wilcox for what shall appear due at next Ct at the suit of Thomas Howard. Same being £3:7 1/2.

Charles Jenings' action of debt for £5:2:6 agt George Luke Esqr. Ordered attchmt be continued.

Suit brt by Jno. Smith Senr agt Antho. Armistead gent in action upon the case damage £20. Plt not having his Evidences at Ct & making oath that they were very "meteareall." Ordered suit refd to next Ct to produce evidences.

Henry Batts' action upon the case damage £6 agt Joseph Wragg. Deft pleads he owes nothing. Refd to next Ct for tryall. [Note: This entry repeated by Clerk.]

Cha. Jenings brt an action upon the case damage 3000 lbs tobo agt John Burtell, Admr of James Burtell dec'd, being due for Clerk's fees. Deft prays time to answer. Granted.

Judgmt is confessed by Tho. Roberts for paymt of £1:18:6 unto Tho. Dawk with costs at exec.

John Smith & Edith his wife brt action of trespass for an assault & battery damage £100 sterl agt Henry Irwin gent. Refd to next Ct for tryall.

John Smith brt his action of trespass for assault & battery damage £20 agt Henry Irwin gent. Refd to next Ct for tryal.
[Note: two entries follow for John Smith agt Henry Irwin as above: one for £10 and again for £5.]

Suit brt by Jno. Curle agt Cha. Avery in action of debt for 600 lbs tobo. Deft pleads he owes nothing. Ordered refd to next Ct for trial.

[p 86] Lewis Delany's suit agt William Smelt action of the case damage £30 current money, the former Viewers not agreeing. It's ordered that John Holland & Merritt Sweny view the house where deft now lives to see if work be finished according to their agreemt, which after consent of Parties be submitted to Majr. Holloway for determination. After considering the matter it's ordered suit be dismist.

Barto. Proby Adm of Jas. Proby dec'd agt Jno. Burtell Adm of James Burtell dec'd, action of accot render for £130. Former order for audit not being complied with, ordered that Geo. Walker, Saml. Sweny & Joseph Wragg or any two of them audit acct. Rep to next Ct.

Fra. Ballard's suit agt Tho. Jenings. Action of debt for £10. Accts being submitted to Capt. Henry Jenkins to settle but not performing the same, continued to next Ct.

Henry Robinson's suit agt Edwd. Colwill. Action of debt for £4:10. Plt putting in his replication, deft prays time. Granted.

Wm. Westwood by Cha. Jenings his next friend brought his action of trespass agt James Ricketts for £100 sterl (for trespass committed upon plt's land as it is set forth in the declr.) Ordered that the Sheriff summon an able Jury to meet on land in controversy on 4 Octbr etc. and further order that deft commit no more waste till tryall be ended.

In the suit brt by Edmd. Kerny agt Richard Lewis in an action upon the case damage £20 sterl, the deft pleading, plt prays time. Granted.

Presentmt [of] Grand Jury agt Fra. Malory & Ann Miles etc. ordered refd to next Ct for tryall.

Emanl. Alkin's suit agt Saml. Daniel damage £4, plt not being here, refd to next Ct.

Judgmt granted agt John Burtell Adm of James Burtell dec'd for £30:10 to Saml. Smith with costs, he having proved his debt by Certificate under the Clerk's hand of Norfolk Co.

Dart. Selden's suit brt by Saml. Selden his next friend agt John Roe in action of trespass damage £10 for stopping the Chaine for Surveying the plt's land, and plt failing to prosecute. Non-suit granted deft.

The Court adjourns till tow morrow Ten a Clock. John Holloway signed.

At a Court held 19th day September 1717
Present: Majr. John Holloway, Mr. William Lowery, Mr. Simon Hollier, Mr. Antho. Armistead, Mr. Tho. Wythe, Mr. Mark Johnson - Justices

Majr. John Holloway, Mr. Edmond Kerny and Mr. Wm. Smelt ack a bond for William Dandridge for Coll. Wm. Wilson, Wilson Rascow & Euphan his wife's estate, the wido. of Wilson Rascow, for their estates. Ordered recorded.

Upon petition of William Dandridge for Letters of Adm of Euphan his wife's est and Wilson Rascow's est and Adm unadministered upon by the sd Euphan, ordered petition be granted.

Upon motion of Robert Taylor agt Simon Hollier & Jos. Banister for delivery of James Burtell's est, ordered that Cha. Jenings & Jos. Wragg meet and examine inv, apprsmt, and outcry of the est & ret report to next Ct.

Then the Court adjourns to the Court in Cource. John Holloway.

At a Court held the 3rd Wednesday of October
being the 16th day 1717
Present: Mr. Simon Hollier, Mr. John King, Mr.
Mr. Tho. Wythe, Mr. Mark Johnson - Justices

The last will of Robert Bright Senr proved by oaths of Stephen Lillis, one of the witnesses thereto, who also swears he saw Tho. Naylor dec'd, one of the other witnesses, also sign. Cert of probate to Exec & ordered recorded.

Elizabeth Tabb wido. came into Ct & ack a deed of gift to Edwd. Tabb. Ordered recorded.

The last will of Tho. Tabb Gent dec'd proved by oaths of Henry Howard, William Tabb & Richd. Slater, witnesses. Cert of probate granted to Exec, giving bond etc & ordered recorded. To be appr by Mr. Wm. Lowery, Mr. Tho. Wythe, Mr. Simon Hollier & Mr. Tho. Merry or any two of them. Ret to next Ct, the Extr being sworn according to law.

Wm. Lowery Signe.

At a Court held the 3rd Wednesday of December
being the 16th day 1717

Present: Mr. Wm. Lowery, Capt. Francis Ballard, Mr.
Simon Hollier, Mr. Antho. Armistead, Mr. John
Bayley, Mr. Mark Johnson – Justices

[p 88] Robert Minson came into Ct & ack his deeds for Town land to John Middleton. Ordered recorded.

Power of Atty from Mr. Jno. Croft to his wife is proved by oath of Grisham Salter, that he saw Croft sign, seal & deliver the power & that he saw Thomas Johnson, the other wit, witness the same. Ordered recorded.

Ordered that Mr. Thomas Merry be Surveyor of the Highways to clear from John Merritt's to Scones? Dam the convenient way that he shall think fit.

William Baylis ack his deeds to James Browne & ack bond to Browne for performance. Ordered recorded.

Ordered that Alexander Carver do forthwith clear the road from Scones? Dam to Warwick Co., to Richard Cursell's along the ancient road.

Robert Westlock's ejectmt agt Wm. Symons. Alexander Avery made oath to the service etc of --- declr upon tenant in possession.

Ordered that Charles Cooper be Surveyor for the plantation where Wm. Cox did live to Broad Cr Bridge.

Upon petition of Ann Andrews for her share of est. Ordered she be paid the same according to the Outcry.

Upon presentmt of the Grand Jury agt Francis Mallory & Ann Myhill for living in adultery and they pleading not guilty and two evidences being sworn agt defts. Jury impanneled, namely: Henry Robinson etc [sic] & ret verdict: Vizt: Wee of the Jury doe find the Defendts not Guilty, Jno. Armistead foreman. On motion of defts it is reorded & ordered dismist.

Power of Atty of Wm. Roberts etc [sic] to Mr. Henry Irwin is proved by oath of John Wallace & affirmation of Joseph Wragg, wits. Ordered recorded.

[p 89] Ordered that a Grand Jury be sworn. Eighteen men sworn & received their Charge, went upon their Presentments, but being too Late noe Presentmts returned.

Upon motion of the Sheriff, the Ct appts the Levy to be Laid the 1st day of January next coming and the notice be given.

Upon motion of Wm. Westwood Surveyor from Broad Cr Bridge to Scowins Dam alledging that he has not help sufficient in his persincks to repair the road, ordered that motion be refd to a fuller Ct.

The Court adjourns till Tomorrow Ten a Clock.

At a Court held the 19th day of February being the 3rd Wednesday 1717
Present: Mr. Wm. Lowery, Mr. Antho. Armistead, Mr. John Bayley, Mr. Thomas Wythe, Mr. John King
His Majestie's Justices

Wm. Jones' deeds to James Gilbert proved by oaths of George Yeo, John Selden & Samuel White. Ordered recorded.

Emanuel Alkins's suit agt Blanchett is dismist, plt failing to prosecute.

Order granted agt Peter Baker & Henry Irwin Security for his non-appearance to answer the suit of John Burtell Adm of James Burtell dec'd in an action upon the case for 40 shillings.

Saml. Neale's suit agt Johnathan Cliffe is dismist.

Wm. Allen's suit agt John Smith Junr is dismist.

Edward Ballard's suit agt Thomas Ryland is dismist.

Order granted agt Nicholas Preynton? & Jos. Curle Security for his non-appearance to answer the suit of Thomas Roberts in an action on the case for £8.

John Standley's suit agt Thomas Roberts in an action of the case for £10:7 refd to next Ct, Capt. Jenkins his Atty being sick.

John Wallace's suit agt Robert Mew is dismist.

Cornelius Dorlich's suit agt Robt. Mew is ended.

Order granted agt Jos. Banister & the Sheriff his Security to answer the suit of Alexdr. Meckenzie. Action upon the case £28.

[p 90] Order granted agt Thomas Wilcox & Thomas Wood his Security to answer suit of Charles Jenings in action of debt for £12:16.

Jno. Burtell Adm the suit of Edwd. Roe is ended. [sic]

Idem agt Jno. Burtell is ended

Idem agt Robert Armistead is ended.

Order granted agt Andrew Law & the Sheriff for his non-appearance to answer the suit of Jno. Burtell Adm etc of James Burtell action case £6.

Order granted agt John Smith Senr & the Sheriff for his non-appearance to answer the suit of Charles Jenings in an action upon the case damage 3000 lbs tobo.

Robt. Bright Senr. Last will & testament proved by oath of Charles Cooper, one of the witnesses.

Cornels. Dorlich's suit agt James Marshall is ended.

Richard Nusum's suit agt John Phillips is dismist.

Emanuel Alkins' suit agt Jno. Burtell Adm etc of James Burtell dec'd in an action upon the case damage £10. Refd, Capt. Jenkins his atty being sick.

Richard Hopkins atty of Mary Simons, Admstrx of Ja. Simons. Suit agt Jno. Kimbale in an action upon the case £4:18. Order granted agt Kimbal & Abra. Mitchele his Security for non- appearance to answer the suit.

Jno. Kimball's suit agt Robert Mew dismist.

Samuel Selden's summons by Sire [sic] facias agt Robert Armistead. Upon motion of deft, special imparlence granted him.

John Burtell Adm & of Ja. Burtell dec'd suit agt John Bayley is refd to next Ct by reason Capt. Jenkins who is his atty being sick.

Francis Bracy by Wm. Bracy &. Suit agt Joh. Burtell Adm in an action upon the case £5. Refd to next Ct by reason Capt. Jenkins his Atty is sick.

John Smith Senr agt John Burtell Adm & of James Burtell in an action upon the case damage £80. Refd to next Ct by reason Capt. Jenkins his Atty is sick.

[p 91] Judgmt granted by Nihil Dicett agt Richd. Kirkin to answer suit of Robert Taylor in an action upon the case for 50 shillings.

Upon petition of Jno. Burtell Adm of James Burtell dec'd agt Simon Hollier & Joseph Banister for delivery of Burtell's est. Ordered refd to next Ct, Capt. Jenkins being sick.

Action of debt for $100 sterl brt by Henry Robinson agt Saml. Selden is refd to next Ct, Capt. Jenkins being sick.

Mary Henderson's two actions of trespass salt & batry [sic] damage £10 each agt Emanl. Alkin dismist.

Action brt by Brian Penny agt Joshua Curle Junr action upon the case for £4:10:6. Pltf joyning, deft prays time to consider. Granted.

Tho. Howard brt his action upon the case damage £3 agt John Knott. The plt being very sick, ordered refd to next Ct.

The action upon the case damage £50 sterl brt by Emanl. Alkin agt Fra. Ballard ordered refd, Capt. Jenkins being sick.

Upon petition of Jno. Massenburgh agt Mattw. Small for his wife's est. Small not appearing, ordered the Sheriff take Saml. into Custody for his appearance at next Ct.

Judgmt granted by Nihill Dicet agt Francis Ballard in an action upon the case damage £500 at suit of Antho. Armistead.

Wm. Malory action upon the case damage £1:3 agt Richard Kirkin is ordered refd, Capt. Jenkins being sick.

Fras. Ballard agt Antho. Armistead Senr for 3001 lbs tobo being [due] by specialty, refd to next Ct, plt being sick & he paying the Ct's charge.

Fra. Ballard agt Antho. Armistead Senr in action of debt for 546 lbs tobo, deft prays oyer of the bill. Granted.

Fra. Ballard agt Eliza. Goodwyn & Jno. More Execs of Jno. More dec'd in an action upon the case for £183. Refd by plt's request, he paying this Ct's charge.

Fra. Ballard brt his action upon the case agt Jno. Burtell Adm of James Burtell dec'd damage £40. Refd by plt's request he paying this Ct's charge.

Fra. Ballard brt his action upon the case agt Emanl. Alkin for £13. Refd at plts's request &.

Fra. Ballard brt his action upon the case for 2000 lbs tobo agt Emanl. Alkin. Refd at plt's request &.

[p 92] Fra. Ballard brt his action for £14 agt Jno. Burtell Adm of James Burtell dec'd. Upon motion of Pltf refd to next Ct.

Judgmt is confirmed agt James Servant & Tho. Wilcox for £6 to William Smelt with costs of this suit and the cost of the suit that was depending between Smelt & Thomas Baddely alis Ex.

In the Scire Facias brt agt Fra. Ballard & Jno. King Bayle for Jno. Vanburgh in an action of debt on which Judgmt passed agt him for £100 sterl with costs & no cause being shown why execution thereof should not be done on their land & tenements, goods & chattels, ordered execution to issue to Levy the Judgmt.

Cole Diggs gent agt Jno. Burtell Adm of James Burtell dec'd for £14 action upon the case, deft prays oyer of the acct. Granted.

John Smith Senr agt Marg. Prest Exectrx of James Prest dec'd in action upon the case damage 1288 lbs tobo. Refd, Capt. Jenkins being sick.

Wilson Curle Infant by James Ricketts & Jane his wife next friend & agt John Burtell Adm of James Burtell dec'd damage £70 for rent is dismist. No appearance.

Richd. Kirkin agt Alexandr. Alkins in an action upon the case damage £4. The deft appearing in discharge of his Sec whereupon special bayle being demanded & failing to give such, he pleads in custody and confesses Judgmt for £2:2, being balance of acct with costs &.

Richard Kirkin agt Alexdr. Alkins damage £12. Deft pleaded in custody & confesses judgmt only liberty is given deft to bring in his discount of what work he has done for plt. Wm. Allen, Jno. Roe, & Jno. Cook or any two of them to view the work and report to next Ct.

Upon petition of Tho. Batts for his wife's est in the hands of Tho. Jones. Ordered that Jones be summoned to next Ct to answer.

Wm. Creek agt Tho. Wood damage £9. Debt being left at deft's house, upon motion of plt, attachmt granted him.

John Bordland's action upon the case agt Mary ?Randy? refd to next Ct, Capt. Jenkins being sick.

Order granted agt Tho. Wilcox & Jno. Smith Senr damage £30 to answer suit of Richd. Hopkins.

Order granted agt Wm. Coopland & the Sheriff for his non-appearance to answer suit of Hennr. Cock damage £6

[p 93] Order granted agt Tho. Wood & John Wallace Security in an action upon the case damage £5 for Wood's non-appearance to answer the suit of William Smelt.

Order gramted agt Robt. Tennoch & Cha. Moone Security for his non-appearance to answer suit of Wm. Smelt in an action upon the case £3.

Imparlence granted to Brian Penny to answer the suit of [blotted] Kerny in an action upon the case ----.

Suit brt by Hind Armistead, Hanah his wife & Cha. Tucker Execs of Mattw. Watts dec'd agt Saml. Watts damage £10. Refd to next Ct, Capt. Jenkins being sick.

Saml. Watts' action of trespass damage £40 agt Hind Armistead. Refd to next Ct, Capt. Jenkins being sick.

Upon petition of Francis Ballard agt Mr. Servant's estate to have his acct auditted. Ordered refd.

Tho. Frybus orphan of John Frybus being thirteen years old last Septembr is bound as apprentice to Mathew Small until he comes of age. Small to teach the art of a taylor & likewise to read a Chapter in the Bible & Prayers finding Frybus all necessaries. At time of expiration to pay 3000 lbs tobo & cask.

In the suit brt by Edwd. Lattemore agt Phillip Prescott damage £10 trespass. Deft's papers being not to be had being in the hands of Mr. Robt. Hyde their Atty who being dead, ordered suit refd to next Ct.

Saml. Selden agt Fra. Ballard damage £10 trespass. Ordered refd upon deft's request.

Robt. Wells' suit agt Saml. Bromage in an action on the case. Refd to next Ct, Capt. Jenkins, deft's atty, being sick.

Wm. Allen agt Antho. Armistead Junr wherein Hanah Armistead was admitted deft in an action of trespass damage £10 for trespass committed on plt's land. Verdict being ret & rec & no opposition made, judgmt granted plt according to the Verdict with costs at exec.

The presentments of the Grand Jurt being ret, ord the persons presented be summoned to next Ct to answer.

Court adjourned tell Towmorrow Ten a Clock. Wm. Lowery

[p 94]

At a Court held the 20th Febry 1717
Present: Mr. Wm. Lowery, Mr. Antho. Armistead, Mr. Tho. Wythe, Mr. John Bayley, Mr. John King – Justices

In the suit brt by Wm. Smelt agt Mary Frizell in an action on the case damage 40 shillings. Deft pleads she owes nothing and a Jury impanneled, namely: Jno. Armistead, Saml. Sweny, Jno. Cook, Joseph Harriss, Henry Turner, Brian Penny, Wm. Coopland, John Roe, John Bordland, Robt. Minson, Mathw. Small, Tho. Ryland. Arguments were heard and verdict returned: We of the Jury find for the Pltf 19 shillings. Verdict rec & Sheriff ordered to pay same to Plt with costs.

Ordered that Mary Henderson pay to John Roe for his three days attendance as evidence for her agt Eman. Alkins.

Samuel Riddlehurst came into Ct & choosed [sic] his sister Eliza. Riddlehurst to be his Guardian. Granted giving bond & security.

Charles Chiswell gent agt Saml. Irwin damage £20 in an action upon the case refd to next Ct by consent.

Emanl. Alkin agt Geo. Luke & Mary his wife damage £12. Case refd, Capt. Jenkins being sick.

James Ricketts & Jane his wife in behalf of Wilson Curle infant as next friends brt action of debt for rent for £60 agt Jno. Burtell Adm of James Burtell. Refd for want of a Court.

Tho. Howard brt his action upon the case agt Tho. Wilcox. Ordered refd to next Ct., plt being sick.

Ordered William Jones be fined 350 lbs tobo & pay same to Robt. Armistead for failing to appear as evidence on behalf of our Soveraigne Lord the King agt Wm. Hopkins & Mary Bridge.

Wm. Lowry signe

[p 95] At a Court held the 3rd Wednesday of March being the 19th day 1717
Present: Mr. Wm. Lowery, Capt. Fra. Ballard, Mr. Simon Hollier, Mr. Antho. Armistead, Mr. Tho. Wythe, Mr. John Bayley, Mr. John King – Justices

Richd. Hopkins' suit agt John Vilage damage £50 sterl for trespass. Refd to next Ct by request of Deft he paying this Ct's fees.

John Smith and Edith his wife brt their action of trespass salt & batry damage £100 sterl agt Henry Irwin gent. Dismist. No appearance.
Note: following three entries. John Smith agt Henry Irwin. One action for £20 sterling, one for £10 and one for £5. All dismist. No appearance.

John Curle agt Cha. Avery in action of debt for 600 lbs tobo. Issue being joined, refd to next Ct for tryall.

Bartrand Proby Adm of Thomas Proby agt John Burtell Adm of James Burtell dec'd in acct render for £100. Audit not being ret, ordered refd for audit to be returned.

John Smith's suit agt Antho. Armistead Senr in an action upon the case damage £20. Refd to next Ct for want of deft's evidences, he paying this Ct's charges.

Francis Ballard's action of debt agt Tho. Jenings for £10. Ordered refd to next Ct for Capt. Jenkins to file his report.

Wm. Westwood by Cha. Jenings his next friend agt James Ricketts in an action of trespass damage £100 sterl. Verdict being ret, deft prays time to file his Errors. Granted provided he file them tomorrow morning to be argued.

Judgmt granted agt Edwd. Colwill for £4:10 unto Henry Robinson with costs at exec.

In the suit brt by Cha. Jenings Clk of Eliz. City Co. Ct agt John Burtell Adm of James Burtell dec'd in an action upon the case damage 3000 lbs tobo. Ct settling accts, judgmt granted agt John Burtell for 1504 lbs tobo to be paid out of decedent's est with costs alis Ex.

Edmd. Kerny's suit agt Richd. Lewis damage £28 sterl refd to next Ct.

Henry Jenkins by virtue of a power of atty from William Hatchell and Ann his wife ack deed to Thos. Jones, Cordwindr. Ordered recorded.

Tho. Cornelas came into Ct & ack deeds for land in Hampton Town to Richd. Hopkins. Ordered recorded.

[p 96] William Lowery & Fra. Ballard gent, foeffees, ack deeds for town land to John Cooke. Ordered recorded.

Judgmt confirmed agt Johnathan Clift for £1:8:11 to Tho. Wood with costs at exec.

Emanl. Alkin's suit agt Saml. Daniell damage £4 is by consent of the plt refd to next Ct.

Mrs. Mary Cary's Bill in Chancery agt Mr. William Dandridge for £500 sterl dismist. No appearance.

Last will & testament of Stephen Lillis is proved by oath of John Henry Ramburgh and affirmed by Joseph Wragg, witnesses. Cert for probate granted Exec giving bond.

Last will & testament of Mark Parish proved by oaths of Henry Jenkins & John Bayley gent, wits. Cert for probate gr Execs giving Security &. Ordered recorded.

Edwd. Tabb returned his part of appr of Mr. Tho. Tabb's est. Ordered recorded.

Mr. Robt. Armistead's motion to have Majr. Wm. Armistead's est be appr, ordered that whole est be appr by Mr. Jno. King, Mr. Fra. Ballard, Mr. Tho. Wythe & Mr. Joseph Banister or any three of them and ret to May Ct.

Ordered that Mr. Jos. Banister & Mr. James Ricketts appr the est of Elizabeth Prescott dec'd & ret appr to May Ct.

Sarah Wedgeberry is bound to James Servant & Mary his wife till she come to the age of eighteen years or marries, learning Sarah to read & her prayers & to sew, card, spin, nitt, finding her necessaries during her time.

Susanah Wedgeberry is bound to Abr. Mitchel & his wife till she comes to the age of eighteen years or marries, learning Susanah to read & her prayers &.

Upon petition of James Servant for license to keep an ordinary at Point Comfort giving bond &. Granted.

Judgmt renewed agt Brian Penny for 5 shillings & 31 lbs tobo cost upon the former judgmt & cost of this suit to Joshua Curle Junr at exon.

Attchmt granted to Robert Brough agt est of Tho. Wood for 20 shilling in an action upon the case &.

Attchmt gr to Cha. Jenings Clk agt est of Tho. Wood. Ret to next Ct for further Tryall &.

[p 97] Attachmt granted to Henry Robinson agt the est of Tho. Wood for £12. Ret to next Ct for further proceedings.

Suit brt by Cole Digg gent agt John Burtell Adm of James Burtell dec'd in action of debt for £200. Deft prays oyer of the Bond. Granted.

Order granted agt Tho. Wilcox & William Smelt Security for his non-appearance to answer the suit of Thomas Faulkner in an action upon the case damage £10.

In the action of debt brt by Robert Bright agt Thomas Wood, deft not appearing in defense. Upon motion of the plt attchmt gr him agt Wood's est. Ret to next Ct.

In the action upon the case brt by Margreat Bayley agt Thomas Wood, deft not appearing. Attchmt granted her agt Wood's est. Ret to next Ct.

Special Imparlence gr to Francis Ballard at the suit of William Lowery in an action upon the case damage 1250 lbs tobo.

In an action upon the case brt by Benja. Hill & Eliza. his wife agt Tho. Wood, deft not appearing. Attchmt granted agt Wood's est. Ret to next Ct.

Order granted agt Mary Frizell & Execs of Peter Baker as Security to answer the suit of Margreat Bayley in an action upon the case 40 shillings.

Order granted agt Ralph ?Seba? & James Ricketts his Security to answer the suit of Mathew Small damage 50 shillings.

Order granted agt Tho. Wilcox & Robert Armistead Security to answer the suit of Robert Minson in an action upon the case for 55 shillings.

Suit brt by Brian Penny agt Geo. Pane in an action upon the case damage £5. Deft not appearing, attchmt granted plt agt Pane's est &.

Imparlence granted to James Ricketts to answer the suit of Mathew Small in an action upon the case £4:14.

Judgmt confessed by Robt. Mew for 20 -- to Antho. Armistead Junr with costs at exec.

Judgmt confessed by Robt. Mew for £4:10 to Wm. Newberry with costs at exec.

Order granted agt Sarah Robinson & Cha. Jenings Security to answer the suit of Jno. Burtell Adm of James Burtell. Case damage three pounds.

[p 98] Order granted agt Emanl. Alkin & William Smelt Security for his non-appearance to answer the suit of John Cook & John Roe in an action upon the case damage £30.

Henry Dunn came into Ct & ack his deed of gift for land to his brother John Dunn. Ordered recorded.

In the suit brt by Fra. Ballard agt John Forgison in an action of debt for £4 & suit being heard, ord dismist.

Order granted agt John Poole Senr & Henry Robinson Security for his non-appearance to answer the suit of Bart. Selden assignee of John Wallace in an action of debt for 666 lbs tobo.

Mark Parish orphan of John Parish dec'd being sixteen years old is bound unto Gilbert Wilson until he comes of age, he learning Parish to read & write.

Court ordered to be adjourned till Tomorrow Ten a Clock. Wm. Lowery.

At a Court held the 20th day of March 1717/8
Present: Mr. Wm. Lowery, Capt. Fra. Ballard, Mr. Antho. Armistead, Mr. Simon Hollier, Mr. John Bayley, Mr. Tho. Wythe, Mr. John King - Justices

Upon petition of James Ricketts & Jane his wife in behalf of Pasco Curle about turning a road at Scone Dam. It's ordered that petition be granted, making another road.

In the suit brt by Saml. Selden agt John King in action of debt for £5, plt proving his debt. Judgmt granted agt deft for paymt to plt with costs at exec.

In the suit brt by Wm. Marshall & Eliza. his wife agt John King gent in an action of detinue damage £300. Special bayle being demanded, which the Ct being divided in their opinion. It's ord refd to a fuller Ct.

In the suit brt by Cha. Jenings on behalf of William Westwood agt James Ricketts in an action of trepass damage £100 sterl, deft pleading not guilty. Whereupon a Jury being awarded & verdict being returned & no opposition made, ordered verdict rec & deft to pay plt [award] with costs at exen.

In obedience to an order of Ct Date the Eighteenth Day of September 1717. We of the Jury do find the Trespass came within the Bounds of the Plaintives Pattent to the Plt's Damage £20 sterl. John Armistead, Antho. Armistead Junr, Peter Baker, Thomas Jones, George Waffe, Wm. Winterton, Thomas Howard, Joseph (X) Harriss, Edward Lattemore foreman, John Bordland, Francis Rodgers, William Davis. Octobr the tenth 1717.

In an action upon the case for £1:08 brt by Jno. Burtell Adm of James Burtell dec'd agt Peter Baker & Henry Irwin being Security. Judgmt agt the Principall & Security for what shall appear due at exon, the deft having Lyberty to bring in his Discount.

Tho. Roberts' action upon the case £4 agt Nicho. Bouton, the deft pleading. Plt prays time to answer. Granted.

The action upon the case brt by Alexandr. McKenzie agt Joseph Banister for £14 for the looking after of Negr Coffy's broken leg. Parties referring cause to Ct, it's ordered that deft pay £8 out of Burtell's est in hands of Banister to plt with costs at exec.

Judgmt confessed by Tho. Wilcox for £8:6 to Cha. Jenings with costs at exon.

Judgmt confirmed agt Andr. Laws & the Sheriff for what shall appear due at execution to John Burtell Adm of James Burtell with costs.

Judgmt granted by Nihil Dicet agt John Smith Senr to answer the suit of Cha. Jenings case damage 3000 lbs tobo.

Attachmt granted Emanl. Alkin agt est of Jno. Burtell Adm of James Burtell dec'd in an action upon the case for – – –.

Saml. Selden Scirefacias agt Robert Armistead for £12, deft prays time & arguments being heard whether he should have further time he having been sick. Ordered the deft have time to next Ct.

John Burtell Adm of James Burtell dec'd agt John Bayley gent in an action upon the case damage £12, deft prays time. Granted.

[p 100] Judgmt confirmed agt John Burtell Adm of James Burtell dec'd for payment of four bbls of Tarr to Francis Bracey with costs at exon.

John Smith action upon case damage £80 brought agst Burtell Admr of James Burtell dec'd. Parties consent to refer acctts to audit who makes choyce of Mr. Jos. Banister, Mr. Jos. Wragg and Mr. Saml. Sweney or any two of them. Returnable to next Court.

Judgment confirmed agst Richd. Kirkin for paymt of 25 shillings to Robert Taylor with costs, plt proving his case.

John Burtell's petition agst Mr. Hollier and Mr. Banister for delivery of Mr. James Burtell's estate out of their hands. Ordered petition refd to next Court.

In the action of debt for --- sterling brought agst Henry Robinson by Saml. Selden. Deft prays Liberty to plead as many matters as he things fit. Granted. Plt prays time. Granted.

Brian Penny brought his action upon the case for £5 agt Joshua Curle Junr which is refd to Mr. Joseph Banister to audit. Report same to next Court.

Judgment confirmed agt John Knott, Tho. Wood and Richd. Adams Security for payment of 13 shillings 6 pence being balance of acct to Tho. Howard with costs at execution.

Upon petition of John Massenbird [sic] for his wife's estate in the hands of Mathw. Small. Ordered that Capt. Jenkins do settle the acct and report to next Court.

Order granted agt Richd. Kirkin and Jno. Merrideth Security for payment of what shall appear due at next Court to Wm. Malory Plt, the deft having Liberty to bring in his discount.

Fra. Ballard's two actions agt Jno. More and Eliza. Goodwyn Exectrix of Jno. More gent dec'd is dismist being agreed.

Emanl. Alkins actions upon the case, the one for £31:11 and the other for --- agst Fra. Ballard is by consent of the parties refd to Mr. McKenzie, Capt. Jenkins and Mr. Sweny or any two of them to audit & return to next Court.

The action upon the case brought by Antho. Armistead agst Fra. Ballard damage £500 sterling. Deft pleads he owes nothing and the plt joynes. Ordered refd to next Court for tryall.

Fra. Ballard. Action of debt for 3201 lbs tobo agt Antho. Armistead. Deft prays time. Granted.

Fra. Ballard. Action of debt for 546 lbs tobo agt Antho. Armistead. Deft prays time to plead. Granted.

Fra. Ballard agt Jno. Burtell Admr of James Burtell dec'd action upon case for £17:18. Deft pleads discount. It's ordered that acct be audited by Mr. McKenzie and report to next Court.

Fra. Ballard agt Jno. Burtell Admr of James Burtell dec'd action upon case for 22 lbs tobo refd to Mr. McKenzie for audit. Report to next Court.

Cole Diggs Gent brought his action case for £14 agt Jno. Burtell Admr of James Burtell dec'd. Deft prays oyer of the accott. Granted.

Special imparlence granted to Margt. Prest Exectrx of James Prest dec'd to answer suit of Jno. Smith action case for 644 lbs tobo.

Ordered that rates of lyquor be settled and sold as they were set formerly at [blank].

Evidences in the suit between Saml. Watts and Hind Armistead on behalf of the plt that in case upon tryall the sd Evidences being Dead that then their depositions to be allowed good upon the tryall. Ordered also that Hind Armistead's Evids be sworne Mr. Tho. Jones and Jno. Thedam.

Ordered that James Ricketts be summoned to next Court to give account of what he knows concerning the Standard belonging to the County which was in possession of Col. Wilson.

        Wm. Lowery Signe

At a Court held the 21st of May 1718
Mr. Wm. Lowery, Capt. Fra. Ballard, Mr. Simon
Hollier, Mr. Antho. Armistead, Mr. Tho. Wythe
Mr. John Bayley, Mr. John King – His Majesties
       Justices

Upon petition of Robert Taylor for a license to keep an ordinary in the Town of Hampton. Granted giving bond and Security according to law.

Upon petition of Henry Jenkins for Admstion of John Curle's estate and Josa. Curle opposing same and arguments being heard. Court judged that the sd Curle was not capable of the Admstion. Ord that certificate for Admstion be granted to sd Petitioner giving bond according to law.

Abraham Mitchel and Ann his wife came into Court & ackd certain deeds for town land unto Jno. Henry Romborg. Ordered to be recorded, sd Ann first being examined.

[p 102] Geo. Giggets nuncupative will proved by the oa--- - ----- Coly and William Coly witnesses. Ordered refd to next Court for the heir-at-law & if any be ---

It's ordered that Wm. Smelt & Mr. John Bordland appr the goods of Eliza. Clarke being first examined. Return appr to next Court.

Upon petition of Ann Carver for Adm of her husband's estate. Ordered that certificate for Adm be granted her, she giving bond & Security. Ord estate be appr by Mr. Fra. Rogers, Mr. Tho. Allen, Mr. Tho. Hawkins & Mr. Richd. Nusum or any three of them. Return to next Court. Bond signed acknowledged.

Last will & testament of Henry Batts is proved by oaths of Cha. Jenings & Bright Pharen witnesses. Certificate for probate granted the Exectors giving bond.

Last will & testament of Robt. Johnson proved by oaths of Wm. Spicer, Wentr [?] Whittaker & affirmation of Joseph Wragg Witnesses. Certificate for probate granted the Exec giving bond & sec. The bond signed ack.

Ordered that Tho. Batts & John Batts Execs of Henry Batts do pay to Briget Oharen acc to law for her one day's attendance at Court in proving Batt's will with costs.

Upon petition of Temperance Parish for her thirds of her husband's estate. Ordered that Abraham Parish Exec be summoned to answer the petition.

Upon motion of John Bordland who prayed the estate of Fra. Treadway be appraised. It's ordered that same be appr by Wm. Smelt & Jos. Banister. Return to next Court.

Last will & testament of Tho. Casey is proved by oaths of Richd. Hawkins & Jno. Howard witnesses. Certificate for probate granted the Exec giving bond & security. Ordered estate be appr by Jno. Howard, Hind Armistead, John Skinner & John Jeggetts or any three of them. Return to next Court.

Part of the appraismt of Majr. Armistead's estate being returned, ordered recorded.

Ordered that Wm. Allen Exec of Jno. Springer pay to Fra. Rogers & Jno. Cook for their one day's attendance each as Evidences in probate of sd Springer with costs at exon.

[p 103] Last will & testament of John Springer proved by oaths of Fra. Rogers & Jno. Cook witnesses & certificate for probate granted the Exec giving bond & security. Bond not yet given. Wm Lowery Signe

At a Court held the 3rd Wed of June being the 18th 1718
Mr. Wm. Lowery, Capt. Fra. Ballard, Mr. Simon
Hollier, Mr. John Bayley, Mr. Tho. Wythe
Mr. John King – His Majesties Justices

Upon petition of John Mitchel agst Saml. Reddlehurst for consideration of his maintaynance, sd Reddlehurst absenting himself from Mitchel's servis, Court is of the opinion that the Petition be refd to next Court for Mitchel to make his personal appearance.

Upon petition of Wm. Smelt for Admstion on the estate of his Brother in law Jno. Batt dec'd. Ordered petition be refd to next Court to see if there be any will of sd Batt & also ordered that petitioner take care of his estate in the meantime.

Christopher Davis & Eliza. his wife is appt Gdn to Constantine Umphelt being next of kin.

Last will & testament of Wm. Hopkins is proved by oaths of William Creeke & Mark Powell witnesses & ord refd to next Court for the heir-at-law to come in if any before any [sic] Probate be granted the Exec thereof.

Wm. Tucker, Jno. Bordland & Tho. Watts ack a bond for Tho. Merry's estate. Ordered recorded.

Upon petition of Emanl. Alkin agst Admr of James Burtell dec'd for the care of Negro Coffy's legg. It's ordered that a summons agst sd Alkin to appear at next Court to answer.

Last will & testament of Tho. Merry dec'd is proved by oaths of Simon Hollier gent, John Wilson & Plano Ward witnesses. Bond &c & ordered that estate be appr by Mr. Simon Hollier, Mr. John King, Mr. Edwd. Tabb & Mr. Edmd Hollier or any three of them. Return to next Court.

The action upon case damage £28 brought by Richd. Kirkin agst Alexand. Alkins. It's ordered that the former order in this cause for the Vewing of certain work be renewed. Report to next Court.

[p 104] William Greek [sic] agt Thos. Wood is dismissed. No appearance of either party.

The action upon case for £3:09:08 brought by Jno. Bond agst Mary Randy [?]. She not appearing, order granted agt the Principall by nihill dicet.

Richd. Hopkins suit agt Tho. Wood & John Wallace his security for paymt of £2:07:02 to Wm. Smelt. This order stays till next Court for Petitioner to make out his debt.

The suit brought by Wm. Smelt agt Robt. Tannoch action upon case for £1:15:07 1/2. Judgmt confirmed agt deft for what shall appear due at next Court.

Edmd. Kerny's suit agst Brian Penny action upon case. Ordered dismist.

Hind Armistead & Hanah his wife Execs of Mattw. Watts dec'd agt Saml. Watts action case damages £10, Plts replying. Deft prays time till next Court. Granted.

Saml. Watts agt Hind Armistead damage £40 trespass. Deft pleads not guilty. Ordered refd till tomorrow morning for time to draw up a special verdict.

Fra. Ballard's petition to have his accott agt Mr. Servant's estate audited, the former order not being complyed with, ordered refd & report to next Court.

Edward Lattemore agt Phillip Prescoat action of trespass damage £10 for trespass committed on Plt's lot in Town & issue being joyned but deft not appearing. Judgmt is granted by default and a Jury awarded & sworne namely: Tho. Howard, Barto. Proby, Andr. Laws, Richd. Nusume, Saml. Watts, Jno. Poole, Tho. Jones, Henry Robinson, Geo. Waufe, James Naylor, Wm. Tucker & Nathl. Parker. Returned Verdict in these words. We of the Jury do find for the Plt the deft not appearing, damage six pence. Richd. Nusume foreman. On motion of Plt verdict is recorded & ordered deft pay to plt with costs at exon.

The action of trespass damage £10 brt by Saml. Selden agt Fra. Ballard is by consent refd till tomorrow morning.

[p 105] Robt. Wells's suit agt Saml. Bromage damage £16. Order continued for deft to put in his replyqation.

Cha. Chickwell agst Saml. Sweny action case damage £20 refd to next Court.

Emanl. Alkin agt Geo. Luke and Mary his wife action case damage £12, defts pleading they owe nothing. Refd to next Court for tryall.

James Ricketts & Jane his wife on behalf of Wilson Curle Infant agt Jno. Burtel Adm of James Burtell action case damage £60 lies for want of a Court.

Judgmt granted agt Tho. Wilcox for 13 shillings & 7 pence being balance of accott to Tho. Howard with costs.

Thomas Roberts sworn to his accott agt Nicho. Benton &c.

Ordered Court be adjourned till tomorrow Ten a Clock
Wm. Lowery Signe

[added on left half of page in small script] Upon --- & order of John Bordland agt Alien & McKenzie for divers outrages. Ordered that McKenzie give bond with sec for £20 sterling for his good behaviour towards all his Majestie's Leige People especially toward Bordland and that the Sheriff take him into custody & detaine him till he give such bond and return it to next Court. This is the same Court as above.

At a Court held 7th day of July 1718
Mr. Wm. Lowery, Mr. Simon Hollier, Mr. Tho. Wythe,
Mr. John King – His Majestie's Justices

Mr. John Bayley is this day sworne High Sheriff of Elizabeth City Co. according to the Governor's Commission dated the 4th day of July 1718 and has accordingly given bond & ack the same. Also Jno. Dun is sworn Under Sheriff of sd County. [Signed] William Lowery.

[p 106] At a Court held the 3rd Wed of July being the
15th Day 1718
Mr. Wm. Lowry, Capt. Fra. Ballard, Mr. Antho.
Armistead, Mr. Simon Hollier, Mr. John
King – His Majestie's Justices

Henry Jenkins, Francis Ballard, Antho. Armistead, Thomas Wythe, James Ricketts, and James Servant hath this day taken the Oaths appointed by Law & signed the Test with the Oaths of Justice of the Peace & oath In Chancery according to the Govers. Commission &c.

The Last Laws of Virga. is this Day Published.

The last will & testament of Richard Crusell is proved by oaths of Charles Powers, Wm. Woods & Thomas Delany witnesses & refd for Probate till next Court, giving Security &c.

Upon petition of Joyce Hopkins for Administration of her husband Richd. Hopkins' estate. Ordered that certificate for Adm be granted her, she giving bond & security.

Ordered that the estate of Richd. Hopkins dec'd be appr by James Ricketts, Joseph Banister, Wm. Smelt & Thos. Howard or any two of them. Return to next Court.

Upon petition of Susa. Smith for Adm of her husband Benja. Smith's estate. Ordered certificate of Adm be granted her giving bond & security.

Ordered that Mark Powel, Hind Armistead, Wm. Spicer & Wm. Creek or any three of them appr the estate of Wm. Hopkins dec'd. Return to next Court. Probate granted Mary Bridge, giving bond &c.

Upon petition of Xtopher Davis for the estate of Constantine Umphlet as being her guardian. Ord that Wm. Spicer as having the sd estate do deliver to the sd Guardian all & singular the sd orphan's estate.

Ordered that Richd. Hawkins do appear before Capt. Ballard to take the oath of a Constable of that precinct & that the Clerk give notice of the same.

The appraisal of Tho. Merry's estate being returned, ordered recorded.

The nuncupative will of David James is proved in Court by oaths of Xtopher Davis & Eliza. Davis witnesses &c according to due forms of Law & on motion of the Devisee ordered to be recorded.

[p 107] Upon the motion of Jno. Bordland on behalf of his wife for the canceling a certain bond given by the sd Borland's [sic] wife for her good behaviour. Ord that the Sheriff cancel the same.

Court ordered to be adjourned til tomorrow Ten a Clock
                                        Hen. Jenkins Signe
At a Court held the 17th day of July 1718
Capt. Henry Jenkins, Capt. Fra. Ballard, Mr. Antho. Armistead, Mr. Thomas Wythe, Mr. Jno. King
Mr. Jas. Ricketts, Mr. James Servant
His Majestie's Justices

Mr. Henry Irwin has this day taken the oath appointed by Law and signed the Test together with the oath of Justice of the Peace & oath in Chancery according to the Govers. Commission &c.

An appraisal of Eliza. Clark's estate. Ordered the Sheriff take the estate into his hands & keep the same till further order. And ordered that all persons that have any demands agt the Est bring in their accotts at next Court for each person to be allowed In proportion.

Fra--- Treadway's apprmt is returned & ordered recorded.

Upon motion of John Roe for delivery of the estate of Edwd. Penny's orphan. Ordered that he deliver the estate together with the sd orphan to Bryan Penny her Uncle, he giving bond &c. Ordered also that the estate of Elizabeth Prescott be Delivered to the sd Penny.

Ordered that the estate of Alexdr. Carver be appr by Charles Tucker, Mattw. Small, Thomas Allen & Fra. Rogers or any three of them. Return to next Court.

John Massenburgh's petition agt Matthew Small for his wife's estate is rejected.

Thomas Wright & Jane his wife came into Court and ack their deed for Town land to Robert Minson, she being privately examined. Ordered recorded.

Eliza. Boutwill Exectrx of Wm. Boutwil dec'd. Suit agt Robt. Taylor action of debt for £5. Parties consent of refer the Cause to Mr. Thomas Wythe and his report to be entered at next Court.

Order granted agt John Armistead & Wm. Armistead his Security to answer suit of Peter Morisett action case damage £5.

Order granted agt Henry Irwin gent & Jno. Walless his Security for non-appearance of sd Henry Irwin to answer the suit of Jno. Smith Senr and Edith his wife. Action of debt for £50 sterling.

Antho. Armistead's suit agt Eland Carhill is dismist. No declaration.

[p 108] Order granted agt the late Sheriff for the non-appearance of Wm. Sidwell to answer the suit of Cornel. Dorlich action of trespass damage £20 sterling.

Benjamin Clifton's suit agt Darby Dunnaway is ended.

Order granted agt Richard Kirkin & Charles Jennings his Security for the non-appearance of Kirkin to answer the suit of George Walker action upon the case damage £5.

Upon motion of Charles Jenings attchmt is granted him agt the estate of Richard Kirkin to save himself from the sd Judgmt.

Richard Hopkins' suit agst [blank] Eustice is dismist, the Plt being Dead.

John Curle's suit agt Charles Avery is dismist, the Plt being Dead.

Bertrand Proby, Adm of Thomas Proby, suit agt John Burtell &c of James Burtell account to render £130 sterling. Order refd to next Court to be argued.

Francis Ballard's suit agt Thomas Jenings action debt for $10. Ordered refd to next Court for Capt. Jenkins to return report.

Edmd. Kearny's suit agt Richard Lewis action case damage £28 sterling dismist. No appearance.

Emal. Alkin's suit agt Samuel Daniel is dismist, the Deft being Dead.

Robert Brough's suit agt Thomas Wood is dismist. No appearance.

Charles Jenings' suit agt Thomas Wood. Upon motion of plt attchmt continued to next Court.

Henry Robinson's suit agt Samuel Selden action upon the case damage 1800 lbs of tobo. Deft prays time till next Court to plead. Granted.

Henry Robinson's suit agt Thomas Wood. On motion of plt attchmt is continued to next Court.

Richard Hopkins' suit agt Thomas Wood is dismist. The plaintive being Dead.

Cole Diggs gent. Suit agt John Burtell Adm of James Burtell. Action of debt for £200. Deft prays time till next Court to plead. Granted.

Upon motion of Jno. King & Robt. Taylor &c agt Jos. Banister & Simon Hollier for the delivery of Mr. Burtell's estate in their hands. Ordered that the Sheriff summon the sd persons to next Court to show cause why they do not comply with the former order.

[p 109] James Baker's suit agt Thomas Tucker is dismist, the Deft being Dead.

Thomas Faulkner's suit agt Thomas Wilcox action upon the case damage £10 is refd to next Court by consent of both parties.

Robert Bright attchmt agt Thomas Wood action upon case damage £8 is continued to next Court.

Margrett Bayley's suit agt Thomas Wood action upon the case damage £8. Attchmt continued to next Court.

In the suit brought by Wm. Lowry gent Plt agt Francis Ballard gent action upon the case damage 1250 lbs tobo. Deft pleads he owes nothing. Time is given the plt til next Court to Joyne Issue.

Benjamin Hill & Eliza. his wife. Suit agst Thomas Wood action case. Attchmt is continued.

Margt. Bayley's suit agt Mary Frissill action upon the case damage 40 shillings is refd to next Court for plt to prove her accott.

Matthew Small's suit agt Ralph Lahea action upon the case damage 50 shillings is ended.

Robert Minson's suit agt Thomas Wilcox is ended.

Bryan Penny's attchmt agt George Paine action case damage £5 is continued.

Matthew Small's suit agt James Ricketts action case for £4:14. Deft prays time till next Court to have a copy of the deft's account. Granted.

Judgmt granted agt Charles Jenings as Security of Sarah Robinson for paymt of $1:12:09 to Admr of James Burtell dec'd with costs at exon.

John Cook & John Roe. Suit agt Emanuel Alkin action upon the case damage £30. Deft prays time till next Ct to plead. Granted.

In the action brought by Bart. Selden assignee of Samuel Wallace agt John J. Pool [?] for 660 lbs tobo due by specialty. Plt moves for special bayle, which Henry Robinson enters himself special bayle &c and the deft pleads he owes nothing. Ordered refd to next Ct for tryall.

John Burtell Adm &c of James Burtell agt Peter Baker action upon the case for £1:08. Deft being dead, judgmt granted the plt agt the sd deft according to specialty for £1:08.

Alexdr. McKenzie's suit agt Thomas Wood is dismist. No appearance.

Jno. Burtel Adm &c of James Burtell. Suit agt Andrew Lewis refd to next Ct.

[p 110] John Mitchell presenting Saml. Daniel's will to be proved. Ordered that the will lie in the office till next Ct for proof for the heir to come in if any &c.

Ord that Mr. Wm. Smelt, Mr. Jos. Banister, Mr. Jno. Smith & Mr. Wm. Loyall or any three of them appraise a sloop belonging to Mr. John King & Mr. John Curle dec'd and return appraisal to next Ct.

Ordered that Mr. Wm. Smelt have Admistion on estate of John Pett dec'd, giving bond &c, and that the estate be appr by Robt. Armistead, T--- Read, Fra. Rodgers & Thomas Allen or any three of them & returned to next Ct.

Ordered that Court be adjourned til the Court in Course.

At a Court held the 3rd Wednesday of August
being the 20th day 1718

Capt. Henry Jenkins, Capt. Fra. Ballard, Mr. Antho. Armistead, Mr. Thomas Wythe, Mr. John King, Mr.

Henry Irwin, Mr. James Ricketts, Mr. James
Servant — His Majestie's Justices

Judgment is confirmed agt John Smith Senr for 800 lbs good sweet scented tobo being the balance of the Deft's accot against a bill dated the 13th May 1715 to Charles Jenings with costs, only Jenings is to pay the Deft 18 shillings & 9 pence.

Upon complaint of Henry Irwin gent agt Henry Morrisett for "grosly abussing him and threatening to shoot him with a pistole," and Morrisett confessing the fact. It's ordered that Morrisett be bound to the peace for his good behaviour toward all his Majestie's Leige Subjects & especially toward Irwin til next Ct held for the County & that he appear to answer & that the Sheriff take him into Custody til he give bond & security for £20.

Upon petition of John Walliss for lycense to keep an ordinary at his house in Hampton Towne, granted giving bond &c.

Upon petition of Robert Minson for lycense to keep an ordinary at his house in Hampton Towne, granted giving bond &c.

Upon petition of John Bordland for Adm of Francis Treadway's estate. Granted giving bond & security &c.

[p 111] Upon oath of Mary Gilbert for Letters of Adm of James Gilbert's dec'd estate. Granted giving bond & security &c --- and given.

Ordered that Mr. Wm. Smelt, Mr. James Ricketts, Capt. Fra. Ballard & Mr. Jos. Banister or any three of them appr estate of James Gilbert dec'd. Return to next Ct.

Upon petition of John Bayley Sheriff about the insufficiency of the county gaole. Ordered that the gaole be viewed by Mr. Wm. Smelt & John Cook and report to next Ct whether prison be sufficient or not.

William Hays being fifteen years of age is by consent of his mother Sarah Hays bound an apprentice to Thomas Howard & Eliza. his wife till he is twenty-one & Howard is to learn Hays the art & trade of shoemaker & at expiration of his time to give him a new suit of apparel & a set of Shoemaker's Tooles.

Appr of Alexander Carver's estate being returned, ordered recorded.

John Parish, son of John Parish dec'd, being thirteen years old is bound apprentice to Wm. Carhill till he comes of age & to learn the apprentice the trade of a Cooper & to read & "wright" & at expiration of time to give him a new suit of Cloaths.

Probate of the last will & testament of Richard Crusell dec'd is granted to Mary Crusell his wife giving bond &c. Bond given.

Abraham Parish & Ann his wife & Temperance Parish widdow came into Ct & ack a certain lease & release for land to Thomas Morgan & his heirs, the sd Ann being privately examined. Same order recorded.

Capt. Wm. Boswell's will being presented to the Ct by Ellinor Boswell wido. who declines the Legacies given in the will to her & adheres to what the law gives her, and also the Exership to her therein mentioned. It's ordered that George Walker, one of the Execs of the will mentioned, be summoned to next Ct to show whether he will take the Exship upon him or not & ord that the witnesses to the will be summoned to next Ct to prove the same.

An appraisal of the Sloop between Mr. John King & Mr. Jno. Curle dec'd is returned and on motion of Capt. Henry Jenkins ordered to be recorded.

Upon petition of Edward Andross for his Estate. It's granted.

In the suit brought by John Smith Senr agt Anthony Armistead Senr. In an action upon the case for 1100 lbs tobo, deft pleads he owes Nothing & now being called & one Evidence being sworn for plt & arguments being heard, Court are of the opinion that there is no cause of action. Ordered dismist with costs.

[p 112] Appr of estate of William Hopkins being returned, ordered recorded.

Samuel Selden's Scirefacias agt Robert Armistead. Deft pleading, plt prays time to next Ct to answer. Granted.

John Burtel Adm &c of James Burtell dec'd suit agt John Bayley is dismist.

John Armistead being summoned as an Evidence for John Smith agt Antho. Armistead and being solemnly called did not appear. On motion of plt, ordered that Armistead be fined according to law, except he appear at next Ct & show sufficient cause to the contrary.

John Pett, orphan of John Pett dec'd, is bound to Mr. Wm. Lowry Senr & his heirs or assigns til he come to age of one & twenty years he being now nine years old. Lowry is to learn the orphan a Trade & to read & write.

In the suit brought by Emanl. Alkins agt John Burtel Adm of James Burtel dec'd in action upon the case for £5:09 for medicines expended on James Burtel dec'd & upon settling the acct, the Court were divided in their opinion. It's ordered cause be refd for a fuller Court to be considered.

Martha Pett, orphan of John Pett dec'd, is by consent of her Uncles & Aunts bound to Jane Baker til she is eighteen or married, she being fourteen, & to learn Sarah anything of Woman's Work that she is capable to learn & to give her a new suit of apparel at end of term.

John Smith's suit agt Jno. Burtell Adm of James Burtell, the report being returned, upon motion of plt time is given him til next Ct to have copies of report in order to answer at next Ct.

Henry Robinson's suit agt Samuel Selden action debt for £100, the plt replying, deft prays time to Rejoyne. Granted.

Emanl. Alkins' action agt Francis Ballard is refd for Capt. Henry Jenkins & Mr. Henry Irwin to compleat their auditt & return report to next Ct.

Upon petition of Wm. Langman for lycense to keep an ordinary at his house in Hampton Town which is granted giving bond &c.

In the suit brought by Anthony Armistead agt Francis Ballard in an action upon the case damage £500 sterling is by consent refd to next Ct for Tryall.

Francis Ballard. Two actions agt Anthony Armistead is by consent refd to next Ct for Tryall.

Mr. James Ricketts being sumed [sic] to give accott of the Standard & Weights that was in Collo. Wilson's possession & he appearing & declaring that he knows nothing of them. Ordered th-- be dismist.

[p 113] In the suit brought by Wm. Marshall & Mary his wife agt John King in an action of Detinue damage £300 sterling & it being argued whether deft should give special bayle, the Court are of the opinion that he ought not to be held to bayl. Therefore deft prays special imparlence. Granted.

Mr. Mark Johnson's will is lodged in the office till next Ct to be Proved.

An inv of John Pett's est returned & ordered recorded.

Francis Ballard's two actions agt Emanuel Alkin. Refd to next Ct by consent of plt.

Francis Ballard's action upon the case for £40 agt Jno. Burtell Adm of James Burtell is by consent refd to be audited by Mr. Samuel Sweny, Mr. Jos. Banister & Mr. Jos. Wragg & report to next Ct.

Francis Ballard's action upon the case for 1400 lbs tobo agt John Burtell Adm of James Burtell is by consent refd to be audited by Mr. Samuel Sweny, Mr. Jos. Banister & Mr. Jos. Wragg & report to next Ct.

Emanuel Alkin's suit agt Thomas Pool is dismist, the plaintive paying cost.

Charles Jenings &c suit agt John Smith Senr damage 1600 lbs tobo, deft appears & prays imparlence. Granted.

Charles Jenings &c suit agt John Burtell Adm of James Burtell dec'd. Deft prays imparlence. Granted.

John Burtell Adm of James Burtell, suit agt Jos. Curle gent action case damage £20. By consent of both parties, orderedthat their accots be audited by Jos. Banister, Saml. Sweny, & Jos. Wragg & returned to next Ct.

Order granted agt Jos. Wragg & Jno. Wallace his Security to answer the suit of Charles Jenings action case damage £6.

Order granted agt Richard Kirkirn [sic] & Emanll. Alkin his Security to answer the suit of Thomas Wootten action case damage £5.

Upon motion of Emanl. Alkin & Jos. Wragg Security of Richd. Kirkin attchmt granted agt Kirkin's estate to save Themselves.

Order granted agt Richard Kirkin & James Ricketts his Sec for his non appearance to answer the suit of Edwd. Myhill action case damage 2000 lbs tobo.

Attchmt granted agt Francis Mallory to answer the suit of Jno. Hardiman action case for £4:7:6 current money.

[p 114] Order granted agt Wm. Knight & Gilbert Wilson his Security to answer the suit of Richard Nusum action case damage £6.

Thomas Faulkner's suit agt Thomas Roberts action case dismist. No appearance.

Imparlence granted to John Wallace to answer the suit of Richard Kirkin action detinue dam £10.

Judgmt confessed by Hind Armistead as marrying Hanah the relict of Mattw. Watts dec'd for paymt of £8:04:06 being due on a protested Bill of Exchange to Emanuel Alkin with costs to be paid out of Matthew Watts' estate in hands of Hind Armistead.

Time granted to John Burtell Adm &c to answer the suit of Emanl. Alkin action case damage £4.

Then the Court adjourns til tomorrow Ten a Clock.

At a Court held the 21st day of August 1718
Capt. Henry Jenkins, Capt. Francis Ballard, Mr. Thomas Wythe, Mr. John King, Mr. Henry Irwin, Mr. James Ricketts, Mr. James Servant — His Majestie's Justices

Upon petition of Emanuel Alkin agt John Curle's est for £1:11:06, the Court abating part of the accts. Ordered that he be paid £1:01:06 in the hands of Henry Jenkins Gent with costs.

Judgmt is granted to Cole Diggs Gent agt John Burtell Adm of James Burtell dec'd for paymt of £11:13:07 & 3 farthings with costs.

Upon petition of Thomas Skinner agt the est of John Pett. Mr. Wm. Smelt Adm of Pett's est prays time to next Ct to answer. Granted.

Ordered that Mr. Jos. Banister & Mr. Wm. Smelt pay Eliza. Hill £4:13:06 out of Eliza. Clark's estate, Hill having proved her acct.

Ordered that the Sheriff summon Peter Morisett to appear at next Ct to give acct of what goods he hath in his hands belonging to Jno. Babb dec'd.

Upon petition of Wm. Smelt for ordinary license which is granted &c.

[p 115] Upon petition of Temperance Parish wido. of Mark Parish dec'd setting forth agt the Exec of Mark Parish's will for her thirds. Ended among themselves. Ordered dismist.

John Ellyson's suit agt Emanl. Alkin action upon the case damage £10. Deft pleads he owes nothing. Ordered refd to next Ct for Tryall.

Ordered that Mr. Jos. Banister & Mr. Wm. Smelt pay Emanl. Alkin £2:09:06 our of Eliza. Clark's Est.

Bryan Penny's petition for Edwd. Penny's child. Ordered refd to next Ct.

In the Ejectment brought by Robert Westlock agt James Ricketts who is admitted deft for lands & tenements in the Declr mentioned to witt &c & a Jury Impaneled namely: Hind Armistead, Henry Robinson, Bart. Proby, Abraham Mitchel, John Cooke, Saml. Watts, Francis Rogers, Joseph Banister, Jno. Mitchel, George Wauffe, John Henry Rombough & John

Robinson & being out some time, brought in a Special Verdict which on motion of Plt is recorded & refd to next Court for the points of law to be argued.

Imparlence granted to Henry Jenkins Adm of John Curle dec'd to answer the suit of Henry Hay's action case.

In the suit brought by John Bayley agt Henry Jenkins Adm of John Curle dec'd in an action upon the case for £40:10, the Court is making abatement of the acct. It's ordered that Henry Jenkins Adm &c pay £28:05 out of Curle's est with costs.

Bryan Penny action upon the case agt Joshua Curle for £5:10:06 and being returned, Ordered dismist.

Ordered that John Mitchel deliver certain articles of agreement between Mr. King & Jul. Skinner to the Clerk for the parties to have copies of them if required.

Then the Court adjourns til the Court in Course.

At a Court held the 3rd Wednesday of September
being the 17th day 1718
Capt. Henry Jenkins, Capt. Fra. Ballard, Mr. Thos.
Wythe, Mr. Jno. King, Mr. James Ricketts, Mr.
Henry Irwin, Mr. Jos. Curle, Mr. James
Servant — His Majestie's Justices

Richard Kirkin's suit agt Alexdr. Alkins. £28. Ordered dismist. No appearance.

[p 116] Upon petition of Thomas Howard for keeping the Court House clean &c. Ordered that the expiration of Mr. Bosell's time for cleaning the house, that then Thomas Howard have the cleaning, the same Yearly Allowing to him at the Laying the Levy what shall be thought reasonable.

Upon petition of Celea Langman formerly Cole setting forth of the Ill Usage of Bryan Penny agt her Daughter Martha Cole. It's ordered that Martha be clear from Penny's service.

The suit brought by John Smith Senr agt Margtt. Preist Exectrx of James Preist &c action case for 644 lbs tobo. Deft pleading, plt prays time to next Ct to answer.

The action upon the case for £2:09:08 brought by John Dordland agt Mary Randy. Court settling accts ordered that Randy pay 7 shilling & 1/2 penny, being the bal of accts with costs.

Judgmt is confirmed to Wm. Smelt agt Thomas Wood & Jno. Walles his Sec for paymt of £2:07:03 with costs.

Judgmt is confirmed to Wm. Smelt agt Robt. Tanoch & Charles Moon his Sec for paymt of £1:12:10 with costs.

In the suit brought by Hind Armistead & Hannah his wife Execs of Mattw. Watts dec'd agt Samuel Watts in an action upon the case damage £10 concerning a Still &c, the deft rejoyning, plt prays time to consider. Granted.

The action brought by Saml. Watts agt Hind Armistead damage £40. Time given til the morning to draw the Special Verdict.

Administration with will annexed of last will & testament of Wm. Bosell dec'd is granted to Ellinor Bosell his Relict during the minority of Wm. Boswel one of the Execs mentioned in the will, giving bond &c. Ordered recorded.

The last will & testament of Wm. Boswel gent Dec'd is proved by oaths of Elizabeth Howard & the affirmation of Jos. Wragg, witnesses.

Francis Ballard's accots agt Mr. Servant's est he desires to be returned to next Ct. Granted.

In the suit brought by Wm. Lowry gent agt Francis Ballard gent in an action upon the case for 1000 lbs tobo, deft pleads he owes nothing and a Jury impaneled Namely: Saml. Sweny, Abra. Mitchell, Jno. Cook, Wm. Loyall, Jno. Massenburg, Wm. Coopland, Henry Dunn, Natl. Parker, Jno. Mitchel, Jno. Roe, Tho. Jones & Richd. Kirkin. Upon plt's consideration he withdrawing his action. Suit dismist.

Judgmt granted agt Matthew Small for £5:13:09 to John Massenburgh being the bal of all accotts upon his wife's est which was in the hand of Small, with costs at execution.

Robert Well's suit agt Samuel Bromage action of case damage £10. Plt filing his report. Time is given deft to consider.

Charles Chiswell's suit agt Samuel Sweny action case damage £20 refd to next Ct for Chiswell's appearance.

Emanuel Alkin's suit agt George Luke & Mary his wife action upon the case damage £12. Accts left to Capt. Hen. Jenkins & Mr. Saml. Selden to settle. Return to next Ct.

Cha. Jenings' suit agt Geo. Luke Esqr a debt for £5:02:06. Refd to next Ct.

Nonsuit granted to Thomas Fry agt Matt. Williams according to law. Plt failing to prosecute his action.

Time is given to Tho. & Jno. Batts to answer the suit of Emal. Alkin action upon the case damage £12.

Ordered that Wm. Smelt Adm of John Pett be summoned to Ct to answer Wa. Beane & Richard Nusum.

Samuel Selden's suit agt Kert Norden is dismist.

Kert (?) Whittaker's suit agt Hind Armistead action case is dismist. No prosecution.

Edmond Kearny's suit agt Bryan Penny action debt £30, deft prays special Imparlence. Granted.

Time is granted to Thomas Fry til next Ct to answer the suit of Owen Raine action assault & battery damage £50.

Jno. Bordland's suit agt Alexdr. McKenzie action trespass for assault & battery damage £100. Deft prays time til next Cy to answer. Granted.

Robert Tannoch's suit agt Charles Moone is dismist there being no prosecution.

Wm. Smelt's suit agt Wm. Taylor action upon the case damage £50. Deft prays time to next Ct to answer. Granted.

Jno. Pool Senr. Suit agt Thomas Jones action detinue damage £50 sterling. Deft prays time to answer. Granted.

[p 118] Elizabeth Boutwil Exectrx of Wm. Boutwil. Suit agt Rober- Taylor action of debt for £5, the former order not being complied with. Refd to Mr. Thomas Wythe to judge the difference & report to next Ct.

Judgmt granted agt John Armistead & Wm. Armistead his Security for five barrels of Indian Corne to Henry Morisett with costs at exon.

Cornelius Dorlich's suit agt Wm. Sidwell action of trespass damage £20 is ended.

George Walker's suit agt Richard Kirkin action upon the case damage £5 is ended.

Judgmt is granted agt Thomas Jenings for £10 unto Fra. Ballard with costs at exon.

Bart. Proby Adm of Thos. Proby agt Jno. Burtel Adm of Ja. Burtel action of acct to render for £130. Receipt for £100 being lodged in the office. Ord that Jury be summoned at next Ct to try such matters of fact as shall arise upon the return of the Audittors Report.

Attchmt is continued to Charles Jenings agt est of Tho. Wood for 1000 lbs tobo.

Attchmt is continued to Henry Robinson agt est of Thos. Wood action case damage £12.

Henry Robinson's suit agt Saml. Selden action case damage 1800 lbs tobo, the deft pleads. Plt prays time. Granted.

Simon Hollier and Joseph Banister being summoned to deliver up Mr. James Burtell's est which they have in their hands. It's ordered they deliver est to John King & Robert Taylor Securities of John Burtell Adm of James Burtell dec'd & that they give [Hollier & Banister] sufficient receipt for what they shall recover.

Thomas Faulkner's suit agt Thomas Wilcox action upon the case damage £10 is refd to next Ct.

Attchmt is continued to Robert Bright agt est of Thomas Wood action debt.

Margrett Bayley's attchmt agt Thomas Wood's est action case damage £8 is continued til next Ct.

Benja. Hill & Eliza. his wife attchmt agt Thomas Wood's est action case is continued til next Ct.

Margt. Bayley's suit agt Mary Frissill action case damage 40 shillings is dismist, they being agreed.

[p 119] Bryan Penny's attchmt agt George Paine action case damage £5 continued to next Ct.

Judgmt by Nihil Dicet is granted agt Emanl. Alkin to answer the suit of John Cook & John Roe action case damage £30.

Judgmt is confessed by John Pool for 666 lbs tobo to Bart. Selden assignee of Samuel Wallace with costs.

Samuel Riddlehurst ack a certain indenture on his part to Owen Raine. Ordered recorded.

Matthew Small's suit agt James Ricketts Gent action case for £4:14:0 is refd to next Ct by consent.
Court adjourns til tomorrow Ten a Clock.

At a Court held 18th September 1718
Capt. Henry Jenkins, Capt. Francis Ballard,
Mr. Antho. Armistead, Mr. Thomas Wythe, Mr. Henry Irwin, Mr. James Ricketts, Mr. Joshua Curle,
Mr. James Servant – His Majestie's Justices

Upon an attchmt brought by Daniel Corkerell agt the Ship Mary for £11:11:08 being due for wages & arguments being heard. Court are of the opinion that the Cause ought to be tried before the Court of Vice-Admiralty & ordered suit dismist with costs at exon.

Note: This entry is followed by three more identical entries: one each for Richard Corbett; Thomas Stoneham; and Lazs. Brambles. Each is suing the Ship Mary for wages.

[p 120] Suit brought by Saml. Watts agt Hind Armistead action trespass damage £40, the special verdict on both sides being lodged in the office. Ordered tried next Ct by a Jury.

Judgmt granted to Emanl. Alkin agt John Burtel Adm of Ja. Burtel for £4 with costs at exon, the deft having lyberty to make his discount.

Judgmt granted to Thomas Nelson Gent agt Henry Jenkins Gent, Adm of Jno. Curle dec'd, for what shall appear due at next Ct upon an action case brought by plt for £57:12:11.

Judgmt is confirmed agt Henry Jenkins Adm of Jno. Curle dec'd for £1:11:03 to Jno. L----fee (?) with costs at exon.

Henry Robinson's suit agt Saml. Selden action debt for £100, deft prays time til next Ct. Granted.

The proving Samuel Daniels' will is upon motion of Capt. Jenkins refd to be argued at next Ct.

Judgmt is confirmed agt Andr. Laws for £3:09 to Jno. Burtell Adm of James Burtell dec'd with costs at exon.

Thomas Roberts' suit agt Nicho. Boynton action upon case damage £8 refd to next Ct.

In action of accts to render brought by John Croft Guardian of Abra. & Childermus Croft's his Sons agt Robert Taylor. Taylor not appearing. Upon motion of the plt attchmt is granted him agt the body of Taylor for his appearance at next Ct.

Archibald Blair's suit agt George Lawder [?] dismist they having made up between themselves.

Order granted agt Wm. Mallory Security of Francis Mallory for non-appearance of Francis to answer suit of Charles Jenings action debt for £8:16.

Time is granted to John King gent to answer suit of Jno. Skinner action case Covnt broaken damage £40.

Time is granted to John Skinner to answer suit of Jno. King gent action case Covnt broaken damage £40.

Cornelius Dorlich & Rachel his wife. Suit agt Richd. Allen is dismist.

[p 121] Order granted agt the Sheriff for the non-appearance of Wm. Spicer & Mary his wife in an action upon

the case for 559 lbs tobo to answer the suit of Henry Cary & Jno. Riddlehurst Churchwardens of Denby Parish.

Order granted agt the Sheriff for the non-appearance of James Naylor to answer the suit of Charles Jenings action case damage 1000 lbs tobo.

Judgmt confirmed agt Henry Jenkins Adm of Jno. Curle dec'd for 25 shillings out of Curle's est to Wm. Loyall with costs at exon.

Upon the motion of Wm. Smelt ordered that no further waste be made upon Saml. Daniel's land til the will be proved.

John Coffee a Negro. Suit agt Robert Taylor action trespass for assault & battery damage £10. Deft prays time to next Ct to plead. Granted.

Order granted agt the Sheriff for the non-appearance of Henry Cock to answer the suit of Thomas Jenings action debt.

Emanuel Alkin's suit agt John Mitchel action case damage £6. Deft prays time to next Ct to plead. Granted.

The action of debt brought by Henry Irwin Gent agt Thomas Frye for £7:18:03. Judgmt granted Irwin for what shall appear due at next Ct.

Judgmt is granted Jno. Bordland agt Samuel Wilson for £10:12 being upon an attchmt served in the hands of Richard Hopkins for a coat that belonged to Samuel Wilson & ordered that Mr. Jas. Ricketts & Mr. Thos. Faulkner appr the coat & return to next Ct.

Ordered that Capt. Wm. Boswell's est be appr by Mr. James Ricketts, Mr. Thomas Wythe, Mr. Joshua Curle & Mr. George Yeo or any three of them & ret report to next Ct.

Ordered that the Sheriff summon Thomas House to next Ct to give accott of what he hath in his hands of Timothy Bloodworth's at the suit of Jno. Smith Senr.

Samuel Selden's Scirefacias agt Robert Armistead, the plt replying, the deft prays time to next Ct to rejoyne. Granted.

Jno. Smith Senr action case agt Jno. Burtel Adm &c. Plt prays time to take copies of the auditt. Granted.

Emanuel Alkin action case damage £31 agt Francis Ballard is by consent refd to next Ct.

Anthony Armistead Gent action case damage £500 sterling agt Fra. Ballard Gent is by consent refd to next Ct.

Francis Ballard's action debt 3121 lbs tobo agt Antho. Armistead is by consent refd to next Ct.

[p 122] Judgmt by Nihill Dicet granted agt Jno. King to answer the suit of Wm. Marshall action detinue damage £300 sterling.

Francis Ballard's two actions agt Emanuel Alkin is refd to be auditted according to the former order.

Judgmt granted to Charles Jenings agt John Burtell Adm &c of James Burtell dec'd for 797 lbs tobo with costs.

Charles Jenings' action case damage 1 barl tobo agt Jno. Smith Senr is by consent refd to next Ct.

Jno. Smith & Edith his wife for £50 sterling agt Henry Irwin gent prays oyer of the bond. Granted.

Jno. Burtell Adm &c suit agt Joshua Curle gent. Accotts refd to be audited according to the former order.

Judgmt granted agt Joseph Wragg & Jno. Walless his Sec for £2:19:09 & 31 lbs tobo unto Charles Jenings with costs only four shillings to be discounted.

Alexdr. McKenzie's suit agt Richard Kirkin action upon the case damage £14. Deft prays time to next Ct to bring in his discount. Granted.

Thomas Hotten's suit agt Richard Kirkin action case damage £5. Ord refd to next Ct for tryall.

Judgmt is confessed by Richard Kirkin for 1000 lbs of sweet-scented tobo unto Edward Myhill with costs.

Judgmt is granted John Hardiman agt Francis Mallory for £4:07:06 with costs only deft hath Lyberty to bring in his discount if he hath any.

Samuel Selden & Jno. Smith Senr ack themselves to stand indebted to our Sovrgne Lord the King in the sum of £20 each to be levied upon their good & chattles Lands & Tenements &c. Upon condition the sd Saml. be of good behaviour toward all His Majestie's Leige People & especially toward the sd King for one month &c.

Jno. King & Hen. Jenkins ack themselves to stand indebted to our Sovrgne Lord the King in the sum of £20 each [Note: peace bond, exactly as the above entry.]

At a Court held the 15th day of October 1718
for Laying of the County Levy
Henry Jenkins, Francis Ballard, Antho. Armistead, Thomas Wythe, James Servant, John King, Henry Irwin, Joshua Curle, James Ricketts –
His Majestie's Justices

Francis Ballard ack deeds for half an acre of Towne Land unto Samuel Sweny & the same ordered recorded.

Thomas Cornelius ack deeds for Towne Land unto John Henry Rombough & the same ordered recorded.

Henry Irwin & Josa. Curle Gent are appointed feofees of the Towne Land in the Roome of Capt. Bossell who is Dead and Mr. Lowry who refuses to supply the place.

Judgmt is confirmed agt Thomas Frye in the hands of Alexdr. McKenzie for £7:18:07 to Henry Irwin gent, he having made oath to his debt, with costs at exon.

Look for The Levy in the Ruff Order Book. Hen. Jenkins signe.

At a Court held the 3rd Wednesday of January being the 21st day 1718
Capt. Fra. Ballard, Mr. Antho. Armistead, Mr. Thomas Wythe, Mr. Henry Irwin, Mr. Josa. Curle, Mr. James Servant, Mr. James Ricketts
His Majestie's Justices

Richard Street & Eliza. his wife ack their deeds for land unto Samuel Sweny, Elizabeth being privated examined & same ordered recorded.

John Lowry producing a Commission dated 21 Nov. 1718 to be Surveyor of this County of Eliza. Citty & is accordingly sworn.

Upon petition of John Bordland for lycense to keep an ordinary in Hampton Towne. Granted giving bond & security.

Wm. Mallory ack a deed for land to his son Francis Mallory. Ordered recorded, Francis having first assumed to pay a Bill of Exchange to Collo. Harrison which Capt. Jenkins endorsed.

The last will & testament of James Brown dec'd is proved by oaths of Wm. Baylis & Hanh. Whittfeild witnesses & certificate for probate granted his Executrx giving bond & Sec, to wit, Thomas Wythe Security for the Probate.

[p 124] Moved that when Mr. Nelson's attchmt agt Henry Jenkins Adm of Jno. Curle dec'd is called that he have judgmt for his debt according to the former order.

The nuncupative will of Mikl. Roberts dec'd is proved by oaths of Francis Williams, Eliza. Creek and Eliza. Haslegrove witnesses thereof & certificate for probate granted Exectrx giving bond & sec & ordered recorded.

Upon petition of John Bayley & Josa. Curle for Adm of John Curle's Est, ordered the petition be lodged in the office till next Ct for consideration & if no person opposes it, that Adm be granted to petr.

Henry Hicks, orphan of Henry Hicks, is bound apprentice to Barto. Proby till he comes of age, learning orphan to read & write & to say his Commandments & at expiration of time to give him acc to law.

Thomas Hill & his mother Sarah Hill als Peirce came voluntarily into Ct & ack an Indenture to John Bordland. Ordered recorded.

John Bordland ack his part of Indenture to Thomas Hill & his mother &c & ordered recorded.

Upon petition of Giles Duberry for his est in hands of Thos. Morgan. Ordered that Morgan be summoned to next Ct to answer.

Emanuel Alkins action case brought agt Tempe. Parish is dismist with costs they having agreed.

Judgmt is confirmed agt Wm. Knight & Gilbert Wilson his Sec for what shall appear due at next Ct unto Richd. Nusum with costs at exon.

Judgmt is granted by Nihill Dicet agt John Wallas to answer suit of Richard Kirkin action detinue damage £5.

It's ordered that Mr. James Ricketts & Mr. Jos. Banister appr the remaining part of Eliza. Prescott's est & ret to next Ct.

Emanuel Alkin action case agt Robert Taylor. Capt. Jenkins, Deft's attorney being Dead & having his papers. Ordered refd to next Ct.

Thomas Skinner's petition agt Wm. Smelt Adm of Jno. Pett dec'd. Smelt being sick, ordered refd to next Ct.

Robert Westlake's Ejectmt agt James Ricketts. Capt. Jenkins, deft's attorney being dead, ordered refd to next Ct.

[p 125] John Ellyson agt Henry Jenkins Adm of John Curle dec'd. Dismst, Deft being Dead.

Judgmt granted to Charles Jenings Assigne of Henry Jenkins agt Henry Robinson & Jno. Batts Security of Richd. Kirkin for £6 with costs only the Defts have lyberty to bring in his Discount at next Ct. If not judgmt to be confirmed.

Samuel Selden's action trespass damage £10 agt Francis Ballard. Capt. Jenkins who having deft's papers being dead ordered refd to next Ct.

John Smith Senr Suit agt Margtt. Preist Exectrx of James Preist dec'd action case for 644 lbs tobo. Deft prays time to next Ct. Granted.

Francis Ballard's petition agt Mr. Servant's est is continued to next Ct.

Robert Wells' suit agt Samuel Bromage action case damage £10. Capt. Jenkins who having deft's papers being dead ordered refd to next Ct.

Emanuel Alkin's suit agt George Luke & Mary his wife action case damage £12. Plt prays time to next Ct. Granted. Capt. Jenkins being dead & having his papers & in the meantime the Cause is refd to Mr. Smelt in the room of Capt. Jenkins to compose the difference.

Charles Jenings' suit agt George Luke Esqr a debt for £6:02:06. Former order continued.

Emanuel Alkins's suit agt Jno. & Thomas Batts Execs of Henry Batts dec'd is dismist by consent of the Plt.

Judgmt by Nihill Dicet is granted agt Bryan Penny to answer suit of Edmond Kearny action debt damage £30.

Judgmt by Nihill Dicet granted agt Wm. Taylor at the suit of Wm. Smelt action case damage £50.

Judgmt by Nihill Dicet granted agt Thomas Jones to answer the suit of Thomas Poole Senr action detinue damage £55.

The last will & testament of Peter Baker dec'd is proved by oaths of Jno. Bayley & Susa. Banister witnesses & certificate for probate granted the Exectrx giving bond & security.

Upon petition of Wm. Williams & Mary his wife agt Mary Bridge for detaining a mare and colt &c. Ordered same be dismist.

The Grandjury being summoned & returned their presentments. Ordered that the severall persons be summoned to answer. Except Josa. Curle Junr who being not in his right mind.

[p 126] In the suit brought by Charles Chiswell Gent agt Samuel Sweny action upon the case damage £20. Deft making oath to his accott. Judgmt granted agt deft for £11:13:07 two farthings with costs at exon.

Suit brought by Hind Armistead & Hanh. his wife Execs of Matthew Watts dec'd agt Samuel Watts in an action upon the case damage £10. Ordered refd to next Ct for tryall.

The Court adjourns til tomorrow Ten a Clock

At a Court held the 22nd day of January 1718
Capt. Fra. Ballard, Mr. Thomas Wythe, Mr. John
King, Mr. Josa. Curle, Mr. Henry Irwin, Mr. James
Servant, Mr. James Ricketts –
His Majestie's Justices

The last will & testament of George Wauff Senr is proved by the oath of John Mitchell one of the witnesses & also made oath that he saw Henry Jenkins, one of the other witness, witness the will. Certificate for probate granted the Exec thereof, giving bond & sec, to wit, Henry Irwin & ordered recorded.

Ordered that William Winterton, Exec of Geo. Wauff, will pay to John Mitchel according to law for his one day's attendance at Ct in proving Wauff's will with costs.

Certificate for Adm with the will annexed of Geo. Jeggett's est granted to John Bordland &c giving bond & security, to wit, Cha. Jenings.

In the suit brought by James Ricketts & Jane his wife as guardians to Wilson Curle infant agt John Burtell Adm of James Burtell dec'd in an action of debt for Rent for £60. Capt. Jenkins, deft's attorney having his papers. Refd to next Ct.

Samuel Watts action of trespass d £40 agt Hind Armistead is by consent of parties refd to next Ct.

Elizabeth Bowtell action of debt for Rent for £5 agt Robert Taylor. The Plt being married, ordered the suit be dismist.

Barto. Proby Adm of Tho. Proby dec'd agt John Burtel Adm of James Burtel dec'd for £130 action of accot render. Capt. Jenkins having deft's papers, suit refd to next Ct.

[p 127] Charles Jenings' attchmt agt Thomas Wood action case continued to next Ct.

Henry Robinson's attchmt agt Thomas Wood action case continued to next Ct.

The suit brought by Henry Robinson agt Samuel Selden action case damage 1000 lbs tobo. Plt's lawyer being dead, plt prays time to next Ct. Granted.

Thomas Faulkner's suit agt Thomas Wilcox action case damage £10. Dismist with costs at exon.

Thomas Wilcox ack mortgage for Town Land unto Wm. Smelt. Ordered recorded.

Judgmt confirmed agt Jno. Burtell Adm &c of James Burtell dec'd for £68:03 (the interest being included) unto

Colo. Diggs gent, being bal of bond dated 22 Aug 1716 to be paid out of James Burtell's est with costs at exon.

By virtue of an attchmt from a Justice of the Peace agt John Blyth at the suit of Francis Ballard & he proving his accott. Judgmt is granted for 20 shillings agt Blyth's est to be paid in the hand of Matthew Small which is discharge of 120 lbs tobo & part of debt for 157 lbs tobo with costs at exon.

Robert Bright's attchmt agt Thomas Wood is refd to next Ct.

Margtt. Bayley's attchmt agt Thomas Wood refd to next Ct.

Elizabeth Hill's attchmt agt Thomas Wood refd to next Ct.

Bryan Penny's attchmt agt George Payne is continued to next Ct.

John Cook & Jno. Roe's suit agt Emanuel Alkin damage £30 action case. Deft prays time to next Ct. Granted.

Ellinor Bossell with her Securities Vizt: Jno. Bayley, Josa. Curle & Jas. Ricketts ack a bond for the Adm of Capt. Wm. Bossell's est & ordered recorded.

The Court Adjourns for one hour.

[p 125] William McKartee orphan being seven years of age is bound to John Massenburgh till he comes of age, Massenburg learning him to read & write and at expiration of time to give him according to law.

The petition of Mark Powell for Adm of his Brother Matt. Powell's est is granted giving bond & security.

Adm with the will annext of Thomas Powell's est is granted to Mark Powell his Brother during the minority of the heir giving bond &c.

The last will & testament of Thomas Powell dec'd is proved by oaths of Jno. Howard & Mark Powell witnesses & ordered recorded. Dec'd's est is to be appr by Hind Armistead, Jno. Howard, Mattw. Small & Wm. Spicer or any three of them & ret to next Ct.

It's ordered that Mark Powell [pay] to John Howard for his two days attendance as Evidence to prove Thomas Powell's will with costs at exon.

The last will & testament of Thomas Batts Senr dec'd is proved by oath of Charles Jenings, one of the witness, and also that he saw Eliza. Cole witness same & certificate for probate granted to the Exec thereof giving bond &c.

[Note: Next entry crossed over. Suit brought by Thomas Nelson]

In the suit brought by Thomas Nelson gent agt Henry Jenkins gent Adm of John Curle dec'd. In an action upon the case for £57:12, plt making oath to his accott. It's ordered that the former order shall be fully complied with for payment to plt.

Suit brought by Henry Robinson agt Samuel Selden. In an action of debt for £100 sterling, the deft assuming to put in his Rejoynder in the office within fifteen days ensuing. Ordered refd to next Ct.

Upon motion of John Mitchell to have Samuel Daniel's will proved. Ordered refd to next Ct for proof, Mr. King assuming to take what care he can possibly of the stock [in] the meantime & also ordered that no waste be made on either side.

Thomas Roberts action case damage £8 agt Nicholas Beynton, Capt. Jenkins having the papers. Ordered refd to next Ct for tryall.

[129] The action of accott render brought by John Croft Guardian to Abra. & Childerm. Croft agt Robert Taylor & arguments heard. Deft's attorney obliged himself to put in his pleas seven days before next Ct. Ordered refd to next Ct.

Judgmt granted agt Francis Mallory & Wm. Mallory his Sec for £5:16 to Charles Jenings with costs at exon only execution stayed till Last of May next.

Judgmt by Nihill Dicet granted agt John Skinner to answer the suit of John King Gent in an action of Covenant Broken damage £40.

Upon petition of Thomas Batts for Adm of est of Elizabeth his late wife, orphan of John Sheppard. Granted giving bond & sec according to law.

Ord that Rachel Provine, Elizabeth Hill & Sarah Jones be summoned to next Ct to answer the information of Henry Irwin gent.

Judgmt granted agt James Ricketts for £2:07:06 unto Matthew Small to be paid out of Mr. Nicholas Curle's est with costs at exon.

The Court adjourns Till Nine A Clock Tomorrow morning. F. Ballard signe.

At a Court held the 23rd day of January 1718
Capt. Fra. Ballard, Mr. Thos. Wythe, Mr. Henry Irwin,

Mr. Josa. Curle, Mr. James Ricketts, Mr. James Servant – His Majestie's Justices

Upon the motion of James Servant Gent to have the assignment of his Pattent recorded which is granted.

The last will & testament of Thomas Tucker dec'd is proved by oath of Charles Jenings, one of the witnesses.

Henry Cary & Richard Riddlehurst, Churchwardens of Denby Parish. Suit agt Wm. Spicer & Mary his wife action debt for 259 lbs tobo, defts plead nihill dicet. Refd to next Ct for plt to consider defts' plea.

John Coffee a Negro action assault & battry damage £20 agt Robert Taylor. Deft prays time to next Ct. Granted.

[p 130] Thomas Jenings' suit agt Henry Cocke action debt. It's ordered to be auditted by Mr. Joshua Curle & Capt. Francis Ballard & reported to next Ct.

Emanuel Alkin's suit agt John Mitchell is dismist, deft paying the Clerk of the Ct fees at exon.

Judgmt granted to Charles Jenings agt the Sheriff & James Naylor for what shall appear due at next Ct from Naylor.

Samuel Selden's Scirefacias agt Robert Armistead refd to next Ct upon deft's motion, His attorney being dead.

Upon return of an order of Ct wherein Henry Irwin had judgmt agt Thomas Frye for £7:18:07. It's ordered that unless the Sheriff return a negro boy of Fry's (which was not attached) to next Ct to be appraised that then judgmt shall be confirmed agt the Sheriff.

John Bordland's appr of Samuel Wilson's coat to be returned to next Ct.

John Smith's attchmt agt Thomas House is continued to next Ct.

The suit brought by John Smith Senr agt Jno. Burtell Adm of James Burtell is continued to next Ct, the Deft being Dead.

In the suit brought by Emanuel Alkins agt Francis Ballard gent [Note: part of this is scratched over & part added above the line] in an action upon the case damage £31. Report to next Ct for former order to be complied with (Mr. Henry Irwin & Capt. Hen. Jenkins showed? an accott butt Jenkins being dead). Ord that Mr. Samuel Sweny or anyone whom the plt shall think fit be in the room of Jenkins & report to next Ct.

The suit brought by Anthony Armistead Gent agt Francis Ballard Gent in an action case damage £500 sterling is refd to next Ct for tryall.

Francis Ballard's action debt for 546 lbs tobo agt Anthony Armistead, the deft's attorney being dead. It's refd to next Ct.

Suit brought by Wm. Marshall & his wife agt John King Gent action Detinue damage £300. Deft's attorney being dead ordered refd to next Ct.

[p 131] Francis Ballard's action case damage £13, deft's attorney being dead. Ordered refd to next Ct.

Francis Ballard's action case damage 2000 toba. Deft's attorney being dead, ordered refd to next Ct.

In the suit brought by Francis Ballard gent agt John Burtell Adm &c of James Burtell dec'd in an action upon the case damage £40 (Capt. Jenkins being dead). It's ordered that the persons who were to audit the accotts viz: Mr. Samuel Sweny, Mr. Jos. Banister & Mr. Joseph Wragg, perform the same & made report to next Ct.

Judgmt is granted agt John Smith Senr for paymt of what shall appead due at next Ct unto Charles Jenings with costs at exon.

Suit brought by John Smith & Edith his wife agt Henry Irwin Gent in an action of debt for £50. Deft's attorney being dead, refd to next Ct.

Judgmt is granted to Alexander McKenzie agt Richard Kirkin for what shall appear due at next Ct.

The former orders in the suit between John Hardiman & Francis Mallory for £4:07:07. It's ordered that same be confirmed with costs at exon.

Martin Bean's petition agt Wm. Smelt Adm of Jno. Pett dec'd, petitioner not appearing. Dismist with costs at exon.

Attachmt granted to Charles Jenings agt the est of Richard Kirkin in an action upon the case damage £8.

Falvy Coopland action assault & battery agt John Faulkner is dismist, plt not having filed his declr.

Samuel White's suit agt Jno. Bayley Sheriff refd to next Ct, Deft's attorney being dead.

In the suit brought by John Burtell Adm &c of James Burtell dec'd agt Thomas Frye action case damage £4, deft being dead. Ordered suit be dismist with costs at exon.

Hanah Roberts action trespass assault & battry damage £20 agt Robert Tannoch. Deft prays imparlence. Granted.

Emanuel Alkin's suit agt Jno. Vaughan action case damage £3 is dismist there being no appearance.

Charles Moone [or Moore] agt Robert Tannoch is dismist with costs at exon.

[p 132] Edward Tabb Exec of Thomas Tabb dec'd action case agt John Merry, there being no declr filed. Ordered that suit be dismist with costs at exon.

Willm. Lowry action case damage 1000 lbs tobo agt Andr. Laws refd to next Ct upon plt's request.

Emanuel Alkin's Scirefs agt James Naylor for 27 shillings, deft not appearing & the Sheriff undertaking for his appearance at next Ct. Imparlence granted him.

Upon the Information of Joshua Curle Gent ord that persons informed against be summoned to next Ct to answer.

Then the Court adjourns to the Court in Course.

F. Ballard signe.

At a Court held the 3rd Wednesday of Febry being ye 18th day 1718
Capt. Fra. Ballard, Mr. Antho. Armistead, Mr. Thomas Wythe, Mr. Josa. Curle, Mr. Jno. King, Mr. Hen. Irwin – His Majestie's Justices

Upon petition of Mary Jenkins for Adm of her dec'd husband Capt. Hen. Jenkins est, certificate for Adm granted her giving bond & security.

Judgmt confessed by Hind Armistead for £3:07:06 to Emanuel Alkin with costs at exon.

Emanuel Alkin's suit agt Mary Bridge, they having agreed. Ordered dismist with costs.

James Servant gent action upon the case damage – – – agt Robert Tannoch & parties not appearing. Ordered dismist with costs at exon.

Samuel Sweny's suit agt Thomas Watts, plt not appearing to prosecute. Ordered dismist with costs at exon.

Edward Myhill's action debt agt Thomas Delany and the – – – – not appearing. Ordered dismist with costs at exon.

Samuel Sweny's suit agt Florence Dreskell & they not appearing. Ordered dismist with costs at exon.

Capt. Francis Ballard having sworn to his accott agt James Burtell dec'd est. Ordered that he have judgmt when the action is called.

Joshua Curle's suit agt William Deandridge, Curle not appearing. Ordered dismist with costs at exon.

[p 133] Order granted agt Thomas Delaney, James Chapple his Sec & the Sheriff for the non-appearance of Delaney to answer the suit of Samuel Sweny in an action upon the case damage £5.

Upon the motion of John Bayley Sheriff, attchmt is granted him agt the est of Thomas Delany for the above sum to save himself.

Order granted agt the Sheriff for the non-appearance of Thomas Baylis to answer the suit of Paul Phillips action trespass damage £20.

Order granted agt Henry Hays & Joseph Wragg his Sec for his non-appearance to answer the suit of Eliza. Hill action assault & battry damage £20.

Richard Kirkin's suit agt John Burtell Adm of James Burtell dec'd & no accott appearing. Ordered suit dismist with costs at exon.

James Roscow Esqr suit agt Ellinor Boswell Adm of Wm. Boswell &c in an action upon the case damage £500 & no declr being filed which upon motion of deft nonsuit is granted her with costs at exon.

Judgmt confessed by Elizabeth Hill for £8:08:01 1/2 unto Jno. Bordland with costs at exon.

Upon petition of Mary Jenkins for Adm on John Curle's est. It's ordered that certificate for Adm be granted her giving bond & security.

It's ordered that the est of Capt. Henry Jenkins dec'd be appr by Mr. Henry Irwin, Mr. John King, Capt. Francis Ballard & Mr. Jos. Banister or any three of them & ret to next Ct.

It's ordered that the est of John Curle dec'd by appr by Mr. Henry Irwin, Mr. John King, Capt. Francis Ballard & Mr. Jos. Banister or any three of them & ret to next Ct.

Richard FitzWilliams Esqr enters himself Security to pay all costs & damages if lost in a suit brought by Matthew Hilliard agt Cornelius Dorlich & Rachel his wife action case damage £7.

Matthew Hilliard's power of atty to Richd. FitzWilliams Esqr is proved in Ct & ordered recorded.

Special Imparlence granted to Cornelius Dorlich & Rachel his wife to answer the suit of Matthew Hilliard action case damage £7.

John Smith Junr suit agt Henry Jenkins Adm of Jno. Curle dec'd action case damage £4 the deft being dead. Ordered dismist with costs at exon.

Samuel Selden's action case agt James Thompson they having made up. Dismist with costs at exon.

Bart. Selden and Archily his wife [Note: added above line – Adm &c] suit agt Joseph Wragg action case damage £10. Deft prays time to next Ct. Granted.

[p 134] Epaphroditus Williams' action case damage £6:5:5 agt Robert Fletcher is dismist. No appearance.

Mary Jenkins, Thomas Wythe, Joshua Curle & Jno. Bayley ack a bond for Adm of Capt. Henry Jenkins est. Ordered recorded.

The last will & testament of Wm. Minson dec'd is proved by oaths of Samuel Selden, Thomas Jones, & Jno. Bushell witness & certificate for probate granted to Exectrx giving bond & Sec.

The last will & testament of Mark Johnson Gent dec'd is proved by oaths of Charles Jenings & Wm. Westwood witnesses & certificate of probate granted Exectrx giving bond & Sec.

It's ordered that the est of Mark Johnson dec'd be appr by Mr. Thomas Wythe, Mr. John King, Mr. Edward Tabb & Mr. Joseph Banister or any three of them. Ret to next Ct.

The King's Information agt Rachel Provine & Sarah Jones is discontinued for want of proof.

The King's Information agt Elizabeth Hill who pleads not Guilty. It's ordered refd to next Ct for tryall.

The Court adjourns til Tomorrow ten a Clock.

At a Court held the 19th Day of February 1718
Capt. Francis Ballard, Mr. Antho. Armistead, Mr.
Thomas Wythe, Mr. John King, Mr. Josa. Curle,
Mr. Hen. Irwin, Mr. James Servant –
His Majestie's Justices

Upon petition of Wm. Short for Turning the Road. It's ordered that Mr. Jno. Bayley & Capt. Francis Ballard view the road & report to next Ct.

Upon petition of Wm. Short for lycense to keep an ordinary at the Watering place. Granted giving bond & sec.

Upon petition of John Noblin to choose his guardian who makes choyce of Mickl. Draper & ordered Noblin's est in his hands provided he give bond & sec.

Charles Jenings' suit agt Robert Bright action case damage 600 lbs tobo. Refd to next Ct.

Order granted agt Thomas Wilcox & John Cook his Sec for his non-appearance to answer the suit of Wm. Greek action case damage £4.

John Wallass' suit agt Owen Raine action case damage £3 they having made up. Ordered dismist.

[p 135] Order granted agt George Wilson & Emanl. Alkin his Sec for his non-appearance to answer the suit of Cornelius Dorlich & Rachel his wife action of assault & battery damage £10 current money.

Order granted agt Robert Tucker, Jno. Wallas & Thos. Jones his Sec for his non-appearance to answer the suit of Cornelius Dorlich & Rachel his wife action trespass for an assault & battery damage £20.

Henry Hays action agt the Sloop Hampton is dismist.

George Waffe's warrant agt Richard Casey is dismist there being no prosecution.

John Bayley & Joshua Curle's petition for Adm on John Curle's est is dismist.

Upon petition of Giles Duberry for his est in the hands of Thomas Morgan. It's ordered that Morgan pay petitioner the same according to apprsmt.

Richard Nusum's suit agt Wm. Knight action case damage £5 the plt not appearing. Ordered dismist.

Ordered that apprsmt of Capt. Wm. Bosell's est be returned to next Ct.

Judgmt is confirmed agt Jno. Wallas in an action of Detinue damage £10 for a Horse &c in the declr mentioned at the suit of Richd. Kirkin, but because it is unknown to the Ct what damage the plt has sustained, it's ordered that a writ of inquiry issue.

It's ordered that appraismt of the remainder of Elizabeth Prescott's est be returned to next Ct.

Upon petition of Emanuel Alkin agt Robert Taylor for £10 for the cure of Negr Coffey's Legg. Ordered that petition be dismist.

Upon petition of Thomas Skinner agt Wm. Smelt Adm of Jno. Pett dec'd for £6:01:04 for keeping of Pett's child, Smelt not appearing. Upon motion of plt refd to next Ct.

The Ejectmt brought by Robert Westlake agt James Ricketts for lands & tenements mentioned in the declr, deft not being present. Refd to next Ct, he paying this Ct's fee.

The suit brought by John Ellyson agt Emanuel Alkin in an action upon the case damage £10, jury being impanneled, namely: Henry Robinson, Willm. Coopland, James Naylor, Thos. Jones, Hind Armistead, Thomas Baylis, George Waffe, Jno. Cook, Willm. More, John Howard, Falvy Coopland, Wm. Spicer, Wm. Baylis & Samuel Sweny. [Jury's verdict] in these words. We of the Jury find for the plt damage £5. Samuel Sweny foreman
[p 136] and upon motion of plt verdict is ordered recorded & judgmt granted agt deft for paymt with costs at exon.

The appraismt of Thomas Powell's est being returned. Ordered that same be recorded.

Judgmt is granted to John Smith agt Margtt. Preist Exectrx of James Preist dec'd in an action upon the case for 654 lbs tobo. Because it is unknown what damage plt hath sustained, it's ordered that writ of inquiry be awarded to inquire into damages at next Ct.

The nuncupative will of James Dixon is proved by oaths of George Guy & James Cousens witnesses.

In the action upon the case damage £12 brought by Charles Jenings assigne of Henry Jenkins agt Richard Kirkin [who] exhibits an accott, the Ct settling the same. Ordered the deft with his Securities pay £4:11:04 with costs at exon.

It's ordered that the est of Thomas Tucker dec'd be appr by James Naylor, Wm. Coopland, Edward Lattemore & James Naylor or any three of them & returned to next Ct.

Mary Jenkins & her Securities ack a bond for Adm of John Curle's est & ordered to be recorded.

The last will & testament of Samuel Daniels dec'd is proved by oath of Nicho. Parker & affirmation of Joseph Wragg witnesses & certificate for Probate granted to John Mitchell Exec giving bond & Security.

It's ordered that John Mitchell pay to Joseph Wragg & Nicholas Parker for their three days attendance each as Evidences to prove Saml. Daniels' will with costs at exon.

Upon petition of Julian Daniel widow of Saml. Daniel dec'd to decline her part to the will & adhere to what the law allows her. Ordered that petition be granted.

The presentments of the Grand Jury agt Richard Hawkins for stopping a road by his house & he appearing and excusing himself, ordered fine be remitted paying costs at exon.

The presentment of the Grand Jury agt Thomas Needham for not coming to Church, he appearing & excusing himself. Ordered fine be remitted with costs at exon.

[p 137] Note: the following persons were presented by the Grand Jury for not coming to Church. Those not excused were to be fined 5 shillings or 50 lbs tobo to be paid to the Churchwardens of this Parish at the laying of the next Levy for use of the Poor of the Parish with costs at exon. Fines were remitted for those who appeared and excused themselves.
   Henry Cock – fined.
   Thomas Baylis – fined.
   Fleet Cooper – fined.
   Thomas Britten – fined.
   Mickl. Peirce – fined.
   Jno. Whifield – excused.
   Thos. Pool Senr, he being Infirme. Fine remitted.
   Wm. Browne, not appearing. Fined.
   Jno. Poole Jur – excused.
   Jno. Pool, Sawyer – excused.
   Andr. Bully – fined.
   Wm. Peirce – fined.

[p 138] John Wallas – fined.
   Richard Rowton – fined.
   Richard Ellis – fined.
   It's ordered that the Sheriff summon James Floyd and John Martin to next Ct to answer the presentment of the Grand Jury.
   Job. [?] Thomas – fined.
   Wm. Lowry & Jno. Lowry – fined.
   Thomas Watts – fined.

Upon motion of Robert Armistead Deputie atty &c. Ordered that Sarah Robinson & Cornelius Dorlich & Rachil his wife be summoned to next Ct to answer the Information &c of Henry Irwin Gent.
   John Noblin, orphan, by his own consent bound apprentice to Charles Cooper until he comes of age, he being fifteen years old next Oct coming. Cooper to learn him to read & write & trade of carpenter & at expiration of term to give Tools necessary to build a house &c.
   It's ordered that the est of Samuel Daniel Dec'd be appr by Mr. Jos. Banister, Mr. Samuel Sweny, Mr. Joseph

Wragg & Mr. Wm. Loyall or any three of them & return to next Ct.

Then the Court adjourns till the Court in Course.

F. Ballard Signe

[p 139]

At a Court held the 3rd Wednesday of Aprill being the 15th day 1719
Francis Ballard, Jno. King, James Servant, Joshua Curle, Henry Irwin – His Majestie's Justices

Edwd. Ballard ack his lease & release for 1/2 acre Town Land to Cha. Jenings, also Eliza. his wife ack deed, she being privately examined in the Business & same ordered recorded.

Tho. Williams' Power of Atty to Rebeca his wife was proved by oath of Christopher Hindes one of the witnesses & same ordered recorded.

Rebeca Williams wife of Thos. Williams by virtue of a power of atty from Thos. ack certain deeds in land to Wm. Allen, she being privately examined. Same ordered recorded.

Upon petition of Ann Lowry for lycense to keep an ordy [ordinary] at her house in Hampton Town. Granted giving bond & Sec.

Upon petition of Jane Baccus for her est in the hands of Thos. Howard & Howard appearing chooses Mr. Curle & the sd Jane chooses Mr. Servant to settle accotts between them & ordered to make report at next Ct.

The last will & testament of Robert Minson dec'd is proved by affirmation of Joseph Wragg & oath of Robert Tannoch witnesses. Certificate for probate granted to Exec [or Execs] giving bond &c.

John Davis, orphan, by his own consent being eleven years old the 19th of Jan last past is bound apprentice to Joseph Wragg till he comes of age, he learning apprentice to "wright" & to cypher & also to learn him his trade & at expiration of time to give him according to law.

F. Ballard Signe

[p 140]

At a Court held the third Wednesday of May being the 20th day 1719
Capt. Francis Ballard, Mr. Anthony Armistead, Mr. Thomas Wythe, Mr. John King, Mr. Joshua Curle, Mr. Henry Irwin, Mr. James Servant, Mr. James Ricketts – Justices

The last will & testament of Edward Myhill dec'd being presented to be proved which is opposed. It's therefore ordered refd to next Ct for the heir at Law to come in if any.

Nicholas & Nathaniel Parker ack an agreement between them each to the other. Ordered recorded.

Upon motion of Thomas Wilcox for auditors to settle the accotts between him & the est of Elizabeth James dec'd. Ordered that Mr. Charles Jenings be added in the room of Capt. Wm. Bossell dec'd & report to next Ct.

Upon motion of Elizabeth Tabb [inserted above line & very blurred "wido. of --- Tabb"] Gdn to two of her children vizt Edward & Martha Tabb [also added above line - "and to have their est in her possession"]. Ord that petition be granted giving bond & Sec & that Mr. Edwd. Tabb Exec of Tabb's will pay all & singular their Estates to the Petitioner.

The last will & testament of Edmund Hollier dec'd is proved by oaths of Thomas Wythe & Edward Tabb witnesses & certificate for probate granted Exec giving bond & Sec.

It's ordered that the est of Edmund Hollier dec'd be appr by Mr. William Lowry, Mr. Edward Tabb, Mr. Wm. Tucker & Mr. Wm. More or any three of them. Return appr to next Ct.

The last will & testament of Margrett Preist dec'd proved by oaths of Thomas Parris & Ann Pirkett witnesses & certificate for probate granted Exec giving bond & Sec.

Ordered that Mr. Edward Tabb, Mr. Simon Hollier, Mr. Merritt Sweny & Mr. Antho. Armistead Jur or any three of them appr est of Margrett Preist dec'd. Ret to next Ct.

Walter Ress Servant to Andrew Laws is adjudged to be fifteen years of age & to pay Levy according to law.

The Court ordered that there be an Orphans' Court held every October.

It's ordered that William Williams be summoned to next Ct to give Security for the est belonging to the orphans of John Roberts dec'd.

It's ordered that Mr. Edwd. Lattemore, Mr. James Naylor, Mr. Wm. Coopland & Mr. John Bushell or any three of them appr est of Humphrey Baylis dec'd & return to next Ct.

Upon motion of William Smelt to have the remaining part of John Pett's est. It's ordered that the appraisers appt in former order return appr to next Ct.

Note: the Grand Jury made presentments for not coming to Church agt the following persons. If they were not excused, a fine of 5 shillings or 50 lbs tobo was to be paid to the Churchwardens of the Parish at the laying of the Levy to be used for the Poor of the Parish. If they were excused, fine was to be remitted with costs at execution.

Francis Mallory – not excused.
Wm. Marshall – excused.
Edward Tabb – excused.
Wm. Fling [?] – not excused.
Florence Driskell, not appearing. Sheriff ordered to summon him to next Ct.
William More – excused.
Wm. Walker – excused.
Thomas Randoll, not appearing. Fined.
Thomas Allen, not appearing. Fined.
It's ordered that Wm. Allen pilot be summoned to next Ct to answer the presentment of the Grand Jury.
Charles Allen – not excused.
Thomas Skinner – not excused.

[p 142]
Thomas Baccus – not excused.
Francis Massenburgh – not excused.
Emanl. Alkin, not appearing. Fined.
Falvy Coopland – not excused.
Thomas Wilson, not appearing. Rined.
Henry Dunn, not appearing. Fined.
John Dunn – excused.
Wm. Scott, not appearing. Fined.
John George, not appearing. Fined.
John George, Junr – excused.
Matthew Small – not excused.
Abraham Pirkett – not excused.

Ordered that the Sheriff summon Francis George to appear at next Ct to answer the presentment of the Grand Jury for having a bastard child borne of her body.

Ordered that the Sheriff summon Mary Floyd to appear at next Ct to answer the presentment of the Grand Jury for having a bastard child borne of her body.

Presentment of the Grand Jury agt Richard Casey for breaking the Sabbath & he not appearing. Ordered he be fined according to law [no amount given] & pay to the

Churchwarden &c if he does not appear at next Ct & excuse himself.

Robert Wells action case damage £10 agt Samuel Bromage. Judgmt granted the plt according to declr & a Writ of Inquire awarded.

Judgmt granted agt George Luke & Mary his wife for £1:19:06 being the balance to Charles Jenings with costs at exon, the plt having made oath to his accot.

Edmond Kearny's suit agt Bryan Penny damage 1000 lbs tobo & deft pleading. Plt prays time to next Ct to answer. Granted.

Capt. Francis Ballard's petition agt Servant's est. Ordered accotts be audited according to former order & report to next Ct.

John Pool Senr a Detinue agt Thomas Jones damage £55, deft pleads the Genll Issue. Refd to next Ct for tryall.

Henry Robinson's suit agt Samuel Selden action case dam 1800 lbs tobo. Plt prays time to next Ct to reply. Granted.

John Cook & John R--s action case damage £3 agt Emanuel Alkin. Cont to next Ct upon deft's motion.

Charles Jenings' suit agt Thomas Wood action case. Attchmt continued to next Ct for further proceedings.

Henry Robinson's suit agt Wm. Taylor action case damage £50. There being no appearance ordered suit dismist with costs at exon.

Eliza. Hill's attchmt agt Thomas Wood is dismist. No appearance.

[p 143] Suit brought by Samuel Watts agt Hind Armistead in action of trespass damage £40. Two evidences each for plt & deft being heard and Jury impanneled namely: Bryan Penny, Thomas Baylis, Wm. Coopland, William Thurkett, Thomas Jones, John Cook, Falvy Coopland, Thomas Howard [foreman], Thomas Batts, George Wauffe, Nathl. Parker & John Pool. Special verdict returned: Hind Armistead did enter into the close & freehold of plt and broke down the brickwall whereto the still was fastened & insloped & carried away the still contrary to the will of the plt. We also find that the still was so fixed when the plt purchased the land of Matthew Watts who brought syder to Samuel to still during his lifetime & paid for the distilling. Matthew Watts sold the still as appurtenance and about three weeks before he died, said the still should never be removed off that plantation. Upon execution of the deeds of lease &

release from Matthew to Samuel Watts, the Jury finds the still to be esteemed, reputed & taken to be & set upon land of Matthew Watts which he sold to the plt. We find Mr. Hind Armistead, deft, intermarried with Hannah the widow of sd Watts & ... that he left all his personal estate to his wife & children & made wife Exectrx. We find the sd Watts in his last sickness ordered that the still be brought home for the use of his family & [that in his life he has said] if he sold his land he would remove the still, being asked what he had for the use of the still, after, he answered nothing but his Craw full of drink when he went there. We find Watts sent for Thomas Jones to make his will & being asked what he would do with the still, he said there was no occasion to make mention of it for it would go with the rest of his personal estate to his wife & children. We do not find that Watts made any conveyance of the still to anyone & if upon the whole matter Law be with Pltf, We find for the plt £12 current money damage. Otherwise we find for the deft. Ord recorded & refd to next Ct for matters of Law to be argued.

Hanah Roberts' action trespass assault & battery damage £10 agt Robert Tannoch. Continued to next Ct at deft's costs.

Henry Robinson's action debt for £100 sterling agt Samuel Selden plt rejoyning. Deft prays time to next Ct. Granted.

John Croft Gdn &c action accot render agt Robert Taylor deft pleading. Plt prays time to next Ct. Granted.

Henry Cary & Richard Riddlehurst Churchwardens of Denby Parish. Suit agt William Spicer & Mary his wife action debt for 559 lbs tobo. Defts' atty being sick. It's ordered that suit be refd to next Ct upon defts' cost.

Henry Irwin gent. Suit agt Thomas Frye is dismist.

[p 145] John Coffee action assault & battery agt Robert Taylor damage £10. Deft pleads to which plt joynes. Refd to next Ct for tryall.

Emanuel Alkin's suit agt Francis Ballard action case damage £31. Refd to next Ct for accotts to be settled.

Francis Ballard's action upon case damage £13. Refd to next Ct for accotts to be settled.

Francis Ballard's action case damage 2000 lbs tobo. Refd to next Ct for accotts to be settled.

Judgmt granted agt John Smith Senr for 1202 lbs tobo unto Charles Jenings with costs at exon, plt having proved his accott.

Judgmt confirmed agt John Burtell Adm &c of James Burtell for £6 one farthing current money & 76 bushells & a halfe of Sault & 605 lbs tobo to Francis Ballard Gent according to auditors' report to be paid out of est of James Burtell dec'd with costs at exon. If assets are not sufficient then the cost out of the proper estate of John Burtell.

Emanuel Alkin's Scirefacias agt James Naylor for £1:07. Order renewed, deft making what just discount he can with costs at exon.

Richard Kirkins' power of atty to Joseph Wragg proved by oaths of Nicholas Parker & Wm. Brough witnesses. Ordered recorded.

Joseph Wragg by virtue of a power of atty made to him by Richard Kirkin ack deeds for Town land to Richard Nusum. Ordered recorded.

Special imparlence granted to Ellinor Boswell Admtrx of Wm. Bossell [sic] dec'd &c to answer suit of James Rascow Esqr action case damage £500 sterling.

Special imparlence granted to Mary Jenkins Admtrx &c of Henry Jenkins dec'd to answer suit of Richard Fitzwilliams Esqr action debt for £45:06:03.

Special imparlence granted to Mary Jenkins Admtrx &c of Henry Jenkins dec'd to answer suit of Richard Fitzwilliams Esqr action case for £4:6:8.

Judgmt granted agt Mary Jenkins Admtrx &c of Henry Jenkins for £133:05 unto Thomas Nelson gent, it being due for protested bills of Exchange, he saying that he never received any satisfaction. To be paid out of Decedant's est.

Judgmt granted agt Mary Jenkins Admtrx &c of Henry Jenkins dec'd for £170:03:11 3 farthings to Thomas Nelson gent, he having proved his accotts. To be paid out of decedant's est with costs at exon.

[p 146] Special imparlence granted to John Burtell Adm of James Burtell dec'd to answer suit of Richard Bland action case £17:01:11.

Imparlence granted to John Faulkner to answer suit of Falvy Coopland in action tressp for an assault & battery damage £10.

Upon petition of Richard Nusum for lycense to keep an ordinary at his house in Hampton Towne. Granted giving bond & security.

Upon petition of Rachel Dorlich for lycense to keep an ordinary at her house in Hampton Towne. Granted giving bond & security.

Upon petition of Elizabeth Hill to keep an ordinary at her house in Hampton Towne. Granted giving bond & security.

The Court adjourns till Tomorrow ten a Clock. F. Ballard signe.

At a Court held the 21st day of May 1719
Capt. Francis Ballard, Mr. Thomas Wythe, Mr. Antho.
Armistead, Mr. Jno. King, Mr. Joshua Curle,
Mr. James Servant, Mr. James Ricketts — Justices

It's ordered that John King gent be paid £8 according to the agreement for making the Ducking Stool &c who hath the money in his hands at exon.

Samuel Skinner chooses his father Thomas Skinner his gdn & also prays that his est left him by his grandmother Ann Daniels dec'd might be put in his father's hands &c. John Mitchell Exec of Samuel Daniels' will prays time to next Ct to answer petition. Granted.

Upon petition of Sarah Hays for Adm of her son Hays dec'd [sic]. Ordered petition be granted giving bond & security.

Upon petition of Hind Armistead & William Spicer to be discharged from being Securities for Mary Bridge's probate of Hopkin's est. It's ordered that Mary Bridge be summoned to next Ct to answer petition.

It's ordered that Samuel Watts pay to Isaac Preedy according to law for his 28 days attendance as an Evidence for Watts agt Hind Armistead with costs at exon.

Upon petition of Wm. Winterton & Joseph Wragg to be discharged from being Securities for Mary Gilbert's Adm of James Gilbert's est. It's ordered that Mary Gilbert be summoned to next Ct to answer petition.

[p 147] Judgmt is confirmed agt George Luke & Mary his wife for £3:10 to Emanuel Alkin with costs at exon.

Hind Armistead & Hanah his wife Exectrx action case damage £10 agt Samuel Watts. Refd to next Ct.

Presentment of the Grand Jury agt John Martin for not coming to church, he not excusing himself. Ordered fined 5 shillings or 50 lbs tobo to be paid to the Churchwardens for the use of the Poor of the Parish.

Mark Powell with his Security ack bond for Adm with will annext of Thomas Powell dec'd. Ord recorded.

Thomas Roberts' action case damage £8 agt Nicholas Beynton. Judgmt confirmed agt deft according to declr and a writ of Inquire awarded to inquire damages.

Charles Jenings' suit agt James Naylor action case continued to next Ct.

Imparlence granted to Mary Jenkins Admtrx of Henry Jenkins to answer suit of Charles Jenings action case damage 2000 lbs tobo.

Richard Kirkin's action case agt Cely Langman deft pleads she owes nothing. Refd to next Ct for tryall.

Imparlence granted to Samuel White to answer suit of John & Thomas Batts Execs of Henry Batts dec'd.

John Burtell Adm &c agt Thomas Frye action case damage £4 current money, sd Frye being returned not found within the Bailiwick. Upon motion of plt attchmt agt deft's est returned to next Ct for further proceedings.

Emanuel Alkin's action case damage £10 agt John & Thomas Batts Execs &c. Defts pray time to next Ct to answer. Granted.

John & Thomas Batts, Execs of Henry Batts dec'd, suit agt Joseph Wragg action case damage £6, defts pray time to next Ct. Granted.

Bryan Penny action assault & battery damage £10 agt Henry Jenkins, plt failing to prosecute. Upon motion of deft non suit granted. Ordered plt pay 5 shillings to deft with costs at exon.

Order granted agt Thomas Wilcox & John Wallas his Security for his non-appearance to answer suit of Jacob Talbert action debt damage £2 current money.

Emanuel Alkin's action case damage £10 current money agt Mark Powell, deft pleads he owes nothing. Refd to next Ct for tryall.

Imparlence granted to John More to answer suit of Robert Taylor action trespass damage £100 sterling.

[p 148] John Bordland action case damage £15 curt money agt Cornels. Dorlich, deft not appearing. Upon motion of plt attchmt is granted agt deft's est with costs returnable to next Ct for further proceedings to be had.

Order granted agt Eliza. Hill & Charles Jenings her Security for her non-appearance to answer suit of Robt. Taylor action case damage £5.

Emanuel Alkin's action case damage £8 current silver money agt Wm. Barber & Susanh. his wife. Defts pray time to next Ct. Granted.

Order granted agt the Sheriff for non-appearance of Thomas Wilcox to answer suit of James Servant a debt for £3:10.

Judgmt confessed by Joseph Milby for 225 1/2 lbs tobo to Francis Ballard Gent with costs at exon.

Order granted agt the Sheriff for the non-appearance of Wm. Browne to answer suit of Saml. Selden assigne of Mary Floyd.

John Croft &c agt Robert Taylor, bil Chancery, deft pleading, the plt prays time to next Ct to consider deft's plea. Granted.

William Smelt action case damage £10 agt Richard Nusum & Plt not appearing. Ordered suit dismist.

William Robinson a debt for £50 bills Exa [Exchange] agt Mary Jenkins Admx &c of Henry Jenkins dec'd, plt not appearing. Upon motion of deft nonsuit is granted & ordered plt pay damage 5 shillings with costs at exon.

William Robinson's action case damage £50 curt money agt Mary Jenkins Admx &c, plt not appearing. Upon motion of deft nonsuit is granted & ordered plt pay damage 5 shillings with costs at exon.

George Waffe action case damage £6 agt Willm. Winterton & Jane his wife Execs of Geo. Waffe dec'd. Deft prays time to next Ct. Granted.

Order granted agt John Liles & Alexdr. McKenzie & Jos. Curle his Securities for his non-appearance to answer suit of Emanuel Alkin action case damage £5 curt money.

Order granted agt Henry Irwin gent Security of Jno. Battersby for Battersby's non-appearance to answer suit of Samuel White action case damage £6.

It's ordered that Hind Armistead pay to Thomas Jones for his 26 days & to Jno. Theadam for his 27 days attendance according to Law, as Evidences for him agt Saml. Watts with costs at exon.

[p 149] In the suit brought by John Smith agt John Burtell Adm &c of James Burtell in an action upon the case damage £80 current money. Auditors' report returned approving

£12:03:10, 200 bushels of Indian corn & 1 barrel of tarr. Ordered paid out of decedant's est with costs at exon.

In the suit brought by Anthony Armistead gent agt Francis Ballard gent in an action upon the case damage £500 sterling. By consent ordered accotts be audited by Mr. Thomas Wythe, Mr. Simon Hollier & Mr. Edward Tabb or any two of them. If either of the parties does not meet to acct before the audittors, then judgmt shall be entered at next Ct for what shall appear due.

Francis Ballard's action debt for 506 lbs tobo agt Anthony Armistead is refd to the same audittors above mentioned [sic].

Francis Ballard's action debt for 3021 lbs tobo refd to same audittors as above [sic].

Bartrand Proby Adm of Thomas Proby dec'd suit agt John Burtell Adm &c of James Burtell dec'd an accott render for £130 and auditors report being returned & audit & writ being found erroneous, the plt hath Lyberty to amend paying cost & ord suit refd to next Ct for to be amended & that they come to tryall at next Ct for the costs.

Hind Armistead ack a certain deed for land to Charles Tucker, also Hanah wife to Hind Armistead relinquishes her right of dower, she being privately examined. Ordered recorded. And also they ack deed & bond to Tucker & ordered recorded.

James Ricketts & Jane his wife as guardians to Wilson Curle infant a debt agt Jno. Burtell Adm &c of James Burtell for £60. Plts not having accott ready, upon his motion it's ordered refd to next Ct he paying costs.

Bryan Penny's atcht agt George Paine is refd to next Ct by consent.

In the Scirefacias brought by Samuel Selden agt Robert Armistead as bayl for Chr. Phillipson for £12:18:02 & 303 lbs tobo. Ct are of the opinion & do order suit dismist, for that George Luke Esqr who was also bail for Phillipson ought to have been mentioned in the scirefacias, from which order plt appeals to the seventh day of the Honeabl the Genl Ct next coming. Granted giving bond &c (to witt) Jno. Smith.

[p 150] Judgmt granted agt Henry Irwin Gent for £50 sterling according to bond & dated 19 Oct 1717 unto John Smith Senr with costs at exon, only deft hath lyberty to put in a plea before signing of the order.

Ordered that the Liste of Tythables be taken on 4 June next coming by the Gent hereafter named Vizt: Capt. Francis Ballard Salter's Creek &c. Mr. James Servant the east side of Hampton River, Harrisses Creek & ---- to Hampton river bridge. Mr. Joshua Curle his Towne. Mr. Antho. Armistead the north side of Back River. Mr. Wythe & Mr. John King along the east side of Back River.

Judgmt by nihill dicet is granted agt Henry Cock for £20 unto Thomas Jenings.

Judgmt is granted agt Thomas Delany for 7 shillings & 4 hogsheads of Cyder to Samuel Sweny with costs at exon.

Paul Phillips action of trespass agt Thomas Baylis damage £10. Dismist with costs at exon.

Appraismt of Capt. Henry Jenkins & John Curle's estates is continued to next Ct.

Matthew Hilliard's action case damage £7 agt Cornelius Dorlich & Rachil his wife there being no appearance. Ordered dismist.

Bartholomew Selden & Archiley his wife Adm &c action case damage £10 current money agt Joseph Wragg. Deft pleads he owes nothing in manr & forme &c. Ordered refd to next Ct for tryal.

Appraismt of Mark Johnson dec'd est is continued to next Ct to be performed according to former order.

Henry Irwin gent information agt Elizabeth Hill, deft pleading not guilty. It's ordered refd to next Ct for tryall.

William Marshall & his wife's suit agt Jno. King gent action detinue damage £300, deft pleading not guilty. it's ordered refd to next Ct for tryall.

William Short's petition for to turn the Road continued to next Ct for former order to be complied with.

Judgmt by nihill dicet is granted agt Thomas Wilcox to answer the suit of Willm. Greek action case damage £4.

Appraismt of Capt. Bossell's est continued to next Ct for the former order to be complied with.

Appr of Prescott's est is continued to next Ct.

[p 151] John Pool's ejectmt agt James Ricketts is refd to next Ct, deft paying this Ct's costs.

Appraismt of Thomas Tucker's est is continued to next Ct for the former order to be complied with.

Samuel Selden's action trespass damage £10 agt Francis Ballard is refd to next Ct for a fuller Ct.

It's ordered that the appraismt of Samuel Daniel's est be returned to next Ct.

It's ordered that the Sheriff take Sarah Robinson & Rachel Dorlich into custody til they give bayle & security for their appearance at next Ct to answer the information of Henry Irwin gent.

Upon the petition of Thomas Skinner agt William Smelt Adm of John Pett dec'd estate for paymt for keeping & nursing of Pett's child, the Ct finds the balance £10 current money. Ordered Smelt to pay petitioner out of Pett's est with costs at exon.

Imparlence granted to Mary Jenkins Admx &c of John Curle & ordered to answer suit of Charles Jenings action case damage 1000 lbs tobo.

John Bordland action case damage £60 current money agt Mary Jenkins Admx &c of Henry Jenkins dec'd, plt not appearing to prosecute. Upon motion of deft nonsuit is granted agt plt & ordered he pay 5 shillings to deft with costs at exon.

Imparlence granted to Mary Jenkins Admx of Henry Jenkins to answer suit of Jno. King Gt a c d [sic] £50 current money.

Imparlence granted to Mary Jenkins Admx of Henry Jenkins to answer suit of Jno. King Gt a c d [sic] £100 sterling.

Thomas Howard's action case damage £9 current money agt Mary Jenkins Admx &c of Henry Jenkins dec'd, plt not appearing. Upon motion of deft nonsuit is granted her & ordered plt pay 5 shillings to deft with costs at exon.

Ellinr. Bossell Admx &c action case damage £9 current money agt Mary Jenkins Admx of Henry Jenkins dec'd. Imparlence granted deft who prays oyer of the writing mentioned in the declr.

[p 152] John Smith Junr action case damage £10 current money agt Mary Jenkins Admx &c of Henry Jenkins dec'd, plt not appearing. Ordered suit dismist.

Imparlence is granted to Mary Jenkins Admx &c of Henry Jenkins dec'd to answer suit of Joshua Curle action case damage £150.

James Ricketts & Jane his wife & George Walker surviving Execs of Nicholas Curle dec'd action case damage £140 [added above line – agt Mary Jenkins Admx &c of Henry Jenkins dec'd] deft pleads the genl Issue. Refd to next Ct for tryall.

Special imparlence granted to Mary Jenkins Admx &c of Henry Jenkins dec'd to answer suit of James Ricketts action case damage £10 current silver money.

Phillip Smith action &c debt for £57:8:5 agt Mary Jenkins Admx &c of Henry Jenkins dec'd. Deft prays oyer of the bills. Granted.

Richard FitzWilliam Fitzwilliam [sic] Esqr action debt for £500 good & lawful money of Great Britain agt Andrew Mead. Deft prays oyer of the bond which is granted.

Henry Irwin gent Naval Officer of the Lower District of James River action of debt agt Jno. Smith Senr. Deft prays imparlence which is granted.

Emanuel Alkin's action case agt Edward Ballard. Deft prays time to next Ct. Granted.

Imparlence granted to Mary Jenkins Admx &c of Henry Jenkins dec'd to answer suit of Simon Hollier action case damage 1228 lbs tobo.

Upon petition of Jane Baccus for her est in hands of Thomas Howard. It's ordered that Howard pay her accotts to appraisal.

Thomas Batts Adm &c Bill in Chancery agt Thomas Jones. Deft prays time to next Ct. Granted.

Judgmt renewed agt Mary Jenkins Admx of Jno. Curle dec'd for £28 current money with costs of former suit to Jno. Bayley Gt with costs at exon.

Sarah Pett orphan of John Pett dec'd is bound as an apprentice to John Mitchell & Hanah his wife till she be of age or married learning her to Card Spinn Knitt & Household Work & when free to give her a suit of apparel &c according to law.

Capt. Francis Ballard ack deed for Town Land to Charles Jenings. Ordered recorded.

[p 153] At a Court held the 3rd Wednesday of June
be the 17th Day
Fra. Ballard, Antho. Armistead, Thos. Wythe,
John King, James Servant, Henry Irwin
His Majestie's Justices

Judgmt granted to Charles Jenings agt est of Eliz. Prescott for 204 lbs tobo to be paid by Brian Penny who has est in his hands with costs at exon.

Upon petition of Jno. Merrideth for license to keep an ordinary at his house in Hampton Towne. It's granted giving bond & security &c.

Edwd. Tabb having returned an accott Dr & Cr of est of Thomas Tabb gent dec'd. The Ct regulating the accott ordered the same be recorded he having made oath to the same.

Simon Hollier gent having returned an appraismt of est of Edmd. Hollier dec'd, ordered recorded.

Upon petition of Francis Malory & Ann his wife late wife of Edward Mihill dec'd praying liberty to decline such a part of Edwd.'s will as related to her & adhere to what the law gives & also prays to have her Due Share & portion of Edwd.'s est as by Law She ought to have. It's ordered granted.

Edward Mihill's last will & testament is proved by oaths of Jaret [or Janet] Roberts, Edward Ward & Edwd. Ward Junr witnesses & certificate for probate granted the Execs giving bond & secuity. Ord est appr by Mr. Simon Hollier, Mr. Edwd. Tabb, Mr. Jno. Lowery & Mr. Merritt Sweny or any three of them. Retun to next Ct.

The last will & testament of Fras. Rogers dec'd is proved by oaths of Robert Armistead & Brian Penny witnesses & certificate for probate granted the Exec giving bond & Security &c. Ordered est be appr by Cha. Tucker, Tho. Allen, Tho. Read & Jno. Roe & returned to next Ct.

[p 154] An account of Henry Jenkins' est being returned. Ordered that Capt. Ballard divide the same between his wife and three children equally & report same to next Ct.

Upon return of audit between Thos. Wilcox & est of Eliza. James dec'd, and found in Favour to Wilcox [for] £133:06:08. Ordered that Wilcox be paid out of dec'd's est & ordered audit be recorded.

Robin a Negr boy belonging to William Allen is adjudged to be twelve years of age.

Hanah Negr Girle belonging to William Allen is adjudged to be twelve years of age.

Court adjourns till Tomorrow morning Nine a Clock

At a Court held the 18th Day June 1719
Fra. Ballard, Thos. Wythe, Antho. Armistead,
John King, James Servant, Henry Irwin,
Josa. Curle — His Majestie's Justices

John Bayley is this day sworn High Sheriff of Elizabeth City County according to the Governor's Comssion dated &c & entered into bond &c. Jno. Dunn sworn his under Sheriff.

Upon petition of William Barber and Susanah his wife late Susa. Smith for Adm on her Daughter Susana Smith's est. Ordered certificate for Adm be granted them giving bond & Security according to law.

The action of debt damage 200 lbs tobo brought by Edmd. Kerny agt Brian Penny. Cause refd --- for tryall & further consented to that cause not to try unless deft's atty be present. Refd at Plt's cost.

Capt. Fra. Ballard's petition agt Mr. Bertd. Servant's est to have auditors appointed. Refd to next Ct.

Henry Robinson agt Saml. Selden action case damage 1800 lbs tobo. Deft joynes in Demurrer. Refd to next Ct for tryall.

[p 155] Suit brought by Jno. Roe & Jno. Cook upon an action of the case damage £33 agt Emanl. Alkin. Judgmt granted plt for what shall appear due at next Ct.

In the suit brought by Saml. Watts agt Hind Armistead in action of trespass damage £40, Special verdict being argued. Ct are of the opinion that Law be with the Deft. It's therefore ord suit be dismist with costs at exon. Plt appeals to the 7th day of the Honorble the General Ct next coming. Granted giving bond & Security according to law (to witt) Thos. Watts for plt.

Henry Robinson brought his action of debt for £100 sterling agt Saml. Selden. Deft prays time to next Ct & ---- his plea having paid cost which is granted.

John Croft Gdn to his two sons Abra. & Childemus agt Robert Taylor action of accott render damage £50. Plt prays time to next Ct. Granted, he paying this Ct's charge.

Henry Cary & Richd. Riddlehurst, Churchwardens of Denby Parish, brought their suit agt William Spicer & Mary his wife action of debt. Deft joyning in Demurrer. Ordered refd to next Ct for tryall.

Jno. Coffy Negr brought his action assault & battery agt Robt. Taylor damage £10. Plt prays time to next Ct to provide his Evidences. Granted.

Emanl. Alkin's suit agt Francis Ballard action upon the case damage £31 is by consent dismist.

Francis Ballard's two actions agt Emanl. Alkin is ended, deft to pay cost of both suits at exon.

In the suit brought by James Roscow Esqr agt Elinor Bosell Admx &c of William Bosell dec'd in an action upon the case damage £250, deft pleading the genral Issue. Refd to next Ct for tryall.

Richd. Fitzwilliam Esqr agt Mary Jenkins Admx &c of Henry Jenkins dec'd action of debt for £45:06:03. Deft hath liberty to plead as many Matters as she Thinks Convenient. Plt prays time to next Ct. Granted.

[p 156] Richd. Fitzwilliams Esqr agt Mary Jenkins Admx of Henry Jenkins dec'd action case for £4:04:08. Deft hath liberty to plead as many Matters as she Thinks Convenient. Plt prays timt to next Ct. Granted.

Richd. Bland gent agt Jno. Burtel Adm &c of James Burtel action case for £17:01:04. Deft pleads n--- Refd to next Ct for tryall.

In the suit brought by Falvy Coopland agt John Falkner action case for assault & battery damage £10, deft pleading not guilty. Refd to next Ct for tryall.

Upon petition of Thos. Skinner Gdn to Saml. Skinner his son for his est in hands of John Mitchell which was left him by his grandmother Ann Daniell. It's ordered that Mitchell Exec of Saml. Daniel's will pay the est to the Gdn.

Hind Armistead's suit agt Saml. Watts a detinue damage £10 is by consent continued to next Ct.

Judgmt granted by Nihill Dicet agt Mary Jenkins Admx of John Curle to answer suit of Charles Jenings action case damage 1000 lbs tobo.

Judgmt is confirmed agt Cely Langman by Default for 40 shillings to Richard Kirkin.

Judgmt by Nihill Dicet is granted agt Samuel White to answer suit of John & Thomas Batts Execs of Henry Batts dec'd action case damage £4.

John Burtell Adm of James Burtell dec'd agt Thomas Frye action case damage £4. Attchmt being returned executed upon the goods left in the hands of Mrs. Croft, she not appearing. Upon motion of plt ordered that the Sheriff take her into Custody till she enters into bond &c for her appearance at next Ct to give account of Fry's est in hands.

Judgmt by Nihill Dicet granted agt John & Thomas Batts Execs of Henry Batts to answer suit of Emanuel Alkin action case damage £10.

John & Thomas Batts Execs of Henry Batts dec'd action case damage £6 agt Joseph Wragg, the deft alleging that that there is some work left undone by Henry Batts dec'd according to agreement. It's ordered that the work be viewed by Jno. Merideth & Abra. Mitchell & value same. Report to next Ct.

Jacob Talbort action debt agt Thomas Wilcox damage £20, deft appearing, plt prays Spl Bayle & he not giving any, the former is continued. Refd to next Ct & ordered that Thomas Roberts be sworn as an Evidence & his deposition allowed to be good upon tryall at next Ct.

Robert Taylor action trespass damage £10 sterling agt John More, deft pleading. Plt prays time to next Ct. Granted.

Judgmt granted agt Eliza. Hill & her Security for £1:16:02 unto Robert Taylor with costs at exon.

[p 157] William Marshall & his wife agt Jno. King Gent a Detinue damage £30 is by consent agreed to come to tryall the first day of next Ct. Ordered refd til Then.

It's ordered that Samuel Watts pay Thomas Watts according to Law for his twenty days attendance as an Evidence agt Hind Armistead with costs at exon.

Judgmt is confessed by Thomas Wilcox for £3:10 current money to James Servant Gent with costs at exon.

Samuel Selden assigne of Mary Floyd action case damage £5, the deft appearing & Special Bayle being required which Barto. Proby enters himself Special Bayle. Deft prays time to next Ct. Granted.

John Crofts Gdn &c agt Robert Taylor, bil Chancery, the respondent making oath to the accott, the Complainant prays time to consider the same. Granted.

George Waffe action case damage £6 agt Willm. Winterton &c Exec of Geo. Waffe dec'd is refd to Ct for tryall. There appears due to the plt 30 shillings. It's ordered that deft pay out of Dec'd est with costs at exon.

John Dunn making oath of the serving of an ejectment brought by Wm. Smelt agt Julian Daniel. It's ordered that the common order be made &c.

Saml. White action case damage £6 agt Jno. Battersby, Geo. Walker enters himself Specl Bayle for the deft. Lycense granted him to plead as many matters as he think fit. Plt prays time to next Ct. Granted.

Bartrand Proby Adm of Thomas Proby action accott render for £130 agt Jno. Burtell Adm of James Burtell, last order being complied with. Parties take time to next Ct for tryall.

James Ricketts & Jane his wife Gdns to Wilson Curle infant brought action of debt for £60 agt John Burtell Adm of James Burtell dec'd. Plt not appearing to prove their accotts. Refd to next Ct.

Thomas Jenings brought his action of debt for £20 agt Henry Cock. Refd to next Ct for accotts to be audited.

Brian Penny brought his action agt George Paine damage £5. Continued to next Ct for accotts to be audited.

In suit brought by Bart. Selden & Achily his wife Execs of Saml. Selden Junr dec'd action case damage £10 agt Joseph Wragg. [Ct decides] there appear to be due 27 shillings & 6 pence. Ordered deft pay same with costs at exon.

Judgmt granted agt Thos. Wilcox for 25 shillings unto William Greek Greek with costs at exon.

Richd. Fitzwilliams Esqr agt Andr. Mead action debt for £500 sterling. Deft prays oyer of bond. Granted.

Emanl. Alkin agt Mrk. Powell action case damage £12 is by consent refd to next Ct.

[p 158] Upon petition of Elizabeth Reddlehurst for a cow and calf left her by her grandmother. It's ordered that John Mitchell Exec of Saml. Daniel's est will pay and deliver the cow and calf to petitioner.

Ordered that the Churchwardens summon a Vestry forthwith in order to appoint Processioners to procession the lands in the county.

In the suit by Antho. Armistead gent agt Fras. Ballard gent in an action upon the case damage £500 sterling, the auditors' report in this cause being returned & the Councill's arguments heard. It's upon Capt. Ballard's promising to give the plt a full acctt of tobo. he has rec'd and what he has not received of the Parish. It is agreed by the Parties, ordered & decreed that he deliver unto Armistead a just and perfect accot of all tobo by him rec'd and from whom also which of the Parish tobo is still outstanding and not collected by him as Churchwarden with the plt and the deft further consenting to bear his part of the loss sustained by Insolvents. Plt is to return a list thereof to the next Ct to which time the Cause is continued.

Francis Ballard gent his two actions agt Antho. Armistead gent is by consent of parties refd to next Ct.

Upon motion of Matthew Wiles to have Francis Ballard & James Servant gent sworn concerning the legacie given by Barto. Servant dec'd to Frans. George his grand daughter which they accordingly made oath that the legacy was paid John George her father for the use of the Child by Fras. Ballard out of dec'd's est.

The last will & testament of Eliza. Tucker dec'd is proved by oaths of Charles Jenings & William Westwood wit thereto. Certificate for probate granted the Execs giving bond &c & ordered recorded.

The last will & testament of Thos. Tucker dec'd is proved by oath of John Batts & certificate for Adm with will annext granted to Jno. More & Charles Cooper giving bond &c & ordered recorded.

Upon motion of Jno. King gent to take the depositions of Robt. Taylor & wife as Evidence for him agt Wm. Marshall, Mr. Ricketts or some other of His Maj's Justices is desired to take deposition & [they] to be allowed good Evids upon tryall.

[p 159] Judgmt by Nihill Dicet is granted agt Mary Jenkins Admx of Henry Jenkins dec'd action debt for £11:13:06 to answer suit of Charles Jenings.

Richd. Fitzwms. action debt for £500 sterling brought agt Andr. Mead. Deft prays liberty to plead as many matters as he thinks convenient. Granted whereupon he demurs. Plt joyned. Time tomorrow is given to argue demurrer.

Henry Irwin Naval Officer of the Lower District of Jas. River brought his action debt agt Jno. Smith Senr for £10. Deft pleads. Plt joins. Ordered refd to next Ct for tryall.

The suit brought by Emanl. Alkin agt Edwd. Ballard case for £3 the deft bringing in his discount & there appears due to the plt £1:04:09. Judgmt granted agt deft for paymt with costs at exon.

Thos. Batts Adm of Eliza. Batts formerly Eliza. Shepperd agt Thos. Jones & Sarah his wife Execs of Jno. Shepperd dec'd Chancery. Respondents making oath to their answers, Complainant prays time to next Ct. Granted.

In the suit brought by James Ricketts & Jane his wife Execs of Nicho. Curle gent dec'd agt Mary Jenkins Admx of Henry Jenkins gent dec'd in an action upon the case for £125:07. Last Ct parties pled the genll Issue. A jury impanelled namely: Josa. B---- senr, Saml. Sweny, Henry Robinson, Jno. More, Jno. Batts, Geo. Waffe, Mrk. Powell,

Jno. Jones, Jas. Naylor. [Jury] returned a special verdict. James & Jane swear that is a true copy of an acctt which they found in their testator's book in which Henry Jenkins was charged with £89:07 current money. The accott is [dated] the same day Testator made his last will & testament & appointed Henry Jenkins one of his Execs. Henry Jenkins survived to become Exec & received £35 lawful money of this Dominion, the proper estate of the Testator. Jenkins died intestate. Depending on matters of law, if Henry Jenkins being one of Nicho. Curle's Execs, such Adm bring his goods to be a release in Law Extinguishment or Discharge of the sum of £84:07, then we find for the plt £35 current money damage & do move if otherwise the sum of £124:07 current money. Jos. Banister foreman. Refd to next Ct for mattrs of Law arising to be argued. It's ordered that Verdict be recorded. Mr. Saml. Selden Entrd Atty for Plts & Maximillian Boush Entrd Atty for Defts.

[p 160] James Ricketts gent action upon the case damage £10 brought agt Mary Jenkins Admx of Henry Jenkins dec'd is by consent refd to next Ct.

John Burtell Adm of James Burtell dec'd agt Thos. Wilcox action upon the case damage £6. Deft pleads. Plt prays time. Granted.

Upon petition of William Short for turning a certain road that runs along the Ditch where Short now liveth the same be viewed. Ordered petition be granted.

Thos. Walk brought his action of debt for £16:07:10 agt Mary Jenkins Admx of Henry Jenkins dec'd. By consent of both parties refd to next Ct.

Mary Jenkin's power of atty to Mr. Robert Armistead is ordered recorded.

Judgmt granted agt Mary Jenkins Admx of Henry Jenkins dec'd for £12 & 94 lbs tobo & the sum of £1:05 current money unto the Exec of Christopher Cocks dec'd. Mr. Boush one of the Execs made oath that he never recd any sattisfaction nor noe body Else to his Knowledge. To be paid out of decd's est with costs at exon.

Judgmt granted agt Mary Jenkins Admx of Henry Jenkins dec'd for 2869 lbs tobo & £13:06:09 current money to Maxl. Boush to be paid out of dec'd's est with cost at exon.

Special imparlence granted to Mary Jenkins Admx of Henry Jenkins dec'd to answer suit of John Bordland case damage £60 current money.

Imparlence granted to Henry Jenkins to answer suit of Brian Penny action trespass, salt & battery damage £10 current money.

Imparlence granted to John Mitchell to answer suit of Julian Daniel in an action of trespass upon the case damage £30.

Maximilian Boush action case damage £5 is by consent of the plt refd to next Ct.

Imparlence granted to Baldwin Shepperd to answer suit of Thomas Batts in an action upon the case damage £30 current money.

Judgmt is granted agt Richard Nusum for £4:16 unto Wm. Smelt with costs at exon.

Judgmt is granted agt John Burtell Adm of James Burtell dec'd for £42:08:08 according to audit returned. To be paid out of the decd's est unto James Ricketts & Jane his wife Execs of Nicho. Curle dec'd with costs at exon.

Imparlence granted to John Smith Senr to answer suit of Jane Rowton in an action upon the case damage £5.

Imparlence granted to Mary Jenkins Admx of Henry Jenkins dec'd to answer suit of Henry Irwin gent action case.

[p 161] In the suit brought by Francis Ballard gent agt Benja. Rolfe in an action of debt for £14:01:09 sterling for protested Bills of Exchange & two Evidences being sworn for the deft that they heard Thomas Wilcox who was the ----- of sd bills say he had received of deft's friends in England £10, part of the bills, whereupon Wilcox sworn for the plt declared that he nor noe person for him ever received any part of the bills. Ct do order that deft pay sd sum to plt with costs at exon.

Imparlence granted to Mary Jenkins Admx of Henry Jenkins dec'd to answer suit of Archibald Blair action debt.

Special imparlence granted to John Walless & Susa. his wife to answer suit of Thomas Wilcox Adm of Elizabeth James dec'd in an action upon the case damage £20.

Imparlence granted to Mary Bridge Exectrx of William Hopkins dec'd to answer suit of Francis Ballard gent action upon the case for £3:09:09 & 369 1/2 lbs tobo.

In the suit brought by Henry Jenkins agt Brian Penny in an action upon the case damage £20, plt failing to file his declr in time. Which upon motion of deft nonsuit is granted him & ordered plt pay deft 5 shillings with costs at exon.

Julian Daniell action Chancery agt John Mitchell Exec of Samuel Daniel dec'd. Respondent prays time to answer which is granted.

Henry Robinson's action agt Saml. Selden damage 1800 lbs tobo is by consent refd to next Ct to argue the demurrer.

Judgmt by Nihill Dicet is granted agt Mary Jenkins Admx of Henry Jenkins dec'd to answer suit of Samuel Sweny action case damage £200 money.

Judgmt by Nihill Dicet is granted agt Mary Jenkins &c to answer suit of Simon Hollier & Joseph Banister a debt for £13:10.

Judgmt by Nihill Dicet is granted agt Mary Jenkins &c to answer suit of Philip Smith action debt for [blank].

Judgmt by Nihill Dicet is granted agt Mary Jenkins &c to answer suit of Saml. Selden action debt.

Simon Hollier action case damage 1228 lbs tobo agt Mary Jenkins &c is by consent refd to next Ct.

William Holloday action case damage £100 agt Mary Jenkins &c the plt not appearing to prosecute his suit. Upon motion of deft ordered suit be dismist.

John Pool Senr a Detinue damage £55 agt Thomas Jones the plt's Evids not being summoned. Therefore prays time til next Ct to provide those which upon Mr. Selden's consenting to pay this Ct's charge is granted.

[p 162] John Cook & John Roe action case damage £30 agt Emanuel Alkin is ended.

Henry Robinson's action debt for £100 agt Samuel Selden. Plt prays time to consider til next Ct. Granted.

Richard Fitzwilliams Esqr agt Mary Jenkins Admx of Henry Jenkins dec'd action case £45:06:08, plt replying. Deft prays time to consider. Granted.

Richard Fitzwilliams agt Mary Jenkins Admx of Henry Jenkins dec'd action case 4--5, plt replying. Deft prays time to consider. Granted.

In the action of assault & battery brought by Falvy Coopland agt John Faulkner & two Evidences being sworn for plt &c. Jury impanneled namely: Jos. Banister, Saml. Sweny, John House, Hen. Robinson, Thomas Batts, John Batts, Thomas Jones, Jno. More, James Naylor, Thomas Howard, Wm. Loyall & Geo. Waffe, but not returning their verdict before the Ct break up.

Judgmt by Nihill Dicet granted agt Mary Jenkins Admx of Henry Jenkins dec'd action case damage £40 to answer suit of Jno. King gent.

Judgmt is granted by Nihill Dicet agt Mary Jenkins Admx of Jno. Curle dec'd action case damage £100 current money to answer suit of Jno. King gent.

Hind Armistead a Detinue agt Samuel Watts refd to next Ct by consent of both parties.

Robert Taylor action case damage £4 agt Thomas Frye. Mrs. Crofts being summoned to give an acct of what estate belonging to Frye she hath in her hands, she appearing & making oath to an accott of Dr & Cr which she produces agt Frye as also what goods she hath of Fry's in her custody. It's therefore ordered that the goods be appraised by Mr. Saml. Sweny, Mr. Jos. Banister & Mr. Wm. Loyall or any two of them & return to next Ct.

Then the Court adjourns til tomorrow Ten a Clock
F. Ballard signe

At a Court held the 16th Day of July 1719
Capt. Fra. Ballard, Thos. Wythe, Mr. Henry Irwin,
Mr. James Ricketts, Mr. Jas. Servant, Mr. Jos. Curle,
Mr. Jno. King – His Maj's Justices

In the suit brought by Henry Cary & Richard Riddlehurst late Churchwardens of Denby Parish agt Wm. Spicer & Mary his wife in an action of debt for 559 lbs tobo. Demurrer argued. Ct are of the opinion that Demr is sufficient & order that plts recover the sum according to the judgmt of Warwick Ct with costs at exon.

[p 163] Thomas Woods power of atty to Samuel Selden is proved & ordered recorded.

The Jury between Falvy Coopland & Jno. Faulkner being yesterday sworn but not returning their verdict in time now return verdict. We find for the plt damage six pence. Joseph Banister foreman, which on motion of plt is ordered recorded & ordered deft pay same to plt & being urged for full cost which deft opposing. It's ordered refd to next Ct for matter of Law to be argued.

In the suit brought by James Roscow Esqr agt Elinor Bosell Admx of Wm. Bosell dec'd in an action upon the case damage £500 sterling and one Evidence being sworn for the plt and four for the deft and a Jury being impannelled and sworn to try the issue. Jury returned verdict: We find for the plt damage £153:03:09 & three farthings. Edward Tabb foreman. Upon motion of plt verdict is recorded & ordered deft pay same out of dec'd estate with costs at exon.

Samuel Selden by virtue of a power of atty made him by Thomas Wood came into Ct & ack deeds for town land to John Pugh. Ordered recorded.

John and Thomas Batts Execs of Henry Batts dec'd action case agt Samuel White. Deft putting in his plea, plt prays time to next Ct. Granted.

Judgmt granted agt Andrew Mead for £116:00:10 being balance of a bond unto Richd. Fitzwilliams Esqr with costs at exon.

In the suit brought by Wm. Marshall and his wife agt John King gent in an action of detinue damage £300 for detaining several negroes from the plt as is set forth in the plt's declr and a Jury impannelled and sworn namely: Jos. Banister, Edwd. Roe, Wm. Tucker, Thomas Jones, Geo. Waffe, George Cooper, John Cooper, Jno. Batts, Richd. Nusum, Wm. Loyall, Bartd. Proby and Thomas Batts. Jury returns special verdict. We find that Eliza. the wife of Wm. Marshall, one of the plts, is the only child of Wm. Merritt, eldest brother to Mary late wife of Jno. King the deft. We find that sd Mary Taylor was seized & possessed of seven slaves to witt: Dick, Jack, Tony, a melatto boy called Johnne, ole Mary, Sara and Kate when sole and before her marriage with the deft and that they were in the deft's possession and that the mellatto was disposed of in her lifetime and that the others were in Mr. King, the deft's, custody. At and after the sd Mary's death he doth detain them and still hath all of the other six except Tony which died about three months after his Mistress in the deft's custody. We find the Act of Assembly which exacts and makes negroes a Real Estate. We find that that Act was in force some years before and at the time Mary was married to the deft. We find that Mary is dead and that she never had any issue. We also find that Mary was the wido of Capt. Daniel Taylor dec'd and when a sole possessed of all the negroes in the declr specified by virtue of the last will & testament.

[p 164] We find by the oath of Madm. Wallace that she heard Mary in her last sickness say she had never made over any negroes to Mr. King nor never would and that there was a paper offered to her for that purpose to sign but she never did for she had married him and if the Law gave them to him they were his and that when she was dead believed that

paper would appear against her and desired the Deponent if she outlived her she would testifie what she told her. We find the deposition of Robt. Taylor hereunto annext to which we refer. We find the affadavit of Mr. Edward Tabb that Mary Taylor who was his Aunt called him out of doors the day before she was married to Mr. King and told him that except she made some instrument of writing to Mr. King before marriage, he could not have the negroes, but they would fall to the next heir after her decease and thereupon bid the Deponent tell Mr. King that she was free and willing to make and sign any that he should desire to make them secure to him. Upon which Mr. Bard. Coudart who put his name as a witness to the deed went into the J---s Room and went to writing, Mr. King and his Aunt being in company with him, and after that took up a paper importing Bill of Sale which was lying amongst severall other papers, which he read & saw that she had sold thereby all the negroes she had for a consideration therein mentioned not before given away which is all that was left and that he knows his Aunt's hand & Mr. Schlater's & Mr. Cowdart's hands who has attached the same & believes it to be her and their hands and also believes he saw her sign it with several other papers at that time, but believes she did not know it to be paper importing a deed to the deft and that he was present and took notice of the delivery and sealing of the other papers that then were executed, but did not see any paper sealed or delivered by her to the deft. We find the affadavit of Barnard Cowdart who deposed that the day before she was married he writt a bill of sale for negroes mentioned in a writing now in Court produced unto him at the request of the afsd Mr. Taylor unto Mr. Jno. King and believes the name of Mary Taylor affixed thereto is her hand and his own name to be in his hand and did hear Mr. King say there was no need to call in the negroes and deliver them as a cow or a horse and that he writt the same by her orders, also that Mr. King paid him for so doing but he never saw Mrs. Taylor sign, seale or deliver the paper produced, but believes it was put in among the other papers unknown to her. We find these negroes mentioned in the writing are one the same now sued for by the plt. And if upon the whole matter the Ct shall adjudge the Law to be with the plt, We find for them damage £10 current money, if otherwise then for the deft. We also find the five slaves to be worh £105 current money. Joseph Banister foreman. Which upon motion of the Parties, verdict is ordered recorded & refd to next Ct for the mattrs of Law arising therefrom to be argued.

Saml. Hunter came into Ct & consents that his two sons named John being fourteen years old and his son Andr. being twelve years old shall serve Mr. Henry Irwin according to custom of the country unless Hunter do perform a certain agreemt made between Irwin and him. Which when performed the sd boys to be free from service.

[p 165] Ordered that Jno. King gent pay to Bard. Cowdart for four days attendance as an Evidence agt William Marshall &c being twelve miles distance from his own house in Poquoson in York Co. and for his coming twice and going twice with costs at exon.

Mr. James Schlater being an Evidence from Poquoson in York Co. for Jno. King gent agt Wm. Marshall &c. Ordered he be paid for three days attendance being twelve miles distance & for his coming three times and going three times with costs at exon.

Ordered Jno. King gent pay to Edwd. Tabb for three days attendance as an Evidence for him agt Wm. Marshall with costs at exon.

Ordered that the Court be adjourned Tell the Court in Course.

At a Court held the 3d Wednesday of August being the 19th Day 1719
Fras. Ballard, Antho. Armistead, Thos. Wythe, John King, James Ricketts, James Servant
His Majt's Justices

Thomas Jenings ack release for land to Charles Jenings and ordered recorded.

Upon petition of Jno. Standly agt Mary Jenkins Admx of Henry Jenkins dec'd for £15 being for building Jenkins a Sloop. Jenkins atty consents that the petitioner shall have judgmt for same. It's ordered that plt have judgmt granted him for £15 and that Mary pay out of decedant's estate.

Upon the petition of John Nobbs agt Thos. Faulkner and Martha Taylor concerning his service. Ordered that Faulkner and Taylor be summoned to answer petition.

In the ejectment brought by Thos. Poole agt James Ricketts and Jane his wife, guardians to Pasco Curle infant, for lands and tenements in the declr mentioned to witt: the special Verdict in this Cause being argued, Ct are of the opinion that the Law is with defts. Therefore upon motion of deft ordered plt be nonsuited and that he pay 5 shillings with costs at exon.

Judy Negr girl belonging to Thos. Morgan is adjudged to be nine years of old and to pay according to Act.

[p 166] Thos. Howard bringing to Ct John Price his servant who having been Runaway from his Master's service the time of two days and three nights. It's ordered that Price serve his Master double the time after his indenture expires and a futher time of six months, it being for £3:08:06 which Howard paid for bringing home the servant being at the rate of 800 lbs of tobacco per years service.

Jno. Crofts guardian to his children Abraham and Childermus agt Robt. Taylor action accot render. The deft being dead, ordered dismist with costs at exon.

Jno. Coffy &c agt Robert Taylor action upon the case of assault and battery damage £10. The deft being dead, ordered dismist with costs at exon.

John Crofts &c agt Robert Taylor Chancery. The deft being dead, ordered dismist with costs at exon.

Robert Taylor's action trespass damage £100 sterling agt John More. The plt being dead, ordered dismist.

It's ordered that William Williams return an appraisal of John Roberts' estate to next Ct.

It's ordered that Wm. Smelt return an appraisal of John Petts' estate to next Ct.

Edmond Kearny's action case debt damage 1000 lbs tobo agt Bryan Penny the plt demurring. Ordered suit refd to next Ct for deft to consider the Demurrer.

Upon petition of Peter Thibout agt Henry Morriset for his freedom. Ordered that Morriset be summoned to next Ct to answer petition.

Then the Court adjourns til the Court in Cource.

Antho. Armistead signe

[Note: p 167 contains accounts of the estate of Mr. Thomas Tabb, dated 1717. The following names occur on the page.]
Debits column on left hand side of page:
Jno. Berry, Charles Nightingale, Mr. Emanl. Alkin, Lazarus Sweny, Mrs. Margt. Boucher, James Burtin, Anthony Butts, William Walker, James Callohill, Mr. Thomas Nelson, Reba. Groome, Mr. Phillip Lightfoot, John Dunn, Henry Parks, Mr. Simon Hollier, Simon Wootten, Mr. Robert Phillipson, Daniel Mackintosh, Francis Minis, Eliza. Tabb Wido of Thos.

To cash paid by order of York Co. Ct being due to the Orphans of Henry Hayward dec'd.
Total paid - £175:07:06
Credits column on right hand side of page:
Thomas Burnam, Mr. Edwd. Tabb, Robt. Sheild, Josiah Russill, Edmd. Hollier, John Bordland, James Baker, Charles Haines, Simon Hollier, Richard Baker, Jno. George, Wm. Cook, Wm. Caddo [?], Mr. John Armistead, George Paine, Margt. Preist, Thomas Roberts, Mr. John Gibbins, Mr. James Schlater, Mr. Gerrard Roberts, Wm. Moss, Wm. Tucker, Sarah Burnham, Massenburd, Wm. Tabb, Merrit Sweny, Saml. Groves, Thomas Read, Wm. Marshall, Wm. Armistead, Jno. Patrick, Jno. Drury, Saml. Sweny, Edmd. Sweny, Wm. Walker.
Total receipts - £441:18:01 1/4
Balance due estate - £266:10:06 3/4
Errors excepted 8 June 1719 per Edwd. Tabb
Recorded by order of Ct dated 17 June 1719
Recorded 19 Sept 1719. Test: Cha. Jenings CCur

[p 168] Upon petition of John Bayley for Adm on John Dun's estate. Order granted giving bond &c. Ordered appraisal by Tho. Batts, Brian Penny, John Chandler & Tho. Read or any three of them.

William Westwood is this day sworn Under Sheriff, John Dun late Under Sheriff being dead.

Upon petition of John Mitchell on behalf of his daughter Ann for a legacy of 20 shillings sterling left her by her grandmother Ann Daniel dec'd. Ordered that Mitchell Exec to Saml. Daniel pay the sum to Ann with costs at exon.

Upon petition of Joseph Prince to choose his guardian who chooses Cha. Jenings. Ordered that guardian receive his estate.

Upon petition of Tho. Skinner for a legacy left by Saml. Daniel. Ordered that John Mitchell Exec of Daniel's estate be summoned to next Ct to answer petition.

Upon return of audit in the suit depending between John Burtell Adm of James Burtell & Josa. Curle for £12:19:05 & three farthings but some things being refd to Ct and they making abatement. Ordered that deft pay £10 current money being the balance with costs at exon.

In the suit brought by Emanl. Alkin agt John and Thos. Batts Execs of Henry Batts in an action upon the case for £6:09:06. [After arguments] Ct ordered that Exec pay plt £3:10:06 with costs at exon.

The suit brought by Jno. and Thos. Batts Execs of Henry Batts dec'd action case damage £3 the former order for certain work not being complyed with. Ordered deft to pay [ ] of Nov &c. [sic]

Judgmt granted agt Joseph Wragg for £3:06 and a penny farthing unto John & Thos. Batts Execs of Henry Batts dec'd with costs at exon.

Judgmt granted agt Mark Powel for £5 current money to Emanl. Alkin with costs at exon. Execution stayed five months.

Judgmt granted agt Wm. Brown for 1055 lbs tobo unto Saml. Selden assign of Mary Floyd with costs at exon.

Judmt granted agt John Lillo, Josa. Curle and Alexandr. McKensie his Security for 40 shillings to Emanl. Alkin he having made oath to his accot with costs at exon.

In the suit brought by Jacob Talbart agt Thos. Wilcox in an action of debt for £14:16:06. Deft produces his accot for £10:16:06 and also note drawn upon Capt. Jenkins for £4 payable to plt. Refd to next Ct for plt to make oath whether he recd the same.

Antho. Armistead Senr and Elizabeth his wife ack deeds for land to Robt. Armistead Junr & ordered recorded.

Saml. White's suit agt John Baddesby action upon the case damage £6 plt replying. Deft prays time till next Ct. Replyquation granted.

The appraisal of John Curle's estate continued to next Ct to be finished and John More to be added in the room of Mr. King and Hind Armistead in the room of Capt. Ballard.

Brian Penny agt Geo. Paine action upon the case for £1:6:3 former order for audit not being complied with. It's ordered that same be performed by Mr. Antho. Armistead Senr. and Mr. Jno. King next Saturday the 19th instant & ordered that if deft appears not, then the audittors proceed Ex partie.

Ordered that Jos. Banister and Saml. Sweny, Tho. Howard & Wm. Loyall or any three of them appraise estate of Robt. Minson dec'd & return to next Ct.

Antho. Armistead signe

[p 170] At a Court held the 17th Day of Septembr 1719
Antho. Armistead, Thomas Wythe, John King,
James Ricketts, Joshua Curle, James Servant –
His Majestie's Justices

Upon petition of Tho. Tucker to choose his guardian who makes choice of John More and ordered guardian receive his estate giving bond & security.

Judgmt granted agt John Burtell Adm of James Burtell for £5:01:11 unto Richd. Bland gent having proved his accotts to be paid out of James Burtell's estate with costs at exon.

Cha. Jenings agt Mary Jenkins Admx of Henry Jenkins dec'd case damage 1000 lbs tobo by consent of parties refd to next Ct.

Imparlence granted to Thomas Curle to answer suit of William Barber case damage £26.

Upon the summons in Chancery brought by Fra. Malory and Ann his wife agt Lockey and Joshua Mihill, respondents pray time to next Ct. Granted.

Wm. Barber brought his action upon the case damage £8 agt Saml. Watts, deft pleading nonsuit. Refd to next Ct for trial.

Emanl. Alkin's suit agt John Mitchell Exec of Saml. Daniel dec'd action upon the case damage £8 is refd to next Ct by consent.

Upon the summons by scire facias brought by William Smelt agt John King, deft prays liberty till next Ct to bring in his discount.

Robt. Tannoch agt Cornelas Dorlich and Rachel his wife a detinue damage £10. The suit is ended, deft paying costs at exon.

The action of debt for 26 shillings brought by Robt. Tannoch agt Rachel Dorlich. Deft prays oyer of the bill. Granted.

Upon summons in Chancery brought by Matthew Hilliard agt Cornelas Dorlich and Rachel his wife. Respondent prays time to next Ct to answer. Granted.

Mr. Joshua Curle's information agt Eliza. Chambers for having a bastard child born of her body. Mr. Poole the deft's atty prays time to next Ct to answer. Granted.

[p 171] Upon the information of Josa. Curle Churchwarden agt Mary Frizell & Mary Randy for having bastard children born of their bodies, they not appearing to answer. Ordered that an attchment issue against their bodies for their appearance at next Ct.

The action of detinue damage £55 brought by John Poole Senr agt Tho. Jones is refd to next Ct for want of Evidences.

Tho. Batts Adm of Eliza. his wife lately dec'd formerly Eliza. Sheppard exhibited his bill in Chancery agt Thos. Jones & Sarah his wife, the complainant excepting agt their answer & also joining. Time given the respondents to consider. Granted.

The suit brought by John Burtel Adm of James Burtell dec'd agt Tho. Wilcox action upon the case damage £6, the deft's Evidences being sick. Refd to next Ct.

In the action of trespass brought by Julin Daniel agt Jno. Mitchel damage £30 deft pleads not guilty. It's ordered refd to next Ct for trial.

The Ct appoints Mr. Saml. Selden guardian to Baldwin Sheppard to defend a suit between him and Thomas Batts.

Tho. Batts Adm of Eliza. his wife brought his action upon the case damage £30 agt Baldwin Sheppard. The plt mending his declr having paid cost to which deft pleads. Plt prays time. Granted.

In the suit brought by Henry Irwin Naval Officer of the lower District of James River agt John Smith Senr for £10 on an action of debt. Issue being joined, parties consent to put the Cause to the Ct for trial & deft producing a Proclamation repealing the Act for Importing Persons into this Colony & arguments being heard. It's ordered that suit be dismist.

In the suit brought by Jane Rowton agt John Smith Senr upon an action of the case damage £5, deft pleading the Genll. Issue. Refd to next Ct for trial.

Joseph Banister & Simon Hollier brought their action debt for £13:10 agt Mary Jenkins Admx of Henry Jenkins dec'd. Plt consents to let the suit fall.

The action of debt for £100 brought by Henry Robinson agt Saml. Selden. Deft prays time to next Ct to answer.

Judgmt by Nihill Dicet granted agt John Wallace to answer the suit of Tho. Wilcox Adm of Eliza. James action case damage £20.

[p 172] In the suit brought by Falvy Coopland agt John Faulkner damage £10 Salt & Battry the cause being continued for a matter of Law to be argued. It's ordered that defts pay plt the sum assest by the Jury which was six pence and pay cost of suit at exon.

Judgmt granted to Jno. Burtel Adm of James Burtel agt the estate of Tho. Fry in the hands of Mrs. Croft for 40 shillings with cost at exon.

John & Thomas Batts agt Saml. White action case for -- --. Dismist.

In the suit brought by William Marshall and Eliza, his wife [note: part of this is scratched over & word Mary is lined through with Eliza, added above the line] agt John King gent in an action of Detinue damage £300 current money for Negrs in the declr mentioned.

The Jury's verdict being refd for the mattr of Law arising. The Ct are of the opinion that the Law is with the deft. It is therefore ordered suit be dimist with costs at exon from which judgmt plt appeals to the seventh day of the Honorable the Genll. Ct next coming. Granted giving bond & security. Saml. Selden per Plt.

Certain deeds & bond from William Winterton to Henry Irwin gent is proved in Ct by oaths of Mr. William Brand, Mr. Godfrey Poole & Isaac Rambow wits. [They swear] they saw Winterton sign seale & deliver. Ordered recorded.

Tho. Wythe signe

At a Court held the 3d Wednesday of Novr being the 18th day 1719
Fra. Ballard, Thomas Wythe, Joshua Curle, Henry Irwin, Jas. Servant, Jno. King – His Majestie's Justices

Pompey, negro boy belonging to Mr. George Walker is adjudged to [be] thirteen years of age.

Soldier, negro boy belonging to Mr. George Walker, is adjudged to be twelve years of age.

The Feoffees ack deeds for Town land to Abraham Mitchell & ordered recorded.

[p173] Thos. Balis swears to the service of an Ejectment agt Thomas Lee tenant in possession.

Dina, negro girl belonging to Mr. Joshua Curle Senr, is adjudged to be seven years old.

Upon petition of John Tabb to choose his guardian who chooses Mr. Henry Howard. Granted.

Moll, negro girl belonging to Mr. Cha. Cooper, is adjudged to be seven years old.

Betty, negro girl belonging to Mr. Joseph Banister, is adjudged to be nine years old.

The Grand Jury being sworn returned presentments. Persons being presented are ordered to be summoned to next Ct.

Upon petition of Mrs. Ann Wallace and Tho. Wythe gent that Letters of Adm might be granted on the estate of Mr. Andr. Thomson Clk dec'd. Certificate for Adm granted them giving bond & security & the estate to be appraised by Mr. Saml. Selden, Mr. Geo. Yeo & Mr. Jno. King & returned to next Ct.

Upon petition of William Carhill to be allowed for burying a poor man who died at his house. Ct ordered that petitioner receive whatever debts the dec'd person hath due to him in this county for the defraying charge & trouble in burying the person.

Upon the action of debt damage 1000 lbs tobo brought by Edmond Kerny agt Brian Penny, deft joining a demurrer. Refd to next Ct to be argued.

Judgmt case agt Henry Cock for £1 & five pence half penny unto Thomas Jenings with cost at exon.

Upon the ejectmt brought by Robert Westlock agt Julian Daniel admitted deft in the room of William Symons for land & tenements in the declr mentioned. Whereupon the deft appeared and confessed Lease Entry and Ouster. It is ordered that unless she appear at next Ct & come to trial & insist upon the title only, that then his Majt. writt of Haberefacias Possessionem will issue to put the plt in possession of premises.

[p 174] Imparlence granted to Roseanah Hunt at suit of Martha Taylor action upon the case for slander damage £500.

Judgmt is [by] Nihill Dicet granted agt Jno. King gent to answer suit of Miles Cary gent debt for 50 shillings.

Imparlence granted to Robert Tannoch to answer suit of Richd. Adams in an action upon the case damage £5.

Special imparlence granted agt Mrs. Mary Jenkins to answer suit of Sarah Hayes Admx of Henry Hayes dec'd case damage £12.

Mrs. Martha Taylor & Tho. Faulkner desires time till next Ct to plead to the petition of John Nobbs exhibited agt them.

The action upon the case brought by Francis Ballard gent agt Charles Moore is by consent dismist, deft paying costs at exon.

Imparlence granted to John Amory to answer suit of Francis Ballard gent action upon the case damage £10 current money.

Imparlence granted to John Smith Senr to answer suit of Charles Jenings action upon the case damage £30.

Special imparlence granted to John King gent & John Burtell to answer suit of John Coffy action of trespass for an assault & battery damage £10 current money.

Imparlence granted to Richd. Kirkin to answer suit of Francis Ballard gent action upon the case damage £22:16:07.

Imparlence granted to Henry Irwin gent to answer suit of Ellinor Bosell trespass upon the case damage £50 current money.

In the suit brought by Saml. Selden agt Fra. Ballard gent action of trespass damage £10. Continued til next Ct.

In the suit brought by Antho. Armistead agt Fra. Ballard gent on hearing what each party has to offer & allowing deft 512 lbs tobo, the plt half part of the Parish Insolvents, also 1284 lbs tobo in the hands of several persons whose names & particular debts were contained in a list returned by the plt to this Ct that are indebted for their Parish dues & have agreed to pay the plt, which he accepts, and by the deft's consent he is to receive from them, which with 2592 lbs tobo due from plt to deft by two bills under his hand discounted doth reduce plt's claim of 9333 lbs tobo to 4942 lbs tobo which deft is hereby ordered to pay with costs at exon, from which deft appeals to the 7th day of the Honorable Genll Ct. Granted giving bond & security.

At a Court held the 19th of Novembr 1719
Fra. Ballard, Antho. Armistead, Thomas Wythe, John King, James Servant – His Majestie's Justices

Robin, a negro boy belonging to James Rascow Esqr, is adjudged to be ten years of age.

Deria, a negro boy belonging to Mrs. Martha Taylor, is adjudged to be ten years of age.

The last will & testament of Robert Taylor is proved by oaths of Joshua Curle, Saml. Sweny and the affadavit of Joseph Wragg wits thereto and is refd to next Ct for the Heir at Law to come in if any.

Upon petition of Jane Bloodworth for license to keep ordinary. Granted giving bond & security.

Mr. Jno. Bayley exhibiting an attchmt agt John Dunn's estate, the Ct regulating the same do order that Bayley be paid out of estate 2045 1/2 lbs tobo & 18 shilling & four pence in money being sworn to his accot.

Bryan Penny brought his action of trespass upon the case an assault & battery damage £10 agt Henry Jenkins. Deft pleads the Genll Issue. It's ordered refd to next Ct for tryall.

In the suit brought by Jane Rowton agt John Smith Senr action upon the case damage £5 current money & arguments heard. Ct order that deft pay plt 25 shillings with costs at exon. Boush atty per deft. Mr. Yeo for plt.

Ordered that Jane Rowton pay to Sarah Hayes for her two days attendance as an Evidence agt Jno. Smith with costs at exon.

Ordered that Jane Rowton pay to Rachel Dorlich for her two days attendance as an Evidence agt Jno. Smith with costs at exon.

In the suit brought by Saml. White agt Jno. Baddesby in an action upon the case damage £5 current money & two Evidences being sworn for deft & Jury impanneled, namely: Tho. Jones, Bart. Proby, Jno. Smith Junr, John Bordland, W---- Coopland, Nicho. Parker, John Mitchel, Tho. Batts, Saml. Watts, Joseph Banister, Saml. Sweny, Robt. Bright. [Jury] brought in verdict: "Noe verdict not before Court break up, being to late."

Ordered that William Winterton be sworn Constable in the Town of Hampton for one year in the room of Abraham Mitchel &c.

At a Court held the 3d Wednesday of Janry
being the 20th Day 1719
Capt. Fra. Ballard, Mr. Thos. Wythe, Mr. John King, Mr. Antho. Armistead, Mr. Jos. Curle - Justices

The Foefees ack their deeds for town land to Geo. Walker & ordered recorded.

Reba. Avera wido ack her deeds for town land to Joseph Wragg & ordered recorded.

Sarah Hicks chooses Jno. Jones her guardian which is granted giving bond &c security &c.

Upon petition of Tho. Delany for the delivery of the orphans estate of Richd. Cursell dec'd. Order rejected.

Upon motion of Jno. Lowery Surveyor for an allowance for laying out the streets. Order every freeholder in town pay the surveyor six pence per lot towards his charge & Geo. Waffe for carrying the chayne.

Upon petition of Thos. Faulkner for license to keep an ordinary. Granted giving bond & security & paymt of fees.

Upon petition of Martha Taylor for to decline such a part of her husband's will as relates to her part & desires to be restored to what the Law gives her. Granted.

Probate of the last will & testament of Robt. Taylor dec'd granted to Martha Taylor, giving bond & security & ordered estate appraised by Capt. Ballard, Mr. Banister, Mr. Wragg & Mr. Curle Senr or any three of them &c.

Upon return of the processioners of the Town persinks. Ordered recorded.

[p 177] The suit brought by Fra. Ballard agt Mary Bridge Exectrx of Wm. Ho----- dec'd upon an action of the case for £3:9:8 & 369 1/2 lbs toto, the deft demurring. Time is given plt to joyne or consider. Deft prays liberty to plead as many pleas as he things fitting. Granted.

Cha. Jenings & Capt. Ballard's attchmt agt Tho. Brittan's estate in the hands of Willm. Copeland is refd to next Ct for persons concerned to appear at Ct.

Our Soveraigne Lord the King & Henry Irwin agt John Smith Senr in action of debt damage £10 for the breach of a penal law is dismist, declr being blank.

Imparlence granted to Fras. Malory to answer the suit of Thos. Batts debt for £7:15:06.

Ellinor Bosel wido brought her action upon the case damage £50 agt Henry Irwin gent. Dismist by plt's consent.

Court adjourns tel Tomorrow Ten a Clock. Fra. Ballard signe.

At a Court held the 20th of Janry 1719
Fra. Ballard, Tho. Wythe, Josa. Curle, John King –
His Majestie's Justices

Upon petition of Jo---- Parish for his estate in the hands of John Cooke & Edward Lattemore which was left him by his grandfather Richd. Hurshly. Ordered that Cook & Lattemore pay the petitioner his estate according to division with costs.

Upon petition of Susanah Prince, orphan of Edwd. Prince, to choose her guardian who chooses Joyce Simmons wido & ordered she receive the orphan's estate giving bond & security. Matthew Small Security.

Dunn Armistead deeds for land to Antho. Armistead Senr proved by oaths of witnesses subscribed & ordered recorded.

Ct appoints Mr. John Bayley guardian to John Roberts, orphan of John Roberts dec'd.

Judgmt confessed by Jno. Bayley Adm of Jno. Dun dec'd for 1400 lbs tobo unto John Bordland he having proved his accotts with costs at exon. Execution stayed by consent seven months.

James Ricketts brought his action upon the case agt John Bayley Adm of John Dun dec'd for £10:07:07. Refd to next Ct.

[p 178] John Wallace agt John Bayley Adm of John Dun dec'd action upon the case damage £18 refd to next Ct.

Judgmt granted by Nihil Dicet agt Thomas Curle to answer suit of William Barber & Susa. his wife action case damage £26 1/2.

In the suit brought by Wm. Barber & Susa. his wife agt Saml. Watts in an action upon the case damage £6 (and put to trial) Ct [decides] £2:02 due to plts. Judgmt granted agt deft for paymt of sd sum with costs at exon.

Ordered that Wm. Barber pay to Richd. Nusum for his four days attendance as an Evidence agt Saml. Watts with costs at exon.

Robert Tannoch brought his action case of debt agt Cornelius Dorlich & Rachel his wife, plt not appearing. Ordered dismist.

Matthew Hilliard agt Cornelas Dorlich & his wife in Chancery, the respondents putting in their answer. Complainant takes time to next Ct to reply &c.

John Poole Senr agt Thos. Jones action detinue damage £55, plt's Evidences not being here. Refd to next Ct.

Tho. Batts Adm of Eliza. Sheppard his late wife agt Thomas Jones & Sarah his wife Adm of Jno. Sheppard dec'd in Chancery. Respondents pray time. Granted.

Judgmt granted agt Tho. Wilcox for paymt of £4 money unto Jacob Tabort with costs at exon.

Henry Robinson agt Samuel Selden action of debt for £100 sterling is dismist, plt being dead.

The action upon the case damage £20 brought by Tho. Wilcox Adm of Eliza. James agt Jno. Wallace, deft pleading. Deft prays time. Granted.

The Jury between Saml. White & Jno. Baddesby not appearing to return any verdict. Ordered new tryall at next Ct.

Hind Armistead agt Saml. Whatts [sic] dec'd £10 detinue, plt not appearing which upon motion of deft nonsuit granted him with costs at exon.

Wm. Allen fined according to law upon presentment of the Grand Jury for not coming to Church with costs at exon.

Bryan Penny agt Geo. Paine damage £5. Ordered former order be continued for acctts to audit between this and next Ct.

[p 179] Julian Daniel agt Jno. Mitchell Exec of Saml. Daniel &c in Chancery, having made oath to his answer. Refd for complainant to reply &c.

Ordered that Robt. Wells pay to George Waffe & Abraham Mitchell for their thirteen days each as Evidences agt Saml. Bromage with costs at exon.

Andrew Laws being presented by the Grand Jury for turning the High Way and being thought not reasonable. Ordered that his fine be remitted paying cost at exon.

Fra. Ballard signe.

At a Court held the 17th of Febry
being the 3d Wednesday 1719
Fras. Ballard, John King, James Servant, Josa.
Curle, James Ricketts – His Majestie's Justices

Upon petition of Wm. Allen for turning of a road that runs through his land. It's ordered petition be granted upon his promising to make the other road passable.

Thomas Wilcox ack deed for land to Isaac Velline & ordered recorded.

Upon complaint of several gentlemen as well as the Inhabitance of this county the Scones Dam Bridge is not passable for Man nor Horse &c. Ordered complaint lie till next Ct for consideration.

The Court adjourns till the Court in Course. Fra. Ballard signe.

[p 180] <center>At a Court held the 3d Wednesday of March
being the 16th Day 1719
Antho. Armistead, Henry Irwin, James Ricketts, James Servant, John King – His Majestie's Justices

Martha Taylor returning an appraisal of her husband's estate. Ordered recorded.

The last will & testament of Francis Ballard is proved by oaths of Robert Armistead and Mary Jenkins and the affirmation of Joseph Wragg wits subscribed thereto & certificate for probate granted the Execs named giving bond & security &c. Ordered estate be appraised between this & next Ct by Joseph Wragg, Mr. James Ricketts, John Bordland & returned to next Ct.

Upon petition of Elizabeth Chambers for license to keep an ordinary. Granted giving bond & security.

Upon motion of Tho. Poole setting forth that one of his witnesses in the case of ejectment depending agt James Ricketts is very aged & not able to come to Ct, prays he may make oath before some Justice. Granted & to be allowed upon tryall as Evidence.

Mr. Edmond Kearny ack deeds for town land to Mr. William Lowery & ordered recorded.

Upon petition of severall gentlemen of this Country for to have a good & passable road made through Sawyers Swamp & some sums of money being raised toward the same. It's ordered Surveyor together with Tho. Allen, Mr. Antho. Armistead, Mr. Robert Armistead, Mr. Jno. King & Mr. Henry Irwin do survey & lay out a convenient & nearest road through the Swamp to Finces [?] Dam & surveyor be paid. Further ordered that surveyor meet at Mr. Robt. Armistead's on Monday the 28th instant if fair if not on the first fair day & perform same.

[p 181] Upon petition of James Servant gent to have the care & tuition of the children of Francis Ballard dec'd as being their Uncle. Granted.

Upon petition of Jane Robinson wido that whereas her husband Henry Robinson became Security for Mary Gilbert, prays she may be discharged. Ordered Mary be summoned to next Ct to answer petition.

It's ordered that Richd. Haney [or Harvy] be added to Frans. Malory to procession land in this county &c, the Processioner before appointed refusing.

Mr. Lockey Mihill is ordered to repair Finces [?] Dam Bridge & what charge he is at to be allowed at the Laying of the next Levy & to make good the road to Allen's Swamp with the assistance of the male laboring tythables in his Persinkes.

Mr. Antho. Armistead is appointed Surveyor from Allen's Swamp to the Mill.

Mr. Josa. Curle is appointed Surveyor from the Church to the Town to Capt. Ballard's along James River to the Halfway Tree Road.

Ordered that the rates of lyquors be set & sold at the prices set formerly by this Ct.

Upon motion of Lockey Mihill to take the affadavit of Edmd. Ward who is an Evidence between him & Fras. Malory. It's ordered that some Justice of the Peace of this county [take his oath] between this & May Ct giving deft notice & to be allowed upon trial as good Evidence.

The Ct represents to the Honble Gov. Mr. Tho. Wythe, Mr. Jno. King & Mr. Irwin, either of which to be fit & proper persons as Sheriff of Elizabeth City Co. for the ensuing year.

The Ct recommends to the Honble Gov Mr. Saml. Selden to be Judge, Mr. James Rascow, Mr. Robt. Armistead, Mr. McKenzie together with the rest last represented to be Justices.

Antho. Armistead Signe.

[p 182] At a Court held the 3d Wednesday of May being the 18th Day 1720
Saml. Selden, James Rascow, James Ricketts, Henry Irwin, Joshua Curle, James Servant, Saml. Sweny — His Majestie's Justices

Saml. Selden, James Rascow, James Ricketts, James Servant, Joshua Curle, Henry Irwin, Tho. Wythe & Saml. Sweny hath taken the several oaths appointed by Law of the Justices of the Peace &c & also in Chancery & Subscribed the Tests according to the Govs. Commission dated the 5th day of May 1720.

Tho. Wythe gent is this day sworn High Sheriff of this County & Fra. Malory Under Sheriff & Henry Dunn Balife.

Mr. Tho. Wythe ack his Sheriff's bond & ordered recorded.

Upon petition of Matthew Williams to be discharged from the estate of his brother Wm. Williams dec'd. It's ordered that the Sheriff take care of the estate & return an inventory to next Ct.

Upon petition of Mrs. Ann Lowery for license to keep an ordinary which is granted giving bond & security &c.

Upon petition of Timothy Lee [?] for to be Levy free. Ordered petition be granted, it appearing to the Ct that he is an impotent person.

Upon petition of Servant Ballard to choose his guardian who makes choice of his Uncle James Servant. Granted giving bond & security.

Mr. Andr. Thomson's estate not being appraised. Ordered Mr. Jno. Lowery & Mr. Simon Hollier be added in the room of Mr. King & Mr. Yeo, the former appraisers neglecting to attend.

Upon petition of John Byresee for license to keep an ordinary. Granted giving bond & security &c.

In the ejectment brought by Robert Westlock agt Wm. Simmons, the common order is entered to which the deft pleads.

Order granted agt Alexandr. McKenzie for the non-appearance of Robt. Harr [or Warr] to answer Jno. Smith Senr damage £50.

[p 183] William Smelt ack receipt for paymt upon a debt of mortgage for Town land made by Tho. Wilcox to Smelt. Therefore ack same & ordered recorded.

Judgmt granted agt John Mitchell Exec of Saml. Daniel dec'd for paymt of six shillings to Wm. Smelt Adm of Jno. Pett dec'd with costs &c.

The last will & testament of John Bayley is proved by oaths of Joshua Curle & Margt. Needham wits thereto & certificate of probate granted the Exectrx giving bond & security &c & ordered recorded & further ordered estate be appraised by Mr. Jos. Banister, Mr. Sweny, Mr. Robt. Armistead & John More or any three of them. Return to next Ct.

Hind Armistead is appointed Constable in the room of Richd. Hawkins.

Imparlence granted to Jane Baker to answer suit of William Smelt Adm of Jno. Pett dec'd case damage £3.

Imparlence granted to John Kimbal to answer suit of Wm. Smelt case for 29/6.

Upon attchmt brought by Saml. Sweny agt Tho. Brittain & being attached in the hands of Wm. Coopland & he appearing & confessing he had in his hands sufficient to pay the debt. It's ordered he pay same to the plt, he having proved his acct with costs at exon.

Imparlence granted to Richd. Kirkin to answer suit of Wm. Smelt case damage £10.

Wm. Smelt brought his action of ejectmt agt Julian Daniel for land & tenements mentioned in the declr which is ended.

Martha Taylor agt Jno. King, deft having paid the debt. Ordered dismist, deft paying costs at exon.

Miles Cary agt Jno. King. Deft having paid debt. Ordered dismist, deft paying costs at exon.

Richd. Adams' suit agt Robert Tannoch is dismist.

[p 184] Judgmt is granted by Nihill Dicet agt Mary Jenkins Admx of Jno. Curle dec'd to answer suit of Sarah Hayes Admx of Henry Hays case damage £12.

Upon petition of John Kobbs [or Hobbs] agt Tho. Faulkner & Martha Taylor, defts pleading. Plt prays time. Granted.

John Coffy agt Jno. Burtell & John King for his freedom action of the case damage £20 is dismist, the plt being "gon".

Cha. Jenings agt John Smith Senr. Deft prays time to next Ct to bring in his discount. Granted.

Doglas Bogal als Reed [?] his deeds to Tho. Lattemore for land proved in Ct by oaths of Edwd. Lattemore & James Baker wits. Ordered recorded.

The Foeffees ack deeds for Town land to Edwd. Lattemore & ordered recorded.

Brian Penny's suit agt Henry Jenkins trespass d --- refd for the Defendts coming in to Virga.

Nonsuit is granted to Cha. Chapman agt Jos. Brown, the plt not appearing.

Attchmt granted agt Jno. King gent at the suit of Joseph Wragg case --- [sic]

Nonsuit granted agt Tho. Jones [inserted above Cordwind.] he failing to prosecute his suit of Brian Penny upon an action of trespass case damage £---

Imparlence granted Mr. Henry Irwin to answer suit of Richd. Nusum case damage £5.

In the suit brought by Brian Penny agt Jno. Kimbal case damage £6 deft prays oyer of the bill. Granted.

Saml. Selden agt Jno. King damage £200 is dismist by consent of the plt, the deft assuming to pay costs at exon.

John Wallace agt Emanl. Alkin damage £28. Dismist. No appearance.

[p 185] In the suit brought by James Ricketts & Jane his wife & Geo. [torn] vs Jenkins surviving Exec of Nicho. Curle dec'd agt Mary Jenkins Admx of John Curle damage £80, deft pleading not guilty. Refd to next Ct for tryall.

Francis Ballard's petition agt Mr. Servant's estate to have his accotts auditted is ordered dismist, plt being dead.

Court adjourns til tomorrow ten a clock

At a Court held the 19th day of May 1720
Saml. Selden, James Rascow, Henry Irwin, James Ricketts, James Servant, Saml. Sweny – His Majestie's Justices

Saml. Selden's suit agt Francis Ballard action trespass damage £10 dismist, deft being dead.

Foefees ack deed for Town land to James Rascow Esqr. Ordered recorded.

Lean [?] Bean is sworn Constable in the room of Francis Malory. He is therefore discharged.

Hind Armistead is sworn Constable in the room of Richd. Hawkins. He is therefore discharged.

William Dandridge gent came into Ct & ack deeds for Town land to Henry Irwin gent & also ack bond for same. Ordered recorded.

Upon petition of John Bowland for license to keep an ordinary which is granted giving bond &c.

Upon petition of Jno. Kimball for license to keep an ordinary which is granted giving bond &c.

Upon petition of James Barrett for license to keep an ordinary which is granted giving bond &c.

Matthew Hilliard agt Cornelas Dorlich & Rachel his wife refd to next Ct by consent in Chancery.

Tho. Wilcox agt John Wallace is dismist they being agreed, case damage £20.

Upon petition of John Green agt his Master Joshua Curle gent for his wages, deft prays time to next Ct to put in his answer. Granted.

[p 186] Irwin's Informations agt Rachel Dorlich, Eliza. Hill & Sarah Robinson refd to next Ct for want of Informant's Evidences.

Mr. Geo. Yeo returning the remaining part of an inventory of Capt. Wm. Bosell's estate. Ordered the things contained in inventory be appraised except those articles marked to be appraised by the former appraisers & return same.

The Grand Jury being sworn. It's ordered that the several persons presented be summoned to next Ct to answer except Mr. Irwin & Eliza. Chambers.

Judgmt by Nihill Dicet granted agt Mary Jenings [sic] Admx of Henry Jenkins dec'd to answer suit of Joshua Curle gent case damage £50.

James Ricketts & Jane his wife Execs of Nicho. Curle agt Fra. Ballard is ordered dismist, deft being dead.

Cha. Jenings agt Mary Jenkins Admx of John Curle damage 1000 tobo, deft pleading prays time. Granted.

Upon petition of William Smelt for license to keep an ordinary which is granted giving bond & security &c.

John King agt Mary Jenkins Admx of Henry Jenkins is dismist, plt not appearing action case damage £40.

In the suit brought by John Poole Senr agt Tho. Jones in an action of detinue damage £55 for one Negr man slave called Paul. Four Evidences sworn for the plt & two for deft. Jury impanelled namely: Edwd. Roe, Wm. Tucker, Jno. Bushell, Bartd. Proby, Edward Lattemore, Jno. Batts, Lend. Whiting, John More, Wm. Barber, Jas. Baker & Abra. Mitchel. Jury returnes verdict in these words viz: We of the Jury do find for the deft. Edwd. Lattemore foreman. Verdict ordered recorded & ordered dismist with costs at exon.

It's ordered that Jno. Poole pay to Wm. Coffield of Nansemond Co. for his ten days attendance as an Evidence for Poole agt Tho. Jones & for five times coming & going twenty miles with the necessary charges of ferriages with costs at exon.

[p 187] In the suit brought by James Ricketts & Jane his wife --- Nicho. Curle dec'd agt Mary Jenkins Admx of Henry Jenkins --- action case damage £140 continued to argue matters of Law --- upon the Verdict.

James Ricketts agt Mary Jenkins Admx of Henry Jenkins dec'd case damage £10 refd to next Ct for the other action between the parties to be tried first.

Tho. Walk agt Mary Jenkins Admx of Henry Jenkins dec'd debt for £16:07:08 continued.

Jno. Bordland agt Mary Jenkins Admx of Henry Jenkins dec'd case damage £-- refd to next Ct.

Maxl. Boush agt Mary Jenkins Admx of Jno. Curle dismist.

Ordered that Thos. Jones pay to Wm. Frazey for ten days attendance agt John Poole with costs at exon.

Ordered that Jno. Poole pay to Matthw. Small for his five days attendance as an Evidence agt Tho. Jones with costs at exon.

Ordered that Jno. Poole pay to Ann Roe for six days attendance as an Evidence agt Tho. Jones with costs at exon.

Ordered that Jno. Poole pay to Jane Rowton for six days attendance as an Evidence agt Tho. Jones with costs at exon.

Harry, Negr boy belonging to Edwd. Lattemore, adjudged eight years old.

Upon considering the new Commission of the Peace, ordered that the Sheriff give the Gent. notice that is appointed in Commission to be at next Ct to take the Oaths & if not to give their reasons.

Upon motion of Mr. Wythe Sheriff that the prison of this county is insufficient, ordered that he repair same & bring in his charge at next Levy.

Ordered that the Clerk of the Ct do provide to get him an office built in the Court House as soon as convenient & that he remove the records thereto in three months.

Lists of tythables to be taken on the 20th June &c. Orphans Ct to be held the second Tuesday in June &c.

Court adjourns to the Court in Course.

[p 188]   At a Court held the 15th of June 1720
being the third Wednesday
Henry Irwin, James Ricketts, James Servant, Joshua Curle, Saml. Sweny – His Majestie's Justices

Upon petition of John Merrideth for license to keep an ordinary at his house in Hampton which is granted giving bond & security &c.

Upon petition of Tho. Delany for an allowance for the keeping of Richd. Crusell's orphans. Ordered petition rejected & that the person that hath the estate in possession do bring in an inventory at next Ct.

Upon petition of Thos. Francis for to keep one of the children of Moses Davis dec'd he being their Grandfather. Ordered that sd child remain with Francis together with his plantation & if he learn him to read and wright and when the child is able to be bound out to a Trade that then he deliver him up to the Court &c.

Upon the petition of Easter Francis for to keep one of the orphans of Moses Davis dec'd she being Aunt. Ordered that child remain [with her] & if he learn him to read and wright and when the child is able to be bound out to a Trade that then she deliver him up to the Court &c.

Wm. Brough one of witnesses to Mr. Saml. Selden's will made oath on the holy Evangeless [sic] that he saw Selden sign seale & deliver the same & that he was in perfect sense & memory to the best of his knowledge.

John King, Jno. Lowery & James Wallace has this day taken the Oaths & signed the Test also taken the Oaths of Justice of the Peace & Chancery.

Upon motion of Cha. Jenings to record a platt or survey of certain lands surveyed for one John Hales. Ordered recorded.

[p 189] Sarah Teemo malato binds her child called James unto William Brooks & his wife Eliza. & their heirs until he comes of age.

Upon petition of Elinor Edghill agt Elinor Wanless for her --ly. Ordered she be summoned to next Ct to answer.

Upon petition of Mary Bridge to have the care of Ann Williams, orphan of Wm. Williams dec'd & to have the estate being nearest of kin. Ordered that Mary have Ann together with her estate giving bond & security &c & that she pay the Sheriff his charge for taking estate into custody & that Mattw. Williams give the estate up upon oath & als ordered that same be appraised by Brian Penny, Richd. Nusum & Tho. Batts & returned to next Ct.

Upon petition of James Robinson agt Mary Gilbert [to give] new Security. Ordered that Mary have liberty to next Ct to give Security &c.

Upon petition of John Lawson agt Joshua Curle gent. Ordered Curle be summoned to next Ct to answer.

In suit brought by Bartd. Proby Adm of Thos. Proby dec'd agt Jno. Burtell Adm of James Burtell dec'd acctt render for £100. Ordered refd to next Ct. Mr. Selden the plt's atty being dead.

Henry Irwin gent agt Mary Jenkins Admx of Henry Jenkins dec'd action upon the case damage £20, deft not appearing. Judgmt granted by Nihill Dicet.

Judgmt granted by Nihill Dicet agt Mary Jenkins Admx of Henry Jenkins dec'd to answer suit of Archibald Blair debt.

John King gent agt Mary Jenkins Admx of John Curle dec'd. Deft prays to plead as many pleas as she thinks convenient which is granted & the plt prays time to answer. It's granted.

Judgmt granted agt Mary Jenkins Admx of Henry Jenkins dec'd to answer suit of Saml. Sweny gent action case damage ----.

The suit brought by Elinor Bosell agt Mary Jenkins Admx of Henry Jenkins dec'd action case is ordered dismist, plt being married.

Philip Smith brought his action of debt agt Mary Jenkins Admx of Henry Jenkins dec'd dismist, plt not appearing.

Saml. Selden gent a [blotted] brought agt Mary Jenkins Admx of Henry Jenkins is dismist, plt being dead.

Judgmt granted agt John Bayley late Sheriff as Security for Cha. Pyne for £3:10 to James Servant with costs at exon &c, plt having prove his acct.

Judgmt granted agt Mary Jenkins Admx of Henry Jenkins dec'd by Nihill Dicet to answer suit of Cha. Jenings case for 1080 lbs tobo.

Upon suit in Chancery brought by Francis Malory & Ann his wife late wife of Edwd. Mihill dec'd. It's agreed that a Justice of the Peace take depositions of witnesses & return same to next Ct to which Cause is refd for trial.

Judgmt by Nihill Dicet granted agt Mary Jenkins Admx of Henry Jenkins dec'd to answer Cha. Jenings debt for £13:11:06.

Judgmt granted agt John Mitchel Exec of Saml. Daniel dec'd for £5;09:06 out of Daniel's estate, deft making his just discount to Emanl. Alkin with costs at exon, he having made oath to his acct.

Wm. Smelt agt Jno. King gent by Scirefacias. Ordered judgmt be renewed for one Barrel of Tarr at Nansemond with costs of both sides to Wm. Smelt at exon.

Judgmt confirmed agt Tho. Wilcox Adm of Eliza. James for £3:09:09 to John Burtell Adm of James Burtel dec'd with costs at exon.

Thos. Batts Adm of Eliza. Sheppard dec'd agt Baldwin Sheppard case damage £30 is refd to next Ct, Mr. Selden his atty being dead.

Tho. Skinner's petition agt John Mitchel Exec of Samuel Daniel dec'd is dismist, the plt not appearing.

Edmond Kearny agt Brian Penny action of debt, the plt's atty being dead. Ordered refd to next Ct.

Joshua Curle Junr his two actions agt Mary Jenkins Admx of Henry Jenkins & Jno. Curle dismist, plt not appearing.

The action upon the case brought by Wm. Barber & his wife agt --- Curle damage 26 shillings is refd to next Ct, Mr. Selden his atty being dead.

Tho. Batts Adm of Eliza. Sheppard dec'd agt Tho. Jones & Sarah his wife Chancery is continued to next Ct, the parties being upon complyance.

Saml. White agt Jno. Baddesby is dismist, plt not appearing.

[p 191] In the suit brought by Brian Penny agt George Paine action upon the case, the auditors reporting 9 shillings due. It's ordered that he pay same to plt with costs at exon.

The suit brought by Julian Daniel agt John Mitchel Exec of Saml. Daniel dec'd Chancery is refd to next Ct, deft's atty being dead.

John Poole brought his action of ejectmt agt Pasco Curle infant wherein James Ricketts gent was admitted deft. Plt not appearing, ordered dismist.

In suit brought by Jno. Smith Senr agt Robert Kerr in an action upon the case damage £50, plt not appearing to prosecute which upon motion of deft nonsuit granted him & it's ordered that the plt pay the nonsuit with one atty's fee with costs at exon.

Wm. Smelt brought his action upon the case agt John Kimball which by consent of parties is dismist, deft paying cost of suit at exon.

William Smelt brought his action upon the case agt Richd. Kirkin which by consent of the parties is refd to next Ct.

Note: The following three entries are exactly alike, except for referring to three different persons.

Upon the Information brought by Joshua Curle gent one of the Churchwardens of this Parish of Eliza. City agt Mary Frizell for committing of fornication & having a bastard child born of her body & she appearing & confessing the fact. It's ordered that Mary be fined 500 lbs tobo or 50 shillings paid to the Churchwardens at the laying of the next Parish Levy for the use of the Poore of sd Parish &c with costs at exon, or receive 25 lashes well laid on, on her back &c.

Same entry re Mary Randy.
Same entry for Eliza. Chambers.

[p 192] It's ordered that the Sheriff take Mary Frizell, Mary Randy & Eliza. Chambers into custody till they give security for the payment of their several fines &c.

Judgmt granted agt Thos. Wilcox Adm &c of Eliza. James dec'd for £3:09:09 unto Jno. Burtell Adm of James Burtell dec'd with costs at exon.

The suit brought by Thos. Batts Adm of Eliza. Sheppard agt Baldwin Sheppard action upon the case damage £30 is by consent refd to next Ct, Mr. Selden being dead.

Upon petition of Thos. Skinner agt John Mitchel Exec of Saml. Daniel dec'd for a legacy &c dismist, plt not appearing.

The remaining part of John Pett's appraismt is ordered continued till tomorrow to be returned.

In the action of debt damage 1000 lbs tobo brought by Edmd. Kerny agt Brian Penny, plt's atty being dead, refd to next Ct.

The two actions upon the case brought by William Barber agt Thos. Curle is refd to next Ct, his atty being dead Mr. Selden.

The suit in Chancery brought by Tho. Batts Adm of Eliza. Sheppard dec'd agt Tho. Jones & his wife is continued to next Ct, the Parties being upon a complyance.

The action upon the case damage £6 brought by Saml. White agt John Baddesby is dismist, plt not appearing.
[Note by scribe: --- from the Top Our to this last is Recorded already ---]

Upon the presentment of the Grand Jury agt Fras. Williams & Mary Bridge for living under the notion of man & wife and the Presentment being wrong. It's ordered dominion [?] pay costs at exon.

Upon the presentment of the Grand Jury agt Wm. Knight for a common swearer & he appearing but not excepting himself, ordered to be fined & that he pay Churchwardens at laying of the next Levy for the use of the Poore of the Parish with costs at exon.

Robt. Armistead takes time to plead to the presentment of the Grand Jury.

[p 193] Presentment of the Grand Jury agt Thos. Curle for firing of Gunns on the Sabbath Day, he appearing but not excepting himself. Ordered fined &c.

Presentment of the Grand Jury agt Reba. King for having a bastard child born of her body & Mr. Josa. Curle having fifty shillings the sd fine in his hands. It's ordered he pay same to Churchwardens &c.

Presentment of the Grand Jury agt Job Thomas for a Common Swearer – fined &c.

Presentment of the Grand Jury agt Elizabeth Chambers for having a bastard child &c.

Presentment of the Grand Jury agt Ellinor Wanless for having a bastard child, upon which Joseph Wragg & Cha. Moone came into Ct & assumed to pay the fine.

Presentment of the Grand Jury agt John Harris & Dorothy Carter for living in Common Adultery, she appearing & making no legal defense. Ordered fined &c.
[Note: two lines are here crossed out.]

The Jurors for our Sovreigne Lord the King upon their oaths presenting John Pugh & Jane Bloodworth for living in adultery & the sd Pugh appearing & not making any legal defence & Jane failing to appear. It's ordered that each be fined 1000 lbs tobo to be paid as the Law directs with costs at exon, which order the deft appeals to the 7th day of the Honorable the Genll Ct next coming. Granted giving bond & security &c. Joseph Wragg Security.

[p 194] Upon presentment of the Grand Jury agt Mary Savoy [?] for having a bastard child, she confessed the fact and is fined 500 lbs toto or 50 lbs to be paid to the Churchwardens &c & that she remain in the Sheriff's custody till she give bond & security & to keep the Parish harmless from maintaining the child.

Presentment of the Grand Jury agt Wm. Spicer for a Common Swearer and he not excepting himself. Ordered fined &c.

Presentment of the Grand Jury agt William Knight for a Common Swearer and he not excepting himself. Ordered fined &c.

Presentment of the Grand Jury agt Wm. Spicer for killing of Hoggs under pretense of Wild ones, he appearing & making no legal defense. Ordered fined to be paid to our Sov. Lord the King with costs at exon.
Henry Irwin

At a Court held the 16th day of June 1720
Henry Irwin, James Ricketts, James Servant, Mr. King,
Saml. Sweny – His Majestie's Justices

In the suit brought by Martha Taylor agt Roseanah Hunt case for slander damage 500 lbs tobo. Refd to next Ct, plt's atty being dead.

Sarah Hayes Admx of Henry Hayes dec'd agt Mary Jenkins Admx of John Curle dec'd. Deft prays liberty to plead as many pleas as he [sic] thinks convenient which is granted, whereupon he pleads. The plt prays time to answer. Granted.

Upon petition of John Nobbs agt Thos. Faulkner & Martha Taylor, Mr. Selden the petitioner's atty being dead. It's ordered refd to next Ct.

[p 195] Judgmt granted agt John Smith Senr for £8:03:06 being the balance of a bill to Charles Jenings with costs at exon.

Brian Penny brought his action of trespass for Salt & Battery damage £10 agt Henry Jenkins. Dismist, parties being agreed.

Joseph Wragg's his two actions agt John King gent ordered dismist, the debts being paid.

Matthew Hillard agt Cornelas Dorlich, complainant putting in his demurrer. Respondent prays time to consider. Granted.

Judgmt granted by Nihill Dicet agt Mary Jenkins Admx &c of Henry Jenkins dec'd to answer suit of John Bordland.

Tho. Read being summoned to Ct to answer the Contempt for not obaying the Constable at last Ct & now appearing & making no defense. It's ordered he be fined 5 shillings with costs at exon.

Upon petition of Bridget Jenkins for her thirds agt Mary Jenkins Admx of Henry Jenkins dec'd. Ordered that petition be dismist being thought fit not to lie before the Ct upon the petition.

Saml. Selden's action of trespass agt Wm. Cunningham is ordered dismist, plt being dead.

Joseph Selden brought action of tresspass agt Geo. Walker. Special imparlence granted the D---

Order granted agt Wm. Acrill & John Bordland his security for his non-appearance to answer suit of Martha Taylor.

Upon the suit in Chancery brought by John Nixon agt Wm. Barber and Susa. his wife. It's refd to next Ct, complainant's atty being dead.

The action upon the case brought by Martha Taylor agt Emanl. Alkin. Deft prays oyer of the bill. Granted.

Order granted agt Tho. Faulkner & Jno. Faulkner & Jno. Merrideth their Security to answer suit of Saml. Sweny gent damage £28.

Order granted agt the Sheriff for the non-appearance of Michl. Peirce to answer suit of Saml. Sweny.

Attchmt granted to the Sheriff agt estate of Michl. Peirce. Sweny's suit agt Peirce.

Order granted agt Mattw. F--- & Hind Armistead his security to answer suit of Saml. Sweny.

[p 196] Upon summons by Scirefacias brought by William Smelt agt Mary Frizell for the renewing of a former judgmt for 19 shillings & 216 lbs tobo. It's ordered that the former order be renewed.

In the suit brought by Thos. Jones Cordwinder agt Brian Penny in an action of trespass damage £20, plt failing to file his declaration which upon motion of deft nonsuit is granted him agt plt's estate & ordered that plt pay nonsuit to deft with costs at exon.

Order granted agt William Taylor & Saml. Sweny his security for his non-appearance to answer suit of Emanl. Alkin.

Imparlence granted to Richd. Adams to answer suit of James Barrett.

In the suit brought by Cornelas Dorlich & Rachel his wife agt Sarah Reding a trespass damage £10, plt failing to file declaration. Upon motion of deft nonsuit is granted & plt ordered to pay to deft with costs at exon.

Order granted agt the Sheriff for the non-appearance of Tho. Delany to answer suit of Samuel Sweny. Upon motion of Sheriff attchmt granted him agt Delany's estate.

In the suit brought by Richd. Adams agt Jos. Barret & no declr being filed. Upon deft's motion nonsuit is awarded & ordered plt pay same with one atty's fee to deft with costs at exon.

Nonsuit and one atty's fee ordered to be paid by Jno. Foster to Cha. Moone, Foster not filing declr with costs.

Nonsuit granted agt Mary Frizel & ordered she pay same to Mary Randy, plt not filing declr with costs at exon.

Upon motion of the Sheriff attchmt granted him agt Tho. Delany's estate at suit of Andr. Johnson.

It's ordered that Mr. Henry Irwin provide weights and seals for a standard for this county & to keep in the county & he will be paid at laying of the next Levy.

It's ordered that the Inhabitance of the Town & the People adjoining do clear the roads to Tho. Reads & from thence ... along Jas. River to clear to Scone Dam Bridge & from there to Holmes Bridge to Mr. Ricketts Surveyor.

At a Court held the 3d Wednesday of July
being the 20th day 1720
James Rascow, John King, Henry Irwin, James Servant, James Ricketts, John Lowery, James Wallace, Joseph Banister, Saml. Sweny, Mr. Joshua Curle

Mr. Joseph Banister is this day taken oaths appointed by Law & also the oaths of Justice of the Peace & Chancery & signed the Test &c.

Alexdr. Kennaday & his wife & Richard Casy being committed to prison upon suspicion of assisting & aiding certain persons out of prison which was committed upon suspicion of Pyresey [Piracy] the prisoner[ers] being brought to the Barr & arguments heard, the Ct are of the opinion that the prisoners ought not to be discharged but to have their tryall upon that mittemus & upon hearing of witnesses the Ct are of further opinion the prisoners be discharged paying costs at exon.

In the suit in Chancery brought by Francis Malory & Ann his wife late wife of Edward Mihill dec'd agt Lockey Mihill & Joshua Mihill Execs of Edward for 1/3 part of Edward's personal estate. Ct having heard defts' pleas with depositions produced in behalf of both Parties & arguments from both Councills, decree that suit be dismist with costs at exon. From which order complainants appeal to the Honorable the Genll Ct next coming on the 10th day thereof. Granted giving bond & security.

The last will & testament of Saml. Selden gent is proved by oaths of Geo. Yeo & Margt. Welch witnesses & certificate for probate granted Execs thereof giving bond & security. Ordered recorded.

The last will & testament of Margt. Bayley dec'd is proved by oaths of Jno. Selden & Thos. Jones witnesses thereto and certificate for probate granted to Margt. Needham one of the Execs giving bond & security. Ordered recorded.

In the suit brought by James Ricketts & Jane his wife Execs of Nicho. Curle gent dec'd agt Mary Jenkins Admx of Henry Jenkins dec'd in an action upon the case damage £140. The Mattrs of Law arising from the special verdict in the

Cause being argued. It's considered by the Ct the plts recover £35 damage out of decedant's estate with costs at exon.

Court adjourns til Tomorrow - a Clock. Jas. Rascow signe.

[p 195]   At a Court held the 21st day of July 1720
James Rascow, Henry Irwin, Joshua Curle, James Servant,
Saml. Sweny, James Ricketts, Jno. Lowery, Joseph
Banister - His Majestie's Justices

Ordered that the remaining part of Capt. Bosell's Inventory be appraised by the former appraisers except the wearing apparel & those things markt.

Upon petition of John Roberts agt Mrs. Judeth Bayley. It's ordered she be summoned to next Ct to answer petition.

Julian Daniel agt John Mitchell Exec of Saml. Daniel dec'd trespass damage £30, deft prays time to next Ct. Granted.

Mr. Francis Malory Sheriff having returned an inventory [on] Wm. Williams estate. Ordered recorded.

Judgmt by Nihil Dicet granted agt Henry irwin gent to answer suit of Richd. Nusum case for £5 damage.

Upon petition of John Green agt Joshua Curle gent his Master for wage. Ordered dismist.

In the suit brought by Josa. Curle gent agt Mary Jenkins Admx of Henry Jenkins dec'd action upon the case damage £150, plt proving his acct. It's ordered that deft pay £27:17:02 out of Decedant's estate with costs at exon.

In the suit brought by Martha Taylor agt Roseanah Hunt action upon the case for slander damage £55, deft plead not guilty & Evidences being heard & Jury Impanneled namely: Bartd. Proby, Thomas Batts, Richd. Nusum, Richd. Kirkin, John Faulkner, Wm. Cunningham, Thos. Howard, Jno. Pugh, Thos. Jones, Jno. Jones, Jno. Nixson & Brian Penny ... & returned this verdict: We of the Jury doe find for the plt damage six pence, which on motion of plt verdict is recorded & ordered deft pay six pence to plt with noe more costs at exon.

It's ordered that Roseanah Hunt pay to Thos. Wilcox for his two days attendance as Evidence for her agt Martha Taylor with costs at exon.

It's ordered that the estate of William Williams pay to Brian Penny for his two days in appraising the estate.

It's ordered that the estate of Wm. Williams pay to Richd. Nusum & Thos. Batts for their two days attendance each in appraising estate with costs at exon.

Imparlence granted to Henry Irwin gent to answer suit of Martha Taylor action upon the case damage £30.

Martha Cole daughter of Cela Cole is bound apprentice to Richard Rowton & his wife until she comes of age or marries, they learning her to read a Chapter in the Bible & her Prayers & to Card & Spin, Sew & to Nitt & to give her when free what the law allows.

[p 199] Jno. Lawson's petition agt Joshua Curle gent & he not appearing to prosecute. It's ordered dismist with costs of Clk's & Sheriff's fees.

Mr. Tho. Wyth's accott agt Mr. Andr. Thompson's estate is allowed he making oath to the same & inventory of estate & ordered recorded.

Mr. Jno. Bayley by appraisers being returned it's ordered recorded.

William Williams by appraisers being returned it's ordered recorded.

John Faulkner bringing James Crafford his servant who had absented himself from his Master's service fifteen days. It's ordered that he serve his Master double the time & pay £2:01 for charges expended & that he serve his Master the time of five months for the same after Time is expired by indenture at the rate of 800 lbs tobo per year.

Judgmt granted agt Henry Irwin gent for £3:06 to Martha Taylor she having proved her acct with costs at exon.

Bartd. Proby Adm of Thos. Proby agt Jno. Birtell Adm of James Birtell accott render for £100. Plt prays oyer of the receipt. Granted he paying this Ct's charges.

Henry Irwin gent agt Mary Jenkins Admx of Henry Jenkins. Time is given deft to plead as many pleas as she thinks convenient.

Archibald Blair gent agt Mary Jenkins Admx of Jno. Curle. Time is given deft to plead as many please as she thinks convenient.

John King's suit agt Mary Jenkins Admx of Jno. Curle. Plt prays time. Granted.

Saml. Sweny gent agt Mary Jenkins Admx of Henry Jenkins. Time is given for deft to plead as many pleas as she thinks convenient.

Tho. Batts Adm of Elizabeth Sheppard agt Baldwin Sheppard action upon the case damage £30. Refd, parties being upon complyance.

In the suit brought by Edmond Kearny agt Brian Penny action of debt damage 1000 lbs tobo, plt prays time. Granted.

Judgmt granted by Nihil Dicet agt Thomas Batts Adm of Eliza. Sheppard agt Tho. Jones & Sarah his wife, respondents in Chancery which by consent of Parties it's desired that Mr. Josa. Curle & Mr. Saml. Sweny settle the accotts & return report to next Ct.

It's ordered that the appraisers of Jno. Pett's estate be summoned to next Ct to shew cause why the appraismt is not returned.

Julian Daniel agt Jno. Mitchel Exec of Saml. Daniel dec'd Chancery. Deft prays time. Granted.

[p 200] In the suit brought by Wm. Smelt agt Richd. Kirkin action upon the case damage £20. It's agreed by both parties that their accotts be auditted by Mr. Joseph Banister & Cha. Jenings & report to next Ct.

John Whitfield being presented by the Grand Jury for Stopping of the Road & he not appearing. Ordere that he be fined & pay to Churchwardens at the laying of the next Levy for the use of the Poor in the Parish.

Sarah Hayes Admx of Henry Hayes agt Mary Jenkins Admx of Jno. Curle dec'd £12 case, plt replying. Deft prays time. Granted.

John Nobbs' petition agt Thomas Faulkner & Martha Taylor. Ordered dismist "Not be Brought Regular."

In the suit in Chancery brought by Matthew Hilliard agt Cornelas & Rachel Dorlich his wife. Deft prays time. Granted.

Thos. Walk agt Mary Jenkins Admx of Henry Jenkins gent dec'd is by complainant dismist.

In suit brought by John Bordland agt Mary Jenkins Admx of Henry Jenkins, deft prays liberty to plead as many pleas as she things convenient in the action of case damage £60. Plt prays time. Granted.

Joseph Selden bringing his action of trespass damage £20 agt George Walker is by consent dismist.

Martha Taylor agt William Acrill case damage £10 deft not appearing. John Bordland his security prays time till next Ct. Granted.

Jno. Nixson's bill in Chancery brought agt William Barber is by consent of the complainant dismist.

Judgmt granted by Nihill Dicet agt Emanl. Alkin to answer suit of Martha Taylor damage £8 case.

Judgmt confirmed agt the Sheriff Security for Michl. Peirce for £5:12:06 to Saml. Sweny & one atty's fee with costs at exon.

Judgmt confessed by Thomas & Jno. Faulkner for £15 current money & one atty's fee to Saml. Sweny with costs.

Judgmt confessed by Matthew Tual for 31 shillings and one atty's fee to Saml. Sweny with costs.

Judgmt granted agt Wm. Taylor & Saml. Sweny gent his security for £1:06:06 with one atty's fee & costs.

Judgmt confessed by Richd. Nusum for £2:05:02 farthing to James Barret with costs at exon.

Judgmt confirmed agt Tho. Delany & the Sheriff for £4:16:10 current money to Saml. Sweny with one atty's fee with costs at exon.

Upon motion of the Sheriff the attchmt granted him last Ct agt Tho. Delany's estate might be confirmed for £4:16 & the same of Saml. Sweny with costs at exon.

Judgmt confirmed agt Tho. Delany for 200 lbs sweet scented tobo to Andr. Johnson with costs at exon.

Upon motion of the Sheriff his attchmt agt Tho. Delany's estate is confirmed to pay 200 lbs sweet scented tobo at Andr. Johnson's suit with costs.

James Ricketts & Jane his wife Execs of Nicho. Curle dec'd agt Mary Jenkins Admx of John Curle dec'd. Case dismist, plt not prosecuting.

James Ricketts agt Mary Jenkins Admx of Henry Jenkins dec'd action case damage £10. Dismist, plt not prosecuting.

Upon motion of the Sheriff his attchmt agt Michl. Peirce's estate confirmed for £5:12:06 at Saml. Sweny's suit with costs.

Upon the information brought by Henry Irwin gent agt Eliza. Hill for selling drink contrary to law to which deft pleads not guilty. Evidences being heard & Jury impanneled namely: Brian Penny &c. Returned verdict. We of the Jury find the deft Not Guilty. Wm. Westwood foreman. On motion of deft verdict is ordered recorded & suit dismist with costs.

Joshua Curle & Servant Ballard Execs of Fra. Ballard dec'd agt Tho. Roberts in an action upon the case damage £14 & 400 lbs tobo. Deft prays oyer of accotts. Granted.

John Bordland agt Andr. Laws damage £10 case is dismist, deft paying costs at exon.

Upon the action by Scirefacias brought by Jno. Bordland agt James Barret & Eliza. his wife formerly Eliza. Hill for the renewing of a judgmt granted agt Eliza. Hill, deft having paid some of the judgmt & plt making oath to the true balance. Ordered that judgmt be renewed for £5:18:03 & one atty's fee with costs at exon.

Imparlence granted to James Barret to answer suit of Richd. Adams case damage £14.

Imparlence granted to Wm. Winterton at suit of John Whitfield action trespass damage £50.

Special imparlence granted to Wm. Cunningham to answer suit of John Bordland action of the case damage [blank]

Order granted agt the Sheriff for the non-appearance of Brian Penny to answer Thomas Jones' action of trespass damage with ---

[p 202] Order granted agt Hind Armistead & Cornelas Dorlich & Rachel his wife to answer suit of John Pugh case damage [blank]

It's ordered that Wm. Coopland pay to Joshua Curle & Servant Ballard Execs of Fra. Ballard dec'd for 147 lbs tobo & 5/8 out of Geo. Brittan's estate provided he hath so much in his hands with costs at exon.

The action upon the case for 500 lbs tobo brought by Richd. Nusum agt Brian Penny is by consent refd to next Ct.

Henry Irwin his Infomations agt Rachel Dorlich & Sarah Robinson is dismist they not being brought right.

Court adjourns til tomorrow 9 a clock.

At a Court held the 22nd of July 1720
James Rascow, Henry Irwin, Joshua Curle, James Ricketts, Joseph Banister, Saml. Sweny

Richd. Tuckerman's Power of Atty to Henry Irwin is proved by oaths of Fra. Malory & Saml. Sweny witness thereto that saw Tuckerman sign seal & deliver. Ordered recorded.

Upon motion of Mr. Henry Irwin about the new road through Sawers Swamp. It's ordered that every male labouring tythable person of the county & town do go or send & meet the Overseer & there to work two days each upon the road towards the clearing & making the same.

Upon the motion of the Gent of the Town of Hampton that a Watch should be kept in town. It's ordered that every Constable of the Town ... do duly keep a Watch Every Night according to usual hours & be paid for his service by the Dwelers & Proprietors & that a Watch House be built ten foot square near or on the common key & that Mr. Sweny ... to build the same & bring in his accott at next Levy.

Ordered that Mary Bridge who have Wm. Williams Executorship in her hands do pay Matthew Williams £4:03 he having proved his accott with costs at exon.

Jno. Roe being by the Sheriff presented by a Warrant from John Curle & Saml. Sweny to go to Mr. Kings &c and he continuing the sd Power, it's ordered that he be find 5 shillings for his Contempt
[p 203] & that he pay with costs at exon.
James Rascow

At a Court held the 3d Wednesday of Augst
being the 17th day 1720
James Rascow, John King, John Lowery, Henry Irwin, James Ricketts, Jas. Curle, Saml. Sweny, Joseph Banister, James Servant & James Wallace

Hannah Booker her Power of Atty to Mr. William Lowery Senr if proved by oaths of Peter Manson & Wm. Lowery witnesses & is admitted to record.

Wm. Lowery by virtue of Mrs. Booker's Power of Atty to him ack deed for land to Thomas Kirby Junr & is ordered recorded.

Wm. Lowery ack deed of gift for land to his son William Lowery & ordered recorded.

Wm. Lowery & Joshua Curle gent foeffees ack deed for wast land in Town bounds to Joseph Banister gent & ordered recorded.

Wm. Lowery & Joshua Curle gent foefees ack deed for wast land in Town bounds to John Bordland and ordered recorded.

Upon petition of Matthew Williams desiring to have the keeping & bringing up of Ann Williams orphan of his brother Wm. Williams dec'd, he promising to keep the child without any charge to her estate. Granted.

The order last Ct for the former appraisers to appraise the remaining part of Capt. Bosell's estate not being complied with. Order same be performed & report to next Ct.

John Robert's petition agt Mrs. Judeth Bayley is by consent of the petitioner refd to next Ct, they paying this Ct's continuance.

Judith Daniel brought her action of trespass damage £30 agt John Mitchel Exec of Saml. Daniel dec'd. Refd to next Ct.

Richd. Nusum agt Henry Irwin gent action upon the case. Refd to next Ct.

Judgmt granted agt Mary Jenkins Admx of Henry Jenkins dec'd for £25:07:06 to Henry Irwin gent he having made oath to his accot to be paid out of decedant's estate.

[p 204] In the suit brought by Bartd. Proby Adm of Tho. Proby agt Jno. Birtell Adm of James Birtell dec'd accott render for £100, plt not appearing. Ordered dismist. Upon reading of the orders plt prays cause might be continued offering to pay all the costs of suit to this time. It's ordered continued to next Ct.

In the action of debt brought by Archibald Blair granted agt Mary Jenkins Adm of Henry Jenkins dec'd is by consent refd to next Ct.

In the action upon the case damage £80 brought by Saml. Sweny gent agt Mary Jenkins Admx of Henry Jenkins dec'd, refd to next Ct.

Tho. Batts Adm of Elizabeth Sheppard agt Baldwin Sheppard case damage £30 refd to next Ct.

Edmd. Kearny brought his action of debt damage 1000 lbs tobo agt Brian Penny continued to next Ct.

In the suit brought by William Barber agt Thos. Curle in an action upon the case damage £26 & at last Ct judgmt passed agt deft by Nihill Dicet & now being called & not appearing. Judgmt is confirmed for £16:08:03 with costs.

The suit in Chancery brought by Thos. Batts Adm of Eliza. Sheppard agt Thomas Jones & Sarah his wife, respondents setting forth for part of Sheppard's estate as marrying Eliza., the accott being put to audit & returned report. Ct orders that deft pay to complainant £6:09:11 with costs at exon.

Judgmt granted agt Henry Irwin gent for 19 shillings & 11 pence to Martha Taylor Exectrx of Robt. Taylor dec'd, she having made oath that she found it so stated in the Testator's books, with costs at exon only deft has liberty to bring in his discount.

Judgmt granted agt Mary Jenkins Admx of Henry Jenkins dec'd for £2:15:11 being balance due for protested Bills of Exchange to be paid our of decedant's estate.

Judgmt granted agt Mary Jenkins Admx of Henry Jenkins dec'd for 1080 lbs tobo with costs at exon.

The remaining part of John Pett's appraisal to continue to next Ct to be returned.

In the suit in Chancery brought by Judieth Daniel agt Jno. Mitchell Exec of Saml. Daniel dec'd is by consent refd to next Ct.

Wm. Smelt agt Richd. Kirkin action upon the case damage £20 is continued so Mr. Banister & Charles Jenings [may] audit & make report to next Ct.

[p 205] Sarah Hayes Admx of Henry Hayes dec'd action upon the case agt Mary Jenkins Admx of John Curle dec'd is by consent refd to next Ct.

Matthew Hilliard's suit in Chancery agt Cornelas Dorlich & Rachel his wife is by consent refd to next Ct.

Jno. Bordland's action upon the case damage £60 agt Mary Jenkins Admx of Henry Jenkins &c refd to next Ct.

Martha Taylor Exectrx of Robt. Taylor dec'd agt Wm. Avrill action upon the case refd to next Ct.

Judgmt granted agt Emanl. Alkin for £4 with one atty's fee to Martha Taylor with costs at exon.

Josa. Curle & Servant Ballard Execs of Fras. Ballard dec'd agt Thos. Roberts action on the case for 286 lbs tobo & £8:06, deft producing his discount & nothing appearing due. Ordered dismist.

The action upon the case damage £14 brought by Richd. Adams agt James Barret by consent refd to next Ct.

John Whitfield agt Wm. Winterton damage £50 trespass is by consent refd to next Ct.

John Bordland's action upon the case agt William Cunningham is refd by consent to next Ct.

Thos. Jones Cordwinder agt Brian Penny damage £10 trespass assault & battery, deft pleading not guilty which is refd to next Ct for tryall.

Judgmt confirmed agt Cornelas Dorlich & Rachel his wife & security for 26/4 to Jno. Pugh with costs at exon.

Judgmt granted agt Brian Penny Exec of Eliza. Prescot for 500 lbs tobo & cask to Richd. Nusum late School Master of Eaton's School being due for rent to be paid out of Decedant's estate he having sworn to his account.

Alexandr. Honaday agt Jno. Kimbal action upon the case damage £5 sterling costs for -- atty --.

In the action upon the case damage £30 brought by Jno. Lawson School Master of Eaton's free school agt Jos. Curle gent, plt failing to file his Declr which upon motion of deft nonsuit is awarded him & ordered plt pay same to deft with costs at exon.

Order granted agt Jno. Armistead & Jno. King gent security for his non-appearance to answer suit of Antho. Armistead gent debt per £6.

Order granted agt the Sheriff for the non-appearance of Wm. Lattemore to answer suit of Jno. Wallace Senr case £5 damage.

James Barret agt Jno. Kimbal debt for £4:02:06 continued to next Ct, the deft being very sick.

[p 206] Order granted agt John Armistead & John King gent for his non-appearance to answer suit of Edmd. Kearny gent damage £12 case.

Upon petition of Fra. Riddlehurst and his wife agt Jno. King gent for a legacy given his wife by the will of Ann King dec'd. it's ordered that King be summoned to next Ct to answer.

Mr. Wm. Lowery one of Foeffees ack deed for wast land in Town to Henry Irwin & ordered recorded.

Upon petition of John Wallace for license to keep ordinary which is granted giving bond &c.

Upon petition of Robt. Armistead for license to keep ordinary which is granted giving bond &c.

Upon complaint made by Henry Irwin gent agt Josa. Curle about Eaton's free school land of wast being made of Timber &c. It's ordered that the Clerk bring Eaton's will & deed to next Ct concerning the premises & a copia of the Vestry order where Curle had land granted to him.

Mr. Henry Irwin producing deeds for wast land in the Town bounds to be signed which Mr. Jos. Curle one of the Foefees refused & giving his reason because it hindered his passing to and from his lot adjoining thereto.

James Rascow

At a Court of Claims held the 19th of October 1720
Henry Irwin, Antho. Armistead, Ja. Ricketts,
J. Banister, Ja. Wallace

It's ordered that the Court be adjourned till Ten a Clock

Saturday next it being now too late to proceed about business. H. Irwin

[p 207] Gentlemen – A copy of the Govs. Letter to the Justices – Williamsburgh Janry 7th 1720
    Last Wednesday I received by hands of Mr. Samuel Sweny your J[ustices] letter with the Interrogations & affadavits relating to the dispute between Major Henry Irwin & Mr. Charles Jenings and haveing the next day given afurther [?] to both partys I not only concur with you in judging the conduct of Jenings to be a great T--y [?] but am also satisfied that he has with some malice cast groundless aspersions upon Mr. Irwin, Nay and I observe by Jenings Interrogatories that my Character's attacked and that he would make you & the Country believe that I obliged the Clerks to purchase their places, under colour of presents to Mrs. Cook [or Cock]. Whereupon as the said Jenings, by offering to Injure my Character with false Insinuations little Deserves from me such a favour as the Renewing his Commission, soe I can not but in Justice to Mr. Irwin &c show some Publick mark of Displeasure towards Jenings, and for these reasons, as well as for his notorious Imprudence in most Passages of his life, I have thought fitting to Commission an other person in his Roome. However, I have had regard to the notice you take of his place being the Principal Subsistence of the Family and have therefore Injoyned his Successor to make him the allowance Exprest in the In----- Bond, which you may observe is as much as he himselfe had actually disposed of his place for.
    Thus you may perceive that I did not look upon the character you gave one of your Late Clerks being a Silly person, to be any recommendation for his Continuance & that I have fully complyed with what you Intimated to me in his behalfe, namely his Poverty, Soe that I hope the Present Clerk, under my appointment will meet your Countenance & favour, which can not but be very pleasing to – Gentlemen –
        Yor most affectionate humble Servant. A. Spotswood.
    This letter was delivered the Justices on the Eleventh Instant in John Bordland's house where they appointed to receive the same but they voted it should be referd till the Court day in Cource and then Mr. James Servant, John Lowry & James Wallace three of the Justices voted against my being admited Clerk or Sworn tho I showed them likewise my Comission from the Governr. and ---dectly they rose up &

went away out of Court which Disabled the rest from Complying with the Letter.

[Note: there is no page numbered 208. There was simply an error when modern pagination was entered.]
[p 209] January 20th 1720. Present John King, Joshua Curle, Samuel Sweny, Joseph Banister.

This day the above Justices having mett in Town in order to Swear me their Clerk and admit me in compliance to the Governrs. Letter & Comission in the Room of Charles Jenings and being accordingly mett they Repaired to the Court house of thie County & in their Passage thither they met with Mr. John Lowry one of the Justices & asked him if he would join with them to have me sworn byt he rudely answered no whereupon they went in and then administerd the following oath.

You Henry Irwin dow swear that you shall well and truly and faithfully demean yourself as Clerk to this Court of Elizabeth City County and shall at time when Required give your attendance on his Majesty's Justices of the afsd County you shall Diligently and truly take due care of and Endeavor the preservation of the county Records that shall be committed to your care, as after faithfully make Entry of all orders and other matters as you shall from time to time receive command and Directions from the said Justices. You shall without favour or Objection Issue upon all Accions due Process as by Law directed. You shall delay no person for any maner of reward, or any by respect Whatsoever or take more or other fee than by the Laws of this County or by consent or rule of this Court shall be allowed you. You shall well and truly doe all other things belonging to the office to the best of your Skills, Judgment and knowledge without favour Partiality or any by respect Whatever Soe help you God.

Eliz. City Co. John King Judge then – At a Court held for Laying the County Levys Janry 31st 1720. Present John King, Joshua Curle, Saml. Sweny, Joseph Banister, James Wallace and John Lowry.

Claims vizt allowed

Mr. Irwin's claim for a Standard for the County	1866
To the Secretary for a writ to -- Burgess	0510
To Mr. Wyth Sheriff for Ex – b – and Cask	1080
To Mr. Jenings late Clerk for Last year Do	1080

To Mr. Robert Armistead for 3 Inquests as Coror.	0390
To James Baker for Sumd two Jurys per do	0100
To John Jones for Sum one Jury per do	0050
Mr. Wm. Westwood for persons over listed and Insolvents	0267 1/4
To Mr. Joshua Curle Claim fer 2 barls of Tarr & Tarr Chests	0200
To Thomas Howard for Cleaning the Court House 6 mos.	0100
To Mr. Jenings further Claim for Private Courts	0400
To Mr. Curle's further Do fer a Person over listed	0017 3/4
	6055
By C allowed the Sheriff for Collecting the same	0605 1/2
By 10 pound per poll on 667 Tythables 6670 pd	6660 1/2

[p 210]

Mr. Thos. Wythe Sheriff to have the Sundry Claims as in the other side To an overpayment which the Sherf is Dr to be allowed the next Laying of the Levys to the County – 20 To Mr. Rascow's 3 Tythes for County and Parish not listed this year	By 10 pound To of Tobacco pr poll for audit 667 tythables 6670

                                               144
                                               164

    Ordered that the Sheriff receive the ten pounds tobo caskd on each tythable being due for the county claims this last year as appears by the several Claims on the other side and upon their nonpayment to make Distrib for same.

    Ordered that Charles Jenings late Clerk deliver to Mr. Henry Irwin in the presence of any two or more Justices of the County all the Records and other papers in his custody relating to the County and Court or Clk's office & that the Justices in Company with Irwin our new Clk goe and demand the same who are hereby Impowered to Examine Inspect and to receive. [signed] John King

The 3d of Febry 1720

    To Mr. Jenings & sent a copy of the order of Ct to him & desired he would let me know when we should come for the records &c & that the Justices would be ready on the Saturday following to goe for to receive them. Upon which he sent his son in law Wm. Westwood to acquaint me that his Brother Thomas Jenings dyed & that on Monday he would be ready to deliver the books &c. On Monday according to appointment the Justices got ready but Mr. Jenings coming to Town begged we would defer going till the next day saying his house was harried his Brother being but lately Burried which was agreed to, and went the next day to the house of Jennings, but he contrived to be from home. Whereupon I sent a boy on Horse back for him to Mrs. Robersons and after about five hours they came and upon demanding the Records he plainly told us he had further advised and would not deliver any of them for that order nor any other until the Order of Court in Course and upon that the Governers' order and his bond should be delivered up which he gave the Sheriff at his being commissioned Clerk upon which answer we parted and came home, but soon after sent his Son to Major Holloway for advice, & upon Holloway's advice came himselfe and brought some of the Dockets & Laws and told me I might goe to receive the rest when Interested, which I refrd doing till I should obtain an other order of Court. [signed] H. Irwin

[p 211] At a Court held February 15th 1720/21
John King, Samuel Sweeny, Joshua Curle, Joseph Banister

The former order for appraising remaining part of Capt. Boswil's est not being complied with, it's continued to next Ct to be brought in.

John Robert's petition agt Judith Bayley nobody appearing to speak. Ordered dismist.

Richd. Newsom's action of case agt Henry Irwin his Lawyer not being at Ct. Refd to next Ct.

Upon action of Detinue brought by Thomas Batts Adm of Elizabeth Batts agt Baldwin Shepherd. Refd to next Ct.

Edmond Kearny's action of debt for 1000 lbs tobo vs Bryan Penny is by consent refd to next Ct.

Martha Taylor vs Henry Irwin action of case is likewise refd to next Ct for Discounts.

Thomas Curle presented deeds for land to Mathew Williams & ack them. Ordered recorded.

John Batts being ordered to return an Inv of his brother's est which is not yet done. Ordered same be done to next Ct.

Upon auditor's report settling accts between Wm. Smith agt Richd. Kerkin. Balance of £4:11:10 1/2 found. Judgmt agt Kerkin with one Lawyers fee & costs at exon to be paid to Smith.

Wm. William's will presented but M. Bush Lawyer moved referral to next Ct for heir at law to be present. Ordered refd.

Sarah Hays action on the case agt Mary Jenkins damage £12. Mr. Poole her Lawyer not being down, it's refd to next Ct.

Matthew Hilyard agt Cornelius & Rachel Dorlich his wife suit in Chancery. Mr. Poole being absent is continued to next Ct.

John Bordland agt Mary Jenkins Admx of Henry Jenkins dec'd action upon the case damage £60 continued for Mr. Poole's coming to next Ct.

Martha Taylor Exectrx of Robert Taylor dec'd agt Wm. Ackrill action of case damage £50. Refd for Mr. Poole's coming to next Ct.

Richd. Adams vs James Barret action of case damage £14 is likewise refd for Mr. Poole the Lawyer.

John Whitfield vs Jon. Winterton action case damage £50. Refd by consent.

A Granjury to be summoned to next Ct.

[p 212] The action of Ct brought by John Bordland vs Cummingham is by consent dismist.

The action of case brought by Thomas Jones vs Bryan Penny also dismist being agreed.

Alexdr. Kennedy's action upon the case damage £5:2:6 vs John Kimble nobody appearing to prosecute or defend, is dismist.

Anthony Armistead's action vs Anthony Armistead they being agreed, is dismist.

John Wallace Senr action vs Wm. Latemore. Nobody appearing. Dismist.

Mr. Edmond Kearny's action upon the case vs John Armistead damage £12 Mr. Robert Armistead appearing for the deft. Ordered Mr. Saml. Sweny & Mr. Joseph Banister audit acct & report to next Ct, but that former bayle be discharged.

James Barret & Elinr. his wife action of debt vs John Kimble damage £4:2:6. Judgmt granted by nihill dicet.

Francis Ridlehurst's petition vs John King to oblige King to prove his late wife's will. Refd to next Ct.

A former order being granted for writ of Inquire to Richd. Kerkin vs John Wallace Senr for a Horse &c. Ordered confirmed for writ to determine damage & report to next Ct.

John Bordland vs Henry Irwin who pleads non assumpsit it being for the Jury's charge on the school land.

Alexdr. McKenzie's action of case vs John Kimble dismist, being agreed.

Petition of John Lawson vs Joshua Curle for wages pretended to be due for keeping a School on Eaton's land granted for a free school for use of orphans &c born in this county & he having a lease of the same from the Vestry. Mr. Poole being absent & nobody appearing to second petition. It's therefore dismist & nonsuit granted deft.

[p 213] John Burtell Adm of James Burtell dec'd vs James Ricketts action upon the case damage £100 and no execution nor writ returned nor motion or Declr filed. Ordered dismist.

Martha Taylor vs John Mitchel. No declr. Dismist.
Christian McKenie vs Hugh Ross. No declr. Dismist.
John Byracy vs Wm. Tayler. No declr. Dismist.

Thomas Howard next friend to Wm. Brough action case damage £200. Ordered special imparlence.

Wm. Lowry gent vs Thomas Francis action case being agreed. Dismist.

George Walker vs Charles Irwin the same.

Robert ---vy vs Robt. Byracy do.

A Negro Boy called Scotland belonging to Mr. Joseph Banister adjudged ten years old.

Upon action of case brought by Emanuel Alkin vs John Mitchel damage £5. Order granted agt Security, no body appearing.

Suit brought by Emal. Alkin vs John Kimble, nobody appearing for deft. Order granted agt him & the Sheriff who pray'd attachmt. Granted.

Robert Armistead's action case damage £10 sterling. Same order is granted as in the last agt Sheriff & Deft & attchmt granted Sheriff.

James Bake [sic] ack deeds for Town land to John Walis. Ordered recorded.

Wm. Loyal petitioned Ct for order that his boy Thomas Hastid that was run away from him should serve time as the Law directs. When indenture is complete he is to serve

Loyal at value of 400 weight of tobo being fourteen days absent from his Master's service.

[p 214] The last will of Wm. Mallory --- by Francis Mallory the Exec therein proved by oaths of John Been & Ann his wife. Admitted to record.

Upon motion of John Bean & Ann his wife, ordered Francis Mallory to pay them for one days attendance to prove will.

Thomas Morgan by Robert Armistead his Atty petitioned to choose a Gdn. [Note: above line is added: "Thomas Dubery he being an orphan."] Refd to next Ct.

Mary Randall's petition for the orphan Thoms. Davis' estate or rent the better to enable her to keep him at Schoole & maintain him. Refd to next Ct.

Upon petition of Jane Bloodworth to keep an ordinary in Hampton Town. Granted giving Clk Security.

This day Jane Baker presented her son Joshua Baker and bound him to Mr. Henry Irwin til Joshua comes of age, Irwin &c him to read & write & finding him clothes & victuals as the law allows.

Upon complaint of James Barret and his wife agt John Walis who was bound to appear at this Ct. Walis is further bound to next Ct for his good behaviour.

Upon complaint of Samuel Sweny agt Henry Moriset being bound over by Mr. Joseph Banister one of the Justices. Moriset having faild, ordered further process agt him for Contempt.

Upon complaint of Mary Randy agt John Walis Junr & John Byracy. Refd to next Ct & ordered that Evidences appear then.

[p 215] John Wyat & Rebeca [blank] vs Alexand. Kennedy. Being agreed, ordered dismist.

Thomas Skinner's petition for a Legacy left his wife by Samuel Daniel in his will. Dismist.

Henry Irwin [recites former order concerning receipt of records from Charles Jenings. See above.] Order not complied with. Now confirmed & ordered Irwin with Mr. King, Mr. Sweeny & Mr. Banister go and demand the records which they are to inspect & see what condition they are delivered in to Irwin.

William Winterton prays relief from serving as Constable in town precinct. Granted & ordered John Henry

Rombough be Constable in his stead and that John Wallace Junr head Borrough in the room of Nicho. Parker.
[Signed] James Rascow

At a Court held the 3d Wednesday in May 1721
John King, Joshua Curle, James Ricketts, James Wallace

A new Commission of the Peace together with a Dedimus to swear the persons named therein & being first publickly read in Open Ct. The following presented & sworn: Anthony Armistead, Joshua Curle, Robert Armistead, Saml. Sweny, John King, James Ricketts, John Lowry, James Wallace, Joseph Selden, John Selden.

[p 216] Mary Randy for having a bastard child.
Ann Floyde for do Judith Preedy and Bett Toomer -- Martha Wilson. [sic]
Richd. Newsom & Elizabeth his wife for common drunkards.
Samuel White for stopping of the Road by information of G. Walker.
Samuel White for not coming to Church.
James Nayler, Michel Pierce, John Pierce, Charles Everett for do.
Wm. B--den for not continuing in Church til Divine Time is Ended.
Christr. McKenzie & Thomas Goodman for not coming to Church.
Margaret Phillips, John House & John Smith Senr for not coming to Church.
John Weymouth petitions for Adm of Peter Burton dec'd as being his father in law. Ordered refd to next Ct.
Upon petition of John Bordland to keep an Ordinary at his house in Town, granted he giving Security &c.
Upon petition of Mrs. Martha Tayler for lycense to keep an ordinary. Granted.
Francis Mallory ack a deed of gift to John Michel Son to his now wife & she appearing relinquishes her right of dower. Ordered recorded.
John Henry Rombow complains that Mongo Rodum grossly abused & beat him in the execution of his office as Constable. Refd til tomorrow.
Upon motion of James Ricketts & Jane his wife Execs of Nicho. Curle dec'd praying to audit accts. Also that Jane's part together with her children orphans of Curle due

parts be computed. Ct orders Mr. Thos. Wythe, Jacob Walker, Samuel Sweny, Joseph Selden & Henry Irwin or any three of them perform same & report to next Ct.

Ordered that the several persons presented by the Granjury be summoned to appear at next Ct.

The Court adjourns till to morrow 9 a Clock.

[p 217] Note: page damaged, top torn.

--- James Rickets, James Wallace, Jacob Walker, Joseph Selden.

Willm. Wilson's will presented by Edward Wilson. Proved by oaths of Edwd. Wilson, George Pain, Jacob Face witnesses. Probate granted Edwd. giving bond.

Thomas Falkner's petition for lycense to keep ordinary in Town. Granted he giving bond & security &c.

Eliza. Chambers petition to keep an ordinary granted she giving bond &c.

Upon petition of Joseph Wragg. Ordered to appraise [estate] of Wm. Merrick. Est to pay him £3:10:05 attchmt. Ordered Abraham Mitchel, Geor- --- & John Massenbergh or any two appraise & return to next Ct.

Present John Selden Justice

Upon petition of Bryan Penny & Richd. Newsom to be discharged as Securities for William William's est in hands of Mary P----. Mary offers William Armistead & Frances Mallory her Securities & Malory appears to be her Baile & she is granted time to next Ct for Armistead to appear. Petitioners as her former Baile dismist.

On yesterday's petition of John Henry Rombough. Ordered Mongo Rodum [to be] taken into Custody by the Sheriff or Constable [and] secured til he give Security & answers the Compalint.

Upon petition of James Barrett to keep ordinary. Ct are of opinion he is not sufficiently qualified. Rejected. Margrt. Armistrong petitions for same. Also rejected.

The remaining part of Capt. Boswel's est to be appraised --- to next Ct.

Upon action of case between Richd. Newsom & Henry Irwin, deft pleads non assumpsit & prays order for a Dedimus issue to examine John Hurst as an Evidence for him, the sd John living out of the county. Granted he giving plt timely notice.

[p 218, torn] Est of Thomas Preby dec'd agt John B------ Adm of James Burtell dec'd the deft render to plt £100 current money the proper money of sd Thomas & in hands of James at the time he was Gdn to Thomas. By consent refd for tryal at next Ct.

In the action upon the case between Thomas Batts & Baldwin Shepherd. By consent refd to next Ct.

In the suit in Chancery brought by Julian Daniel agt John Mitchel. She being married is dismist.

Wm. Lowry & Joshua Curle gent two of the twelve appt to grant lots in town. Ack deeds of lease & release to George Whaffe for a lot lapsed belonging to est of Mr. Nicho. Curle dec'd & addition of some wast land. Ordered recorded.

In the action upon the case between Archibald Blaire & Mary Jenkins Admx of Henry Jenkins dec'd for £16, deft pleading admr. Judgmt granted when assest.

In the action upon the case between John King gent & Mary Jenkins Admx of John Curle dec'd. Refd to next Ct.

-----Saml. G-- & Mary Jenkins. Continued to next Ct.

In action upon the case between Martha Taylor & Henry Irwin. Refd for tryal to next Ct.

Julian Daniel vs John Mitchel she being marryed is dismist.

Sarah Hayes agt Mary Jenkins continued to next Ct.

Martha Hillierd vs Rachel Durlach refd to next Dt.

Martha Taylor vs Wm. Ackrile being agreed is dismist.

[p 219] Richd. Adams action of trespass upon the case & James Barrett. Deft pleads not guilty & refd for tryal.

The remainder of Pett's est was ordered appraised but --- Powell in whose hands the est is said persons appt refused. It's ordered that John Smith Senr, Joseph Wragg & John Bordland appraise & return to next Ct.

John Whitfield action of trespass agt Wm. Winterton. Judgmt by Nihill Dicet granted plt.

James Barrett vs John Kimble action upon the case. Refd to next Ct.

Upon petition of Frans. Ridlehurst vs John King, nobody appearing. Dismist.

In the action of Detinue between Richd. Kerkin & John Wallace Senr. Judgmt granted plt for £4:01 his costs & charges as found by Jury with costs at exon.

Wm. Smelt & Robert Bright moving for an order for their pay as Evidences attending in the suit four days. Granted.

In the action upon the case between John Bordland & Henry Irwin. Deft moves for audit he having a discount. Ordered Mr. Alexdr. McKenzie, Thos. Wythe & Joseph Selden or any two of them [audit] & report to next Ct.

In the action upon the case between Willim. Brough by his next friend Tho. Howard agt Henry Irwin, plt making oath to his acct. Judgmt confessed by deft for 40 shillings with charges for costs &c.

In the action upon the case between Emanuel Alkin & John Mitchel for £2:5:5 due by bills & also 10 shillings due by acct here in Ct produced. Ordered Mitchel pay plt both sums with a lawyer's fee & costs at exon.

[p 220] In the action upon the case between Emanuel Alkin & John Kimble for £4 current money. Deft confessed judgmt upon condition Execution should be stayed til after next Ct. Plt agreed. Ordered John pay the 40 shillings with charges with costs at exon.

In the action upon the case between Edmond Kearny & John Armisteade, Kearny making oath to his accts. Judgmt granted him for £3:11:08, balance due. Ordered Armisteade or his Bail pay to Kearny with a lawyer's fee & costs.

In the action of trespass upon the case between William Brough infant by his next friend Robert Brough, Mr. Pole deft's atty demanding their admission by this next friend & refusing to plead for want of such. Judgmt granted by Nihill Dicet. Plt moves for order the Dedimus should issue to Examine Anthony Pierce to have his deposition taken as Evidence. Granted. Deft prays same order to examine Capt. Vi---t Pearls Comdr of his Majestie's Ship Phenix at New York. Ct are of opinion they have no power or precedence of that nature & refused dedimus.

Hind Armistead & his wife who was first privately examined ack deeds for land to Joshua Curle Senr. Ordered recorded.

Thomas Morgan having petitioned for Gdnship of Thomas Dubery orphan who appears & consents. Ct orders [Morgan] to teach him to read & write & the trade or mistery of a cooper & likewise to take orphan's est he giving bond & security &c.

In the action upon the case between Robt. Armisteade Senr gent & Frans. Williams for £2 sterling, Armisteade making oath to his acct. Judgmt granted agt deft & Sheriff [p 221] but Mr. Armisteade [tells] Ct that Williams has done work for him, the value of which he cannot judge. Ordered John Cook, John Roe & Thomas Read or any two of them to view & value same & return to next Ct.

Upon petition of Mary Randy, Gdn, to have est of Thomas Davis orphan to enable her to maintain him. Granted giving bond & security.

Upon complaint of James Barrett agt John Wallace, complainant appears & says he is satisfied. Ordered dismist with complainant paying costs &c.

Mary Randy being bound to appear for a breach of the peace & not appearing. Same ordered recorded.

---- James orphan of the late widow James being bound to Thomas Wilcox Ship Carpent[er] petitions Ct to be discharged from Wilcox who hath grossly & inhumanely used him. Plt proving such usuage, Master is ordered to give good security for his better usuage before tomorrow night & that Willm. pay to Nath. 40 shillings at the end of his service for "whiping him Naked."

Alexr. Kendy. vs John Kimble being agreed is dismist.

Thos. Skiner vs John Mitchel at deft's motion dismist.

Frans. Mallory took oath of Adm of Wm. Mallory dec'd, his father's est & gave bond (vizt Hugh Ross) for the due Adm of the will. Locky Mihil, Merritt Sweeny, Wm. Moor & Wm. Tucker, sworn before Mr. Antho. Armistead Senr, to appraise est & make return to next Ct.

[p 222] Upon suit in Chancery brought by Martha Taylor agt John Mitchel in behalf of herself & Robert & Martha Taylor infants agt John Mitchel Adm of Saml. Daniel dec'd. Refd to next Ct for deft to put in his answers.

Upon the action upon the case brought by George Whagh agt Christian Makennie who pleaded in custody nihil dicet. Refd to next Ct to prove his discount.

Upon petition of Mary Hursk for her seven days attendance as Evidence in suit depending between Julian Daniel late the relick of Samll. Daniel dec'd & John Mitchel Adm of Samll. Daniel. Ordered she be paid according to law.

The action upon the case brought by Charles Cooper agt Thomas Tucker, they having agreed, ordered dismist.

Do vs Durlach – the same order.

Do vs Watts – the same order.

Do vs Copeland – the same order.

[Note: the three entries above were added in a very small script on the right edge of page.]

Hugh Ross having taken oath for due Adm of Est of Giles Dubery & giving bond ---- Frans. Mallory Adm ---- granted him & ordered that Wm. Armistead, Wm. Allan, John Cook & Thos. Read, first sworn before Robert Armistead, appraise est & return to next Ct.

Upon action of trespass upon the case brought by Charles Whitfield's next friend Thos. Wherwood agt Nicho. Parker. Special imparlence granted [blotted]

In the action upon the case brought by John Burtell Adm of James Burtell dec'd agt James Ricketts, act not being brought right. Ordered dismist at plt's costs.

Upon suit in Chancery brought by Thomas Skiner in behalf of his wife agt John Mitchel who at his request has time to next Ct to put in his answer.

Upon the action of case brought by Mr. Emanuel Alkin agt Wm. Ridlehurst who does not appear. Order granted agt deft & his Security.

The action upon the case brought by John Lawson agt Joshua Curle gent. At plt's motion special imparlence granted.

In the action upon the case brought by Wm. Armistead agt Charles Hobsen. At plt's motion & costs is by his defense dismist.

[p 223] In the action upon the case brought by John Burtell Adm of James Burtell dec'd agt James Ricketts gent for £100 current money. Deft prays oyer of the bill. Granted.

In action upon the case brought by Emanl. Alkin agt Jo. Kimble for £4 current money. Deft confesses judgmt provided execution stayed until next Ct. Ordered that Kimble pay plt at time appointed £2 current money with one lawyer's fee & costs at exon.

In the action of debt brought by Robt. Tucker agt John Wallace Senr for protested Bills of Exchange. At plt's motion dismist, deft paying costs &c.

In action of trespass brought by Samuel Tomkins agt Richd. Harvey for £50 damage. Imparlence granted Petitioner.

In action of debt brought by Christopher Jackson agt James Ricketts gent for £9:01:03 sterling by bill of exchange directed to Messrs. Micajah & Richd. Perry of London Merchants by them protested. Deft confessed judgmt.

Ordered to pay Jackson £9:01:03 sterling with one lawyer's fee & costs at exon.

In the action upon the case brought by Emal. Alkin agt Richard Adams £4 current money. Special imparlence granted plt.

In the action upon the case brought by Thomas Fellows agt Thomas Wyat for 42 shillings current money, deft being returned arrested & Mr. Robert Armistead his Security. Order granted agt him & his Security.

[p 224] In the action upon the case brought by Willm. Parker Merchant agt William Wescoat Mariner for £200 current money. Upon motion of plt imparlence granted.

Abraham Mitchel & Ann his wife & she being first privately examined relinquishing her right of dower, then ack to William Westwood for Town land. Ordered recorded.

On the judgmt obtained by Richd. Kerkin agt John Wallace Senr on the writ of inquiry & brought in by Jury's verdict, Mr. Boush the deft's atty on reading orders moving of a liberty of entering an arrest of that judgmt. Therefore granted & ordered recorded, the plt has time to next Ct to put in his answer.

The Court is adjourned till the next Court in course.
[Signed] Antho. Armistead

At a Court held for Eliz. City Co. the 21st day of June 1721. Joshua Curle, James Ricketts, Robert Armistead, Jacob Walker, Samuel Sweany, Joseph Selden, John Selden

Wm. Loyal brought before the Ct his runaway servant Thomas Eustace who had absented himself seven days & Loyal having been at sundry expenses in the pursuit. Ordered that Eustace serve after time of indenture fourteen days for time of absence & three months fourteen days for costs expended.

Thomas Curle & Ann his wife and Judith Predy (Ann being first privately examined) presented deeds to Joseph Atterson. Admitted to be recorded.

[p 225 On petition of John Randal for his dividend of his mother in hands of Frans. Massenburgh. Ordered Sheriff summon Massenburgh to answer.

John King gent presented a Commission to be Sheriff of this County. Bond for faithful performance with Robert

Armistead & Henry Irwin Securities. King takes the usual oaths & subscribed the Test & therefore admitted Sheriff.

Petition of Richard Newsom for 500 weight tobo & cash in hands of Bryan Penny Exec of Elizbth. Prescot is rejected.

Upon petition of John Merydeth for ordinary license at his house in Hampton. Granted giving bond & security.

Petition of James Barrett for ordinary license. Rejected. Ct finds him not of circumstances sufficient to provide the same.

Petition of Dunn Armistead for ordinary license. Granted giving bond & security.

Simon Hollier, Thomas Wythe, & John Lowry nominated Justices in the late Commission of the Peace took the usual oaths, subscribed the Test & took oaths of Justice of the Peace & likewise Justice of the Co. Ct in Chancery & took their places on the Bench.

At the motion of John King Sheriff, John King Junr & Robert Armistead Junr having taken usual oaths &c now sworn his under Sheriffs.

George Hudson Servant to John Bordland having been committed to the Prison by Samuel Sweeny gent Justice for his misbehaviour to his Master & threatening to burn Hampton & having lain there seven days. It's ordered he serve his Master after the time of his service is finished fourteen days & also the term of nine weeks for the charges his Master expended.

On petition of Edwd. Ballard to keep an ordinary in Mr. Sweeny's house. Granted.

[p 226] The last will & testament of William Cole late of Eliz. City Co. dec'd presented by Henry Robertson Exec named therein & it being proved by oaths of Benjamin Ralph & Joseph Milby two of the witnesses, admitted to record. Certificate granted Exec for probate.

Joseph Otterson & Mary his wife ack deed to William Allen & admitted to record, Mary first being privately examined and relinquishing right of dower.

Former order for appraisal of William Malory's est not being complied with, continued to next Ct.

Robert Armistead gent appt to take the lists of this present year in Eliz. City Parish from Allen's Swamp to Holm's Bridge.

Joshua Curle gent from the Town bounds to the extent of the county upwards to Newport News.

Jacob Walker gent in Hampton Precinct.

Joseph Selden gent in precinct of Strawberry Banks.

James Wallace gent in precinct of Fox Hill & the south side of Back River to the Church.

John Lowry gent from Allen's Swamp to Finch's Dam & so along the Ridge.

On petition of Thomas Morgan Gdn of Thomas Dubery agt Mary Bridge for embezeling the timber of Duberry & John Roberts their land. It's ordered that Sheriff summon Mary to answer petition.

Upon motion of Bryan Penny & Richard Newsom as Securities for Mary Bridge her Gdnship of John Roberts that the est of Roberts is embezeled by Mary. Ordered Sheriff summon Mary to give new Security for the est & also give her notice that if she fail to do the same he will be ordered to seize so much of her est as will amount to a sum sufficient to satisfy the est of John Roberts.

Ordered Court be adjourned till tomorrow morning.

[p 227] At a Court held for Eliz. City Co. 22d day of June 1721. Thomas Wythe, James Ricketts, Robert Armistead, Jacob Walker, James Wallace, Samll. Sweeny, Joseph Selden, John Selden.

In the action upon the case between Richd. Newsom & Henry Irwin by consent of deft is refd to next Ct at the plt's cost.

In the action upon the case between John King Senr gent & Mary Jenkins Admx of est of John Curle dec'd by consent of both parties, James Ricketts, Jacob Walker, Joseph Selden & Henry Irwin gent or any three are appt auditors to examine & settle accts of Admx of Curle's est. To meet in Hampton day before next Ct & report at Ct.

In the action upon the case between Samuel Sweeny gent & Mary Jenkins Admx of est of Henry Jenkins dec'd for £171:12:10 current money. Judgmt when assest is granted him agt Decedant's est for what appears due.

A further inv of Capt. Boswell's est was returned & ordered recorded.

In the action upon the case between Martha Taylor & Henry Irwin by consent of both parties is refd to next Ct.

The action upon the case between Sarah Hayes & Mary Jenkins Admx of John Curle dec'd by consent is refd till the auditors make report of Mary's Admtion.

[p 228] The suit in Chancery between Matthew Hilliard & Cornelius Durlach & Rachel his wife refd to next Ct for complainant to consider & Respondts to answer.

The action of trespass upon the case between Richard Adams & James Barret at plt's cost continued to next Ct.

In the action of trespass between William Whitfield & William Winterton, deft gaving pleaded not guilty & the issue being joyned, refd to next Ct for tryal.

In the action upon the case between James Barrett & Elizabeth his wife & John Kimble for £4:02:03 due by note dated 30 Mar 1720, deft's discount of £1:13:09 being allowed. Judgmt granted plt for £2:08:06 which deft is ordered to pay him together with one atty's fee with costs at exon.

In the action of Detinue between Richard Kerkin & John Wallace Senr. The errors in arrest of judgmt in the cause for the plt given being argued & adjudged good, judgmt is thereupon arrested & set aside & plt ordered to pay costs at exon.

Present Mr. Anthony Armistead

Madam Mary Cary came into Ct & made oath to a deposition concerning a debt due her from Cary Heslett which at her motion is admitted to record.

In the action upon the case between John Bordland & Henry Irwin, order of last Ct not being complied with, is continued & ordered that the same auditors perform the same on the third of July, the summons issue for the witnesses on either side, & the auditors report to next Ct.

[p 229] In the action of acct render between Bertrand Proby Adm of est of Thomas Proby dec'd & John Burtell Adm of est of James Burtell dec'd, that deft render to plt £100 current money, the proper money of sd Thomas & in the hands of James at the time he was Gdn to Thomas. Both parties appearing & arguments upon the auditor's report dated 16 Nov 1717 returned to Ct being heard & the Question Put, judgmt given for the deft & plt is ordered to pay costs.

The action upon the case between Thomas Batts Adm of est of Elizabeth Batts dec'd & Baldwin Shepherd is refd to next Ct for deft to plead.

The action of trespass between William Brough infant by his next friend Robert Brough agt Henry Irwin, atty not being here. At deft's motion continued to next Ct.

The action upon the case between Robert Armistead gent agt Francis Williams. At plt's motion dismist, he paying costs &c.

In the action of debt between Samuel Welden assignee of Thomas Merryman [agt] Thomas Wyn for 660 lbs sweet scented tobo & cask convenient to James or York rivers due by bill under deft's hand & seal dated 28 Mar 1717. Deft confessed judgmt & is ordered to pay with costs at exon.

The suit in Chancery between Thomas Skiner & Elizabeth his wife [agt] John Mitchel Exec of will of Samuel Daniel dec'd. Refd to next Ct for deft to put in his answer.

The suit in Chancery between Martha Taylor in behalf of Robert & Martha Taylor infants [agt] John Mitchel Exec of will of Saml. Daniel dec'd. Refd to next Ct for deft to put in his answer.

[p 230] In the action upon the case between Emanuel Alkin & William Ridlehurst for £7:6 due by note deft not appearing. At motion of plt judgmt is granted agt deft & William Smelt his Security for £7:6. Deft ordered to pay with costs together with atty's fee at exon.

In the action of debt between George Norwell and Hugh Norwell Execs of will of Hugh Norwell dec'd and Christian Makenny for £7:06:07 current money due by note dated 1 July 1718, deft appearing & making oath to a discount of £5:14:06, allowed. Judgmt at plts' motion is granted them for £1:12:01 which deft is ordered to pay with atty's fee.

In the action upon the case between John Lawson & Joshua Curle gent. Deft had at last Ct a special imparlence granted & not this day appearing. Judgmt by Nihill Dicet granted him returnable at next Ct as usual.

In the action of trespass upon the case between Charles Whitferd informing by Thomas Wharwood his next friend and Nicholas Parker. Deft had at last Ct a special imparlence granted & not this day appearing. Judgmt by Nihill Dicet granted him returnable at next Ct as usual.

In the action upon the case between Emanuel Alkin & Richard Adams. Deft had at last Ct a special imparlence granted & not this day appearing. Judgmt by Nihill Dicet granted him returnable at next Ct. as usual.

[p 231] In the suit in Chancery between Samuel Skinner & Darby Skinner infants by their friend Thomas Skinner and John Mitchel Exec of Samuel Danceb [sic] dec'd. At

respondent's motion, time is given to next Ct to put in his defence.

In the action of trespass between Samuel Tomkins & Richd. Harvey for £50 current money for certain lands in controversy. Deft pleads not guilty. Order granted that the Surveyor of this Co. with an able Jury of the Antient Freeholders of this Co. no ways concerned by affinity or consanguinity or liable to any other just exception to be summoned to go on land of petitioner on 5th day of July next ... and survey & lay out the same according to the most known antient & reputed bounds having regard to all Patents & Evidences that shall be produced by either. To make report to next Ct & Surveyor to return a Plot of the land at the same time.

The action upon the case between Mary Bridge & Joshua Curle gent & Issue being joyned. Refd to next Ct. for tryal.

In the action upon the case between Thomas Fellows & Thomas Wyat at plt's motion is dismist.

In the action upon the case between William Parker gent & John Westcoat. Judgmt by Nihill Dicet granted plt returnable to next Ct as usual.

The attchmt obtained by Samuel Sweeny agt est of Thomas Good--- at Sweeny's motion is dismist.

[p 232] Attchmt obtained by Joshua Curle gent agt est of Thomas Goodman at Curle's motion is dismist.

The complaint of Susanna the wife of John Wallace Senr agt John Wallace Junr who was bound over to answer. Complainant not appearing, dismist she paying costs.

The attchmt obtained by Joseph Wragg agt the est of Thomas Goodman continued to next Ct.

In the suit in Chancery between John Ellison & Julian his wife & John Mitchel Exec of est of Samuel Daniel dec'd. Deft given time to answer the bill.

In an action of trespass between John Platt & James White. At deft's motion imparlence granted to next Ct.

In the action of debt between Thomas Walk & Henry Jenkins. At deft's motion imparlence granted to next Ct.

The action upon the case between Joshua Curle & Servand Ballard Execs of Francis Batts dec'd & William Latemore & Abraham Mitchel. At plt's motion dismist, deft paying costs.

Alexander Kennedy being returned arrested at the summons of William Booden & not appearing. At Booden's motion judgmt granted him agt Kennedy & Thomas Wythe gent late Sheriff for what shall appear due unless Kennedy appears at next Ct to answer.

In an action of trespass between John Ellison & Julian his wife agt John Mitchel Exec of Samuel Daniel dec'd. At deft's motion imparlence granted them to next Ct.

[p 233] The action upon the case between Willm. Ford Mariner & Mathew Irland, plt not prosecuting. Dismist.

The action of slander between Richd. Swanly & Mathew Irland dismist for the same action.

In the action upon the case between Thomas Fellows & Cornelius Durlack & Rachel his wife. Imparlence granted him till next Ct.

In the action upon the case between William Dawkins of London merchant & William Tucker Exec of Thomas Merry dec'd. Mr. Maxl. Boush the plt's atty becomes Security for the costs &c. Deft being returned non est inventus & not appearing, at plt's motion attchmt awarded him agt est of Tucker for £2:10:03 sterling returned to next Ct for what appears due.

In the action upon the case between Joshua Curle gent & John Smith Junr. At deft's motion imparlence granted him to next Ct.

In the action upon the case between Wm. Lowry & Florence Dreskill. At deft's motion imparlence granted him to next Ct.

In the action upon the case between Mary Bridge & Thomas Batts. At deft's motion imparlence granted him to next Ct.

In the suit upon a Scirefacias brought by Richard Kerkin to renew a judgmt agt Celia Langman, Sheriff Thomas Wythe made return in these words. "Celia Langman hath nothing whereby she may be summoned in my Bailiwick." Ordered that an Alias Scireficias issue returnable to next Ct.

[p 234] In an action between Joshua Curle & Servant Ballard Execs of Francis Ballard dec'd & John Smith Junr. At deft's motion imparlence granted him to next Ct.

The Sheriff not having made return of the Subpenas issued agt the persons presented by the Grand Jury, same is continued & such of them as have not already been summoned are ordered to be summoned to next Ct to answer.

In the action upon the case between John Burtell Exec of James Burtell dec'd & James Ricketts, deft appearing & not pleading. Judgmt by Nihill Dicet granted plt returnable to next Ct as usual.

The presentment of the Grand Jury agt William Booden for not continuing at Church during Devine Service dismist, he paying costs. It appearing to the Ct that he constantly goes to Church.

Richard Kerkin ack deed for part of his lot to Mary Floyde. Admitted to record.

John Bordland obtained an attchmt agt Wm. Short's est for £75:05:06. Francis Mallory, subsheriff, executed attchmt. Short being called & not appearing, Joshua Curle, James Ricketts, Thomas Wythe gent & Mr. Joseph Wragg or any three are requested to appraise est of Short in hand of Bordland & return appraismt to next Ct.

[p 235] Edward Latimore is appt Surveyor of the High Ways from head of Hampton River to the Meeting Road from Mrs. Wallace's & ordered forthwith to repair the Roads & Bridges in the Presinck.

Jacob Walker gent appt Survey instead of James Servant in the Precinct & ordered that forthwith he repair same.

James Wallace & John Selden gent are appt Surveyors from Mrs. Wallace's gate to the Town Bridge & ordered to repair same.

Joseph Selden gent is appt Surveyor from Mr. Turner's Bridge to the High Road to Mrs. Wallace's.

Joshua Curle gent is appt Surveyor from Hampton up to Spicer's.

Thomas Hawkins is appt Survey from Spicer's up to Newport News.

Ordered that the several other Surveyors of High Ways in this Co be continued in their several Precincts & that they repair & clear their several Roads & the Bridges thereon.

James Ricketts appt Surveyor from Town only to Mr. Armistead's Mill Dam instead of his former Precinct to Holm's Bridge & Schoonsdam Bridge.

A list of the est of Samuel Selden dec'd was returned this day & ordered recorded.

Mary Bridge pursuant to her summons this day appeared & failing to give security for the est of John Roberts in her hands. It's ordered that the Sheriff seize so much of the est as will be of value sufficient to satisfy & pay the est of Roberts & keep secure until she gives bond & security.

[p 236] Order of Justices who have been presented by the Grand Jury of the General Court held at His Majesty's Royal Capitol in the City of Wburgh concerning the impassable condition of the Road through Sawyer's Swamp. Mr. Godfrey Pole spoke for the Eliz. City Justices who understand that it is highly necessary some speedy measures be taken. Wherefore Elizabeth City Ct ordered Joshua Curle, James Ricketts, Jacob Walker, Samuel Sweeny, Joseph Banister, Joseph Selden, John Selden & Henry Irwin gent or any four of them to hire as many labourers as will make the Road passable & will pay in tobacco at the laying of the next Levy. [Signed] Anthony Armistead.

July the 19th At a Court held the 3d Wednesday in July 1721. Simon Hollier, Thomas Wythe, Joshua Curle, James Ricketts, Samuel Sweeny, James Wallace, John Lowry, Joseph Selden.

Upon petition of Abraham Parish for payment for maintaining Thomas Dubery, orphan, one whole year & the same may be paid out of orphan's est. Refd to next Ct for Petioner to bring his acct of charges.

[p 237] This day Henry Jenkins came into Ct & ack deed to Saml. Sweeny gent. Admitted to record.
William Hatchel ack his deed to Thomas Baker. Admitted to record.
In the action upon the case between Richd. Newsom & Henry Irwin. At plt's motion refd to next Ct at his cost.
The action upon the case between Thomas Batts Adm of est of Elizth. Batts dec'd & Baldwin Shepherd is [blotted].
John King Sheriff produced a list of debts & effects as Security for the est of William Williams orphan in hands of Mary Bridge his Gdn. Ordered Sheriff sell at Publick Outcry sd goods & bring acct to next Ct. Clerk to bring a copy of inv to next Ct. Sheriff asks for Ct directions as whether to sell for ready money or whether time should be given. Ct orders a year's time provided Sheriff take security.
In the action upon the case between John King gent & Mary Jenkins Admx of est of John Curle dec'd. Order for

settling accts not being complied with, continued to next Ct.

The action upon the case between Martha Taylor Exectrx of Robert Taylor dec'd agt Henry Irwin, deft proving a discount. Judgmt granted for plt of £1:16:10.

[p 238] In the action upon the case between Sarah Hays & Mary Jenkins Admx of John Curle dec'd est is continued for the audits between John King & Jenkins being finished.

In the suit in Chancery between Mathew Hilliard & Rachel Durlack, time granted to amend her answer to next Ct.

In the action upon the case between Richard Adams & James Barrett. At plt's motion & cost continued to next Ct.

The action upon the case between John Bordland & Henry Irwin former orders not being complied with is by consent continued to next Ct.

Charles Jenings having an order for Adm of his brother's est, took oath, gave Security. Ordered recorded.

Joseph Harris ack deed to William Whitfield & same admitted to record.

Thomas Skiner's suit in Chancery agt John Mitchel. At respondent's motion time is given to next Ct.

In the suit in Chancery between Martha Taylor & Robert Taylor infant by the Exec for Martha Taylor [agt] John Mitchel Exec of Samuel Daniel dec'd continued to next Ct.

In the action upon the case between John Burtell Adm of James Burtell dec'd & James Ricketts, deft pleading nihill dicet & issue being joyned. Refd to next Ct for tryal.

The action upon the case between John Lawson & Joshua Curle at deft's motion is refd for tryal to next Ct.

The action upon the case between Emanuel Alkin & Richd. Adams, deft pleading an assumpsit. Refd for tryal at next Ct.

In the suit in Chancery brought by Thos. Skiner & Elizth. his wife agt John Mitchel Exec of Samuel Daniel dec'd. Time granted deft to next Ct to put in his answers.

In the action of trespass between Samuel Tompkins & Richard Harvey for lands in controversy, former order not being complied with. Continued till 2d of Aug next.

In the action upon the case between Mary Bridge & Joshua Curle plt not appearing. At deft's motion she is non suited & ordered she pay cost.

In the action upon the case between William Parker & John Wescoat. Refd till deft have accts auditted & in the interim pleads no debit & Issue being joyned, refd till he comes for tryal.

Joseph Wragg returned appraismt of William Marweeks' est attached in his hands & praying judgmt for his debt of £3:10 due to him. Judgmt granted.

[p 239] The suit in Chancery between John Ellyson & Julian his wife & John Mitchel Exec of Samuel Daniel dec'd. Mitchel put in his answers to the Bill of Complaint & complainant granted time to next Ct to consider the answers.

This day James Nayler returned appraismt of Thomas Tucker's est. Ordered recorded.

In the action of trespass between John Roe & Samuel White, deft's atty. Granted by Nihill Dicet.

In the action between William Booden & Alexdr. Kennedy, judgmt confirmed agt deft & Security. Ordered to pay plt with costs at exon & one lawyer's fees.

In the action of trespass between John Ellyson & Julian his wife & John Mitchel, judgmt granted plt by nihill dicet.

In the action upon the case between [blotted] & Mary Jenkins, judgmt by nihill dicet granted plt.

John Bordland presented appraismt of Wm. Short's est attached in his hands. Plt receives judgmt for so much as is appraised in his hands & the attchmt be dismist he paying costs.

In the action upon the case between Thomas Fellows & Rachel Durlack. Judgmt by nihill dicet.

In the action upon the case between William Dawkins of London merchant & William Tucker Exec of Thomas Merry for £2:10:03 sterling, deft confessed judgmt. Ordered Tucker pay Dawkins out of Merry's est with costs at exon.

In the action upon the case between Mary Bridge & Thomas Batts, plt not appearing. At deft's motion she is non suited.

In the suit brought by Richard Kerkin by alias Scire Facias [agt] Celia Langman, she appearing & pleaded paymt. Refd to next Ct for tryal.

[p 240 Note: this final page is badly damaged] In the action upon the case between Alexander McKenzie ---- Booden. Plt's lawyer informs Ct that Evidences are going out of County. Ct orders depositions from Evidences about to leave, to be allowable Evidence for either side.

John Randall petitioned last Ct for an order --- Massenburgh should pay him his part of his mother's E-- of the Massenburgh. Ordered Massenburgh be summoned and in complyance Massenburgh appearing & he was willing to pay provided only to be allowed charges in proportion. Ordered Massenburgh to pay unto the --- of his Mother's est only deducting charges on the Adm of Est.

In the action upon the case brought by Joshua Curle -- - Ballard Exec of --- --- & John Smith Junr --- -- dismist deft paying ---.

The action upon the case brought Francis Mallory --- Hobson, plt not appearing --- upon deft's motion nonsuit is granted him --- is ordered to pay the Ct &c.

In the action upon the case between William Smelt --- Mary Bridge plt not appearing & ---.

In the action upon the case between Thomas Howard --- Dunn Armistead, deft being returned arrested --- called & not appearing to answer & sd suit at --- Judgmt is granted him agt Armistead --- Sheriff for what shall appear due --- Armistead appear at next Ct to answer the ---/

In the action upon the case between Thomas Jones ---- Bridge, deft not to be found. Dismist.

In the action upon the case between Thomas Fellows --- Durlach --- Refd to next Ct for tryal.

In the action upon the case between John Byracy --- Dunn, plt not appearing. Ordered to be nonsuited.

In the action upon the case between Emanuel Alkin --- deft not appearing. Judgmt agt him & the Sheriff.

INDEX

The following is an every-name and location index. Military ranks and titles of respect have only been included when the given name is omitted in the text. Sitting Justices are grouped separately under the individual's name. Suffixes indicating "junior" and senior" have been omitted. To retain the accuracy of the verbatim transcript there is an entry for every spelling as it occurs in the text. Names often occur several times per page. Since the various scribes' entries in the original are difficult to decipher and other mistakes in transcription may have occurred, readers are urged to consult the original record for confirmation of any entry.

The name of negroes are listed under "NEGROES" in the main index. Locations are listed separately at the end of the surname index.

ACKRILE, Wm 273
ACKRILL, Wm 268
ACRILL, Wm 252, 257
ADAMS, Richard 81, 280, 281, 286; Richd 138, 166, 235, 243, 253, 259, 262, 268, 273, 277
ALKIN(S), Alexand 169; Alexander 125, 131; Alexder 103; Alexandr 88, 95, 96, 97, 105, 116, 133, 159; Allexander 101; Elexandr 99; Emmannuell 17, 80; Emanuel 156, 157, 175, 179, 180, 182, 186, 187, 189, 190, 192, 194, 196, 199, 200, 205, 206, 207, 209, 210, 214, 217, 223, 269, 274, 276, 281, 286, 288; Emal 115, 174, 182; Eman 160; Emanl 2, 21, 60, 75, 82, 88, 89, 99, 123, 130, 134, 138, 139, 143, 144, 147, 148, 149, 152, 153, 157, 158, 161, 164, 165, 166, 169, 170, 178, 184, 185, 199, 204, 216, 219, 220; Emanll 8, 84, 89, 105, 228, 229, 230, 231, 243, 248, 252, 253, 258, 263; Jane 101, 133

ALLAN, Wm 276
ALLEN, Ann 65; Charles 204; Erwin 21, 144; Molly 1; Mr. 69; Richd 195; Susa 114, 122, 132; Susanah 122; Tho. 114, 116, 119, 125, 151, 168, 215, 240; Thomas 135, 173, 175, 201; Thos. 32, 33, 122; William 1, 11, 14, 21, 25, 30, 31, 32, 34, 43, 46, 108, 113, 132, 144, 215, 278; Willm 101; Wm 2, 3, 71, 95, 122, 128, 132, 143, 151, 156, 159, 160, 168, 202, 204, 239; —— 171
ALLIN, Wm 48, 49
AMORY, John 234
ANDREWS, Ann 155; Edwd 16; Eliza 16, 123, 127, 128; Mary 124
ANDROSS, Edward 144, 177
ARMISTEAD, Ann 21, 143; Antho xiii, 2, 7, 8, 13, 14, 17, 20, 21, 51, 53, 60, 70, 78, 81, 91, 95, 97, 103, 113, 114, 116, 118, 122, 124, 126, 129, 132, 134, 135, 136, 143, 145, 149, 151, 152, 158, 160, 164, 165,

166, 171, 173, 177, 186, 203, 212, 219, 230, 235, 238, 240, 241, 263; Anthony x, xi, xii, 7, 8, 9, 11, 25, 40, 58, 83, 86, 87, 89, 100, 178, 186, 195, 211, 268, 271, 280; [Justice Anthony 75, 76, 77, 79, 85, 89, 90, 91, 94, 100, 106, 107, 109, 111, 116, 120, 122, 124, 129, 140, 141, 144, 154, 155, 156, 160, 161, 164, 167, 171, 172, 175, 184, 187, 188, 196, 198, 202, 208, 214, 215, 225, 230, 235, 236, 237, 263]; Anthoy 136; Dun 119; Dunn 60, 238, 278, 288; Dunne 14, 55,; Edwd 7; Elizabeth 58, 230; Hanah [Hannah & Hanh] 8, 13, 34, 48, 71, 111, 131, 132, 141, 150, 151, 159, 160, 161, 170, 179, 182, 190, 206, 208, 211; Hind(e) 7, 9, 21, 31, 34, 44, 48, 52, 59, 60, 71, 116, 119, 128, 131, 139, 141, 150, 159, 167, 170, 172, 179, 180, 183, 185, 190, 191, 196, 200, 205, 206, 208, 210, 211, 216, 217, 281, 224, 230, 239, 242, 244, 253, 259, 274; John 2, 7, 8, 9, 17, 89, 97, 119, 165, 173, 177, 183, 229, 274; Jno 116, 119, 155, 160, 263; Moss 7; Reba 2, 7, 57; Rebecca 8; Robert xii, 7, 8, 9, 13, 51, 90, 98, 133, 138, 156, 157, 163, 165, 177, 186, 194, 201, 211, 215, 221, 240, 268, 269, 270, 276, 278, 281, [Justice Robert 277, 279]; Robt. 5, 8, 9, 17, 33, 34, 51, 52, 58, 61, 73, 129, 130, 145, 146, 161, 162, 230, 241, 242, 250, 263, 271, 274; Rt. 40; William xi, 2, 7, 8, 29, 79, 85, 90, 98, 108, 109, 162, 173, 183, 229, 276, [Justice William 79, 83, 85]

ARMSTRONG, Margt 272
ATTERSON, Joseph 277
ATKINS, Mrs. 1
AVERA, Charles 6, 84; Reba 60, 236; Rebeckah 60; Thomas 60; -arles 2
AVERIT(T), Hursley 12; Jane 18
AVERSON, Ann 20
AVERY, Alexander 155; Alexdr 77, 82; Cha 93, 94, 147, 153, 161; Charles 80, 173; Elexder 80, 173
BACKAS, Thomas 133
BACKHOUSE, Elizabeth 11; Joan 11; Thomas 11
BADDELY, Tho 117, 130, 147; Thomas 115
BADELY, Thomas 82, 85, 97
BADDESBY, John 230, 250; Jno. 236, 239, 249
BAILEY, John xi
BAKE, James 269
BAKER, James 58, 62, 63, 112, 174, 229, 243, 266; Jane 38, 56, 71, 178, 242, 270; Jas 245; Joshua 270; Peter 38, 56, 71, 73, 88, 93, 96, 125, 156, 163, 165, 175, 190; Richard 229; Thomas 285; Thos. 74
BALEY, Judeth 62; Walter 62
BALIS, Humphrey 3, 24, 62, 142, 150, 203; Tho. 138; Thomas 24, 92, 212; Thos 233; William 24
BALLARD, Ann 61; Capt 131, 172, 215, 230, 237, 241; Edward 4, 45, 84, 90, 156; Edwd. 107, 125, 131, 134, 202, 220, 278; Eliza 25, 202; Elizabeth 45; F. 22, 52, 59, 60; Fra 11, 21, 30, 31, 33, 37, 48, 53, 56, 57, 84, 96, 98, 102, 103, 104, 117, 124, 127, 131, 135, 136, 138, 142, 145, 158, 159, 151, 153, 158, 160, 162, 164, 166, 167

170, 176, 183, 186, 216, 237, 258, 259; Frances 61, 81; Francis xi, 1, 8, 19, 20, 26, 37, 47, 58, 61, 79, 80, 82, 85, 86, 87, 93, 95, 104, 110, 111, 125, 141, 149, 158, 159, 161, 194, 195, 197, 198, 205, 206, 207, 210, 211, 212, 214, 216, 219, 220, 234, 235, 240, 244, 283; [Justice Francis 76, 79, 82, 83, 85, 91, 92, 100, 106, 107, 109, 120, 124, 125, 126, 127, 129, 130, 135, 140, 141, 144, 147, 155, 161, 164, 167, 169, 171, 172, 175, 180, 181, 184, 187, 188, 191, 193, 196, 198, 202, 208, 214, 224, 227, 233, 235, 236, 239]; Fras 64, 158, 219, 262; Lucey 61; Mary 5, 61; Matt 12; Servant 61, 242, 258, 259, 262, 282, 283; Servt 61

BANISTER, Jo 37, 131; Jos 53, 80 95, 117, 120, 123, 125, 142, 154, 156, 166, 168, 174, 175, 176, 179, 180, 189, 195, 201, 221, 223, 224, 225, 230, 232, 242; Joseph 184, 198, 224, 226, 233, 236, 254, 257, 260, 268, 269, 270, 285; [Justice Joseph 254, 255, 259, 260, 263, 265, 267]; Mr 79, 237, 262; Susa 190; Susana 38

BARBER, Richard 108; Richd 115; Susana 51, 52, 56, 210, 216, 238, 252; William 51, 231, 238, 250, 258, 261; Wm 56, 210, 231, 245, 249, 252

BAREFOOT, Noah 106, 112, 121, 141

BARRET(T), Elinr 268; Eliza 259; Elizabeth 280; James 244, 253, 258, 259, 262, 263, 268, 270, 272, 273, 278, 280, 286; Jos 253

BASFORD, Richard 134, 143, 144
BASNETT, John 26
BATTERSBY, John 25; Jno. 210, 218
BATT(S), Eliza 56, 220, 232, 238 Elizabeth 193, 280; Henry 3, 31, 38, 82, 87, 94, 95, 99, 134, 145, 153, 168, 190, 209, 217, 218, 225, 229; John 31, 39, 72, 168, 209, 217, 218, 220, 223, 225, 229, 230, 233, 267; Jno 3, 41, 169, 182, 190, 220, 225, 230, 245; Mr 49; Tho 31, 19, 159, 168, 182, 229, 232, 236, 238, 247, 249, 250, 261; Thomas 3, 26, 31, 39, 70, 190, 192, 193, 205, 209, 214, 217, 218, 222, 223, 225, 233, 255, 257, 280, 282; Thos 56, 66, 220, 229, 230, 248, 250, 256, 261

BAYLEY, Betty 65 John 8, 15, 16, 20, 38, 43, 44, 62, 65, 70, 75, 79, 124, 129, 130, 157, 162, 165, 171, 176, 177, 181, 188, 197, 199, 215, 229, 242, 248; [Justice John 75, 77, 79, 83, 90, 91, 94, 106, 107, 111, 124, 125, 126, 127, 129, 141, 151, 155, 156, 160, 161, 164, 167, 169]; Jno 28, 57, 66, 190, 192, 195, 198, 214, 235, 238, 256; Judeath 124; Judeth 255, 261; Judith 5, 20, 57, 267; Margaret 20, 65; Margreat 143, 163; Margret(t) 20, 174, 184; Margt(t) 20, 57, 65, 133, 192, 254; Mary 65; Sarah 65; Walter 20, 65, 66; Widdow 9, 35; William 75, 124; [Justice William 141]; Wm 19, 38, 124, 126

BAYLIS, Humphrey 21, 50, 54, 77 Jane 50; Jno 21; Mary 54; Thomas 12, 21, 197, 200, 201

205; William 155; Wm 38, 77, 188, 200
BEAN(E), Ann 70, 270; John 270; Jno 70; Lean(?) 244; Martin 85, 150, 195; Wa 183
BECKETT, Geo 92
BENTON, Nicho 143, 170
BERRY, JOHN 40, 47; JNO 228
BEVERLEY, Robt 137
BIRD, Susa 116; Susanna 122, 125
BIRTELL, Ja 123; James 16, 97, 110, 116, 119, 120, 123, 124, 126, 256, 261, 269; John 16, 269; Jno 124, 256, 261; Mr 125
BLAIR, Archibald 73, 135, 185, 222, 247, 256, 261, 273
BLANCHETT, —— 156
BLAND, Richard 207; Richd 217, 231
BLOODWORTH, Jane 235, 251, 270; Timothy 186
BLYTH, John 192
BOARDLAND, Jno 56; —— 60
BOGAL als REED, Doglas 243
BOND, Jno 169
BOODEN, William 282, 284, 287; —— 288
BOOKER, Edwd 68, Hannah 67, 68, 260
BORDLAND, John 3, 10, 28, 29, 63, 73, 74, 119, 129, 159, 160, 165, 168, 171, 176, 181, 188, 189, 191, 194, 209, 213, 221, 228, 236, 238, 240, 252, 257, 260, 264, 268, 269, 272, 273, 274, 278, 286, 287; Jno 4, 33, 39, 93, 169, 172, 183, 186, 197, 245, 259, 262; Wm 74
BORTHWICK, Jane 119
BOSELL, Agness 36; Elinor (and Elinor) 182, 217, 235, 237, 248; William 1, 10, 11, 20, 75, 82, 83, 217; Wm 10, 14, 16, 17, 21, 22, 79, 92, 118, 123, 125, 129, 130, 135, 182, 199, 224

BOSSELL, Capt 1, 147, 188, 212, 255, 260; Elenor (and Ellinor) 37, 177, 192, 213, 224; Grace 36; WWilliam 5, 6, 9, 36, 37, 80, 100; Wm 36, 84, 99, 120, 177, 192, 203, 207; [Justice William 75, 83, 85, 91, 92, 100, 116, 120, 122, 124, 125, 126, 127, 129, 130; Wm 36, 84, 99, 203
BOSWELL, Capt 72, 269, 272, 279; Ellinor 57, 197, 207; William viii, 8, 9, 19, 104; Wm xi, 8, 14, 20, 36, 55, 120, 145, 177, 145, 182, 186, 192, 197, 107
BOSWORTH, Saml 139
BOUCHER, Margt 228
BOUSH, Maximilian 52, 221, 222; Maxl 221, 245, 283; Mr 221, 277
BOUTON, Nich 165
BOWCOCK, Henry 75, 102, 108, 114, 123
BOWDAL, Edwd 25
BOWLAND, JOHN 244
BOWTELL, Adam 19; Eliza 19, Elizabeth 191, John 19; Sarah 19; William 19; Wm 60
BOUTWIL(L)Eliza 173; Elizabeth 183; Wm 22, 140, 173, 183
BOYNTON, Nicho 185
BRACY (BRACEY), Fra 148; Francis 157, 165; Wm 157
BRAMBLES, Lazs 185
BRAND, William 55, 233; Wm 67
BRASEY, Mary 29; Wm 29
BRIDGE, Mary 4, 38, 51, 56, 65, 69, 70, 101, 108, 115, 139, 146, 151, 161, 172, 190, 196, 208, 222, 237, 247, 250, 260, 279, 282, 283, 284, 287
BRIER, Edwd 112, 121
BRIGHT, Robert 22, 139, 140, 154, 163, 174, 184, 192, 199, 273; Robt 3, 22, 42, 157, 236

BRITTAN, Geo 259; Tho 237
BRITTAIN, John 135; Tho 242
BRITTEN, Thomas 201
BRITTIN, Jno 145; Thomas 123
BROGAL REED, Douglas alias 62, 243
BROMAGE, Saml 142, 151, 160, 170 239; Samuel 182, 190, 205
BROOMAGE, Samll 132
BROOKS, Eliza 247; William 247
BROUGH, Coleman x; Robert 140, 163, 174, 274, 280; William 37, 274, 280; Willim 274; Wm 48, 49, 66, 207, 247, 269
BROWEDGE, Saml 113
BROWIGE, Saml 12
BROWNE(E), Euphan 38; James 24, 38, 55, 119, 188; Jos 243; Margrett 38, 55; Saml 119; Sophia 38; William 38, 87, 98, 103, 108, 155; Willm 104; Wm 62, 95, 97, 210, 210, 230
BRYER, Edward 105
BULLY, Andr 201
BURNHAM, Sarah 229; Thomas 229
BURTEL(L), Edward 14; Ja 139, 144, 157, 183, 185; James 3, 14, 15, 17, 22, 24, 104, 133, 134, 135, 136, 138, 140, 141, 144, 146, 148, 149, 152, 153, 154, 156, 158, 159, 161, 162, 163, 164, 165, 166, 167, 169, 170, 173, 174, 175, 177, 178, 179, 180, 185, 187, 191, 192, 194, 195, 196, 197, 207, 210, 211, 217, 218, 219, 221, 222, 229, 231, 232, 247, 248, 250, 276, 280, 284, 286; John 14, 17, 20, 128, 134, 15, 136, 138, 141, 145, 146, 148, 149, 152, 156, 157, 159, 161, 162, 163, 165, 173, 174, 175, 177, 178, 179, 180, 184, 185, 186, 187, 191, 195, 197, 207, 209, 210, 211, 217, 219, 221, 222, 229, 231, 235, 248, 276, 280, 284, 286; Jno 3, 139, 144, 145, 154, 157, 161, 165, 167, 170, 183, 185, 194, 218, 242, 247, 250
BURTEN (BURTON), James 228; Peter 17, 115, 271
BUSH, M 268
BUSHALL (BUSHELL), Abigall 81, John 203; Jno 45, 46, 198, 245
BUTLER, Elizabeth 9, 91; John 8, 9, 91; Tho 115, 130
BUTTS, Anthony 228
BYRACY, John 269, 270, 288; Robert 96, 269
BYREGEE, John 131
BYREREE, John 150
BYRESEE, John 141, 242
BYRD, William ix
CADDO, Wm 229
CAKE, Henery 82; Mary 82
CALICOTE, James 69, Wm 69
CALLOHILL, James 228
CARHILL, Eland 173; William 176, 234
CARMAN, Martha 90
CARVER, Alexander 32, 155, 176; Alexandr 3; Alexr 151, 173; Ann 3, 32, 168
CARY, Henry 186, 194, 206, 216, 224; Mary 73, 88, 96, 103, 110, 117, 141, 162, 280; Miles 9, 96, 234, 243; Tho 7; Wilson Miles ix
CASEY (and CASY), John 31; Richard 199, 204, 254; Tho 168; Thomas 31, 32
CEELY, Charles 38; William 39
CELY, Charles 28, 34; Wm 29
CHAMBERS, Eliza 231, 245, 247, 272; Elizabeth 250, 251
CHAPPEL (CHAPPLE), James 197; John 82; Mr 81; Wm 24
CHANDLER, John 48, 68, 70, 229
CHAPMAN, Cha 243

CHICKWELL, Cha 152 170
CHISWELL, Charles 134, 143, 160, 183, 190
CLAIBORNE, Elizabeth 40; William 40
CLARK(E), Eliza 41, 168, 172, 180; John 78
CLEFTON, Benjamin 7
CLIFFE, Johnathan 156
CLIFT, Johnathan 139, 146, 162
CLIFTON, Benjamin 173
COCK(E), Henry 36, 87, 95, 159, 186, 194, 201, 212, 219, 234; Mary 87, 95
COCKS, Christopher 221
COFFEE, John 194, 206, 243
COFFIELD, Wm 245
COFFY, John 199, 216, 228, 235
COLE, Ceely 102; Cela 256; Celer 86; Eliza 39, 192; Martha 181, 256; William 278; Wm 72
COLLINGS, James 49
COLNELL, Edmd 139; Edward 130
COLWIL(L) Edwd 146, 153, 162
COLY, William 168
CONLEY, John 90
COOK, John 32, 24, 45, 51, 73, 88, 121, 132, 164, 175, 176, 184, 192, 199, 205, 223, 275, 276; Jno 159, 160, 168, 182, 200, 216; Mrs 264; Wm 229
COOKE, John 26, 99, 113, 162, 180, 237
COOPER, Barbery 4, 42, 45; Carter 52; Cha 42, 56, 116, 119, 140, 233; Charles 4, 22, 41, 45, 52, 155, 157, 201, 220, 275; Elizabeth 41; Fleet 201; George 25, 225; John 225; Jno 63
COOPELAND, William 105; Wm 84
COOPLAND, Chr 92; Christopher 12, 16; Eliza 10, 75, 81, 113, 120, 125; Elizabeth 10, 16, 86, 93, 98; Elyas 12; Falni 12;
Falvi 12, 195, 200, 204; Falvy 205, 207, 217, 223, 224, 232; Hannah 12; William 10, 12, 16, 55, 75, 80, 87, 93, 94, 99, 105; Willm 86, 98, 200; Wm 16, 45, 51, 80, 82, 95, 113, 115, 120, 125, 131, 142, 159, 160, 182, 200, 203, 205, 242, 259
COPLAND, Eliza 2; William 12; Willm 237; Wm 2, 44, 95
CORBETT, RICHARD 185
CORK, Henry 58; Mr Secretary 100
CORKERELL, Daniel 184
CORNELAS, Tho 162
CORNELIUS, Thomas 26, 27, 37, 38, 188
COSINS, James 43
COUDART, Bard 226
COUSENS, James 200
COWDART, Bard 227; Barnard 226; bard 227
COX, Wm 155
CRAFFORD, James 256
CREEK, Eliza 188; William 6, 48, 111, 169; Wm 69, 159, 172
CROFT, John 24, 185, 193, 206, 210, 216, 218, 228; Jno 155, 228; Katherine 14, 24, 54; Madm 217; Mrs 224, 232
CROOK(E), Debra 47; Eliza 38; John 30; Martha 47; Penuell 45, 47, 51; Robert 47; Wm 13, 34
CROFT, Abra 185, 193, 216; Abraham 14, 24, 228; Childerm 193; Childermus 14, 24, 185, 216, 228
CRUSELL, Elizabeth 33; Mary 3, 33, 177; Richard 3, 33, 171, 177; Richd 33
CUMBLIN, Henry 50
CUNNINGHAM, William 262; Wm 252, 255, 259; ⸺ 268
CURLE, Ann 70, 71, 277; Jane 3, 9, 75, 78, 79, 80, 81, 82, 92

Jno 2, 4, 28, 34, 56, 95, 106, 109, 116, 121, 128, 132, 153, 177, 185, 186, 188, 198, 214, 224, 245, 249, 256, 257; John 5, 16, 30, 33, 59, 80, 81, 91, 99, 100, 105, 112, 115, 118, 120, 121, 124, 125, 130, 132, 136, 140, 142, 145, 147, 151, 161, 167, 173, 175, 180, 181, 193, 197, 199, 200, 212, 213, 217, 230, 243, 248, 251, 260, 262, 279, 285, 286; Jos 1, 78, 85, 156, 179, 210, 262; Josa 5, 8, 44, 58, 61, 68, 69, 79, 80, 85, 87, 124, 131, 143, 167, 188, 190, 192, 230, 231, 241, 251, 255, 256, 257, 262, 263, 273; Joseph 55; Josha 47, 59, 68; Joshua xi, xii, a, 5, 9, 43, 44, 57, 63, 64, 68, 71, 72, 75, 81, 82, 87, 92, 94, 95, 96, 99, 116, 131, 133, 148, 152, 157, 163, 166, 181, 186, 187, 194, 196, 197, 198, 199, 212, 233, 235, 241, 242, 244, 245, 247, 249, 255, 256, 259, 260, 266, 269, 271, 273, 276, 278, 281, 282, 283, 284, 286, 287, 288; [Justice Joshua 181, 184, 187, 188, 191, 194, 196, 198, 202, 208, 215, 224, 227, 233, 236, 237, 239, 241, 246, 254, 255, 259, 260, 265, 267, 271, 277]; Mr 202, 237; Nicho xii, 2, 3, 16, 47, 75, 78, 79, 80, 81, 82, 84, 87, 90, 91, 92, 94, 98, 99, 105, 109, 112, 115, 116, 120, 121, 124, 132, 137, 149, 152, 220, 221, 222, 244, 245, 251, 258, 273;Nicholas vii, 5, 8, 9, 11, 26, 83, 193, 214; Pasco xiii, 18, 89, 100, 106, 112, 118, 125, 128, 129, 130, 134, 137, 138, 147, 164, 227, 249; Sarah 5; Thomas 59, 70, 83, 89, 144, 231, 238, 267, 277; Thos 60, 70, 71, 250, 261; Wilson 10, 68, 85, 99, 103, 140, 159, 161, 170, 191, 211, 219

CURSELL, Richard 155; Richd 125, 236, 246
CURSILL, Edwd 113
DANDRIDGE, Euphan 75, 78, 82, 86, 88, 96, 103, 110, 117, 147, 154; William viii, 8, 18, 27, 28, 63, 64, 81, 88, 91, 96, 103, 133, 141, 154, 162, 197, 244; Wm 75, 78, 86, 89, 110, 117, 135, 138, 147
DANIEL(L) [DANIELS], Ann 3, 13, 111, 208, 217, 229; Jude 41; Judith 261, 262; Julian 200, 218, 222, 223, 235, 239, 243, 249, 255, 257, 273, 275; Julin 232; Samuel 12, 13, 41, 44, 50, 56, 174, 185, 193, 200, 201, 208, 213, 223, 186, 187; Saml 3, 13, 139, 162, 153, 175, 186, 200, 217, 219, 231, 239, 242, 248, 249, 250, 255, 257, 261, 262, 275
DAVIS, Christopher 33, 169; Elizabeth 33, 169, 172; John 202; Jno 57; Moses 12, 246, 247; Thomas 270, 275; William 165; Xtopher 172
DAWK, Tho 136, 145, 152
DAWKINS, William 283, 287
DELAWENY, Thos 33
DELANEY, Thomas 197
DELANY, Lewis 138, 145, 153; Tho 236, 246, 252, 258; Thomas 171, 196, 197, 212
DIGGS, Cole 15, 119, 158, 163, 167, 174, 180; Colo 192

DINES, Saml 45
DIXON, James 43, 200
DOLICH, Cornelas 147, 231, 238, 252, 257, 259, 262; Rachel 147
DORLICH, Cornel 173; Cornelas 244, 252; Cornelius 156, 183, 185, 197, 199, 201, 212, 238, 268; Cornels 157, 209; Rachel 185, 197, 199, 201, 208, 213, 231, 236, 238, 244, 253, 257, 259, 262, 268
DRAPER, Micheal 30; Mickl 198
DRESKELL, Florence 47, 98, 101, 196, 204, 282
DRISCOLL, Florance 88, 126
DRURY, Jno 229
DUBERRY, Giles 69, 73, 189, 199, 276; Sarah 65; Thomas 270, 274, 279, 285
DUN[N], Ann 6; Elizabeth 6; Henry 55, 128, 164, 182, 204, 241; John 70, 138, 164, 210, 218, 228, 235; Jno 54, 140, 171, 216, 238; Pasco 26, 60; William 12; Wm 6, 70, 92
DUNAWAY, Darby 100, 106, 112, 173; Eliza 125, 128
DURLACK, Cornelius 283; Rachel 238, 287
DYNES, Samuel 60
EDGHILL, Elinor 247
ELLIS, Richard 88, 101, 102, 201
ELLISON [ELLYSON], John 180, 189, 200, 287, 282, 283; Julian 282, 283, 287
ENGLISH, Katherine 67
EUSTACE [EUSTICE], Thomas 277; --- 173
EVERETT, Charles 271
EWINGS, Eliza 58; Wm 58
FACE, Jacob 42, 43, 70, 115, 130, 272
FAULKNER [FALCONAR], Jam 71; John 114, 195, 207, 217, 223, 232, 255, 256; Jno 224, 253, 258; Tho 93, 96, 146, 234, 243, 252; Thomas 272; Thos 10, 186, 227, 237, 252, 272
FELLOWS, Thomas 277, 282, 283, 287, 288
FINLASON, John 20
FIRMER, Elizabeth 12
FITZGERALD, John 20
FITCH WILLIAMS, Richd 129
FITZ WILLIAMS, Richard 45, 197, 207, 214, 217, 219, 220, 223, 225
FLENN, Wm 47
FLETCHER, Robert 198
FLING, Wm 204
FLOYDE(E), Ann 271; Dority 75, 81 James 78, 201; Jno 29; Mary 72, 97, 104, 108, 115, 204, 210, 218, 230, 284
FORD, Willm 283
FORGISON, John 164; Katherine 6
FOSTER, Jno 253
FRACEY, William 87, 95; Wm 83, 94, 116, 125
FRANCIS, Easter 247; Thomas 18, 118, 269; Thos 34, 246
FRANKLIN, John 100, 106
FRASEY, Mary 16; Wm 95
FRAZEY, Wm 246
FRISSILL (FRISSLE) Mary 104, 174, 184
FRIZEL(L), Mary 97, 99, 105, 110, 112, 115, 120, 125, 126, 133, 151, 160, 163, 231, 249, 153
FRY(E) Thomas 182, 183, 186, 188, 194, 195, 216, 217, 224; Thos 54, 232
FRYBUS, John 159-160; Tho 159-160
FYFE, Wm 74
GEORGE, Frances 101, 102; Francis 204; Frans 220; John 121, 127

204, 220; Jno 229
GERNY, Michel 121
GIBBINS, John 229
GIBINS, John 112, 121
GIBBON, John 99, 105
GIBSON, Donald B. xv
GIGGETS, Geo 168
GIGELS, George 39
GILBERT, James 4, 10, 28, 53, 57, 69, 93, 123, 131, 156, 176, 108; Mary 4, 33, 53, 69, 176, 208, 240, 247
GOODING, Elizabeth 69
GOODMAN, Thomas 271, 282
GOODWYN, Eliza 2, 7, 149, 158, 166
GORAM, Geo viii
GRACE, Isaac xii
GRANT, Katherine 67
GREEN, John 244, 255; Wm 118
GREEK, William 169, 219; Willm 212; Wm 199
GREENWOOD, Wm 57
GREISET, Robert 57
GRIMES, Jane 108, 109
GROOME, Reba 228
GROVES, Saml 229
GUGH, Frans 73
GUILLAM, Peter ix
GUY, George 43, 200
GYER, Hugh 18
HACHELL, William 74
HAILE, John 48
HAINES, Charles 229
HAM, Jerom 137
HAMPTON, John 127
HANEY, Richd 69, 240
HANSON, John ix
HARDIMAN, John 187, 195; Jno 179
HARR, Robt 242
HARRINGTON, Mrs 57
HARRIS(S), John 251; Joseph 18, 73, 74, 125, 160, 165, 286; Jos 128

HARRISON, Collo 188; Josias 67; Katherine 67
HARTWELL, Mary 133
HARVEY, John 46; Richard 276, 282, 286
HASLETT, Cary 73
HASLEGROVE, Eliza 38, 188
HASTID, Thomas 269
HATCHEL(L), Ann 26, 162; Mary 26; William 162, 285; Wm 26
HAWARD, Henry 23
HAWKINS, Richard 32, 200; Richd 31, 32, 168, 172, 242, 244; Thomas 32, 168, 284
HAYES, Francis W. xiii; Henry 24, 123, 234, 251, 257, 262; Sarah 24, 58, 103, 123, 126, 234, 236, 243, 251, 257, 262, 273
HAYLES, John 67, 68; — 48
HAYNES, Elizabeth 102
HAYS, Henry 176, 197, 199, 243; Sarah 176, 208, 268, 286
HAYWARD, F 51; Henry 229
HAYWERD, Francis 23
HENDERSON, Mary 148, 157, 160
HENRY, Edmd 81
HESLETT, Cary 280
HEYMAN, Peter viii
HICKS, Henry 189; Sarah 236
HIDE, James 98
HILL, Benj 149; Benja 163, 184; Benjamin 174; Eliza 93, 149, 163, 174, 180, 184, 197, 205, 210, 218, 244, 258, 259; Elizabeth 144, 192, 193, 197, 198, 208, 212; Justinian 150; Martha 150; Thomas 189
HILL als PIERCE, Sarah 189
HILLIARD (HILLIERD etc), Matthew 45, 197, 212, 231, 238, 244, 252, 257, 262, 268, 273, 280, 286
HIND(ES), Chr 49; Christopher 49, 202

HOBBS, John 243
HOBSEN, Charles 276; —— 288
HOGINS, Frasier 32
HOLLAND, John 153
HOLLIER, Edmd 16, 21, 126, 169, 215, 229; Edmond 30, 46, 51, 53, 203; Edwd 56; Mr 166; Simeon 17, 20, Simon xiii, 16, 22, 23, 24, 29, 30, 47, 51, 53, 54, 56, 62, 63, 64, 67, 68, 74, 75, 79, 91, 119, 126, 127, 140, 141, 148, 154, 157, 169, 174, 184, 2-3, 211, 214, 215, 223, 228, 229, 232, 242, 278;[Justice Simon 141, 144, 147, 150, 154, 155, 161, 164, 167, 169, 171, 285]; Symon xiii
HOLLODAY, William 223
HOLLOWAY, John viii, 15, 20, 27; [Justice John 76, 79, 82, 83, 88, 90, 91, 92, 100, 106, 107, 109, 111, 115, 116, 120, 122, 123, 124, 125, 126, 127, 129, 130, 135, 140, 141, 144, 150, 154; Jno 28, 129; Majr 141, 153, 267
HONADAY, Alexandr 263
HOPKINS, Joyce 4, 17, 31, 171; Richard 17, 26, 32, 133, 140, 152, 157, 173, 174, 186; Richd 4, 88, 96, 123, 128, 133, 143, 159, 161, 162, 169, 171; William 69, 108, 177, 222; Wm 34, 101, 115, 139, 146, 151, 161, 169, 172
HOTTEN, Thomas 187
HOUSE, Ann 54; Anthony 54; Elizabeth 54; John 54, 135, 223, 271; Martha 54; Mary 54; Thomas 54, 186, 194; William 54
HOWARD, Eliza 2, 37, 78, 176; Elizabeth 5, 84, 182; Henry 154, 233; John 31, 39, 131, 192, 200; Jno 21, 128, 168, 192; Tho 2, 4, 5, 9, 37, 47, 78, 104, 110, 116, 119, 125, 134, 143, 157, 161, 166, 170, 230, 274; Thomas 19, 35, 60, 83, 90, 97, 118, 125, 128, 131, 133, 144, 152, 165, 170, 176, 181, 205, 213, 214, 223, 266, 269, 188; Thos 22, 59, 148, 171, 202, 228, 255
HUDSON, George 278
HUNT(T), Rosana 71; Rose 234, 251, 255; Roseanah 234, 251, 255
HUNTER, Andr 227; John 227; Saml 227
HURSHLY, Richd 237
HURSLY, Richd 57-58
HURSK, Mary 275
HURST, John 272
HUSK, Mary 5
HYDE, James 111; Robt 160
INGRAM, John 7
IRLAND, Mathew 282
IRWIN, Charles 269; H. 21, 53; Henry ix, xi, xv, 16, 20, 21, 24, 55, 58, 59, 63, 67, 68, 71, 73, 74, 102, 106, 108, 118, 123, 124, 128, 133, 136k 139, 140, 143, 144, 145, 152, 155, 158, 161, 165, 172, 173, 176, 178, 186, 187, 188, 191, 193, 194, 195, 197, 201, 206, 210, 211, 212, 213, 214, 220, 227, 232, 233, 235, 237, 240, 241, 243, 244, 247, 253, 256, 258, 259, 261, 261, 264, 265, 266, 267, 269, 270, 272, 274, 278, 279, 280, 285; [Justice Henry 170, 180, 181, 184, 187, 188, 191, 193, 194, 198, 202, 214, 215, 224, 233, 239, 241, 244, 246, 151, 255, 259, 260, 263]; Saml Irwin 160
JACKSON, Christopher 276
JAMES, David 33, 172; Eliz 3, 79

84, 93, 125, 130, 138, 215, 232, 248, 250; Elizabeth 10, 15, 18, 80, 85, 94, 97, 100, 116, 122, 203, 222; Nath 97; — - 275

JEELE, Kert 87

JEGGELS, George 56

JEGGETTS, Geo 191; John 168

JENINGS, Cha 1, 4, 9, 10, 13, 15, 16, 17, 20, 21, 25, 27, 31, 32, 33, 35, 37, 38, 39, 40, 42, 47, 50, 51, 52, 53, 57, 58, 62, 64, 67, 68, 69, 71, 82, 88, 97, 104, 111, 115, 118, 129, 132, 134, 138, 142, 143, 146, 147, 153, 154, 161, 162, 163, 164, 165, 168, 182, 187, 191, 202, 229, 231, 237, 143, 245, 247, 248, 257 Charles xi, xv, 10, 11, 12, 23, 24, 32, 34, 43, 45, 47, 51, 57, 63, 72, 99, 100, 103, 105, 107, 131, 132, 138, 139, 144, 145, 152, 173, 174, 175, 176, 179, 183, 186, 189, 190, 191, 192, 193, 194, 195, 199, 200, 205, 206, 209, 210, 213, 214, 217, 220, 227, 235, 248, 252, 262, 264, 266, 286; Eliza 5, 10; Elizabeth 11, 12, 43, 107; Mary 129; Tho 85, 93, 153, 161; Thomas 102, 138, 145, 173, 183, 186, 194, 212, 219, 227, 234, 267; Thos 57, 58

JENKINS, Bridget 39, 252; Capt 119, 130, 156, 157, 158, 159, 160, 161, 166, 173, 188, 189, 190, 191, 193, 195; Cha 126; Hen 17, 39, 182, 187, 188, 194, 196; Henry 1, 2, 4, 5, 8, 9, 10, 15, 16, 20, 24, 26, 28, 33, 40, 43, 44, 52, 53, 56, 71, 73, 82, 83, 88, 89, 91, 93, 99, 105, 106, 109, 113, 114, 116, 120, 121, 124, 132, 138, 140, 143, 146, 151, 153, 162, 171, 177, 178, 180, 181, 185, 186, 188, 189, 191, 193, 197, 198, 100, 207, 209, 210, 212, 213, 214, 215, 217, 220, 221, 222, 223, 227, 2231, 232, 236, 243, 245, 247, 248, 249, 253, 254, 255, 256, 261, 262, 268, 273, 279, 285, 286; [Justice Henry 172, 175, 180, 181, 184, 187]; Mary 5, 10, 43, 44, 52, 56, 58, 61, 82, 93, 196, 198, 200, 207, 209, 210, 213, 214, 217, 220, 221, 222, 223, 224, 227, 231, 232, 234, 240, 243, 244, 245, 247, 248, 249, 252, 254, 255, 256, 257, 258, 261, 262, 268, 273, 279

JOHNSON, Andr 253, 258; Eliza 42; Elizabeth 42, 43; Jane 42; Mark(e) 20, 27, 30, 42, 43, 45, 53, 60, 81, 86, 89, 97, 103, 109, 115, 123, 129, 148, 178, 198, 212; [Justice Mark 75, 79, 82, 85, 89, 90, 91, 92, 94, 100, 106, 107, 120, 122, 124, 125, 126, 127, 129, 130, 140, 141, 144, 147, 150, 154, 155]; Marrye (Mary) 8, 42, 43; Robert 21, 29, 131; Robt 3, 168; Tho 24, 114, 122, 132; Thomas 155; Thos 29

JONES, David 2, 10, 55, 81, 86, 98, 113, 120; Edward 102; Edwd 69, 86, 151; John 10, 28, 84, 99, 105, 112, 120, 266; John Allen 118; Johnathon 86, 95, 102, 110; Jno 132, 142, 221, 236, 255; Makhew 132; Mattw 121; Phillis 26; Roger ix; Sarah 88, 96, 100, 193, 198, 220, 232, 238, 249, 257, 261; Tho 13, 75, 86, 129, 159, 167, 170, 182, 231, 236, 243, 245, 249, 250, 257; Thomas 26, 44, 45, 51, 81, 111, 131, 135, 165,

190, 198, 205, 206, 210, 214, 223, 225, 238, 259, 261, 268, 288; Thos 66, 99, 162, 199, 200, 220, 232, 238, 245, 246, 253, 254, 255, 262; William 161; Wm 28, 156

KEARNEY [KEARNY], Edmd 8, 11, 19, 21, 28, 67, 79, 89, 216, 261, 263; Edmond [Edmund] 27, 63, 85, 106, 139, 183, 190, 205, 228, 240, 248, 257, 267, 268, 274; Michl 19

KELLY, Mde 45

KEMBALL, John 99, 105

KENNADAY, Alexdr 254

KENNEDY, Alexander 282; Alexdr 268, 270, 275, 287

KERBY, Thos 67, 68

KERKIN, Richard 282, 284, 287; Richd 268, 269, 273, 277, 280

KERNY, Edmd 114, 122, 124, 153, 162, 170; Edmond [Edmund] 62, 63, 154, 173, 250; Edward 92, 96, 146, 234

KERR, Robert 249

KERSEY, Edmd 58

KETH, Walter 18

KIMBAL(L), Jo 276; John 242, 249, 268 269, 273, 275, 280; Jno 157, 243, 244, 263

KING, Ann 263; Celia ix; John xii, 8, 10, 13, 16, 17, 20, 30, 37, 47, 53, 55, 57, 60, 73, 97, 104, 105, 110, 121, 124, 127, 129, 130, 147, 149, 164, 169, 175, 177, 178, 184, 185, 193, 197, 198, 208, 212, 218, 225, 227, 231, 233, 234, 235, 243, 245, 247, 248, 252, 256, 263, 268, 271, 273, 277, 278, 279, 285; [Justice John 75, 83, 90, 92, 100, 106, 107, 109, 111, 116, 122, 124, 125, 126, 127, 129, 135, 140, 141, 147, 154, 156, 160, 161, 164, 167, 169,

171, 172, 175, 180, 181, 187, 191, 194, 198, 202, 208, 214, 215, 224, 227, 230, 233, 235, 236, 237, 239, 251, 255, 260, 265, 267, 271]; Jno 116, 128, 141, 158, 162, 174, 187, 212, 213, 220, 224, 227, 240, 241, 243, 262; Mary 225; Mr 181, 193, 226, 230, 242, 160, 170; Reba 251

KIRBY, Tho 7, 90; Thomas 7, 260

KIRKIN, Margreat [Margt] 81, 82, 86, 107, 109, 115, 123; Richard 9, 48, 49, 54, 71, 97, 98, 103, 104, 114, 138, 139, 158, 173, 181, 183, 187, 189, 195, 197, 200, 207, 209, 217; Richd 72, 81, 82, 86, 87, 88, 94, 95, 96, 103, 107, 109, 110, 112, 114, 115, 117, 119, 122, 130, 132, 139, 142, 146, 148, 149, 157, 159, 165, 166, 169, 179, 182, 189, 199, 235, 242, 249, 255, 257, 262

KNIGHT, William 251; Wm 179, 189 199, 250

KNOT(T), John 139, 146, 148, 157, 166

KOBBS, John 243

LAHEA, Ralph 174

LANGMAN, Celia [Cely etc] 181, 209, 217, 283, 287; Wm 178

LASHLEY, Eliza 126

LATTIMORE [LATTEMORE], Edward 55, 80, 85, 97, 125, 131, 140, 151, 160, 165, 170, 200, 237, 245, 284; Edwd 24, 54, 62, 63, 64, 78, 95, 104, 112, 117, 128, 131, 142, 150, 213, 243, 246; John 107; Thos 25, 62; William 282, Wm 263, 268

LAWS, Andrew 133, 156, 203, 239; Andr 165, 170, 185, 196, 259

LAWDER, George 185

LAWSON, John 247, 269, 276, 281

LAYLESS, John 28, Stephen 28
LEE, Thomas 233, 241
LEGHMAN, Jacob 87, 95, 98, 99, 103, 105
LEWIS, Andrew 175, Daniell 80, 105; Danll 84, 89, 98, 99, 105, 115, 130; Geo 62; Rich 21; Richard 139, 140, 153, 174; Richd 146, 162; Tho 86; Thomas 94; Thos 71, 72
LIDDELL, James 18
LIGHTFOOT, John 137; Phillip 85, 228
LILES, John 210
LILLIS, Stephen 3, 22, 97, 104, 110, 111, 154, 162
LILLO, John 230
LOUGHMAN, Jacob 111, 112
LOWERY [LOWRY], Ann 202, 241; Frances 67; Jane 75; John xi, xii, 7, 58, 64, 67, 188, 264, 265, 271, 278, 279; [Justice John 254, 255, 260, 265, 285];Jno 201, 215, 236, 242, 247; Rachell 7; Will x; William 8, 19, 20, 30, 59, 67, 72, 83, 105, 129, 162, 163, 203, 240, 260; Willm 10, 14, 26, 53, 196; Wm xiii, 16, 20, 26, 29, 34, 35, 62, 67, 68, 71, 79, 90, 98, 108, 118, 123, 135, 154, 174, 177, 182, 201, 260, 263, 269, 273, 283; [Justice William 75, 79, 82, 88, 90, 91, 92, 94, 100, 109, 111, 116, 120, 122, 124, 127, 129, 130, 135, 140, 144, 147, 150, 154, 155, 156, 160, 161, 164, 167, 169, 171
LOYAL[L], Elizabeth 35, 150; Jno 141; William 11, 27, 35, 121; Wm 34, 71, 75, 150, 175, 182, 186, 202, 223, 224, 225, 230, 269
LYALL, Wm 93

LUKAS, Richard 132
LUKE, Esqr 67, Geo 75, 80, 114, 34, 143, 144, 152, 161, 170, 182; George 134, 153, 182, 190, 205, 208, 211; Mary 100, 114, 134, 143, 152, 161, 182, 190, 205, 208; Mrs 118
LUPO, Eliz 68
MACKINTOSH, Daniel 228
MAKENNIE [MAKENNY], Christian 275, 281
MALLORY [MALORY], Ann 70, 215, 231, 248, 254; Eliza 81; Fra 40, 48, 69, 71, 72, 78, 86, 108 121, 139, 146, 150, 153, 231, 259; Francis 40, 57, 70, 100, 101, 106, 113, 115, 155, 179, 185, 187, 188, 192, 195, 204, 215, 248, 254, 255, 270, 271, 272, 184, 288; Fras 65, 67, 237, 240, 241, 275; Mary 70; William 40, 81, 85, 87, 95, 98, 99, 105, 107, 112, 121, 278; Wm 60, 70, 149, 158, 166, 185, 188, 193, 270, 275
MANSON, Peter 67, 68, 260
MARKE, James 133, 143
MARLOE, William 77, 80, 84, 86, 98, 218
MARSH, Moses 131
MARSHALL, Eliza 164, 225, 233; James 157; Mary 178, 233; William 99, 105, 212, 227, 233; Wm 51, 78, 87, 164, 178, 187, 195, 204, 220, 225, 229
MARSONE, Robert 18
MARTIN, John 201, 209
MARWEEKS, William 287
MASSENBIRD, John 166, 229
MASSENBURGH, Francis 204, 277; John 35, 58, 149, 150, 158, 173, 182, 192, 272, 288
MATHERS, John 64
MCKARTEE, William 192
MCKENZIE, Alexander 195, 228;

Alexandr 61, 164, 230, 242;
Alexdr 129, 156, 175, 183, 187,
188, 210, 269, 274; Chrisr 269,
271; Doctr 65; Mr 166, 167,
241
MEAD(E), Andrew 214, 225; Andr
45, 219, 220
MECKOVER, Evander 43
MERRICK, Wm 272
MERRIDEL, William 25
MERRIDETH, John 114, 128, 218,
246, 278; Jno 69, 136, 149,
166, 214, 153
MERRITT, John 6, 7, 155; Wm 225
MERRY, Elizabeth 29; John 29,
196; Mary 29; Prettyman 28; Tho
3, 30, 85, 128, 154, 169, 172;
Thomas 28, 29, 30, 101, 131,
155, 183, 187
MERRYMAN, Thomas 281
MEW, Robert 17, 88, 114, 115, 130
140, 156, 157; Robt 156, 164
MEWDEN, Robert 140
MICHEL, John 271
MIDDLETON, 25, 155
MIHILL, Ann 115, 146; Edward 81,
82, 87, 95, 112, 119, 215,
154; Edwd x, 54, 56, 78, 81,
116, 117, 126, 127, 248; Jos
56; Joshua 231, 254; Lockey 56,
231, 240, 241, 254, 275
MILBEE, Jos 113; Joseph 82, 87,
95, 113
MILBY, Joseph 72, 210, 278
MILES, Ann 153; Saml 140
MILLER, James 124, 126
MILNER, Mary 66; Thos 57
MINCHINTON, Walter ix
MINIS, Francis 228
MINSON, Easter 44, 56, 57;
George20; Hester 44; Robert 19,
25, 27, 32, 45, 93, 155, 163,
173, 175, 176, 202; Robt 10,
21, 51, 56, 59, 143, 160, 230;
Thomas 44; William 44, 97, 104;
William 44, 97, 104; Wm 44, 55,
56, 95, 198
MITCHEL(L), Abraham 26, 27, 38,
47, 71, 167, 180, 233, 236,
239, 272, 277; Abra 34, 35, 37,
41, 58, 71, 157, 182, 218,
245;Abr 71, 88, 162; Ann 13,
27, 71, 167, 229, 277; Hanah
41, 421; John 34, 39, 40, 41,
44, 50, 58, 71, 169, 175, 181,
186, 191, 193, 194, 200, 208,
214, 217, 219, 222, 223, 229,
231, 236, 242, 248, 249, 250,
255, 261, 273, 274, 275, 276,
281, 282, 283, 286, 287; Jno
56, 180, 182, 232, 239, 262
MOON, Charles 182, 183, 196
MOONE, Cha 159, 251, 253
MOOR(E), Augn xiii, Charles 234
John 32, 65, 69; Jno 42, 56,
59; William 69; Wm 275
MORE, Ann 4, 6; Augustine x, 68,
98; Daniel 6; Edward 6; Eliza
42; John 4, 6, 7, 23, 27, 32,
78, 80, 90, 94, 102, 209, 218,
228, 230, 231, 242, 245;
[Justice John 77, 83, 85]; Jno
52, 149, 158, 166, 220, 223;
Lazarus 23; Martha; Merritt 6,
128; William 4, 7, 23, 24, 101,
214; @m 2, 23, 128, 149, 100,
103
MORGAN, Reba 46; Thomas 34, 70,
177, 199, 270, 174, 179; Thos
189, 228; William 46, 118
MORGAN als BROOKS, William 2; Wm
46, 71
MORRISETT (MORISET), Henry 36,
41, 176, 183, 228, 270; Peter
173, 180
MORRYSON, Charles 25
MOSELY, Richd 81
MOSS, Robert 140, Wm 229
MOURTON, Ralph 71
MURRIN, ---- 1

MYHILL, Ann 49, 57, 101, 139, 155; Edward 49, 51, 98, 187, 196, 203; Edwd 33, 84, 179; Jos 51; Foshua 49, 50, 54; Lockey 49, 50, 51, 54

NAYLER (NAYLOR), Eliza 3, 11, 20; Elizabeth 19; Ja 116; Jas 221; James 19, 34, 44, 54, 55, 87, 95, 98, 100, 103, 106, 107, 112, 121, 123, 134, 138, 140, 142, 144, 145, 170, 186, 194, 196, 200, 203, 207, 209, 223, 271, 287; Mary 19, 20; Tho 3, 32, 134, 154; Thomas 12, 19, 20, 22, 140; William 11, 19

NEEDHAM, Christopher 65; Margt 18, 19, 57, 65, 66, 138, 242, 254; Tho 26, 138; Thomas 6, 18, 19, 201; Thos 65

NEALE, Kert 133; Samuell 103, 133, 143, 156

NEELE, Kort 118, 143; Saml 88, 96, 110, 125, 143; William 129

NEGROES, Abby 62; Abigail 11; Absalom 42; Adam 62; America 53; Ann 53, Beak 11; Beck 30; Belle 11, 29, 30, 46, 53, 59, 62, 66; Betty 29, 233; Black Betty 22; Bob 62; Bobb 53, 65; Breck 23; Cain 30; Catty 29; Cesar 106; Charles 5; Coffee 15, 142, 165, 169, 186, 199, 216, 228, 235; John Coffee 194, 216; Colb 13; Cuckow 66; Deberah 11; Dempsey 62; Deria 235; Dianna 53; Dick 55, 66, 225; Dina 233; Dogo 11; Fillis 22, 29, 46, 53; Frank 11, 23, 29, 30, 31, 42, 46, 53; Geysa 29; Gomery 62, 65; Grace 38, 42; Guy 13; Hammady 30; Hanah 13, 30, 42, 53, 62, 215; Hannah 11, 23, 46; Hanner 29; Harry 7, 19, 42, 245; Homady 23; Harry 7, 19, 42, 245; Hump 7; Indey 13; Jack 7, 11, 22, 30, 42, 53, 55, 66, 106, 225; James 44; Jamey 13; Janey 65; Janny 140; Japher 11; Jeffery 13, 23; Jemmy 41; Jenny 11, 23, 30, 31, 53, 65, 66; Jessy 30; Johnne 225; Jone 5; Judah 46, 53; Juday 29; Judith 11, 28; Judy 5, 30, 31, 42, 47, 52, 53, 228; Juno 41; Kane 23; Kate 11, 15, 225; Labella 62; Leby 46; Lemmon 29; Lucy 29; Mallachi 29; Bungey Manuell 49; David Manuell 49; Hanah Manuell 49; George Manuell 49; Elizabeth Manuell 49; Nicholas Manuell 49; William Manuell 49; Marea 53; Martha 11; Martin 42, 65; Mary 225; Meriere 92; Mingo 11, 29; Minor 42; Miriam 31; Mole 42; Moll 11, 22, 30, 44, 47, 53, 233; Mount 62, 65; Mundingo Sarah 22; Mundingo 30, Nanney 29; Nanny 11, 22, 30, 33, 62, 65; Ned 11; Nell 65; Thomas Oxford 65; Paul 23, 30, 245; Pegg 30, 66; Pender 37; Perrin 44; Peter 19, 22, 31, 42, 44, 53, 55; Pheby 11; Phillis 11, 23, 30, 92; Pluto 91; Pompey 233; Pompi 66; Prince 62, 79; Rachell 11; Robbin 30; Robin 22, 215, 235; Sam 44; Samson 37; Sara 7, 225; Sarah 10, 11, 23, 29, 30, 37, 42, 44, 53, 55, 65; Sary 29; Scotland 269; Sey 53; Shoreham 11; Soldier 233; Stepney 11, 53; Strumbelo 11; Sue 11, 23, 30; Tena 11; Tenah 47, 53; Titus 64; Tobe 7; Tom 22, 30, 31, 55, 62, 66; Toney 30, 42; Tony 23, 66, 225; Towrey 29; Venus 53, 62, 65; Watt 23; Wilabey 30; Will 11, 13, 22, 23, 29, 30, 31, 62, 65

62, 65, 66, 70; York 7
NELSON, Mr 188; Tho 119; Thomas 15, 185, 193, 207, 228
NEWBERRY, William 89 97, 102, 103 Wm 80, 84, 164
NICHOLSON, Francis xii, 137
NIGHTINGALE, Charles 228
NIXON (NIXSON), John 252; Jno 255 258
NOBBS, John 227, 234, 252, 257
NOBLIN, Henry 52, 69, 198; John 201
NORDEN, Abraham 11; Catherine 28; Katherine 114; Kert 183; Kort 3, 124
NORWELL, George 281; Hugh 281
NEWSOM, Richard 278, 279; Richd 267, 271, 272, 285
NUSUM, Richd 16, 26, 32, 34, 45, 48, 49, 69, 70, 123, 128, 157, 168, 170, 179, 183, 199, 207, 208, 210, 225, 238, 243, 247, 255, 256, 258, 259, 261, 262
OHARREN, Bridget 31, 168
OTTERSON, Joseph 71, 72, 278; Mary 72, 278
PAIN(E), Geo 230, 239; George 47, 70, 175, 184, 211, 219, 229, 249, 272; Mary 70
PALMER, Wm P. vii
PANE, Geo 163
PAYNE, George 192
PARISH, Abra 3, 34, 75, 138, 151; Abraham 28, 105, 108, 114, 132, 168, 177, 285; Ann 34, 177; Edwd 28; Jo— 237; John 150, 164; 176; Mark(e) 28, 34, 147, 162, 164, 180; Mrk 3; Tempe 189; Temperance 28, 34, 147, 151, 168, 177, 180
PARKER, Francis 47; Nathaniel 9, 47, 203; Nathl 28, 35, 76, 99, 170, 182, 205; Nicho 48, 49, 200, 236, 271, 276; Nicholas 41, 47, 200, 203, 207, 281;

Peter 145; William 282, 287; Willm 277
PARKS, Henry 228
PARRIS, Thomas 46, 203
PARSONS, Ann 27; James 27; John 27; William 27
PATRICK, Jno 229
PEARLS, Vi——t 274
PEIRCE, (PEIRSE) Cha 65, 85; Charles 43, 69; Edwd 61; Jean 12; Mary 101, 107; Michl(1) 77, 101, 201, 252, 258; Michael 92, 147; Mycal 12; Susa 61; Tho 124; Wm 201
PENNE, Brian 50, 69; Elizabeth 5; Hanah 5
PENNY, Brian (Brien) 32, 69, 70, 75, 76, 87, 95, 96, 114, 116, 121, 125, 128, 152, 157, 159, 160, 163, 166, 215, 216, 219, 222, 229, 230, 234, 243, 247, 248, 249, 250, 252, 255, 258, 259, 261, 262; Bryan 36, 37, 79, 80, 84, 89, 99, 102, 110, 131, 133, 139, 143, 146, 148, 170, 172, 175, 180, 183, 184, 190, 204, 205, 209, 211, 214, 228, 236, 239, 267, 268, 272, 279; Edwd xvi, 4, 37, 58, 79, 172, 180; Eliza 63; Elizabeth 5, 37
PERRY, Micajah 276; Mr 1, 61; Richd 276; William Stevens x; Wm 68
PETT, Catherine 13; John 4, 73, 79, 175, 177, 178, 180, 183, 203, 213, 214, 228, 250, 262; Jno 33, 134, 189, 195, 199, 242, 257; Martha 13, 71, 178; Sarah 13, 178, 214
PHAREN, Bright 168
PHILLIPS, Ann 135; John 77, 157; Margaret 271; Nicho 92, 135; Nicholas 80, 84; Paul 197, 212
PHILLIPSON, Christopher 80; Chr

35, 211; Robert 228
PHRAIRS, William 12
PHRASEY, Mary 12; William 12
PIERCE, Anthony 274; John 271; Michel 271
PIRKETT, Abraham 204; Ann 203
PLATT, John 282
POLE, Godfrey 55, 69, 285; Geoffrey 40, 64; Mr. 274
POOL(E), Ann 12; Jane 18, 137, 138; John 95, 119, 125, 135, 137, 164, 184, 105, 212, 223, 238, 245; John J. 175; Jno 116, 131, 170, 183, 210, 231, 246; Mr 231, 268, 269; Tho 21, 77, 118, 129, 142, 140; Thomas 18, 37, 80, 111, 136, 138, 179, 190; Thos 137, 210; William 137
POWEL(L), Hanah 38; Mark(e) 39, 52, 56, 169, 192, 209, 230; Mrk 34, 219, 220; Mathew 38, 56; Matt 192; Tho 78, 80, 85, 94; Thomas 31, 38, 39, 52, 102, 192, 100, 209; Thos 56; —— 273
POWER(S), Cha 150; Charles 33, 150, 171; Thomas 44
PREEDY, Ann 71; Daniel 96; Danl 71, Isaac 208; Judith 71, 271, 277; Robt 71
PREIST, Anfilady 46; James 46, 190, 200; Margrett 46, 48, 53, 139, 190, 200, 203, 229; Martha 46; Thomas 46
PRESCOTT (PRESCOAT), Eliza 54, 189, 214, 262; Elizabeth 162, 173, 199, 278; Phillip 78, 79, 80, 85, 97, 104, 110, 117, 131, 142, 151, 160, 170
PREYNTON, Nicholas 156
PREST, Margt 56, 146, 167; Mary 159; James 159, 167
PRICE, John 228
PRIEST, James 17, 181; Margt 17, 181
PRINCE, Edwd 237; Joseph 229; Susanah 237
PROBY, Bart 69, 180, 183, 236; Bartd 45, 56, 128, 138, 142, 225, 245, 247, 255, 256, 261; Barto 3, 28, 51, 86, 111, 125, 145, 151, 153, 170, 189, 191, 218; Bartrand 2, 26, 45, 51, 72, 98, 104, 131, 161, 173, 211, 218, 280; Jas 153; John 45; Mary 45; Peter 2, 98, 104, 131, 151; Petr 142; Tho 3, 128, 145, 191, 261; Thomas 161, 173, 211, 218, 271, 280; Thos 183, 247, 256; —— 81
PROVINE, Rachel(l) 75, 82, 112, 120, 125, 126, 193, 198; Rashell 99, 105
PUCKETT, Ann 46
PUGH, John 54, 55, 225, 251, 259; Jno 255, 262
PUKETT, Abrahas 47
PURIFIE, Frances 67; Thos 67
PURSILL, Edward 121
PYNE, Cha 248
RABB, John 50
RAINE, Owen (Owin) 36, 183, 184, 199
RALPH, Benjamin 26, 72, 278
RAMBOW, Isaac 55, 233
RAMY, Thomas 54
RANDY, Mary 81, 159, 169, 181, 231, 250, 253, 270, 271, 275
RAGG, Josa 74
RANDAL(L) (RANDOLL), John 277, 288; Mary 270; Thomas 204
RASCOW (RASCOE), Euphan 5, 27; James 64, 207, 224, 235, 241, 244, 253; [Justice James 241, 244, 254, 255, 259, 260]; Mr 266; Wilso 78; Wilson 27, 82, 86, 110, 117, 154
READ, Ann 134, 143; T 175; Tho 5, 33, 52, 109, 134, 136, 215,

229, 275; Thomas 143, 229, 275
Thos 50, 63, 138, 276
REED, Douglas alias Brogal 243,
62; Richd 62
REDING, Sarah 253
RESS, Walter 203
RICHARDS, Edward 13
RICHARDSON, Edward 107
RICKETTS, J 55; James xii, 9,
10, 16, 18, 29, 31, 34, 35, 45,
51, 57, 64, 69, 73, 79, 85, 88,
89, 90, 92, 94, 95, 98, 99,
100, 103, 105, 106, 109, 111,
112, 113, 115, 116, 118, 119,
120, 121, 124, 125, 126, 132,
134, 136, 140, 144, 146, 147,
152, 159, 161, 162, 163, 164,
167, 170, 171, 175, 178, 180,
184, 186, 191, 192, 199, 211,
212, 213, 214, 219, 220-221,
222, 227, 238, 240, 241, 244,
245, 249, 254, 258, 269, 271,
272, 276, 279, 284, 285, 286;
[Justice James 172, 176, 180,
181, 184, 187, 188, 191, 194,
202, 208, 224, 227, 230, 239,
241, 244, 246, 251, 255, 259,
260, 263, 271, 272, 277, 279];
Jane 9, 10, 18, 79, 85, 88, 89,
92, 94, 98, 99, 100, 105, 106,
109, 112, 115, 116, 118, 119,
120, 130, 132, 134, 136, 139,
152, 153, 159, 161, 164, 170,
191, 211, 213, 219, 220-221,
222, 227, 244, 245, 254, 258,
271; Jas 54, 73, 186, 192; Mr.
220, 254; --- 37
RIDDLEHURST (REDDLEHURST), Eliza
160; Elizabeth 13, 219; Fra
263; Francis 268; Frans 273;
Jno 186, 216; Richard 194, 216,
224; Saml 169; Samuel 36, 160,
184; William 281; Wm 276
RIDDOUCH, Wm 51
RIDGE, Elizabeth 39; Mary 39

ROBERTS, Gerrard 229
ROBERSON, Mrs 267
ROBERTS, Hanah 195, 206; James
32; Jaret 215; John 203, 228,
238, 255, 261, 267, 279,
284; Jno 38; Michael 52, 55;
Michl 38, 39, 78, 188; Myhill
69; Saml 29; Tho 84, 88, 96,
118, 134, 153, 165, 258; Thomas
80, 81, 89, 103, 112, 133, 143,
145, 156, 170, 179, 185, 193,
209, 218, 229; Thos 60, 149,
262; Wm 25, 155
ROBERTSON, Henry 278
ROBINSON, Henry 26, 32, 53, 72,
79, 84, 93, 95, 102, 111, 120,
125, 127, 128, 130, 139, 146,
148, 153, 155, 157, 162, 163,
164, 166, 170, 174, 175, 178,
180, 183, 184, 185, 189, 191,
193, 200, 205, 206, 216, 220,
223, 232, 238, 240; James 247;
Jane 240; John 21, 48, 280-
181; Jno 49, 144; Sarah
150, 164, 175, 201, 213, 244,
259; Wil xiii; William 210
RODUM, Mongo 271, 272
ROE, Ann 19, 246; Edwd 156, 225;
John 9, 17, 19, 32, 34, 52, 86,
114, 119, 129, 147, 153, 160,
164, 172, 175, 184, 223, 275,
287; Jno 31, 116, 139, 159,
182, 192, 215, 216, 260;
William 45; Wm 62
ROGERS (RODGERS), Ann 50; Bathia
50; Eliza 51; Fra 30, 33, 52,
119, 125, 168, 175; Grancis 14,
16, 31, 50, 15, 109, 116, 134,
165, 173, 180; Frans 56, 215;
John Addeston 107, 139, 146;
Johnathon 135; Richd 88;
William 78, 100, 107; Wm 80,
84, 93, 114, 130
ROLFE, Benja 45, 202
ROOTE, Tho 83

ROSCOW (ROSCOE), James 197, 217; Wilson 75, 88, 96, 103
ROSE, Fr 56; Fra 146; Fran 127; James 119
ROSS, Fra 139; Frances 101; Francis 46, 48; Hugh 46, 48, 53, 107, 269, 275, 276
ROWIN, Cha 7; Charles 90
ROWTON, Jane 222, 232, 236, 246; Richard 201, 256; Richd 77, 118
ROYALL, Henry x, xiii
RUSELL, Joseph 131
RUSSILL, Josiah 229
RYLAND, Eliza 57; Tho 128, 133, 143, 160; Thomas 156
RUMBAGH (ROMBOW, ROMBOUGH ETC), John (and Jno) Henry 27, 28, 37, 162, 167, 180, 187, 270-271, 272
SALTER, Grasinham 24; Grisham 155
SAMPSON, John 81, 84, 87, 95, 98, 114, 126, 127, 130, 138, 146
SANDWICH, Henry 77, 81
SAVOY, Mary 147, 251
SCHAVERALL, Jno 141
SCHLATER, James 229; Mr 226
SCOTT, Hanah 97, 104, 113, 121, 123, 141; Wm 204
SCULLIE, Joane 2
SEBA, Ralph 163
SEETON, Margreat 148
SELDEN, Archiley (Archily) 198, 212, 219; Bart 114, 130, 153, 164, 175, 184, 198, 219; Bartholomew 6, 66, 83, 86, 94, 102, 108, 147, 212; Eliza 134; Elizabeth 25, 26, 66; John xii, 66, 156, 271, 272, 284, 285; [Justice John 277, 279]; Jno 28, 66, 69, 254; Jos 54, 55; Joseph xii, 62, 63, 66, 69, 72, 252, 257, 271, 272, 279, 284, 285 [Justice Joseph 272, 277, 279, 285]; Mary 57; Mr 1, 75, 110, 249, 250; Reba 66, 69; Rebeckah 6, 26, 72, 82; Samuel(1) 6, 8, 25, 26, 37, 66, 83, 84, 89, 102, 104, 107, 115, 137, 157, 177, 178, 183, 186, 187, 189, 191, 193, 194, 198, 205, 206, 211, 212, 218, 223, 224, 225, 238, 284; [Justice Samuel 241, 244]; Saml(1) 16, 24, 45, 54, 55, 57, 69, 72, 79, 80, 82, 84, 86, 93, 94, 96, 102, 108, 109, 111, 114, 117, 119, 120, 123, 127, 130, 134, 139, 142, 147, 148, 151, 153, 157, 160, 164, 165, 166, 170, 182, 184, 185, 210, 216, 219, 221, 230, 232, 233, 234, 235, 241, 243, 244, 248, 252, 254
SERVANT, Bartd 141, 216, 220; Bartram (Bertram) x, xi, 40; James xi, 2, 4, 10, 21, 34, 85, 92, 98, 114, 117, 122, 132, 147, 149, 151, 158, 162, 163, 171, 194, 196, 210, 212, 218, 220, 240, 241, 242, 264; [Justice James 172, 176, 180, 181, 184, 187, 188, 191, 194, 198, 202, 208, 214, 215, 224, 227, 230, 233, 236, 239, 241, 244, 246, 251, 255, 260]; Lucy 45; Mary 45, 162; Sidwell 45
SESMAN, Markem 106
SETON, Margtt 131
SHEPPARD (SHEPPERD), Baldwin 232, 248, 250, 261, 267, 273, 280; Eliza 56, 220, 232, 238, 248, 249, 250; Elizabeth 257, 261; John 193; Jno 56, 220, 238
SHEILD, Robt 229
SHELLS, James 127
SHERLEY, Mr 68
SHIPWRIGHT, Parrish 58

SHORT, William 212, 221; Wm 198 284, 287
SIDWELL, Ralph 12; Wm 173, 183
SIMMONS, Joyce 237; Wm 242
SIMONS, Ja 157; Joyce 61, 62; Mary 157; William 118; Wm 111
SKINER, Elizabeth 281; Elizth 286; Joseph 111; Thomas 276, 281, 286; Thos 275
SKINNER, Ann 13; Darby 13, 281; Eliza 13; Elizabeth 41; Jno 65, 185; John 19, 31, 140, 168, 185, 193; Johnthana 13; Jul 181; Martha 13; Mary 13; Samuel 13, 217; Samuel 41, 208, 281; Tho 114, 122, 229, 248; Thomas 13, 180, 189, 199, 214, 218, 213, 270, 281; Thos 217, 250
SLATER, Richard 23; Richd 154
SMALL, Matthew 61, 62, 78, 80, 8185, 94, 149, 159, 163, 174, 175, 182, 184, 192, 193, 204, 237; Mattw 44, 87, 95, 158, 160, 166, 173, 192, 246
SMALLHANE, George 25
SMELT, William 4, 6, 11, 63, 85, 97, 99, 104, 112, 130, 131, 133, 143, 147, 149, 153, 158, 163, 164, 203, 210, 213, 231, 242, 245, 253, 288; Wm 10, 16, 17, 27, 34, 35, 40, 41, 57, 73, 75, 80, 92, 105, 108, 109, 110, 115, 116, 121, 123, 125, 128, 131, 138, 141, 145, 150, 151, 154, 159, 160, 168, 169, 170, 171, 175, 176, 180, 181, 182, 183, 187, 189, 190, 191, 195, 199, 222, 228, 243, 248, 257, 262, 273
SMITH, Ban 14; Benja (Benjm) 4, 52, 82, 88, 89, 109, 130, 134, 143, 171; Benjamin 17, 60; Edith 128, 136, 145, 152, 161, 173, 187, 195; Joan(e) 47, 76, 103; Johana 76, 103; Jno 15, 51, 60, 136, 145, 152, 159, 173, 175, 186, 187, 214, 220, 242, 249; John 72, 73, 79, 82, 85, 87, 90, 92, 95, 96, 98, 99, 103, 105, 106, 111, 112, 120, 133, 134, 136, 145, 152, 156, 157, 159, 161, 165, 166, 176, 177, 178, 181, 190, 194, 195, 198, 100, 216, 210, 211, 213, 222, 232, 235, 236, 237, 243, 252, 270, 273, 283, 299; Phillip 214, 223, 247; Saml 146, 153; Samuel 139; Sarah 51; Susa 56, 171, 216; Susanah 4, 216; Wm 268
SMYTHE, Joan 35
SNIGNELL, Saml 17
SORRELL, Wm 53
SPICER, Cassander 13; Mary 185, 194, 206, 216; William 206, 208; Wm 29, 32, 33, 34, 44, 52, 93, 114, 116, 119, 151, 168, 172, 185, 192, 194, 200, 216, 252; ⸺ 284
SPISER, Wm 102
SPOTSWOOD, A 15, 264; Alexander 18; Alexdr 130; Elexander 89; Governor xi
SPRINGER, John 168
STANDL(E)Y, John 149, 156; Jno 227
STAC(E)Y (STASEY), Simon 95, 102, 110, 116, 118; Symon 86
STARKE, Wm 87
STENSVAAG, James T vii
STONEHAM, Thomas 185
STORES, John 83
STREET, Eliza 40, 41, 188; Richard 6, 40, 41, 85, 188; Richd 92, 113, 116, 119, 122
STRINGER, Daniel(1) 30; Jno 3; John 30, 31
STUCKEY, Edmond 47; Elizabeth 46, 47; Mary 46, 47; Simon 47
SWANLY, Richd 282

SWEATMAN, John 75
SWEETMAN, Jno 79, 80, 89, 97, 110; John 84, 85, 94, 96, 99, 103, 105, 117, 131, 142
SWENY (SWEENY), Edmd x, 229; Lazarus 228; Merritt 23, 51, 145, 153, 203, 215, 229, 175; Mr 166, 242, 278; Saml(1) xii, 51, 59, 73, 75, 124, 126, 127, 134, 143, 144, 147, 152, 153, 160, 166, 170, 182, 220, 224, 229, 230, 235, 241, 242, 253, 256, 257, 258, 259, 260, 261, 268; Samuel 23, 37, 40, 50, 67, 179, 187, 188, 190, 194, 195, 196, 197, 200, 201, 212, 223, 270, 272, 282, 285; [Justice 241, 244, 246, 251, 254, 255, 259, 260, 265, 267, 277, 279]; Sarah 65; [Justice Wm 129]
SYMMONS, William 96
SYMO, Hago 103, 106
SYMON, Hage 87; William 78, 82, 234; Wm 89, 155
TABB, Diannah 22; Edward 22, 47, 51, 53, 195, 198, 203, 204, 211, 225, 226; Edwd 3, 23, 30, 154, 162, 169, 215, 227, 229; Eliza 228; Elizabeth 23, 51, 154, 203; Henry 22; John 22, 23, 233; Martha 23, 51, 203; Mary 23; Rachel 23; Tho 3, 154, 162; Thomas 8, 22, 23, 196, 215; Thos 228; [Justice 75, 76, 79, 83, 89, 90, 91, 92, 100, 109, 111, 124, 125, 126, 129, 130, 140]; William 154; Wm 23, 229
TABORT, Jacob 238
TALBERT (TALBORT), Jacob 209, 218, 230; James 75
TAYLOR (TAYLER), Cathern 59; Daniel 59, 225; Martha 14, 41, 57, 59, 123, 126, 133, 136, 227, 234, 235, 237, 270, 243,
251, 252, 255, 256, 257, 258, 261, 262, 267, 268, 269, 271, 275, 279, 281, 286; Mary 225-227; Mrs 62; Robert 10, 14, 37, 41, 57, 76, 80, 81, 85, 92, 100, 107, 110, 114, 117, 123, 124, 133, 135, 148, 154, 157, 166, 167, 184, 185, 186, 189, 191, 193, 194, 199, 206, 209, 210, 216, 218, 224, 226, 228, 235; Robt xiii, 16, 17, 59, 62, 77, 78, 103, 127, 128, 130, 136, 142, 149, 173, 174, 220, 236, 261, 268, 275, 281, 286; Sarah 59; Tho 77; William 253; Wm 183, 190, 205, 258, 269
TANNOCH (TANOCH), Robert 182, 183, 195, 196, 202, 234, 238, 243; Robt 133, 148, 170, 231
TEEMO, James 247; Sarah 247
TENNECK, Robert 45
TENNOCH (TENNOCK), Robert 133; Robt 45, 159
THEADAM (THEADOM), Jno 93, 167, 210
THIBOULT (THIBOUT), Peter 64, 228
THOMAS, Job 201, 251; John 88
THOMPSON (THOMSON), Andr 57, 64, 65, 234, 242, 256; James 141, 198; Tho 130
THURKETT, William 205
TIDMARSH, Giles 107
TOMKINS, Samuel 276, 282, 286
TOMPSON, James 24
TOMSON, Thomas 18
TOOKERMAN, Richd 67
TOOMER, Bett 271
TOW, Jonas 62
TRAC(E)Y, John 78; Wm 82
TREADAWAY, Fra 168; Francis 172, 176; T—— 4
TUAL, Matthew 258
TUCKER, Cha 52, 128, 136, 159, 215; Charles 13, 32, 47, 52,

63, 173, 211; Eliza 52, 56;
Elizabeth 42, 220; Mary 42, 52;
Robert 140, 199; Tho 11, 22,
63, 112, 126, 220, 231; Thomas
41, 42, 45, 52, 240, 274, 293,
200, 212, 275; William 29, 283,
287; Wm 3, 34, 45, 53, 169,
170, 203, 225, 245, 275
TUCKERMAN, Richd 259
TUELL, Matthew 48
TURNER, Capt 1; Henry 2, 27, 28,
34, 113, 114, 116, 122, 125,
129, 132; Sidwell 17, 18, 129
UMPHELT, Constantine 169, 172
VANBURGH, Jno 158, John 150
VAUGHAN, Jno 196
VELAGE, John 152
VELLINE, Isaac 60, 239
VILAGE, Jno 143; John 161
VUELAGE, Jno 133
WADE, Elizabeth 31, 39
WAFFE, Geo 210, 218, 220, 223,
225, 236; George 1, 39, 56,
165, 199, 200, 210, 218, 239;
Rebecca 39
WAITE, Peter ix
WALIS, John 269, 270
WALK, Tho 245; Thomas 282; Thos
221, 257
WALKER, Eliza 126; Elizabeth 42;
G. 271; Geo 85, 142, 145, 153,
218, 236, 252; George x, 16,
37, 59, 68, 79, 84, 90, 91, 92,
106, 107, 109, 116, 124, 126,
131, 140, 173, 177, 183, 213,
233, 257, 269; Jacob 272, 279,
284; [Justice Jacob 272, 277,
279]; Margt 57; Mr 110; Tho 75,
78, 81, 87, 95, 110, 116;
Thomas 79, 84, 102; William 99,
101, 105, 135, 228; Wm 96, 112,
124, 126, 132, 204, 229; — 4,
9
WALLACE, Ann 57, 64, 65, 75, 97
101, 104, 234; Ja 8, 9; James

x, xi, xii, xv, 8, 9, 15, 38,
75, 97, 104, 247, 264, 271,
272, 279, 284; [Justice James
254, 260, 263, 271, 272, 279,
285]; Jno 179, 238; John 25,
92, 114, 115, 133, 150, 155,
156, 159, 174, 169, 179, 232,
238, 243, 244, 263, 268, 271,
273, 276, 277, 282; Madam 141,
225; Mr 14; Mrs 284; Samuel
175, 184; Susanna 282
WALLASS, John 199
WALLES(S), Jno 173, 181, 187;
John 222; Susa 222
WALLARD, John 131
WALLIS, John 71, 176
WAN(D)LESS, Elinor 57, 247, 251
WARD, Edward 50, 215; Edwd 215,
241; Hans 29; Pasco 50; Plano
169; Thomas ix
WATSON, Ro 49
WATTS, Anne 12, 13; Matthew 12,
13, 21, 60, 77, 111, 131, 140,
141, 179, 190, 205, 206; Mathw
150, 159, 170, 179, 182; Saml
12, 13, 71, 72, 77, 99, 111,
131, 136, 141, 150, 159, 167,
170, 180, 182, 185, 210, 216,
217, 231, 238; Samuel 105, 182,
190, 191, 215, 216, 218, 224;
Tho 169, 216; Thomas 196, 210,
218
WATTS als ARMISTEAD, Hannah 3
WAUFF(E), Geo xiii, 16, 176;
George 9, 10, 68, 91, 120, 139,
130, 191, 205
WAYSLOCK, Robt 80
WEDGEBERRY, Sarah; Susanah 162
WELCH, Margt 66, 254
WELDEN, Samuel 281
WELLS, Robert 113, 121, 132,
182,190, 205; Robt 142, 151,
160, 170, 239
WEST, Wm 131
WESCOAT, William 277

WESTCOAT, John 282, 287
WESTLAKE, Robert 96, 118, 189, 199; Robt 18, 83, 89
WESTLOCK, Robert 128, 136, 155, 180, 234, 242; Robt 111
WESTON, William 89, 110; Willm 103; Wm 84, 117, 142
WESTWOOD, Tho 2, 113, 114, 122, 132; Thomas 4; W 60; Wil 51; Willm 70; William 11, 17, 20, 31, 43, 107, 127, 129, 144, 164, 220, 229, 277; Wm 13, 35, 52, 63, 71, 132, 139, 146, 153, 155, 161, 198, 258, 266, 267; Worlich 17
WETHERSBY, Elizabeth 30
WAYMOUTH, Jno 38
WEYMOUTH, John 271
WHAFFE, George 272
WHAGH, George 275
WHATTS, Saml 239
WHARWOOD, Thomas 281
WHERWOOD, Thos 276
WHITE, James 282; Saml(1) 26, 28, 218, 230, 233, 239, 249, 250; Samuel 156, 195, 209, 210, 217, 225, 236, 271
WHITFERD, Charles 281
WHITFIELD, Charles 276; Hannah 38, 188; Jno 21, 201; John 77, 142, 247, 259, 262, 268, 273; Matthew 117; William 280, 286; Wm 73
WHITING, Leonard 71; Lendr 245
WHITTICAR, Catherine 29
WHITTAKER, Kert 29, 183; Wentr 168
WILES, Matthew 220
WILCOX [WILLCOX], Elizabeth 58, 60; Mr 97; Tho 3, 15, 60, 75, 104, 109, 112, 114, 115, 116, 121, 125, 130, 134, 135, 144, 146, 149, 152, 158, 159, 161, 165, 170, 232, 238, 242, 244, 248; Thomas 18, 41, 58, 63, 93, 97, 97, 99, 105, 107, 110, 122, 138, 156, 174, 175, 184, 191, 199, 203, 209, 210, 212, 218, 222, 239, 275; Thos 131, 215, 221, 230, 250, 255
WILLIAMS, Ann 17, 69, 247, 260; Epaphroditus 198; Fra 38; Francis 188, 281; Fras 250; Frans 274; Hanah 49; Mary 190; Matthew 70, 241, 260, 267; Mattw 182, 247; Phillip 31; Reba 45, 46; Rebeca 2, 202; Tho 46, 202, 260; Thomas 2, 45, 48, 49; Thos 71, 72, 202; William 17, 203, 228, 255, 256, 272, 285; Wm 5, 65, 69, 190, 241, 247, 255, 256, 260, 268
WILLISWOOD, 52
WIL(L)SON, Col 14, 21, 167, 178; Edward 70, 272; Jane 70; Martha 70, 271; George 199; Gilbert 164, 179, 189; James 24; Jno 29, 98; John 42, 65, 70, 77, 169; Samuel 186, 194; Thomas 204; William xiii, ix, x, 12, 27, 70, 77, 153; Willm 86, 272; Wm xiii, 14, 47, 71, 73, 78, 80, 84; Willis ix, x
WILWESTWOOD, 43, 48
WINFREE, Waverly K. xii
WINSTON, John 76
WINTER, William 28
WINTERTON, Jane 39, 56, 210; Jon 268; William 9, 39, 55, 91, 191, 233, 236, 270, 280; Willm 210, 218; Wm 33, 56, 74, 165, 208, 259, 262, 273
WMWESTWOOD, 53
WOOD, Ann 4, 24, 45, 229, 123, 133; Francis 111; Henry 20; Th 96; Tho 24, 63, 84, 106, 110, 112, 117, 119, 121, 133, 138, 146, 159, 162, 163, 166; Thomas 4, 54, 55, 97, 99, 104, 105, 123, 131, 139, 141, 156, 174

175, 181, 184, 191, 192, 210, 224, 225; Thos 45, 99, 123, 142, 148, 169, 183; William 31; Wm 33, 171
WOOTEN, Simon 228; Thomas 179
WRAGG, Jo 9, 24, 29, 35, 37, 41, 54, 58, 59, 60, 62, 71, 72; Jos 55, 132, 134, 144, 154, 166, 179, 182; Joseph 18, 21, 25, 26, 28, 33, 45, 48, 49, 50, 60, 61, 64, 73, 75, 80, 84, 85, 89, 97, 99, 102, 103, 104, 106, 111, 113, 114, 115, 117, 121, 125, 134, 145, 152, 153, 155, 162, 168, 187, 195, 197, 198, 200, 201, 202, 207, 208, 209, 212, 218, 219, 230, 235, 236, 240, 243, 251, 252, 272, 273, 282, 285, 287; Mr 237; —— 4
WRIGHT, Fra 128; Jane 32, 173; Mary 113, 121; Tho 25, 32; Thomas 32, 173
WYAT, John 270; Thomas 277, 282
WYN, Thomas 280
WYTHE, Tho 16, 20, 23, 30, 47, 53, 63, 64, 70, 72, 73, 108, 112, 116, 124-125, 142, 145, 154, 162, 234, 241, 256; Thos 10, 43, 44, 65, 70, 141, 266, 272, 274; Thomas 8, 15, 40, 57, 71, 123, 131, 171, 183, 186, 188, 198, 203, 211, 278, 283, 285; [Justice 75, 77, 89, 90, 91, 92, 107, 109, 111, 122, 124, 126, 130, 135, 140, 141, 144, 150, 154, 156, 160, 161, 164, 167, 169, 171, 172, 175, 180, 181, 184, 187, 188, 191, 193, 196, 198, 202, 208, 214, 215, 224, 227, 230, 233, 235, 236, 237, 279]
YEO, Geo 54, 60, 234, 244, 254; George 6, 26, 28, 57, 66, 69, 156, 186; Leonard 66; Mr 242; Mrs 72; —— 236

YOUNG, John 57

LOCATIONS

Note: Elizabeth City County, Elizabeth City Parish and the town of Hampton are not indexed since they occur with such frequency in the text.

AFRICA ix
BARBADOES ix, 11, 67
BERMUDA (Barmoodas) ix, 17
CHARLES TOWN, SC 24
COUNTIES, Glocester (Gloster) 60, 68, 78; Isle of Wight (Ile White) 47, 118; King William 63; Nansemond xiii, 36, 54, 55, 62, 63, 245, 248; Princess Anne xiii; Warwick (Warrick) 64, 74, 115, 117, 135, 155, 224
CREEKS AND RUNS, Broad Cr 68; Col Wilson's Cr 63; Gullett Run 7, 34; Harris Cr 16, 211; John's Cr 107, 109; Mill Cr 25; Pagan Cr 118; Point Comfort Cr 7; Potomack Cr 66; Price's Cr 68; Salter's Cr 212; Slippery Pine Granch 68; Tarpitt Springs 68
DAMS AND BRIDGES, Armistead's Mill Dam 284; Broad Cr Bridge 144, 155; Cener Dam 58; Finches (Finces) Dam 240, 279; Hampton R Bridge 211; Holmes Bridge 254, 278, 284; Little Mill Dam 28; Mill Dam 100, 126; Mr. Turner's Bridge 284; Scones Dam 135, 155, 164, 239, 254; Scowins Dam Bridge 144; Shoonsdam Bridge 284; Town Bridge 284
ENGLAND ix, 43, 58
GLASGOW x
GREAT BRITTAN 28

KECOUGHTAN vii
KIRKWALL 18
LEIGH 18
LIVERPOOLE 24
LONDON 283, 287
LANDMARKS, Black Walnut Ridge 24, Capps Point 40, Church 241, Eaton's Free School 262, 263, 269; Fort George vii, Fox Hill 19, 279; Halfway Tree Road 241; High Road 284; Meeting Road 284; Old Ditch 40; (Old) Point Comfort vii, 123
MARRY LAND (Maryland) 18
NEW YORK 274
NEWPORT NEWS 118, 119, 278
NORFOLK xiii, 36
NORTH CAROLINA 45, 48, 62, 76
ORKNEY 18
PARISHES, Abbingdon 68; Charles 23, 27, 68; Denby 186, 194, 206, 216, 224
POQUOSON 227
PRESINKE [PRECINCT] OF PASQUOTANK NC 48

RIVERS, Back 12, 27, 34, 48, 62, 67, 71, 212, 279; Elizabeth 36; Hampton 25, 40, 126, 212, 284; James xiii, 68, 117, 118, 119, 241, 281; Southampton vii, 14, 15, 37, 49, 57, 58, 64, 71, 73; York 280
SOUTH CAROLINA 67
SWAMPS, Allen's 240, 241, 278, 279; Gray's 17, 35; Sawyer's (Sawer's) 240, 259, 285
TRACTS, Back R Plantation 26, 66, Black Ground 7; Buckroe 25, 66 Burton's Quarter 8, Down's Field 5; Eaton's School Land 35; Fort Field 10, 28; Glebe 28; Leanffields 57; Old Fields 25, 67; Old Fortes 66; Ridge of Land 60; Strawberry Banks 5; Tony's Quarter 7; Wils Quarter 67
WEST INDIES ix, 18
WILLIAMSBURGH 15, 124, 285
YORK TOWN 15

VESSELS

ANN & HANAH 8
BATCHELLOUR ix
ELEANOR 24
HAMPTON 53, 59, 199
JANE & MARGARET ix
MAIDSTONE viii
MARY 53, 184, 185
MIGHTINGALE ix
PEARLE 43
PHENIX 274
RYE viii
ST JOHNS ix
SOUTHAMPTON xiii
STROMBULO xiii

www.ingramcontent.com/pod-product-compliance
Lightning Source LLC
Chambersburg PA
CBHW050334230426
43663CB00010B/1856